A. von Ravensberg

Practical Grammar of the German Language

With Conversational Exercises, Dialogues, Idiomatic Expressions... Third Edition

A. von Ravensberg

Practical Grammar of the German Language
With Conversational Exercises, Dialogues, Idiomatic Expressions... Third Edition

ISBN/EAN: 9783337277703

Printed in Europe, USA, Canada, Australia, Japan

Cover: Foto ©Thomas Meinert / pixelio.de

More available books at **www.hansebooks.com**

PRACTICAL GRAMMAR

OF THE

GERMAN LANGUAGE

WITH

CONVERSATIONAL EXERCISES, DIALOGUES,
IDIOMATIC EXPRESSIONS,
A COMPLETE VOCABULARY FOR THE EXERCISES
AND A SELECTION OF READING LESSONS

BY

A. von RAVENSBERG, F. E. I. S.,

GERMAN MASTER OF THE ROYAL HIGH SCHOOL AND
THE PHILOSOPHICAL INSTITUTION, EDINBURGH.

THIRD EDITION
CAREFULLY REVISED, IMPROVED AND ENLARGED.

WILLIAMS AND NORGATE,
14, HENRIETTA STREET, COVENT GARDEN, LONDON;
AND 20, SOUTH FREDERICK STREET, EDINBURGH.
1882.

PREFACE
TO THE THIRD EDITION.

THIS Edition has been very carefully revised and considerably enlarged. The following are some of the changes and additions that have been made: An Alphabetical List of all Strong and Irregular Verbs has been added. In the Grammatical Exercises many Adjectives have been introduced in the sentences, in order to afford the student an increased opportunity of becoming familiar with the Declension of this part of speech. The Dialogues and Phrases have likewise been altered and added to, wherever experience, gathered for many years in practical teaching, suggested, and lastly, a number of Reading Lessons have been added to the book, principally to teach the proper *Reading* of German, the demonstration of which has been attempted by the introduction of *hyphens* and *accents*, a number of the Reading pieces, moreover, have been furnished with grammatical notes.

The Author has spared no trouble in rendering the new edition still fitter for the use of schools and private study and hopes that it will continue to meet with the favour of an appreciative public.

Royal High School, Edinburgh, July 1882.

PREFACE
TO THE FIRST EDITION.

The author has attempted in this grammar to combine sound theory with simple practice. He has limited the rules for the Gender to such as have few or no Exceptions, having learnt by experience that long lists are a stumbling-block to pupils. He has admitted only three Declensions of Nouns, in each of which the Rules of the Singular, Plural and Modification of the Vowel are contained, the necessary lists of Exceptions being in metre with Examples inserted for facility of learning. The Declension of the Adjective has been expressed in a few Simple Rules intelligible to the youngest pupil.

One Conjugation has been adopted for the Verbs, which have been divided into Weak and Strong, the latter being subdivided into Twelve Classes according to the change required in the radical vowel.

With respect to Compound Verbs the author has chosen the terms of Quasi- and Real-Compound Verbs instead of Separable and Inseparable, as he finds the difficulty of the Separable Verbs removed by considering them as *two distinct words* and paying attention to the construction of sentences accordingly.

The rules for the government of Prepositions are given in metre and difficulties explained by contrast.

The Syntax is as short as the necessity of completeness allowed, particular attention being paid to the Construction of Sentences, which is given in a few simple but comprehensive Rules.

The Author feeling that, notwithstanding the great trouble he has taken in making his grammar as perfect a possible, errors may have occurred, would be grateful for any corrections or suggestions for the second edition.

Edinburgh. September 1868.

PREFACE
TO THE SECOND EDITION.

The success which has attended the publication of this Grammar has enabled the author at so early a date to publish a new edition.

The whole work has been subjected to a thorough revision before passing into the hands of the printer. Many rules have been remodelled and new ones added, as experience derived from pratice suggested.

The exercises which in the first edition formed a separate part, have now been incorporated with the Grammar. They also have been altered and improved.

The author has thought it advisable to furnish a complete Vocabulary of all the words occurring in the exercises and sincerely hopes that with these improvements this edition will meet with as much success as the first.

Edinburgh, September 1870.

Contents.

FIRST PART.

INTRODUCTION.

	Page
The German A B C	1
1—6. The 26 letters, vowels, diphthongs, modified vowels and diphthongs, consonants and combined consonants	1—2
The Pronunciation	2
7—11. *General Rules* of pronunciation	2
12—13. The pronunciation of the *vowels* and *diphthongs*	4—5
14—28. „ „ of the *simple consonants* . .	6
29—40. „ „ of the *combined consonants* .	9
41—43. **The Accentuation of Words and Sentences** .	11

THE ARTICLE.

44. The Articles	12
45. The *Definite* Article	12
46. Observations on the same	12
47. The inflections of the same (strong terminations) .	13
48. The Definite Article contracted with Prepositions	13
49. The *Indefinite* Article	13
50—51. Observations on the Indefinite Article	14

THE PRONOUN.

52—53. The Pronouns	14
54. The **Personal** Pronoun	14
55. Observation on the Pronouns used in addressing .	15
56. The Pronoun *es* contracted	16
57. The Personal Pronouns followed by Prep. with Gen.	16
58. **Reflective** Pronouns	17
59. **Reciprocal** Pronouns	17
60. The **Demonstrative** Pronouns	18
61—62. The **Determinate** Demonstrative Pronoun . . .	18

		Page
63.	Pronouns agree with their Nouns	19
64.	The Genitives **Dessen** and **Deren** add -t	19
65—67.	The **Indeterminate** Demonstrative Pronoun	19—20
68.	**Wer, was,** used for the Dem. Indeterm. *and* Rel. Pron. together	21
69.	The **Possessive** Pronouns	21
70—72.	The *Conjoined* Possessive Pronouns	21—22
73.	Observation on the Conventional Possessive Pronouns	22
74.	**Dessen, deren** and **derer** used for **sein** and **ihr**	23
75—79.	The *Disjoined* Possessive Pronouns	23—25
80.	The same used as predicate	25
81.	The same in the plural with certain meanings	25
82.	The **Interrogative** Pronouns	25
83.	The *Disjoined* Interrogative Pronoun	25—26
84.	The Adverb **wo** used for the neuter of the interrogative Pronoun	26
85.	Interrogative Pronouns used *relatively*	26
86.	About the *relative* „**was**"	26
87.	The *Conjoined* Interrogative Pronoun	26—27
88.	**Wer, was, welcher** used as *Indefinite* Pronouns	27—28
89.	*What kind of*, **was für ein**	28
90—92.	The **Relative** Pronoun	28—30
93.	Observation on the *relative* properties of „**was**"	30
94.	The Genitives **welches, -er, -es,** used exceptionally	30
95.	The **Indefinite** Pronouns	30—31
96.	*Additional* Pronouns	31
97.	**Derselbe, dieselbe, dasselbe**	31
98.	**Aller, alle, alles**	32
99.	**Solcher, solche, solches**	32
100.	**Mancher, manche, manches**	32
101.	**Jeder, jede, jedes**	33
102.	**Kein, keine, kein**	33

THE NOUN.

103.	The Noun	33
104.	**The Gender of the Noun**	34
105—106.	Of the *Masculine*	34—35
107—108.	Of the *Feminine*	35
109—110.	Of the *Neuter*	36
111.	Nouns with *varying* gender	36
112.	Nouns with more than one gender	37—38
113.	**The Declension of the Noun**	39
114.	The **First** Declension	39
115—117.	„ „ „ Sing. & Plur. (general rule)	39—41
118.	„ „ „ Nouns modifying the Vowel	41
119.	„ „ „ Exceptions to Rule 118	42—43
120.	„ „ „ „ to the Plural	43

	Page
121—123. The **First** Declension, Exceptions (*First* Class, *no* inflection)	43—44
124. The **First** Declension, Exceptions (*2nd* Class, **-er**)	45—47
125. The **First** Declension, Exceptions *3rd* Class, **-en**)	47—48
126—127. The **Second** Declension	49—51
128—129. The **Third** Declension	51—52
130. „ „ „ . Exceptions to the *Plural*	52—54
131. Nouns occurring in the Plural only	54
132. Declensions of *Adjectives* used *substantively*	54—55
133. **Table of the Declensions of the Noun**	56
134—138. The *Compound* Noun	57—58
139—141. *Foreign* Nouns	58—59
142. *Foreign Proper Names*	59
143. **Proper Names**	60
144. Observations on the same	60
145. Names of *men* (Plural)	61
146—148. Formation of *Feminine* Terms	61
149—153. **Substantive Diminutives** or Petwords	62—64

THE ADJECTIVE.

154. The Adjective	64
155—157. **The Comparison** *of the Adjective*	65
158. Adjectives that do *not modify the vowel* in comparison	66
159. The same, abbriged list	66
160. Adjectives that vary in the modification	66
161. The Adjective „**lange**" compared	66
162. Than, **als, denn**	67
163. The—the, **je—desto**	67
164. The **Superlative** used *adjectively* and *adverbially*	67
165. Adjectives with *irregular Comparison*	67—68
166. Some *peculiar* Comparatives and Superlatives not implying direct comparison	68
167. The Comparison of **erst** and **letzt**	68
168. The Comparison of *Participles*	68
169. **Aller**, used to strengthen the *Superlative*	68
170. The *Superlative not* used in an *absolute* sense	69
171. **The Declension of the Adjective**	69
172. The Adjective *not* declined when predicate	69
173. The Adjective *declined* when *epithet*	69
174. a. Two or more Adjectives declined	70
174. b. Comparatives and Superlatives declined	70
174. c. Intervening adverbs	70
175. The *strong* terminations	70
176. Articles and Pronouns with regard to strong terminations	70

		Page
177.	The *weak* terminations	71
178.	The Adjectives „hoch"	71
179.	Adjectives in -er from names of towns	71
180.	Inflections dropped in declined Adjectives; strong termination -es, substituted by the weak -en . .	71
181.	*Table* of *strong* and *weak* terminations for the Declension of the Adjectives	71
182—190.	*Examples* on the Declension of the Adjective .	72—75
191.	Derived Adjectives	76
192.	Adjectives derived from Proper Names of Persons, Towns etc.	76
193.	" " " words denoting substances	77
194.	" " " Adverbs or Prepositions	77—78

THE NUMERAL.

195.	The Numerals	78
196.	The Cardinal Numbers	78—80
197.	The Ordinal Numbers	78—80
198.	The Same	80
199—202.	*Declension* of Numerals	81—82
203.	The *Ordinals* used with *names* and *dates* . . .	82
204.	" " " *adverbially*	82
205.	Der, die, das wievielte	83
206.	The *Multiplicative* Numerals	83
207.	The *Reiterative* "	83—84
208.	" " " (*Adverbs*)	84
209—210.	The *Fractional*	84
211.	About the use of halb	85
212.	*Variative* Numerals	86
213.	Words in connection with variative Numerals . .	86
214.	Je—je;—weise; the *time* in German . . .	86—87

THE VERB.

215—216.	The Verb	87
217.	**The Regular Verb**	87
218.	Strong Verbs characterized	88
219.	Weak Verbs characterized	88
220.	*Preliminary* Remarks on the *Conjugation* . . .	89
221.	**The Conjugation**	88
222.	Derivation of simple tenses	88
223.	The Infinitive of the Present	88
224.	The Root of Verbs	88
225.	The **Active** Voice (*Simple* tenses)	90—93
226—229.	The **Active** Voice (*Compound* tenses) . . .	92—99
230—233.	The **Passive** Voice	98—103
234.	*Verbs* used as *Nouns*	102

		Page
235.	The *Infinitive* formerly *declined*	102
236.	**The Strong Verbs** classified	103
237.	Class I. (i — a — u)	104—105
238.	„ II. (i — a — o)	105
239.	„ III. (e — a — o — i, or ie)	105—107
240.	„ IV. (e — a — e — i, or ie)	107—108
241.	„ V. (a — u — a — ä)	108—109
242.	„ VI. (a — i, or ie — a — ä)	109—110
243.	„ VII. (ei — i — i)	110—111
244.	„ VIII. (ei — ie — ie)	112
245.	„ IX. (ie, or e, or ü, or au, or ä, or ö—ŏ—ō)	112—114
246.	„ X. (ie, or e, or ö, or au, or i, or a—ŏ—ŏ—ie, or äu)	114—116
247.	„ XI. (*various* changes of radical vowels)	116—117
248.	„ XII. (*change* of radical vowel *and* inflections of *weak* verbs)	117
249.	Observation (mahlen, ſpalten, ſalzen)	118
250.	**The Irregular Verbs**	118
251—253.	„ „ „ The *auxiliary* Verbs (ſein, haben, werden)	119—122
254—259.	„ „ „ The *auxiliary* Verbs of *mood* (dürfen, können, mögen, müſſen, ſollen, wollen)	122—124
260.	„ „ „ The Verb wiſſen	125
261—264.	**The Impersonal Verbs**	125—128
265.	**The Reflective Verbs**	128
266.	„ „ „ Example with *Accus.*	128—129
267.	„ „ „ Example with *Dative*	129
268.	List of *Reflective* Verbs with *Dative*	129—130
269.	**The Compound Verbs**	130
270—271.	The *Real-* (or Inseparable) *Compound* Verbs; Meaning of the Prefixes be, ent, etc.	130—131
272—276.	The *Quasi-* (or Separable) *Compound* Verbs	132—134
277.	Verbs, *being both* real- and quasi-compound	135
278.	Compound Verbs with miſs	135
279.	Verb Diminutives	135

THE ADVERB.

280.	Adverbs	136
281.	**Adverbs of Quality or Kind**	136
282.	„ „ „ „ „ (denoting *number, order* or *extent*)	136—137
283.	„ „ „ „ „ (denoting *comparison* and *estimation*)	137
284.	„ „ „ „ „ (denoting *degree of strength*)	137

		Page
285.	**Adverbs of Quality or Kind** (denoting *question, relation, affirmation, negation, supposition, feeling* etc.)	138
286.	**Adverbs of Place**	138—139
287.	**Adverbs of Time**	139—140
288.	*Comparison* of Adverbs	140—141
289.	Adverbs not to be rendered in English	141

THE PREPOSITION.

290.	Prepositions	142
291—292.	Prepositions with the **Genitive**	142—144
293—294.	„ „ „ **Dative**	144—146
296—297.	„ „ „ **Accusative**	146—147
298—299.	„ „ „ **Dative & Accusative**	147—149
300.	Adverbs used to strengthen the Preposition	149
301—304.	THE CONJUNCTION	150—152
305—307.	THE INTERJECTION	153

SYNTAX.

308.	**The Construction of Sentences**	154
309.	*The Order of Words*	154—155
310—316.	Observations on the position of the *Verb*	155—159
317.	**Agreement** of Articles and Pronouns with their Nouns	159—160
318.	**Apposition**	160—161
319.	**The Articles** (The use of)	161—163
320—321.	*The Definite Article* used in German and *not* in English	163
	Government of Words	163
322.	**The Nominative** (The Subject)	163
323.	The Nominative for the Latin *Vocative*	163—164
324—325.	The Nominative with certain *Verbs*	164
326—328.	Observations on **sein, werden, heißen, schelten**, etc.	164
329—331.	**The Genitive**	165
332—333.	Words of *quantity* or *measure* (Nom. and Gen.) *Observation*, how to translate the English „*of*"	165—166
334.	*Verbs* governing the Genitive	166
335.	*Neuter* Verbs governing the Genitive	166—167
336.	*Reflective* Verbs governing the Genitive	167
337.	*Transitive* Verbs with *two* cases, one of a *person* (Accusative), one of a *thing* (Genitive)	167—168
338.	*Adjectives* and *Adverbs* with the Genitive	168
339.	*Nouns* used *adverbially* in the Genitive	169
340.	**The Dative**	169
341—342.	*Verbs* governing the Dative	170—171

		Page
343.	*Verbs* used with **the Dative** in *some* cases and with **Prepositions** in *others*	171
344—345.	*Verbs* used with the **Dative** and **Accusative** *indifferently*	172
346.	*Adjectives* governing the Dative	172
	Observation, Adjectives requiring a *Preposition*	172
347.	*Dative* of a *Noun* or *Personal Pronoun* instead of *Possessive Pronouns*	172
348.	*Dative of Pers. Pron.* as Particle (ethic Dative)	173
349.	**The Accusative** (The Object	173
350.	*Verbs* governing the Accusative	173
351—352.	*Nouns* used adverbially in the Accusative	173—174
	The Use of the Verb	174
353.	*Agreement*	174
354.	Exceptions to Agreement	174
355.	Observations on Agreement	174
	1) Collective Nouns followed by the Singular	174
	2) Personal Pron. with relative Clause in different person	175
356—358.	**The Use of auxiliary Verbs haben, sein and werden**	175—176
	Note. About the use of thun, to do, as *auxiliary*	176
	The Use of the Voices	176
359.	*The Active Voice*	176
360.	*The Passive Voice*	176
361—363.	Observation on the Passive Voice	176—177
361.	The Passive instead of the Impersonal Active	176—177
362.	*Reflective form* instead of *passive*	177
363.	How to translate *to be*	177
	The Use of the Moods	177
364.	*The Indicative*	177
365.	*The Subjunctive*	177—178
366.	Observation about *Indirect Speech*	178
	Examples to Rules 364—366	178—180
367.	*The Imperative*	180—181
368.	*The Conditional*	181
369.	Observation about Imperfect Subjunctive instead of Conditional	181
370.	*The Infinitive*	181
371—372.	The Infinitive used in German and *not* in English	181—182
373.	Accusative with Infinitive	182
374.	The Infinitive *with* and *without* zu	182
375—377.	„ „ „ „ „ „ cases differing from the *English*	182—183
378.	Observation on Infinitive clauses beginning with *as*	183

	Page.
379. Infinitive sentences indicating a *purpose* (*in order to*: **um zu**)	183
380. „ taken substantively (*for*: **zum**)	183—184
The Use of the Participles	184
381. *The Present Participle*	184
382. *The Perfect Participle*	184
383. „ „ „ its *different* use from the *English*	184
384—385. „ „ „ replaced by the *Infinitive*	185
386. The *English Participles* rendered in German	185—186
The Use of the Tenses	186
387. *The Present Tense*	186
388—391. „ „ *differing* from the *English*	186—187
392. *The Imperfect Tense*	187
393—394. „ „ „ *differing* from the *English*	187
395. *The Perfect Tense*	187
396. *The Pluperfect Tense*	187—188
397. *The Future Tense*	188
398. Observation, how to render *shall, should, will, would*	188
399. **Punctuation**	189
400. Examples on Punctuation	189
Alphabetical List of Strong and Irregular Verbs	190—196

SECOND PART.

Conversational Exercises	196—284

THIRD PART.

Useful Dialogues and Idiomatic Phrases	285—313

FOURTH PART.

Vocabulary for reference and revisal.

English-German	313—332
German-English	332—349

FIFTH PART.

Reading Lessons.

a. Specimens showing how the text should be prepared etc.

I. Die Sternthaler. The star-dollars	350
II. Märchen von der Unke	353
III. Rechnungs-Exempel. Arithmetical Puzzles	355

b. Specimens for Reading etc.

I. Die Erzählung des thüringischen Candidaten	358
II. Böser Markt. A Bad Bargain	366
III. Der silberne Löffel. The Silver Spoon	369
IV. (For Recitation.) Hero und Leander	371
V. Amor als Landschaftsmaler	378

THE
GERMAN GRAMMAR.

と せ

FIRST PART.

THE GERMAN ABC.
Das deutsche Abc.

.1. The German language has 26 letters, namely:

German Type.		Roman Type.		Pronunciation.
Small.	Capital.	Small.	Capital.	
a	𝔄	a	A	ah
b	𝔅	b	B	bay
c *1	ℭ	c	C	tsay
d	𝔇	d	D	day
e	𝔈	e	E	ay
f	𝔉	f	F	eff
g	𝔊	g	G	gay
h	ℌ	h	H	hah
i	ℑ	i	I	ee
j	𝔍	j	J	yay *or* yott
k	𝔎	k	K	kah
l	𝔏	l	L	ell
m	𝔐	m	M	emm
n	𝔑	n	N	enn
o	𝔒	o	O	oh
p	𝔓	p	P	pay
q *	𝔔	q	Q	koo
r	𝔖	r	R	err
ſ, s	𝔖	s	S	ess
t	𝔗	t	T	tay
u	𝔘	u	U	oo
v	𝔙	v	V	fow
w	𝔚	w	W	vay
x *	𝔛	x	X	ix
y *	𝔜	y	Y	ipsilon
z	𝔷	z	Z	tset

¹) Those marked * are of foreign origin and might be dispensed with altogether in German words.

A. v. Ravensberg, German Grammar. 3d Ed.

2. The **Vowels** (Selbstlaute) are *five* in number, viz., a, e, i, o, u; to which must be added the Greek letter y, which is pronounced like ü, according to some like i (ee).

3. The **Diphthongs** (Doppellaute) are: ai[1], ei[1], au, eu and äu (compare rule 4), also ui[1] and oi[1] which latter two, however, occur in a few words only.

4. **Modified vowels and diphthongs** (Umlaute) are produced by the blending with e of the letters a, o, u and au into ä, ö, ü and äu[2]; thus the number of simple vocalic sounds is *eight*, viz., a, ä, e, i, o, ö, u, ü.

5. The **Consonants** (Mitlaute) are: b, c, d, f, g, h, j, k, l, m, n, p, q, r, s, t, v, w, x, z.

6. The **Combined Consonants** (Doppelmitlaute) are: ch, chs, ck, pf, ph, pf, sp, sph, ss, ß, st, sch, th, tz.

THE PRONUNCIATION.
Die Aussprache.

7. *Note.* It may be stated here that pronunciation can be well acquired only by practice; therefore, after the sound of each letter has been learned and the principal differences of pronunciation have been mentioned, the pupil ought at once to proceed to spelling and reading, the master merely referring to the rules given below in cases of difficulty.

---

1) ai, ei, oi and ui are sometimes spelled ay, ey, oy, uy.

2) The modified vowels are, when capitals, represented either by putting two dots on the top, viz., Ä, Ö, Ü, Äu, or by joining the letter e to them, viz., Ae, Oe, Ue, Aeu; the former mode is more practical.

8. All letters are pronounced, with the exception of e and h when they occur to indicate a long vowel; as, viel *(much)*, pronounced *feel*, wohl *(well)*, pronounced *vōl*, That *(deed)*, pronounced *tāt*. In many of the books printed at the present time these, especially the h, are altogether omitted: wol, Tat.

9. All vowels have a long and a short sound; when followed by *one* consonant, they are *long*, when followed by *two* or more consonants, *short*; whilst diphthongs and double vowels are always long.

Exceptions.

10. A. 1) Long remain all syllables which have been contracted from two by the dropping of an e; especially Perfect Participles, Present and Imperfect Tenses of Verbs; as, gelebt from gelebet, bebst from bebest, bebte from bebete.

2) Long are also the following words: Art, f., *manner*; Bart, m., *beard*; Erde, f., *earth*; erst, *first*; Geburt, f., *birth*; Herd, m., *hearth*; Herde, f., *herd*; Husten, m., *cough*; Kloster, n., *cloister*; Krebs, m., *crab*; Mond, m., *moon*; nebst, *with*; Obst, n., *fruit*; Oster, f., *easter*; Pferd, n., *horse*; rösten, *to roast*; Schwert, n., *sword*; stets, *continually*; todt, *dead*; Trost, m., *consolation*; Wüste, f., *desert*; zart, *tender*; Buch, n., *book*; suchen, *to seek*; fluchen, *to swear*; Kuchen, m., *cake*; hoch, *high* (short in Hochzeit, f., *wedding)*; Nachen, m., *skiff*; Schmach, f., *disgrace*; Tuch, n., *cloth*; werden, *to become*, etc. etc.

11. B. 1) Short are: ab, *off*; an, *on, to, at*; am, *at the*; bin, *am*; bis, *until*; das, *the, that*; des, *of the*; es, *it*; hat, *has*; in, *in*; im, *in the*; man, *one*; mit, *with*; um, *about*; von, *of, from*; vom, *of the, from the*; weg[1] (pronounced wed), *away*; was, *what*; zum, *to the*; also in the compounds: Herzog, m., *duke*; Herberge, f., *shelter*; Urtheil, n., *opinion, judgment*; Vortheil, m., *advantage*; vierzehn, 14; vierzig, 40.

2) Short are also all inflections of Nouns, Adjectives and Verbs, and prefixes like be, ent, er, ge, etc.

---

[1] Weg, m., *way*, *road*, is pronounced in the regular way (see pronunciation of g).

The Vowels.

12. **A, a,** *long* is pronounced with mouth quite open[1], like *a* in *father*. Ex.: Vater, Name.

A, a, *short* is pronounced with mouth rather open, like *a* in *command*. Ex.: Hand, hatte.

E, e, *long* " " with half open, broad mouth, like *ay* in *day*. Ex.: geh, leb'.

E, e, *short* " " with slightly less open, broad mouth, like *e* in *better*. Ex.: besser, Vetter.

J, i, *long* " " with mouth same as short e, only less open, like *ee* in *bee*. Ex.: mir, dir.

J, i, *short* " " with mouth same as short e, still less open, like *i* in *in*, or *fill*. Ex.: ich, mich, sich.

O, o, *long* " " with mouth round, like *o* in *pole*. Ex.; hol, so, wol.

O, o, *short* " " with mouth round but slightly farther open, like *o* in *rock*. Ex.: Stock, voll.

U, u, *long* " " with mouth round and somewhat projected, like *u* in *sure*. Ex.: du, Hut.

U, u, *short* " " with mouth same as for long u, only a little farther open, like *u* in *bush* or *butcher*. Ex.: stumm, Luft.

Ä, ä, *long* " " with mouth half open and broad, like *a* in *bade*. Ex.: Käs', jäh; but generally like simple e.

---

2) No pure **a** can be pronounced with closed lips, the sound thus produced will only be that of *a* in English *hand*, but not of *a* in German „Hand".

Ä, ä, *short* is pronounced with mouth same as short e. Ex.: gält', fällt.

Ö, ö, *long* „   „ with mouth round and somewhat pointed, like *e* in *herd, but lengthened;* or like „*eu*" in the French word „*feu*". Ex.: Öb', schwör', hör'.

Ö, ö, *short* „   „ with mouth same as long ö, like *e* in *herd*. Ex.: Mörder, Körner.

Ü, ü, *long* „   „ with mouth round and very pointed, like „*u*" in the French word „*vu*". Ex.: üb', schüb', Mühle.

Ü, ü, *short* „   „ with mouth round and pointed like „*u*" in the Scotch word „*gude*" (good). Ex.: Würde, Müller.

Y, y,   „   „ like ü or i. Ex.: Tyrann.

The Diphthongs.

13. The diphthongs are pronounced with the sound of each vowel, though so fast, as to present only one sound, viz.:

ai like **a** and **i**, or like *ay* in the Scotch word *aye!* Ex.: Hai, Mais, Waise; but commonly like ei.

ei like **e** and **i**, or like the English personal pronoun *I*. Ex.: Hei! Reis, Weise.

au like **a** and **u**, or like *ou* in *house*. Ex.: Haus, Maus, aus, Braut.

eu, **äu** and **oi** like *oi* in *oil*. Ex.: euch, Häuser, Mäuse, Broihan.

ui like **u** and **i**, or like the English personal pronoun *we*. Ex.: hui, pfui!

The Simple Consonants.

14. *Note.* The pronunciation of the consonants is not quite the same all over Germany, but the rules, here laid down, are in accordance with the pronunciation of the Prussians; however, when there is a difference of pronunciation in other parts of Germany, it will be noticed.

15. F, f; K, f; L, l; M, m; N, n; P, p; Q, q; T, t are pronounced *the same as in English.* Ex.: Falke, kamen, Mann, Nipp, Quappe, Quart, Torf.

16. B, b and D, d, at the *beginning* of words and syllables, are pronounced the same as in English; as, babe, binde, Daube; at the *end* of them, however, they are pronounced hard, *i. e.* like *p* and *t* respectively[1]; thus, Hand is pronounced *hant,* (in the plural, Hände, the d retains its natural sound, it now being at the *beginning* of a syllable), Band like *bant,* ab like *ap,* Staub like *staup;* also bs, ds, bst like *ps, ts, pst*. When, however, followed by an apostrophe, the soft sound must be preserved; as, hab', red'.

17. C, c[2], *before* ä, e, i, eu is pronounced like *ts;* before a, o, u, au it is pronounced like *k;* it is used also together with k instead of double k, viz., ck. Ex.: Cäsar, Cecilie, Carl, Caucasus, Conrad, Reck, Sack, Hecke; before consonants it is like *k;* as, Classe or Klasse.

18. G, g, at the beginning of *roots,* as well as at the beginning of all *first* and *second* syllables of words is pronounced hard[3], *i. e.,* like the Saxon *g* in English;

---

1) Some German Grammarians hold, that b and d should be pronounced with their natural sound, i. e. *soft,* even at the end of words.
2) Compare the pronunciation of z.
3) According to some, g at the beginning of prefixes, such as the augment ge, may be pronounced like *yay,* so that „gegeben" might be pronounced *yaygayben;* though this is not allowed as yet to be grammatically correct, it is certain, that there exists at present a tendency to abolish the hard g altogether, which shows itself in the fact, that in some places the *people* pronounce most words beginning with g as if spelled with j, *i. e.,* yay.

as, gut, geben, gegeben, Gabe, Gift. At the beginning of any *further* syllable it is pronounced like *y* in *yes*: as, derjenige, Königin; and at the *end* of words and syllables like *ch* in Scotch *loch*, but it does not shorten the vowel like „ch"; as, Berg, Weg, König, wenig, Tag, bog, Betrug.

19. -ng at the *end* of words is pronounced *hard* like *nk*; as, Ring like *rink* (if such a word occurs in a compound, as Ring-finger, the ng retains its hard sound). *Within* words -ng- is pronounced *soft*, so that Finger sounds like *fing-er*, not like English *fin-ger*; consequently it is precisely opposed to the English pronunciation. Ex.: German: jung, pronounced like *yoonk*, English: *young*; German: jünger, pronounced like *yüng-er*; English: *younger*.

Observations.

20. a. g has never the soft sound of the French *g*, except in foreign words; as, Genie, pronounced as in French.
b. g at the end of words, *not* preceded by n, *must* be pronounced hard *if e has been elided*; as, trag', pronounced like *g* in *bag*; whilst for example Vertrag is pronounced: *Fertrach*.
c. In some parts of Germany the ng is pronounced exactly the same as in English.
d. -ng at the end of words that have dropped an e [1] is pronounced soft; as, lang', *long* (speaking of *time*), instead of lange, pronounced like *ng* in the English *long*; whilst lang, *long* (speaking of *space*) is pronounced *lank*; gering', *little*, fang', *catch*.

21. H, h is always aspirated at the beginning of words and syllables; at the end and within syllables it serves to indicate a long vowel (compare Rule 8). Ex.: Habe, fahen, Höhle, höher.

22. J, j, which is the letter i, *used as consonant*, is pronounced like *y* in *yes*; as, ja, jung, Jahr.

23. S, s, at the beginning of words and syllables is pronounced like English *z*; as, Sohn, so, sein, Saal;

---

1) Though the elision of e ought to be marked by an apostrophe, this is not always done by writers.

at the end of words and syllables it always has the hissing sound¹; as, 𝔊las like *glass*, 𝔊ras like *grass*; also in double -ſ (ſſ), the second has the hissing sound, as, beſſer, pronounced *bess-ser*.

24. *Note.* In some parts of Germany ſ is pronounced at the beginning of words and syllables the same as in English.

25. 𝔙, v, is pronounced in all *Germanic* words like f; as, 𝔙ater, ver-, voll, von, 𝔙ogel, vor; in *foreign* words like *vay*, *e. g.*, 𝔙ictoria, 𝔙enus; at the end of words it sounds hard like f; as, brav like braf; however when shifted from the end to the beginning of a syllable, it resumes its original w-sound; as, braver like brawer, excepting 𝔙ers (pronounced *fers*), 𝔙ice, vice, (pronounced *featsé*), and 𝔙esper, vesper (pronounced *Fesper*).

26. *Note.* The German v may be considered a superfluous letter and might well be abolished along with c, q and x; the learner should at once commit to memory those roots and words which begin with v, their number being very small; they are: der 𝔙ater, *the father;* die 𝔙ehme, *a certain kind of mediæval lynch court;* das 𝔙eilchen, *the violet;* 𝔙eit, *Vitus* (a name); der 𝔙eitstanz, *St. Vitusdance;* the prefix ver; die 𝔙este (or 𝔉este), *the fortress;* der 𝔙etter, *the cousin;* das 𝔙ieh, *the cattle;* viel, *much;* vier, *four;* voll, *full;* der 𝔙ogel, *the bird;* der 𝔙ogt, *the overseer;* das 𝔙olk, *the people;* von, *of;* vor, *before;* and their derivatives and compounds.

27. 𝔚, w, is pronounced like the English *v;* as, 𝔚elle, wird, 𝔊ewalt, wollte, wurde; but after ſch and z it should be pronounced like u, as, ſchwimm like ſchui̅mm, zwar like zua̅r.

28. 𝔷, z, is pronounced like *ts*. Ex.: 𝔷ahl, 𝔷opf, zu, zehn, ziehen, 𝔏anze.

---

1) The reason why certain words such as 𝔊ras, 𝔊las are not spelled with the hissing sound ſz or ſs is, that the simple s is preferred, because it also occurs in the oblique cases and the plural; as, 𝔊ra-ſes, 𝔊rä-ſer; whilst for example 𝔉aſs is declined 𝔉aſſes and 𝔉uſz, 𝔉uſzes.

The Combined Consonants.

29. Ch, ch never occurs at the beginning of *German* words (excepting Charfreitag, where it is pronounced like k); it is always pronounced like the Scotch *ch*, having a *soft* or palatal sound, as in *nicht* and *richt*, and a *hard* or guttural sound as in *focht*. It is sounded *softly* after the vowels ä, e, i, ö, the diphthongs äu, ei, eu, and if preceded by a consonant; as, Nächte, Recht, Licht, möchte, Schläuche, Leiche, euch, Furcht; *harshly* after a, o, u, au. Ex.: Nacht, Docht, Fuchtel, Schlauch, Flucht.

Ch, ch, in foreign words, is pronounced in three different ways, viz.:

a) If they are of *Greek* origin, introduced directly from that language, it has the *German* sound; to this class belong all Greek names; as, Achilles, and recently-formed words; as, mechanisch, mechanic.

b) If they are of *Greek* origin, but introduced *through Latin*, ch is pronounced like *k*; to this class belong all names in connection with the New Testament and others; as, Christus, Chor(us).

c) If they are of *French* origin, they are pronounced *sh*; as, Champagner, Champignon.

30. -chs is equivalent to x; as, Wachs (pronounced vax), wachsen, Fuchs, Füchse.

31. -ck is pronounced like *k* and serves to indicate a short vowel; if it stands at the end of a line and requires to be divided, k takes the place of c; as, Zucker divided Zuk=ker (compare Rule 17).

32. Pf, pf is pronounced so that both letters are distinctly heard; as, Pferd (horse) like P=ferd; but also like -f.

33. Ph, ph is pronounced like *f* and often substituted by that letter; it occurs almost only in words and names of Greek origin; as, Philipp, Philip.

34. 𝔓𝔰, 𝔭𝔰 is pronounced so that both letters are distinctly heard; it occurs only in words of foreign origin; as, 𝔓𝔰𝔞𝔩𝔪, 𝔓𝔰𝔞𝔩𝔱𝔢𝔯.

35. 𝔰𝔰, 𝔰𝔷, 𝔷[1] are the characters which represent the *hissing* sound, of which 𝔰𝔰 and 𝔰𝔷 ought to be used to indicate a *short* vowel (𝔰𝔰 in the middle and 𝔰𝔷 at the end of a word or syllable) and 𝔷 to indicate a *long* one.

36. *Note.* In most German books it will be found that 𝔰𝔷 never occurs at the *end* of words and syllables, ß being used instead, both after *long* and *short* vowels; but the learner will only be able to pronounce such words correctly at sight as well as to decline them properly, when spelled in the distinctive way, *i. e.*, when ß is used after *long* and 𝔰𝔰 or 𝔰𝔷 after *short* vowels. This spelling has been observed in this grammar and other publications of the author, so that the reader cannot fail to pronounce correctly words like the following: 𝔑𝔲𝔰𝔷, 𝔉𝔲ß, 𝔡𝔞𝔰𝔷, 𝔉𝔞𝔰𝔷, 𝔐𝔞ß, 𝔤𝔯𝔬ß, 𝔖𝔠𝔥𝔩𝔬𝔰𝔷, 𝔟𝔩𝔬ß, 𝔊𝔢𝔩𝔞𝔰𝔷, 𝔤𝔢𝔴𝔦𝔰𝔷; whilst he has no idea conveyed to him of their length or shortness, when ß is used indifferently.

37. 𝔖𝔱, 𝔰𝔱 and 𝔖𝔭, 𝔰𝔭 are pronounced *at the beginning of roots* with the avoidance of the hissing sound, *i. e.* like 𝔰𝔠𝔥𝔱 and 𝔰𝔠𝔥𝔭, although not spelled thus.

Examples.

𝔰𝔱𝔦𝔩𝔩 *(still),* pronounced like *shtill*,
𝔖𝔱𝔞𝔟 *(staff),* ,, ,, *shtap*,
𝔰𝔭𝔦𝔫𝔫 *(spin),* ,, ,, *shpin*,
𝔖𝔭𝔢𝔢𝔯 *(spear),* ,, ,, *shpare*.

At the beginning of inflections, or at the end of words 𝔰𝔱 is pronounced as in English; as, 𝔟𝔢𝔰𝔱 = best, 𝔉𝔞𝔰𝔱𝔢𝔫 = fasten (not besht, fashten).

38. *Note.* The pronunciation of these combined consonants may appear arbitrary, yet it is based on the above mentioned principal, viz., the avoidance of the hissing sound, and deserves the faithful imitation of the learner. The same will be observed in words beginning with 𝔰𝔠𝔥𝔩, 𝔰𝔠𝔥𝔪, 𝔰𝔠𝔥𝔫, 𝔰𝔠𝔥𝔴, as, 𝔰𝔠𝔥𝔩𝔢𝔦𝔠𝔥𝔢𝔫, 𝔰𝔠𝔥𝔪𝔢𝔯𝔷𝔢𝔫, 𝔰𝔠𝔥𝔫𝔢𝔩𝔩, 𝔰𝔠𝔥𝔴𝔦𝔪𝔪, 𝔖𝔠𝔥𝔴𝔢𝔯𝔱. It is true that, in a small part of Ger-

---

[1] ß properly speaking is a simple consonant, it is a substitute for a wanting simple letter.

many, some of the people are in the habit of pronouncing the said letters as is done in English; but this is denounced as foreign and pedantic by all other Germans.

39. th is pronounced like t, h only serving to indicate a long vowel; as, thun, that, gethan, Wuth (comp. Rule 8).

40. tz stands for zz and is pronounced like z; it indicates a short vowel; as, Satz.

THE ACCENTUATION OF WORDS AND SENTENCES.

41. In Simple Words the *root* is strongly emphatic, except in leben'dig, *living;* prefixes, affixes and inflections are half mute: especially the inflection -en is sounded as if the e in it were elided; as, Garten pronounced like Gart'n. The English language shows the same peculiarity in its Saxon words (garden, etc.).

42. In Compound Words the *first* component has the stress; the other components, *if roots*, are distinctly sounded, *inflections*, however, are half mute.

43. In Sentences that word which has the greatest *importance* is strongly emphatic.

Note. Although this rule is, in a less degree, also applicable to English, the student is apt to overlook it and to lay all the emphasis on the last word. Only a conscious reading of the text, however short and uninteresting, will enable the student to lay the stress on the proper word; special attention should be paid also to the proper *grouping* of words, that is, one should read *in connection* all words that by the sense belong together and on no account *stop* between them; as: Unter-allen-Völkern haben die-Griechen den-Traum-des-Lebens am-schönsten-geträumt; — any violation of this rule produces what is known as *broken* German.

For this last reason and for others more or less important it is urged on the student, never to read a sentence without trying to follow its meaning, which will frequently save the trouble of translation and be a powerful auxiliary to study. A student who observes this, will learn to understand a German book much more rapidly than one who reads everything in a mere mechanical way and gets its meaning only afterwards by translating.

THE ACCIDENCE. Die Formenlehre.

THE ARTICLE.
Das Geschlechtswort.

44. The Article is that part of speech which is used to point out whether the noun connected with it is to be taken in a *definite* or *indefinite* sense. Thus there are two kinds of Articles in use, viz.;

The Definite Article and *The Indefinite Article*.

45. (A.) THE DEFINITE ARTICLE.
Das bestimmte Geschlechtswort.

	SINGULAR.				PLURAL.	
	Masc.	Fem.	Neut.		For all genders.	
Nominative.	der,	die,[1]	das,	the,	Nom. die,[1]	the,
Genitive.	des,	der,	des,	of the,	Gen. der,	of the,
Dative.	dem,	der,	dem,	to the,	Dat. den,	to the,
Accusative.	den,	die[1],	das,	the;	Acc. die,	the.

Observations.

46. a) It will be seen from the above, that
1) In the Nominative Singular each Gender has a *different* inflection, viz., -er, -e, -s.

---

1) Pronounce *dee*.

2) The Genitive and Dative of the *Neuter* des, dem, are the *same* as the Genitive and Dative of the *Masculine* des, dem.
3) In the *Masculine* each case has a different inflection, viz., -er, -es, -em, -en.
4) The *Accusatives* of the Feminine (die), of the Neuter (das) and of the Plural (die) are the same as their corresponding *Nominatives*, viz., die, das, die.
5) The *Genitive* and *Dative* of the Feminine are alike, viz., der.

THE STRONG TERMINATIONS.
Die starken Endungen.

47. b) The Inflections of the Definite Article are called the *strong terminations*; they are:

	SINGULAR.			PLURAL.
	M.	F.	N.	For all genders.
N.	-er,	-e,	-(e)s,[1]	-e,
G.	-es,	-er,	-es,	-er,
D.	-em,	-er,	-em,	-en,
A.	-en,	-e,	-(e)s;[1]	-e.

48. c) The Definite Article is often *contracted* with *Prepositions*; as:

am	for an dem;	an's	for an das;
im	„ in dem;	in's	„ in das;
beim	„ bei dem;	auf's	„ auf das;
vom	„ von dem;	durch's	„ durch das;
zum	„ zu dem;	für's	„ für das;
zur	„ zu der;	um's	„ um das.

Other contractions, such as hinter's for hinter das, unterm for unter dem, are used almost only in conversation.

49. (B.) THE INDEFINITE ARTICLE.
Das unbestimmte Geschlechtswort.

	SINGULAR.			
	M.	F.	N.	
N.	ein,	eine,	ein,	a (an),
G.	eines,	einer,	eines,	of a (an),
D.	einem,	einer,	einem,	to a (an),
A.	einen,	eine,	ein,	a (an).

---

1) The inflection for the nominative and accusative in the neuter is -es in pronouns and also in the strong declension of the adjective, only the *Definite Article*, the *Demonstrative* and *Relative Pronoun* have -as instead of -es, viz., das.

Observations.

50. The Indefinite Article has *no Plural*.

51. The Indefinite Article has, as will be seen from the above, the *strong terminations* in all cases, excepting the *nominative* of the *masculine* and *neuter* and the *accusative* of the *neuter* which have *no* inflection. (Compare the *Numeral Adjective* ein, 199.)

THE PRONOUN.
Das Fürwort.

52. Pronoun is the name in German Grammars applied:

a) to a word used instead of a noun, such as *I, thou*, etc.

b) to adjectives expressing the position of a noun in its relation to the speaker. The latter can be used either *with* nouns *(conjoined)*, such as *this, that*, etc.; or *referring to* nouns *(disjoined)*, such as, *mine, ours*, etc.

53. There are in German *six* kinds of Pronouns:

    1. *The Personal Pronoun,*
    2. *The Demonstrative Pronoun,*
    3. *The Possessive Pronoun,*
    4. *The Interrogative Pronoun,*
    5. *The Relative Pronoun,*
    6. *The Indefinite Pronoun.*

54. THE PERSONAL PRONOUN.
Das Personenwort.

SINGULAR.

First Person.	*Second Person.*
N. ich, I,	du, thou,
G. meiner (or mein), of me,	deiner (or dein), of thee,
D. mir, to me,	dir, to thee,
A. mich, me;	dich, thee;

Third Person.

	Masculine.	Feminine.	Neuter.
N.	er, he,	sie, she,	es, it,
G.	seiner (or sein), of him,	ihrer, of her,	seiner[2] (or sein), of it,
D.	ihm, to him,	ihr, to her,	ihm, to it,
A.	ihn, him;	sie, her;	es[3], it;

PLURAL.

	First Person.	Second Person.	Third Person.
N.	wir, we,	ihr, you or ye,	sie, they,
G.	unser,[1] of us,	euer,[1] of you,	ihrer,[1, 2] of them,
D.	uns, to us,	euch, to you,	ihnen, to them,
A.	uns, us,	euch, you,	sie, them.

Observations.

55. Almost all the above pronouns occur in *addressing*, expressing more or less *politeness, intimacy, contempt, anger*, etc. and as such often convey a meaning which to represent faithfully would need sentences in other languages. However, the *Third Person Plural* is generally used in addressing *strangers* (except children). In this case the Pronouns receive a capital initial. To address *relatives, intimate friends* or *children*, the *Second Person Singular* is commonly used for *one*, and, of course, the *Second Person Plural* for *more* than one. Formerly the Second Person Plural **ihr** was used from politeness (as in English and French), but is now rare, except in litterature. Last century the Third Person Singular was employed from politeness; now-a-days, however, it is used only to express *anger, insult, contempt*, etc. Thus the *most important form* for the student of German is the

---

1) Read Observation 330.

2) The Genitive and Dative of the Neuter and of the Plural occur almost only when referring to *persons*, when referring to *things*, the corresponding cases of the Demonstrative Pronouns **das** or **dasselbe** are used; as, **dessen** or **desselben**, **dem** or **demselben**. Ex.: Ich erinnere mich **dessen** or **desselben** (instead of **seiner**) sehr gut. I remember *(of) it* very well. When in connection with prepositions, corresponding adverbs are preferred; as, **davon** *(thereof)* of it, **dazu** *(thereto)* to it, etc. Ex.: Dies Haus ist sehr groß; es sind zwanzig Zimmer in **demselben** or **darin** (instead of **in ihm**), this house is very big, there are twenty rooms *in it*. Sprechen Sie nicht mehr **davon** (instead of **von dem**), say no more *about it*.

3) es is used sometimes for the English adverb *so*, in phrases like these: ich hoffe **es**, I hope *so*, ich sagte **es** ja, did I not say *so*.

Third Person Plural. It should also be mentioned that in addressing strangers the words Herr, Frau and Fräulein, are used from courtesy before such nouns as Vater, Bruder, Mutter, Schwester, Tochter, without, however, changing the gender of these last words; e. g.:

Familiar: Wie geht es deinem Vater und deiner Mutter? How are your father and your mother?

Polite: Wie geht es Ihrem Herrn Vater und Ihrer Frau Mutter?

Familiar: Hast du deiner Schwester das Buch gegeben? Have you given your sister the book?

Polite: Haben Sie Ihrer Fräulein Schwester das Buch gegeben?

With regard to the spelling of the pronouns it may be taken as a rule, that all *grammatical* forms of pronouns should have a small and all *conventional* forms a capital letter; thus where du is used to address one person and ihr to address more than one, no capital letter is justifiable; whilst where the polite form of address is used, that is to say, where the terms employed are not exactly grammatical, as, Sie, they, for *you* (one or more), Ihr, ye, you, for *you* (one or more), Er, he, for *you* (one), a capital should be used. In *letters* the pronoun of the person addressed is always spelled with a capital; thus, Du, Ihr, you. The previous rule applies also to possessive pronouns; consequently one should write dein for one person, euer for more persons, but Ihr for one person or more when the polite form is intended, i. e. if one or more would, when spoken to singly, be addressed in that form. However, the present fashion to print, Dir, Dein, Du, etc. is decidedly wrong, no capitals being due to such words except as already indicated.

56. The Pronoun es is often contracted with the word before it; as, ich geb's dir, for ich gebe es dir, *I give it thee;* nimm's nicht, for nimm es nicht, *do not take it.*

57. If the Personal Pronouns are followed by one of the Prepositions **halben, wegen, willen,** *on account of,* which govern the Genitive, they add -et to the short form of the Genitive and affix the Preposition to the form thus derived; as,

meinethalben meinetwegen meinetwillen	on my account, for my sake,	ihrethalben ihretwegen ihretwillen	on her or their account, for her or their sake,
	unser(e)thalben unser(e)twegen unser(e)twillen	on our account, or for our sake.	

(Compare also Rule 64.)

THE REFLECTIVE PRONOUN.
Das rückzielende Fürwort.

58. The German Language uses the Personal Pronouns above mentioned also as Reflective Pronouns excepting only the Dative and Accusative of *all Third Persons*, which are not ihm, ihn, ihr, sie, ihnen and sie, but always **sich**[1]. (This form is of modern origin, for *Luther* employs ihn, sie etc. also *reflectively*; as, Gottes Name ist an **ihm** selbst heilig, where we now would say an sich, The name of God is holy in *itself*.)

Examples with Accusative: Er wäscht sich, he washes himself, sie wäscht sich, she washes herself, es wäscht sich, it washes itself, man wäscht sich, one washes one's self, sie waschen sich, they wash themselves.

Examples with Dative: Er, sie, es, man schmeichelt sich, he, she, it, one flatters himself, herself, itself, one's self, sie schmeicheln sich, they flatter themselves.

59. The same Pronouns serve to express *Reciprocity*, although an Adverb may be used instead of them; as, sie lieben sich, or, sie lieben **einander**, they love *one another*; wir umarmten **uns**, or, wir umarmten **einander**, we embraced *one another*. Sometimes we also find *both* Pronoun *and* Adverb in *one* phrase; as, sie liebten **sich einander**, they loved *one another*, which however, should be avoided as redundant, unless the verb is *reflective* and great *emphasis* is wanted in the pronoun; as, liebet **euch unter einander**, love ye *one another* (Bible).

When *one another* is used in the meaning of *one* **with** *the other*, or *one* **on** *the other*, or *one* **against** *the other*, sich cannot be employed, but the *Preposition* with the Adverb **einander** must be employed; as, Karl und Wilhelm spazieren **mit einander**, Charles and William walk *with one another* (*not* mit **sich**). Die Schiffe stießen **an einander**, the ships struck *against one another*

---

1) About the Adverb selbst see Note 2 to Rule 97.

(*not* an **ſich**). **Sie ſind ſehr freundlich gegen einander**, they are very friendly *towards one another* (*not* **gegen ſich**).

Note. The learner should be careful not to employ the reflective Pronoun in cases like these: *He* asked his friend to excuse *him*; for *him* is the Object of the Infinitive *to excuse* and is not *reflective*; thus, **er bat ſeinen Freund, ihn zu entſchuldigen**; whilst, **er bat ſeinen Freund, ſich zu entſchuldigen**, would be, he asked his friend to excuse *himself*.

THE DEMONSTRATIVE PRONOUN.
Das Zeigewort.

60. There are two kinds of Demonstrative Pronouns, viz.:

    a. *The Determinate Demonstrative Pronouns,*
    b. *The Indeterminate Demonstrative Pronouns;*

the former are conclusive in themselves and do not necessitate any further explanation, whilst the latter are *incomplete* and require *a relative clause* or *a possessive case* for their completion.

a. THE DETERMINATE DEMONSTRATIVE PRONOUN.
Das beſtimmte Zeigewort.

61. The German language has three different forms for this kind of pronoun, viz.:

1) **dieſer, dieſe, dieſes**, this, this one (used for *near* objects)
2) **jener, jene, jenes**, that, that one, yon (used for *distant* objects)

    principally used to express a contrast,

3) **der, die, das**, this, that (commonly used *without reference to distance*).

62. The two former, **dieſer** and **jener**, are declined with the *strong terminations* throughout; **der** is declined like the *definite article*, excepting the *genitive singular* and the *genitive* and *dative plural*; namely:

1.
	SINGULAR.				PLURAL.	
	M.	F.	N.		M. F. N.	
N.	dieſer,	dieſe,	dieſes,	(or dies), this,	dieſe,	these,
G.	dieſes,	dieſer,	dieſes,	of this,	dieſer,	of these,
D.	dieſem,	dieſer,	dieſem,	to this,	dieſen,	to these,
A.	dieſen,	dieſe,	dieſes,	(or dies), this;	dieſe,	these.

2.
	SINGULAR.				PLURAL.	
	M.	F.	N.		M. F. N.	
N.	jener,	jene,	jenes,	that, yon,	jene,	those,
G.	jenes,	jener,	jenes,	of that,	jener,	of those,
D.	jenem,	jener,	jenem,	to that,	jenen,	to those,
A.	jenen,	jene,	jenes,	that;	jene,	those.

3.
	SINGULAR.				PLURAL.	
	M.	F.	N.		M. F. N.	
N.	der,	die,	das,	this, that, he, she, it,	die, these, those, they,
G.	deſſen* (or des),	deren* (or des),	deſſen* of	„ him, her, „	derer*, of „	„ them,
D.	dem,	der,	dem,	to „ „ „ „ „	denen*, to „	„ „
A.	den,	die,	das,	„ „ „ „ „	die,	„ „ „

Observations.

63. The above, in common with *all other* pronouns, must agree in number and gender with the nouns which they *precede*.

64. The Genitives **deſſen** and **deren** add -t when followed by the Prepositions halben, wegen, willen, *on account of*; as, deſſenthalben, on its account. (Compare also Rule 57.)

b. THE INDETERMINATE DEMONSTRATIVE PRONOUN.

Das unbeſtimmte Zeigewort.

65. The German language has two forms for this Pronoun, viz.:

1) Derjenige, diejenige, dasjenige;
2) der, die, das, see 62,³ and foot-note.

The *second* form, being the *shortest*, is most commonly used, especially in conversation.

66. *Note.* The *English* language having no special form for this Pronoun, the *third* Person of the *Personal* Pronoun (*he, she*) and the *Demonstrative* Pronouns (*that, those*) as well as their different cases (*him, of her*, etc.) represent this pronoun *when*

---

*) Before nouns these forms are shortened into des, der, des; der, den.

followed by a relative phrase or a possessive case; that, before the possessive case, however, is often *understood*; as: my house and my friend's, instead of, *that* of my friend.

In *French* this Pronoun is represented by *celui, celle; ceux, celles* and *ce (qui* or *que)*.

67. Derjenige is declined like two words, viz., *the Definite Article* and *an Adjective*; as,

	SINGULAR.				PLURAL.
	M.	F.	N.		M. F. N.
N.	derjenige,	diejenige,	dasjenige,	he, she, that,	diejenigen, those,
G.	desjenigen,	derjenigen,	desjenigen,	of him, her, „	derjenigen, of those,
D.	demjenigen,	derjenigen,	demjenigen,	to „ „ „	denjenigen, to „
A.	denjenigen,	diejenige,	dasjenige,	him, her, that;	diejenigen, those.

Examples.

Derjenige (or der), welcher[1] seinen Feinden vergiebt, handelt gut.	He *who* forgives his enemies, acts well.
Ich achte denjenigen (or den), welcher seinen Feinden vergiebt.	I esteem **him** *who* forgives his enemies.
Diejenige (or die), welche bescheiden ist, wird geliebt.	She *who* is modest is loved.
Ich achte diejenige (or die), welche bescheiden ist.	I esteem **her** *who* is modest.
Dasjenige (or das), welches schön ist, ist nicht immer nützlich.	That *which* is beautiful is not always useful.
Diejenigen (or die), welche ehrlich sind, werden belohnt.	Those *who* are honest are rewarded.
Mir gefällt dasjenige (or das) Buch, welches Sie mir gestern zeigten.	I like **that** book *which* you showed me yesterday.
Mir gefallen diejenigen (or die) Bücher, welche Sie mir gestern zeigten.	I like **those** books *which* you showed me yesterday.
Ich spreche von denjenigen (or denen), welche ꝛc.	I speak of **those** *which* etc.
Ich spreche von denjenigen (or den) Büchern, welche ꝛc.	I speak of **those** books *which* etc.
Wir sollen denjenigen (or denen) vergeben, die uns beleidigen.	We are to forgive **those** *who* offend us.
Wir sollen denjenigen (or den) Menschen vergeben, welche ꝛc.	We are to forgive **those** *men who* etc.

---

1) *Observe*, there are two forms for the relative pronoun too, but no notice has been taken of it in these examples, it being explained further on, in Rule 90.

68. The Pronouns **wer, was** and their various cases are frequently used instead of **derjenige welcher,** and **dasjenige welches,** when it is not uncommon to employ in the subsequent clause (apodosis) the corresponding demonstrative pronoun **der, die, das** (correlative) which gives greater emphasis to the sentence.

Examples.

Wer das sagt, (der) spricht die Wahrheit.	*Who* says that, (he) speaks the truth.
Was du nicht willst, das man dir thu', das füg' auch keinem andern zu.	*What* thou wilt not have done to thee, *that* do not do to other men.
Wes Brod ich esse, des Lied ich singe.	*Whose* bread I eat, *his* song I sing.
Wessen das Gefäß ist gefüllt, davon es sprudelt und überquillt. (Wallenstein.)	*Of what* the vessel is full, *of that* it bubbles and wells over.
Wessen (or wes) das Herz voll ist, dessen (or des) geht der Mund über.	*Of what* the heart is full, *of that* the mouth flows over.
Wem das nicht gefällt, (der) mag es sagen.	*To whom* that is not pleasing (who does not like that), *he* may say so.

THE POSSESSIVE PRONOUN.
Das Besitzwort.

69. There are two kinds of Possessive Pronouns, viz., the *Conjoined. i. e.,* those *joined* to Nouns or Adjectives, and the *Disjoined, i. e.,* those *not joined* to Nouns or Adjectives.

a. THE CONJOINED POSSESSIVE PRONOUN.
Das verbundene Besitzwort.

70. The six Conjoined Possessive Pronouns are derived from the Genitive of the corresponding six Personal Pronouns, viz.:

mein,	meine,	mein,	my,
dein,	deine,	dein,	thy,
fein,	feine,	fein,	his, its;
unfer,	unf(e)re,	unfer,	our,
euer¹,	eu(e)re,	euer,	your,
ihr,	ihre,	ihr,	their, her.

71. They are declined like the Indefinite Article, *i. e.*, they *add* the strong inflections in all the cases, except the *Nominative* of the *Masculine* and *Neuter* and the *Accusative* of the *Neuter* which remain uninflected, viz.;

	SINGULAR.			PLURAL.	
	M.	F.	N.	M. F. N.	
N.	mein,	meine,	mein,	meine,	my,
G.	meines,	meiner,	meines,	meiner,	of my,
D.	meinem,	meiner,	meinem,	meinen,	to my,
A.	meinen,	meine,	mein,	meine,	my.

	SINGULAR.			PLURAL.	
	M.	F.	N.	M. F. N.	
N.	unfer,	unfere,	unfer,	unfere,	our,
G.	unferes,	unferer,	unferes,	unferer,	of our,
D.	unferem,	unferer,	unferem,	unferen,	to our,
A.	unferen,	unfere,	unfer,	unfere,	our.

72. These pronouns always *precede* the noun; as, **mein** Vater, *my* father; except in poetry, where expressions like these are met occasionally, viz.: das Herze **mein**, my heart, die Seele **mein**, my soul, as also in the Lord's prayer which is commenced by some: Vater **unfer**, der du bist im Himmel, *our* father who art in heaven.

An analogous use is made of the Pronoun *mine* in English; as, sister *mine*, brother *mine*.

Observations.

73. Ihr, Ihre, Ihr, *your*, is the conventional form of the possessive pronoun; however, **Euer** (**Ew.** abbreviated) the old conventional form, and **Ihro**, the old genitive occur still rather frequently in connection with high titles; as, **Ew.** Majestät, *your* Majesty; **Ew.** Gnaden, *your* Grace; **Ihro** Majestät, *her* or *your* Majesty.

---

1) Pronounce *oir*.

74. In such phrases where the pronoun may be connected with two different nouns, to avoid ambiguity, the genitives of the *Demonstrative Pronoun* (**deſſen, deren** and **derer**) are used instead of the *Possessive Pronoun* ſein, *his*, and ihr, *her*; as, Wir ſahen geſtern Kaufmann B., ſeinen Bruder und **deſſen Frau**, we saw yesterday the merchant B., his brother and *his* (brother's) wife (ſeine Frau might mean *the merchant's* wife). Er erzählte uns von ſeinem Geſchäft und **deſſen Größe**, he told us of his business and *its* extensiveness (ſeiner Größe might mean *his* size or greatness).

b. THE DISJOINED POSSESSIVE PRONOUN.
Das unverbundene oder abſolute Beſitzwort.

75. There are in German *three forms* for this pronoun, which are derived from the conjoined forms in the following way:

The first form by the addition of the *strong terminations* for *all* cases. Ex.: **meiner, meine, meines,**[1] mine.

The second form by the prefixion of the *definite article* and the addition of the *weak terminations*. Ex.: **der** meine, **die** meine, **das** meine.

The third form by the prefixion of the *definite article* and the addition of the syllable -ig with the *weak terminations*. Ex.: **der** meinige, **die** meinige, **das** meinige.

76. Thus the various forms for the six disjoined possessive pronouns are these:

First Form.		*Second Form.*		*Third Form.*	
meiner meine meines	} mine,	der meine die meine das meine	} mine,	der meinige die meinige das meinige	} mine;
deiner deine deines	} thine,	der deine die deine das deine	} thine,	der deinige die deinige das deinige	} thine;

---

1) This form, of course, can differ from the conjoined pronoun only in the *Nominative* of the *Masculine* and *Neuter* and in the *Accusative* of the *Neuter*, which are the only cases in that pronoun, that have not the *strong* terminations.

First Form.		Second Form.		Third Form.	
ſeiner ſeine ſeines	} his *or* its,	der ſeine die ſeine das ſeine	} his *or* its,	der ſeinige die ſeinige das ſeinige	} his *or* its;
unſerer unſere unſeres	} ours,	der unſere die unſere das unſere	} ours,	der unſrige die unſrige das unſrige	} ours;
eurer eure eures	} yours,	der eure die eure das eure	} yours,	der eurige die eurige das eurige	} yours;
ihrer ihre ihres	} theirs *or* hers,	der ihre die ihre das ihre	} theirs *or* hers,	der ihrige die ihrige das ihrige	} theirs *or* hers.

77. *Note.* Ihrer, Ihre, Ihres, etc., is the conventional form for *yours*.

78. The pronouns of the *first* form are declined with the *strong terminations* throughout, those of the *second* and *third* like an *article* and *adjective*; viz.:

	SINGULAR.			PLURAL.
	M.	F.	N.	M. F. N.
1. N.	meiner,	meine,	meines,	meine, mine,
G.	meines,[1]	meiner,	meines,	meiner,[1] of mine,
D.	meinem,	meiner,	meinem,	meinen, to mine,
A.	meinen,	meine,	meines,	meine, mine;
2. N.	der meine,	die meine, das meine,		die meinen, mine,
G.	des meinen,	der meinen, des meinen,		der meinen. of mine,
D.	dem meinen,	der meinen, dem meinen,		den meinen, to mine,
A.	den meinen,	die meine, das meine,		die meinen, mine;
3. N.	der meinige,	die meinige,	das meinige,	die meinigen, mine,
G.	des meinigen,	der meinigen,	des meinigen,	der meinigen, of mine,
D.	dem meinigen,	der meinigen,	dem meinigen,	den meinigen, to mine,
A.	den meinigen,	die meinige,	das meinige,	die meinigen, mine.

79. The pronouns of the first form, being the shortest, are preferred in conversation; but there is no real difference in the value of the three forms.

---

1) The Genitive is rare in this form.

Examples.

Meine Aufgabe ist schwerer als deine, *or* die deine, *or* die deinige.	My task is more difficult than *thine*.
Dieses Haus liegt innerhalb seines Gutes und außerhalb des unseren, *or* des unsrigen.	This house lies within his estate and without *ours*.
Er spricht von seinem Arzte, und ihr sprecht von eurem, *or* dem euren, *or* dem eurigen.	He speaks of his physician and you speak of *yours*.

80. When the disjoined possessive pronoun is used as the predicate in a sentence, it takes no inflection, in conformity with the rules of the adjective; as, der Hut ist **mein**, the hat is *mine*; die Feder ist **unser**, the pen is *ours*; das Land ist **sein**, the country is *his*.

NB. ihr, *her, their*, is never used as a predicate.

81. The plurals **die Meinigen, die Deinigen, die Seinigen, die Ihrigen**, often occur with the meaning of *my, thy, his, her, your* family *or* people; *e. g.*, grüße **die Deinigen**, remember me *to your family;* **das Meinige** occurs also for *my* property, *my* due; *e. g.*, Jedem **das Seinige** (*suum cuique*), to every one *his due*. Er will mir **das Meinige** nehmen, he wants to take from me *my property*.

THE INTERROGATIVE PRONOUN.
Das Fragewort.

82. Two kinds of Interrogative Pronouns are used in German, viz., a. *The Disjoined* (*i. e.*, the one never combined with nouns or adjectives, in English *who?*). b. *The Conjoined* (*i. e.*, the one used before nouns and adjectives, in English *which?*).

a. THE DISJOINED INTERROGATIVE PRONOUN.
Das unverbundene oder absolute Fragewort.

83. This pronoun occurs only in the singular, with *one* form for the *Masculine* and *Feminine* and *one* for the *Neuter*, viz.:

M. F.	N.
N. **wer**, who?	**was**, what?
G. **wessen**, *or* **wes**, whose, of whom?	**wessen**, *or* **wes**, of what?
D. **wem**, (to) whom?	none.
A. **wen**, whom?	**was**, what?

Examples.

Wer ist da?	*Who* is there?
Wer ist dieser Herr?	*Who* is this gentleman?
Wer ist diese Frau?	*Who* is this lady?
Wer ist dieses Kind?	*Who* is this child?
Wer sind diese Männer und Weiber?	*Who* are these men and women?
Wessen Haus ist das?	*Whose* house is that?
Wem gehört dieser Garten?	*To whom* belongs that garden?
Wen lieben Sie am meisten?	*Whom* do you love most?
Was ist einem Knaben am nützlichsten?	*What* is most useful to a boy?
Was thun Sie in der Schule?	*What* do you do at school?

Observations.

84. The *Genitive* of the *Neuter* (**wessen** or **wes**) is now used rarely; the *Dative* of the *Neuter* has long been obsolete.

When connected with prepositions, compound adverbs, of which **wo** forms the first component, supply this wanting Dative; similar adverbs may be used for the Accusative, though the pronoun **was** with a preposition governing the Acc. is correct also; when beginning with a vowel the consonant **r** is inserted to avoid hiatus; thus:

wodurch? or **durch was?** (wherethrough) through what?
wogegen? or **gegen was?** against what?
worum or **warum?** or **um was?** about what?
woraus? *(whereout)* out of what?
womit? *(wherewith)* with what?
wobei? *(whereby)* by what?
worin? *(wherein)* in what?
wonach? *after what?*

85. The above and similar adverbs are also used *relatively*.

86. About the *relative* properties of **was** see Rule 97.

b. THE CONJOINED INTERROGATIVE PRONOUN.
Das verbundene Fragewort.

87. This pronoun is derived from the word **welch** and has the *strong terminations*; viz.:

	SINGULAR.			PLURAL.	
	M.	F.	N.	M. F. N.	
N.	welcher,	welche,	welches,	welche,	which?
G.	welches,	welcher,	welches,	welcher,	of which?
D.	welchem,	welcher,	welchem,	welchen,	to which?
A.	welchen,	welche,	welches,	welche,	which?

Examples.

Welcher Knabe ist fleißig?	Which boy is diligent?
Welche Feder schreibt gut?	Which pen writes well?
Welches Buch ist schön gebunden?	Which book is bound well?
Welcher von diesen Knaben ist faul?	Which of these boys is lazy?
Welche von diesen Federn ist Ihre?	Which of these pens is yours?
Welches von diesen Büchern ist theuer?	Which of these books is dear?
Welchem Knaben gehört dies Buch?	To which boy belongs this book?
Welchem von diesen Knaben gefällt dies Buch?	To which of these boys is this book pleasing?
Welchen Garten finden Sie schön?	Which garden do you find beautiful?
Welche von diesen Gärten finden Sie schön?	Which *(Plur.¹)* of these gardens do you think beautiful?
Welchen von Ihren Freunden leihen Sie Bücher?	To which *(Plur.¹)* of your friends do you lend books?

88. Both Interrogative Pronouns wer, was and welcher occur in an *indefinite sense*, especially the latter (welcher, welche, welches), which in that case means *some*, (not *a little*), whilst wer, in that case, answers to *anybody*, and was² to *something, anything*.

Examples.

Haben Sie guten Wein? Ja, wir haben welchen.	Have you any good wine? Yes, we have *some* (not stating the *quantity*).
Ist da noch Wasser in der Flasche? Ja, es ist noch welches darin.	Is there any more water left in the bottle? Yes, there is still *some* in (not stating the *quantity*).

---

1) It will be seen from the last two examples, that the Plural of this Pronoun cannot be rendered in English, when followed by a Genitive.

2) Was, *something*, is not, as is often supposed, an abbreviation of etwas, but etwas is a derivation of was.

Hat Heinrich Freunde? Ja, er hat **welche**.	Has Henry any friends? Yes, he has *some* (does not say whether *many* or *few*).
Ist **wer** da?	Is *anybody* there?
Haben Sie **was** gesagt?	Did you say *anything*?

89. *What kind of* — (or *what* inquiring the kind) is rendered in German commonly by **was für**;[1] in elevated style, however, and in poetry **welch** is preferable for the singular. The same terms occur also in exclamatory sentences, in which case the sentence is generally expressed *negatively*.

Examples.

Was für ein Mann war Cromwell?	*What kind* of a man was Cromwell?
Was für ein Mann war nicht C.! **Welch** ein Mann war C.!	*What* a man was C.!
Was für Leute waren die Sachsen?	*What kind* of people were the Saxons?
Was für Leute waren nicht die Sachsen!	*What people* were the Saxons!
Was für einen griechischen Autor lesen Sie jetzt in der Klasse?	*What kind* of a Greek author do you at present read in your class?
Was für lateinische Werke haben Sie schon gelesen?	*What kind* of Latin works have you already read?
Welch ein helles Licht schien durch das Zimmer!	*What* a bright light shone through the room!
Mit **was** für einer Feder haben Sie das geschrieben?	With *what kind* of a pen have you written this?
Was für schönes Wetter ist es nicht heute!	*What* fine weather it is to-day!

THE RELATIVE PRONOUN.
Das Bezugswort.

90. The German language has also for this pronoun two different forms, viz., **welcher, welche, welches,**

---

1) When not joined to a noun or adjective, ein has the import of a numeral and is declined as such (see Rule 199); as, Dieser Mann ist Soldat. This man is a soldier. Was für einer ist er? What kind of a *(one)* soldier is he? Or: Ist dieses Pferd nicht sehr schön? Is not this horse very beautiful? Was für eines ist es? What kind of a *(one)* horse is it?

and **der, die, das**, which are distinguished in their application in no other way but, that the latter is used more frequently and especially after Proper Names of Persons.

91. a. **Welcher, welche, welches** is declined with the strong terminations, but commonly has no genitive of its own; the genitive of the *second* relative pronoun is used instead.

b. **Der, die, das** is declined like the demonstrative pronoun **der, die, das**, excepting the genitive plural which is **deren** not **derer**; viz.:

92.

	SINGULAR.			PLURAL.	
	M.	F.	N.	M. F. N.	
a. N.	welcher,	welche,	welches,	welche,	which, who,[1]
G.[2]	dessen,	deren,	dessen,	deren,	of which, of whom, whose,
D.	welchem,	welcher,	welchem,	welchen,	to which, to whom,
A.	welchen,	welche,	welches,	welche,	which, whom;
b. N.	der,	die,	das,	die,	which, who,[1]
G.[2]	dessen,	deren,	dessen,	deren,	of which, of whom, whose,
D.	dem,	der,	dem,	denen,	to which, to whom,
A.	den,	die,	das,	die,	which, whom.

Examples.

Karl hat einen Freund, **welcher** (or **der**) sehr reich ist.	Charles has a friend *who* is very rich.
Das[3] ist eine Feder, **welche** (or **die**) mir zu spitz ist.	That is a pen *which* is too pointed for me.
Wo ist das Buch, **welches** (or **das**) Sie so sehr lobten?	Where is the book *which* you praised so much?
Dies[3] ist der Knabe, **dessen** Vater gestorben ist.	This is the boy *whose* father has died.

---

1) In English the word *who* is used both as a relative and interrogative; in German, however, these two pronouns are different; the learner should therefore be careful in selecting the proper word for it; thus, *who* is there? should be translated **wer ist da?** *who* being used here *interrogatively*; but, the man *who* is downstairs is your brother, must be rendered: **der Mann, welcher** (or **der**) **unten ist, ist Ihr Bruder**; for in this sentence *who* refers back to *man*, and is therefore a *Relative* Pronoun.

2) But compare Rule 94.

3) Compare Rule 317.

Dies ist die Kleine, deren Mutter so krank ist.	This is the little girl *whose* mother is so ill.
Dies ist das Messer, dessen Schneide so stumpf ist.	This is the knife (whose) *of which* the edge is so blunt.
Wo sind die Kinder, deren Bücher dies sind?	Where are the children *whose* books these are?
Hier ist der Mann, welchen (or den) Sie kennen lernen wollten.	Here is the man *whom* you wished to know.
Kannten Sie die Leute, mit welchen (or mit denen) Heinrich ausgegangen ist?	Did you know the people with *whom* Henry has gone out?
Waren das Ihre Häuser, welche (or die) gestern abgebrannt sind?	Were those your houses *which* were burned down yesterday?

Observations.

93. The Interrogative Pronoun **was** is used exceptionally as a *Relative* in the following cases:

1st. When referring to a whole clause; as, er wird heute nicht ankommen, was mir sehr leid thut, he will not arrive to-day, *for which (what)* I am very sorry.

2nd. After the Neuter of Superlatives; as, das beste, was du wissen kannst, darfst du etc., the best (things) *that* you may know, you dare, etc. (Faust.)

3rd. After the words alles, all, etwas, something, manches, many a (thing), nichts, nothing, vieles, much.

4th. At the beginning of exclamatory sentences, in which it must be taken as referring to a *phrase understood* (thence analogous to 1st); as, was Sie nicht alles wissen! (it is astonishing) *what* all you know!

94. The Genitive of welcher (welches, welcher, welches) is used exceptionally when joined to a Noun explanatory of that to which it refers; as, Friedrich der Zweite, welches Helden Namen Jedermann kennt, starb 1786, Frederick the second, the name *of which* hero everybody knows, died in 1786.

Note. The Relative Adverbs will be found among the other *Adverbs.*

INDEFINITE PRONOUNS.
Unbestimmte Fürwörter.

95. There are in German *four* Indefinite Pronouns, viz.: man, one, Jemand, somebody, Niemand, nobody, Jedermann, everybody.

Man, *one*, is indeclinable; its cases are supplied by the Numeral einer, which is, sometimes even in the nominative, used instead of man.

Jemand, *somebody*, and Niemand, *nobody*, are either declined or not, but in the Genitive they must always have an -s.

Jedermann, *everyone*, only inflects the Genitive; viz.:

N. Man, or, einer, one, Jemand, somebody,   Niemand, nobody,
G. eines, of one,   Jemand(e)s, somebody's, Niemand(e)s, nobody's,
D. einem, to one,   Jemand(em), to somebody, Niemand(em), to nobody,
A. einen, one.   Jemand(en), somebody. Niemand(en), nobody.

N. Jedermann, everybody,   D. Jedermann, to everybody,
G. Jedermanns, everybody's,   A. Jedermann, everybody.

96. To these Pronouns must be added the following words, since under certain conditions they have the inflections as well as the grammatical import of pronouns; viz., selb, *self*, *same*, all, *all*, solch, *such*, manch, *many a*.[1]

97. Derselbe, dieselbe, dasselbe, *the same*, is the (*demonstrative*) pronominal form of selb,[2] *self*; it is declined like *two* words, viz.: the *definite article* and an *adjective*, viz.:

	SINGULAR.			PLURAL.	
	M.	F.	N.	M. F. N.	
N.	derselbe,	dieselbe,	dasselbe,	dieselben,	the same,
G.	desselben,	derselben,	desselben,	derselben,	of the same,
D.	demselben,	derselben,	demselben,	denselben,	to the same,
A.	denselben,	dieselbe,	dasselbe,	dieselben,	the same.

---

1) The words etwas, *something*, nichts, *nothing*, viel, *much*, wenig, *little*, einig(er), (e), (es), etlich(er), (e), (es), *some*, and their respective comparatives and superlatives must not be called *pronouns*, although they sometimes resemble, on account of their inflections, the pronouns, for they do not influence the adjective that follows them in the way pronouns do. Ex.: Viel guter Wein, *much* good wine (vieler gute Wein is incorrect); viel(e) gute Freunde, *many* good friends (viele guten Freunde is incorrect).

2) When used in a purely adverbial sense (selbst, or selber), it does not demand the *repetition* of the pronoun as in English. Ex.: Ich habe es selbst geschrieben, I have written it *myself*; this,

Observation. Der nämliche, die nämliche, das nämliche, is another form for *the same*, it is declined like derselbe; it is, however, rather obsolete.

98. Aller, alle, alles, *all*, is the pronominal form of all, *all*;[1] it is declined throughout with the *strong terminations.* (Compare dieser, -e, -s, Rule 62.) Ex.:

> Aller gute Wein, *all good wine*;
> alle gute Milch, *all good milk*;
> alles gute Brod, *all good bread*;
> alle guten Menschen, *all good men*.

99. Solcher, solche, solches,[2] *such*, is the pronominal form of solch, *such*;[3] it is likewise declined with the *strong terminations.* Ex.:

> Solcher gute Wein, *such good wine*;
> solche gute Milch, *such good milk*;
> solches gute Brod, *such good bread*.

100. Mancher, manche, manches, *many a*, is the pronominal form of manch;[3] it is likewise declined with the *strong terminations.* Ex.:

---

of course, does not exclude the possibility of selbst being joined to a pronoun to qualify *it;* ich selbst habe es geschrieben, I *myself* have written it; *not* ich habe es ich selbst geschrieben, though in English, even in this case, *self* cannot stand alone, but must be attached to the corresponding possessive pronoun.

1) When all is used in a purely adverbial sense, *i. e.*, when it *precedes a pronoun*, it should remain uninflected; as, all mein Geld, *all my money*, all meines Geldes, *of all my money*, etc. However, before Pronouns in the Plural it often has the inflection of a pronoun; as, in allen meinen Thaten, *in all my deeds;* nevertheless it is more correct to leave it uninflected even then and to say in all meinen Thaten.

2) solcher, solche, solches and jeder, jede, jedes are also used *adjectively*, namely when preceded by the Indefinite Article ein or the Negative kein. Ex.: N. ein solcher Wein, *such a wine*, G. eines solchen Weines, *of such a wine*, D. einem solchen Wein, *to such a wine*, A. einen solchen Wein, *such a wine;* N. ein jeder Wein, *every wine*, G. eines jeden Weines, *of every wine*, D. einem jeden Wein, *to every wine*, A. einen jeden Wein, *every wine.*

3) solch, *such*, and manch, *many (a)*, remain, of course, uninflected, when used in a purely adverbial sense, for instance when preceding the *indefinite article* ein or when qualifying an adjective.

N. mancher gute Mann, *many* a good man,
G. manches guten Mannes, of *many* a good man,
D. manchem guten Mann(e), to *many* a good man,
A. manchen guten Mann, *many* a good man.

101. Jeder, jede, jedes,[1] *each*, must also be reckoned among the pronouns, with its variations jeglicher, jegliche, jegliches, and jedweder, jedwede, jedwedes, which latter two, however, are little used. These pronouns are also declined with the *strong terminations*. Ex.:

N. jeder gute Mann, *every* good man,
G. jedes guten Mannes, of *every* good man,
D. jedem guten Manne, to *every* good man,
A. jeden guten Mann, *every* good man.

102. The conjoined negative kein, keine, kein, *no*, is declined like mein, meine, mein, see Rule 71. Ex.:

kein guter Mann, *no* good man,
keine gute Mutter, *no* good mother,
kein gutes Haus, *no* good house.

The disjoined negative keiner, keine, keines, *none*, is declined like meiner, meine, meines, see Rule 78. Ex.:

Wie viele Männer? Keiner! How many man? *None!*
Welche Mutter? Keine! Which mother? *None!*
Wie viele Kinder, Häuser ꝛc.? Keine! How many children, houses, etc.? *None!*

THE NOUN.
Das Hauptwort.

103. A Noun or Substantive is that part of speech which expresses something that exists, either material or immaterial. Besides the Substantives proper there are other words which, when used substantively, are

---

1) See note 2, pag. 32.

treated like nouns; adjectives, however, when used as substantives, retain their own forms of declension. Each noun has a gender which often differs from that of the corresponding word in English, and is subject to a declension, with or without change of terminations. All nouns or words used substantively are written with a Capital Initial.

THE GENDER.
Das Geschlecht.

104. There are *three* Genders in German as in English, viz.: *Masculine* (männlich), *Feminine* (weiblich) and *Neuter* (sächlich), which are applied apparently so diversely that, to give rules, comprising all nouns, would be almost impossible or at least impracticable on account of the very numerous exceptions. The rules given here have been limited to those which have few or no exceptions and will be found useful. To facilitate the acquirement of the gender, however, the student of German ought always to learn the noun with *the definite article prefixed*.

Rules for the Gender.
Regeln für die Geschlechter.

105. Of the *Masculine gender* (männlichen Geschlechts) are:
1. Nouns which denote a *male* being.
2. The names of the *seasons, months, days, mountains* and *stones*.
3. Nouns ending in **-all** and **-ing**.
4. Nouns that are the same as the *Imperfect* Indicative of a *strong* verb[1]; as, **der** Gang, *the song*, being also the imperfect indicative of the strong verb singen, *to sing*.

---

[1] They need not have the same vowel; as, Fund, lupf. fand.

106. *Exceptions.* Ausnahmen.

To 1. Die Mannsperson,[1] the (person of a) man,
Das Mannsbild,[1] the (image of a) man,
Die Schildwache,[1] the sentinel;
also all *Diminutives* representing male beings.

To 3. Das Messing, the brass,
Das Metall, the metal.[2]

To 4. Das Schloß, the castle, the lock,
Das Maß, the measure,
Die Burg, the castle,
Die That, the deed,
Das Verbot, the prohibition.

107. Of the *Feminine gender* (weiblichen Geschlechts) are:
1. Nouns which denote a *female* being and the *numbers*.
2. Nouns ending in **-at**, (or **-ath**), **-e**, **-ei**, **-heit**, **-keit**, **-schaft**, **-ung**.

108. *Exceptions.*

To 1. Das Weib
Das Weibsbild } the woman,
Das Frauenzimmer
Das Mensch, the wench;

also all *Diminutives* denoting female beings; thus, Das Fräulein, the young lady, Miss; Das Mädchen, the girl.

To 2. a. Words denoting male beings, ending in **-e**.
b. Das Auge, the eye,
Das Ende, or End', the end,
Das Erbe, the inheritance,
Der Affe, the ape,
Der Falke, the falcon,
Der Hase, the hare,
Der Löwe, the lion,
Der Rabe, the raven,
Der Käse, the cheese,

as well as *Collective Nouns* beginning with **Ge-** and ending in **-e**; as, Das Gewölke, the clouds.

---

1) In these as in other compound words the latter component determines the gender (see Rule 135).
2) Properly speaking Metall is no exception, being a foreign noun and as such preserving its original gender (see Rule 140).

109. Of the *Neuter gender* (fächlichen Geschlechts) are:

1. The names of *metals, countries, towns* and *letters*.
2. Nouns ending in **-jal, -jel**[1] and **-tum** (or thum).
3. *Collective* Nouns beginning with **Ge-**, as, Gewölfe.
4. All *Diminutives* in **-chen** and **-lein**; as, Mädchen, Fräulein.
5. All words, *other* than *Nouns*, taken *substantively*.

110. *Exceptions.*

To 1. Die Platina,[2] the platina, der Stahl, the steel, der Zinf,[3] the zinc.
Die Krim, the Crimea,[4]
Die Levante, the Levant,
Die Moldau, Moldavia, and all ending in **-au**,
Die Schweiz, Switzerland, and all ending in **-z**,
Die Türfei, Turkey, and all ending in **-ei**,
Der Haag, the Hague.

To 2. Der Irrtum, the error,
Der Reichtum, the riches,
Der Pinsel, *(pencil)* the paint brush, simpleton,
Der Stöpsel, the stopper (of a bottle),
Die Trübsal, the distress, grief.

Nouns with Varying Gender.

111. With a few nouns the gender *varies*, some writers using *one*, others *another* gender; as, der and das Wachstum, *growth*; others have a *different* gender with a *different* termination; as, der Quell and die Quelle, *the well*.

---

1) Words ending in **-chsel** (xel) are not included; as, die Achsel.
2) Occurs also as das Platin.
3) Occurs also as *Neuter*.
4) Although names of *countries* are, as a rule, used *without the Article* (except they are preceded by an Adjective, when the article must be used, if it is not an address or an exclamation), all those that are not *Neuter*, require the article.

Nouns with more than one Gender.

112. There are a number of Nouns which have *more than one Gender* with different meanings,[1] viz.:

SING.	PLUR.	MEANING.	SING.	PLUR.	MEANING.
der[2] **Band,**	Bände, *the volume;*		das **Band,**	Bande, *bond, tie* (figurative);	
			das Band,	Bänder, *band, tie, ribbon* (literal);	
†die Bank,	Bänke, *the bench, form;*		die Bank,	Banken, *the bank;*	
der **Bauer,**	Bauern, *the peasant;*		das (or der) Bauer,	Bauer, *the cage;*	
†das Ding,	Dinge, *the thing* (lit.);		das Ding,	Dinger, *the thing* (fig.);	
der **Erbe,**	Erben, *the heir;*		das **Erbe,**	(not used), *the inheritance;*	
†das Gesicht,	Gesichter, *the face;*		das Gesicht,	Gesichte, *the vision;*	

---

1) To avoid repetition, those nouns which have more than one plural, though only one gender, have also been inserted in the list, and are marked with a cross (†), but it suffices, if beginners in the meantime learn the words in black type, reserving the plural for a later period. The less common, obsolete or doubtful nouns of this class are the following:

SING.	PLUR.	MEANING.	SING.	PLUR.	MEANING.
der Buckel,	Buckel, *the hump;*		die Buckel,	Buckeln, *the stud;*	
der Bund,	Bünde, *the confederacy;*		das Bund,	Bunde, *the bundle;*	
der Dorn,	Dörner, *the prickles, thorns;*		der Dorn,	Dornen, *the thorn* (of plants);	
der Haft,	Häfte, *the hold, handle;*		die Haft,	Haften, *imprisonment;*	
der Kaper,	Kaper, *the privateer;*		die Kaper,	Kapern, *the caper;*	
der Mast,	Masten, *the mast;*		die Mast,	Masten, *the mast, feeding;*	
die Mark,	Marken, *the mark, border;*		das Mark,	(not used), *the marrow;*	
der Marsch,	Märsche, *the march;*		die Marsch,	Marschen, *the marsh;*	
der Schwulst,	(not used), *the bombast;*		die Schwulst,	Schwulsten, *the swelling, tumour;*	
der Stift,	Stifte, *the peg;*		das Stift,	Stifter, *the charitable or religious institution.*	

2) The learner should apply to these words the previous rules for the gender which will facilitate his study considerably; thus, Bauer, *peasant*, Erbe, *heir*, Heide, *heathen*, etc., must be masculine, because they denote male beings; Heide, *heath*, Kunde, *news*, feminine, because they end in -e.

SING.	PLUR. MEANING.	SING.	PLUR. MEANING.
die Gift,	Giften, *the gift;*	das Gift,[1]	Gifte, *the poison;*
der Heide,	Heiden, *the heathen;*	die Heide,	Heiden, *the heath;*
der Hut,	Hüte, *the hat;*	die Hut (Huth),	(not used), *the guard, pasture;*
der Kiefer,	Kiefer, *the jaw;*	die Kiefer,	Kiefer, *the pine tree;*
der Kunde,	Kunden, *the customer:*	die Kunde,	Kunden,[2] *the news;*
der Laden,	Läden, *the shop;*	der Laden,	Laden, *the shutter;*
der Leiter,	Leiter, *the guide;*	die Leiter,	Leitern, *the ladder;*
der Lohn,	(not used), *the reward;*	der Lohn,[3]	Lohne (or ö), *the wages;*
der Mangel,	Mängel, *the want;*	die Mangel,	Mangeln, *the mangle;*
der Mensch,	Menschen, *man (male and female);*	das Mensch,	Menscher, *the wench;*
der Messer,	Messer, *the meter, measurer;*	das Messer,	Messer, *the knife;*
der Ort,	Örter, *the place (def. sense);*	der Ort,	Orte, *the place, region (indef. sense);*
der Schild,	Schilde, *the shield;*	das Schild,	Schilder, *the sign, plate (of a door);*
der See,	Seen, *the lake;*	die See,	Seen, *the sea;*
der Sprosse,	Sprossen, *the sprout, offspring;*	die Sprosse,	Sprossen, *the step (of a ladder);*
das Steuer,	Steuer, *the helm, rudder;*	die Steuer,	Steuern, *the tax, duty;*
der Theil,	Theile, *the part (of a whole);*	das Theil,	Theile, *the share (of a fortune etc.);*
der Thor,	Thoren, *the fool;*	das Thor,	Thore, *the gate;*
†das Tuch,	Tücher, *the tie, handkerchief;*	das Tuch,	Tuche, *the cloth;*
der Verdienst,	(not used), *the gain;*	das Verdienst,	Verdienste, *the merit;*
†das Wort,	Wörter, *the word (lit.);*	das Wort,	Worte, *the word (fig.).*

Note. About the gender of **Compound** and **Foreign** Nouns see Rules 135 and 140.

---

1) Der Gift is rare (Goethe's „Faust").

2) Occurs principally in *Compounds;* as, die Urkunde, the document, pl. Urkunden.

3) Occurs also as *Masculine.*

THE DECLENSION OF THE NOUN.
Declination oder Biegung der Hauptwörter.

113. Nouns in German are best arranged under three Declensions.

The First (or Strong) Declension ends in the genitive singular in -ß or -eß, and in the Dative, occasionally, in -e; in the *plural* some words take *no inflection*, some take -e, others take -er, and some -en; of all these a number *modify* the radical *vowel*.

The Second (or Weak) Declension ends in the genitive and in all other cases of the *singular* and *plural* in -n or -en and *never modifies* the vowel.

The Third (or Feminine) Declension has *no* inflection in the *singular*; in the *plural* most words take -en; some take *no* termination and others take -e and *modify* the vowel.

The First (or Strong, or S-) Declension.
Die erste (starke oder S-) Declination.

114. The First Declension contains:
1. All *Neuter Nouns* without exception.
2. All *Masculine Nouns* which *do not* end in -e or which *formerly did not* end in -e ¹.

115. The *Inflections* (Endungen) given to words of this declension in the *singular* are (as stated in Rule 113). -ß and -eß* for the *Genitive*, and -e for the *Dative*² of those Monosyllables that require for the

* *Note.* The -e in the genitive may often be omitted, as, Bots for Botes, Mers for Meres, Theils for Theiles.

---

1) The latter part of the rule is intended to exclude the words mentioned Rule 126, ² and ³.

2) The -e for the dative is not essential, it is generally left out in conversation, and is best applied in writing *with Monosyllabic* or with *Compound Nouns, the last component of which is a Monosyllable, when not followed by one of the weak prefixes* be, ge, ver, zer, *etc.*; on the other hand, it would be incorrect to add an -e to such words as Vater, Fenster, Stiefel.

sake of euphony -es instead of -s in the genitive; in the *plural* they add -e, but for the Dative -en.¹

Examples.

SINGULAR.		PLURAL.	
N. Der Bleistift,	the pencil,	die Bleistift-e,	the pencils,
G. des Bleistift-s,	of the pencil,	der Bleistift-e	of the pencils,
D. dem Bleistift,	to the pencil,	den Bleistift-en,	to the pencils,
A. den Bleistift,	the pencil;	die Bleistift-e,	the pencils.
N. der Tisch,	the table,	die Tisch-e,	the tables,
G. des Tisch-es,	of the table,	der Tisch-e,	of the tables,
D. dem Tisch-e,	to the table,	den Tisch-en,	to the tables,
A. den Tisch,	the table;	die Tisch-e,	the tables.
N. das Gewehr,	the gun,	die Gewehr-e,	the guns,
G. des Gewehr-s,	of the gun,	der Gewehr-e,	of the guns,
D. dem Gewehr,	to the gun,	den Gewehr-en,	to the guns,
A. das Gewehr,	the gun;	die Gewehr-e,	the guns.
N. das Bot,	the boat,	die Bot-e,	the boats,
G. des Bot-es,*	of the boat,	der Bot-e,	of the boats,
D. dem Bot-e,	to the boat,	den Bot-en,	to the boats,
A. das Bot,	the boat;	die Bot-e,	the boats.

116. *Note.* The following nouns are declined as if the noun were ending in -n. Viz.:

Der **Buchstabe**[n],² (des Buchstabens),
der **Friede**[n], (Friedens), **Funke**[n], **Glaube**[n],
Gedanke[n], (des Gedankens), **Haufe**[n],
der **Schade**[n], (Schadens), **Wille**[n], **Same**[n],
Und³ außerdem das Wort der **Name**[n].

Vocabulary.

Der Buchstabe(n), des Buchstabens, the letter (of the alphabet),

der Friede(n), des Friedens, the peace,

der Funke(n), des Funkens, the spark,

der Glaube(n), des Glaubens, the faith, belief,

der Gedanke(n), des Gedankens, the thought,

der Haufe(n), des Haufens, the heap,

 1) It may be noticed here, that the *Dative Plural of all declinable words* must have an -n, so that one is added, if the nominative plural does not end in -n already, except uns, to us, euch, to you.

 2) The learner should commit to memory the words *with* the [n].

 3) Instead of the last line may be learned: "And add to this *the name*, der Name[n].

der Name(n), des Namens, the name,
der Same(n), des Samens, the seed,
der Schade(n), des Schadens, the damage,
der Wille(n), des Willens, the will.

Example.

Sing. N. Der Name(n), the name,   D. dem Namen, to the name,
     G. des Namens, of the name,   A. den Namen, the name.
Plur. die, der, den, die Namen, the names etc.

117. *Observation.* The noun **das Herz**, *the heart*, is declined regular when taken in a *literal* sense, whilst, when taken in a *figurative* sense, it is declined thus:

SINGULAR.	PLURAL.
N. das Herz,	die Herzen,
G. des Herzens,	der Herzen,
D. dem Herzen,	den Herzen,
A. das Herz,	die Herzen.

Der Schmerz, *the pain*, has in poetical language in the Genitive Schmerzens; pl. Schmerzen.

118. Masculine Monosyllables modify the vowel besides adding -e in the plural. Ex.:

Sing. der Arzt, the physician,   Plur. die Ärzte, the physicians,
     der Sohn, „ son,   die Söhne, „ sons,
     der Fuß, „ foot,   die Füße, „ feet,
     der Baum, „ tree,   die Bäume, „ trees.

Also the following Polysyllables modify the radical vowel, viz.:

Altar', Bi'schof, Cardinal',
Her'zog,[1] Palast', General',[1]
Mar'schall, Morast' und Kanal'.

Examples.

Sing. der Altar, the altar;   Plur. die Altäre, the altars,
     der Bischof, „ bishop,   die Bischöfe, „ bishops.

Vocabulary.

Der Altar (Altäre), the altar,
der Bischof (Bischöfe), „ bishop,
der Cardinal (Cardinäle), „ cardinal,
der Herzog (Herzöge[1]), „ duke,
der Palast (Paläste), „ palace,
der General (Generäle[1]), the general,
der Marschall (Marschälle), the marshal,
der Morast (Moräste), the morass,
der Kanal (Kanäle), „ canal.

---

1) Also regular, *i. e. not* modified.

Finally all compound words formed from monosyllabic masculines modify the vowel. Ex.:

Sing. der Gesang, the song,   *Plur.* die Gesänge, the songs,
der Gebrauch, „ usage,   die Gebräuche, „ customs.
custom.

119. The following monosyllables are the most noteworthy of the *exceptions* to the above rule, they only add -e and do *not* modify the vowel; viz.:

Der Aal, (die Aale), Arm, Dolch, Dachs,[1]
Der Halm, (die Halme), Huf, Hund, Lachs,[2]
Der Laut, (die Laute), Mond, Mord, Pfad,
Der Punkt, Schuh, Stoff, Tag, Thron und Grad.

Examples.

Der Arm, the arm.   Der Schuh, the shoe.
Plur. N. Die Arme,   Die Schuhe,
G. der Arme,   der Schuhe,
D. den Armen,   den Schuhen,
A. die Arme.   die Schuhe.

Vocabulary.

Der Aal, die Aale,   the eel,   der Lachs, die Lachse, the salmon,
der Arm, die Arme,   „ arm,   der Laut, die Laute,   „ sound,
der Dolch, die Dolche, „ dagger,   der Mond, die Monde,   „ moon,
der Dachs, die Dachse, „ badger,   der Mord, die Morde,   „ murder,
der Grad, die Grade, „ degree,   der Pfad, die Pfade,   „ path,
der Halm, die Halme, „ stalk,   der Punkt, die Punkte, „ point,
  blade,   der Schuh, die Schuhe, „ shoe,
der Huf, die Hufe,   „ hoof,   der Stoff, die Stoffe, „ stuff,
der Hund, die Hunde, „ hound,   der Tag, die Tage,   „ day,
  dog,   der Thron, die Throne, „ throne.

The others of less importance are:

Der Aar, die Aare,   the eagle,   der Gurt, die Gurte,   the girdle,
der Born, die Borne, „ well,   der Kork, die Korke,   „ cork,
der Docht, die Dochte, „ wick,   der Krahn, die Krahne, „ crane,
der Dom, die Dome,   „ cathe-   der Lack, die Lacke,   „ lac, var-
  dral, dome,   nish,

---

1) Pronounce *dax*.
2) Pronounce *lax*.

der Luchs, die Luchse, the lynx,
der Molch, die Molche, „ salamander,
der Park, die Parke, „ parc,
der Pol, die Pole, „ pole,
der Puls, die Pulse, the pulse,
der Schuft, die Schufte, „ scoundrel,
der Strauß, die Strauße, „ ostrich,
der Takt, die Takte, „ bar (in music).

Exceptions.

120. The *General Rule*, that words of the first Declension form the Plural in -e, suffers *Three Classes or groups of Exceptions*; viz.:

    a. Words that take *no inflection* in the plural;
    b. Words that take -er and *modify the vowel*;
    c. Words that take -n or -en.

    a. First Class of Exceptions, no Inflections.

121. *Words that take no[1] inflection in the plural,* viz., those ending in -e[2], -el, -en and -er.

Examples.

	Der Käse, the cheese.	Der Stiefel, the boot.	Der Degen, the sword.	Das Messer, the knife.
Plur. N.	Die Käse,	Die Stiefel,[3]	Die Degen,	Die Messer,
G.	der Käse,	der Stiefel,	der Degen,	der Messer,
D.	den Käsen,	den Stiefeln,	den Degen,	den Messern,
A.	die Käse.	die Stiefel.	die Degen.	die Messer.

122. However seven take -n[4], viz.:

der Baier, die Baiern, the Bavarian,
der Bauer, die Bauern, „ peasant, farmer,
der Gevatter, die Gevattern, „ godfather, gossip,
der Muskel, die Muskeln, „ muscle,
der Pommer, die Pommern, „ Pomeranian,
der Stachel, die Stacheln, „ prickle,
der Vetter, die Vettern, „ cousin.

---

    1) The *Dative* of the *Plural*, however, must end in -n, as in all declinable words.
    2) Of Masculine Nouns in -e only Käse follows this declension, the others follow the second; rule 126.
    3) Observe also: Stiefeln, boots.
    4) Some of these words formerly followed altogether the *Second Declension*, and especially Bauer is, even now, often met with the inflections of that declension in almost all cases, viz.: des Bauern, dem Bauern, den Bauern.

123. The following words *modify the vowel* though they take no inflection;[1] viz.:

Der Acker, (Äcker), Apfel, Boden,
Der Bruder, (Brüder), Hafen, Bogen,
Der Graben, (Gräben), Garten, Faden,
Der Hammel, (Hämmel), Handel, Hammer,
Der Kasten, Mangel, Mantel, Laden,[2]
Der Nagel, Ofen, Sattel, Schaden,
Schnabel, (Schnäbel), Schwager, Vater, Vogel.
Von[3] Sächlichen allein **das Kloster**.

Examples.

Der Apfel, the apple.   Das Kloster, the cloister.
Plur. N. die Äpfel,   die Klöster,
  G. der Äpfel,   der Klöster,
  D. den Äpfeln,   den Klöstern,
  A. die Äpfel,   die Klöster.

Vocabulary.

Der Acker, die Äcker,	the acre, field,
der Apfel, die Äpfel,	„ apple,
der Boden, die Böden,	„ bottom, garret,
der Bogen, die Bögen,	„ bow (arch),
der Bruder, die Brüder,	„ brother,
der Faden, die Fäden,	„ thread,
der Garten, die Gärten,	„ garden,
der Graben, die Gräben,	„ ditch,
der Hafen, die Häfen,	„ haven, harbour,
der Hammel, die Hämmel,	„ wether,
der Hammer, die Hämmer,	„ hammer,
der Handel, die Händel,	„ quarrel,
der Kasten, die Kästen,	„ chest,
der Laden, die Läden,	„ shop,
der Mangel, die Mängel,	„ want, defect,
der Mantel, die Mäntel,	„ cloak,
der Nagel, die Nägel,	„ nail,
der Ofen, die Öfen,	„ oven, stove,
der Sattel, die Sättel,	„ saddle,

---

1) See note 1, pag. 43.
2) About its other plural or plurals see Rule 112.
3) Instead of the last line may be said:
   Of *neuter nouns* but one: **das Kloster**.

der Schaden, die Schäden, the damage,
der Schnabel, die Schnäbel, „ beak,
der Schwager, die Schwäger, „ brother-in-law,
der Vater, die Väter, „ father,
der Vogel, die Vögel, „ bird,
das Kloster, die Klöster, „ cloister.

b. Second Class of Exceptions.

124. *Words that take* **-er** *in the plural and modify the radical vowel; viz.:*

1. All nouns ending in **-tum**.
2. The following monosyllables:

Der Geist, (die Geister), Gott, der Leib,
Der Mann, (die Männer¹), Ort,² der Rand,
Der Strauch, (die Sträucher³), Wurm³ und Wald.

Das Amt, (die Ämter), Bad, Band,² Bild,
Das Blatt, (die Blätter), Brett, Buch, Schild,²
Das Ding,² Dach, (Dächer), Dorf, Ei, Feld,
Das Fach, Holz, (Hölzer⁴), Glied, Grab, Geld,
Das Faß, (die Fässer), Glas, Gras, Korn,⁴
Das Gut, (die Güter), Haupt, Haus, Horn,⁴
Das Huhn, (die Hühner), Kalb, Kleid, Land,⁵
Das Kraut, (die Kräuter), Lamm, Lied, Pfand,
Das Licht, (die Lichter), Loch, Maul, Rind,
Mensch,² Nest, (Nester), Rad, Reis, Rind,
Schwert, Schloß, (Schlösser), Stift,² Wort,² Mahl,⁴
Tuch,² Volk, (Völker), Wamms, Weib, Thal.⁵

---

1) A *second* plural, Mannen, is obsolete, except in some *Compounds* and in *poetry*; as, Normannen, Normans; a *third* plural, Leute, must be used with *Compounds*, unless the word is particularly to express the *male sex*; as, Kaufmann, merchant, pl. Kaufleute; but, Ehemann, pl. Ehemänner, married *man* in contradistinction from Eheleute, which would express "a married couple", see also Rule 317, note 2.
2) See 112, pag. 37.
3) Occurs also with *modified vowel* and -e.
4) Occurs also regular, *i. e.* with -e; and without modification; as, Holz, plur. Holze.
5) In elevated style or poetry used also regular, *i. e.* with -e; as, Land, plur. Lande.

3. The following polysyllables:

Das Regiment', das Hospital', Gewand', (Gewänder'), das Tent'mal,[1] Gemüth', Geschlecht', Gesicht',[2] Gespenst', Gemach', (Gemächer), das Gast'mahl.

Examples.

Der Reichtum,	Der Mann,	Das Amt,	Das Gewand,
the riches.	the man.	the office.	the garment.

Plural

N.	Die Reichtümer,	Die Männer,	Die Ämter,	Die Gewänder,
G.	der Reichtümer,	der Männer,	der Ämter,	der Gewänder,
D.	den Reichtümern,	den Männern,	den Ämtern,	den Gewändern,
A.	die Reichtümer.	die Männer.	die Ämter.	die Gewänder.

Vocabulary.

Der Geist, die Geister, the ghost, spirit, mind, genius,
der Gott, die Götter, the God,
der Leib, die Leiber, „ body,
der Mann, die Männer, „ man,
der Ort, die Örter, „ place,
der Rand, die Ränder, „ edge,
der Strauch, die Sträucher, „ shrub,
der Wurm, die Würmer, „ worm,
der Wald, die Wälder, „ wood,
das Amt, die Ämter, „ office,
das Bad, die Bäder, „ bath, watering-place,
das Band, die Bänder, „ tie, ribbon,
das Bild, die Bilder, „ picture, image,
das Blatt, die Blätter, „ leaf,
das Brett, die Bretter, „ board,
das Buch, die Bücher, „ book,
das Ding, die Dinger, „ thing,
das Dorf, die Dörfer, „ village,
das Ei, die Eier, „ egg,
das Fach, die Fächer, „ compartment,
das Faß, die Fässer, the barrel, vessel,
das Feld, die Felder, „ field,
das Geld, die Gelder, „ money,
das Glas, die Gläser, „ glass,
das Glied, die Glieder, „ member,
das Grab, die Gräber, „ grave,
das Gras, die Gräser, „ grass,
das Gut, die Güter, „ estate, possession,
das Haupt, die Häupter, „ head,
das Haus, die Häuser, „ house,
das Holz, die Hölzer, „ wood,
das Horn, die Hörner, „ horn,
das Huhn, die Hühner, „ chicken,
das Kalb, die Kälber, „ calf,
das Kind, die Kinder, „ child,
das Kleid, die Kleider, „ dress,
das Korn, die Körner, „ corn,
das Kraut, die Kräuter, „ herb,
das Lamm, die Lämmer, „ lamb,
das Land, die Länder, „ land,
das Licht, die Lichter, „ light,
das Lied, die Lieder, „ song,
das Loch, die Löcher, „ hole,

---

1) See note 5 pag. 45.
2) See note 2 pag. 44.

das Mahl, die Mähler, the meal,
das Maul, die Mäuler, „ muzzle,
das Mensch, die Menscher, „ wench,
das Nest, die Nester, „ nest,
das Pfand, die Pfänder, „ pledge, forfeit,
das Rad, die Räder, „ wheel,
das Reis, die Reiser, „ twig,
das Rind, die Rinder, „ cattle,
das Schild, die Schilder, „ sign-board,
das Schloss, die Schlösser, the castle, (door)lock,
das Schwert, die Schwerter, „ sword,
das Stift, die Stifter, „ institution (charitable or religious),
das Thal, die Thäler, the dale,
das Tuch, das Tücher, „ cloth,
das Volk, die Völker, „ people,
das Wamms, die Wämmser, the jerkin,
das Weib, die Weiber, the wife,
das Wort, die Wörter, „ word.

Das Denkmal, die Denkmäler, the monument,
das Gastmahl, die Gastmähler, „ banquet,
das Gemach, die Gemächer, „ chamber,
das Gemüth, die Gemüther, „ mind, heart,
das Geschlecht, die Geschlechter, „ sex, gender,
das Gesicht, die Gesichter, „ face,
das Gespenst, die Gespenster, „ spectre,
das Gewand, die Gewänder, „ garment,
das Hospital or Spital, die Hospitäler, „ hospital,
das Regiment, die Regimenter, „ regiment.

Note. The following are the less common words of the same kind:

das Aas, die Äser, the carrion,
das Joch, die Jöcher, „ yoke,
das Trumm, die Trümmer, „ ruin,
der Bösewicht, die Bösewichter, „ scoundrel,
der Vormund, die Vormünder, „ guardian.

c. *Third Class of Exceptions.*

125. *Words that take* -n *or* -en *and never modify the vowel.* viz.:

1. Foreign nouns denoting males, ending in **-or**, as, der Doktor, der Professor.

2. Der Dorn, (die Dornen¹), Diamant,
Der Fink, (die Finken), Forst,² der Mast,
Der Nachbar,³ Psalm, Quell, Reif, der Schmerz,
Der See, Sporn, (Sporen⁴), Strahl, der Staat,
Der Zins, der Vorfahr, Unterthan.

---

1) See note 2 pag. 44.
2) See note 4 pag. 45.
3) Nachbar, plural Nachbarn.
4) Observe the irregularity of Sporen.

3. Das Auge, (Augen), Bett, Herz,[1] End',
Das Leib, Insect', das Ohr, das Hemd'.

Note. A number of the above words, especially Diamant, Fink, Vorfahr, Unterthan may also be declined after the second declension, *i. e.*, with -n or -en both for the singular and plural.

Examples.

1. Der Doc'tor, the doctor.	2. Der Dorn, the thorn.	3. Das Auge, the eye.
Plur.	*Plur.*	*Plur.*
N. Die Docto'ren,	N. Die Dornen,	N. Die Augen,
G. der Docto'ren,	G. der Dornen,	G. der Augen,
D. den Docto'ren,	D. den Dornen,	D. den Augen,
A. die Docto'ren.	A. die Dornen.	A. die Augen.

Vocabulary.

Der Diamant, die Diamanten, the diamond,
der Dorn, die Dornen, the thorn,
der Fink, die Finken, „ finch,
der Forst, die Forsten, „ forest,
der Mast, die Masten, „ mast,
der Nachbar, die Nachbarn, the neighbour,
der Psalm, die Psalmen, the psalm,
der Quell, die Quellen, „ well, source,
der Reif, die Reifen, „ ring,
der Schmerz, die Schmerzen, the smart, pain,
der See, die Seen, the lake,
der Sporn, die Sporen, „ spur,
der Staat, die Staaten, „ state,
der Strahl, die Strahlen, the ray (of light), jet (of water),
der Unterthan, die Unterthanen, the subject,
der Vorfahr, die Vorfahren, the ancestors,
der Zins, die Zinsen, the interest;
das Auge, die Augen, the eye,
das Bett(e), die Betten, „ bed,
das End(e), die Enden, „ end,
das Hemd(e), die Hemden, „ shirt,
das Herz, die Herzen, „ heart,
das Insect, die Insecten, „ insect,
das Leid, die Leiden, „ suffering, pain,
das Ohr, die Ohren, „ ear.

Note. The following are the less common words of the same kind:

Der Dä'mon, die Dämo'nen, the demon,
das Juwel', die Juwelen, „ jewel,
der Konsul, die Konsuln, „ consul,
der Lorbeer, die Lorbeeren, „ laurel,
der Pfau, die Pfauen, „ peacock.

---

1) Compare Rule 117.

The Second (or Weak, or N-) Declension.
Die zweite (oder schwache oder N-)Declination.

126. The Second Declension contains:

1. *All Masculine Nouns* ending in -e (except der Käse, which follows the first).

2. *All Masculine Nouns* which *formerly* ended in -e, viz.:

Der Ahn, (des Ahnen), Bär, Bull, Fürst,
der Geck, (des Gecken), Graf, Prinz, Christ,
der Held, (des Helden), Herr,[1] Hirt,[2] Mohr,
der Mensch, Narr, Nerv, Ochs,[2] Pfaff, der Thor,
und noch Genoß,[2] Gesell[2] und Hagestolz,
doch außerdem Leu, Spatz und Schenk; auch Oberst, doch jetzt seltener.

3. All Masculine *Nouns* that have a tendency to end in -e; viz., those denoting *males* taken from a *foreign* language and ending in a *long* or emphatic syllable, as, Protestant', Astronom', Infanterist' etc. (Except those of French origin ending in -ier -on, and än and those in -al, which follow the first declension. Ex.: Der Offizier, G. des Offiziers, etc.; der Postillon, G. des Postillons, etc.; der Kapitän, G. des Kapitäns, etc.; der General, G. des Generals.)

4. Also the following:

Der Brillant', der Consonant',
der Paragraph',[3] der Elephant',
Komet', (Kometen), der Foliant',
Planet' (Planeten), der Quadrant',
auch Basilisk' und der Quotient'.

Vocabulary.

Der Ahn, des Ahnen, the ancestor,
der Bär, des Bären, the bear,
der Bull, des Bullen, „ bull,
der Christ, des Christen, the christian,
der Fürst,[4] des Fürsten, „ prince,

---

1) Herr takes -n in the sing. and -en in the plural.
2) Used more frequently with -e (Hirte).
3) And others of the same kind, as Telegraph etc.
4) There is this difference between Fürst and Prinz, that the former means a sovereign or heigh dignitary, the latter denotes the *son* of a Fürst.

der Geck, des Gecken, the dotard,
der Gesell(e), des Gesellen, „ fellow, partner,
der Genoss(e), des Genossen, the companion,
der Graf, des Grafen, the count.
der Hagestolz, des Hagestolzen, the bachelor,
der Held, des Helden, the hero,
der Herr, des Herrn, „ gentleman, lord, sir, mister, master,
der Hirt(e), des Hirten, the herd(sman),

der Leu, des Leuen, the lion,
der Mohr, des Mohren, „ negro,
der Mensch, des Menschen, „ man,
der Narr, des Narren, „ fool,
der Nerv, des Nerven, „ nerve,
der Pfaff(e), des Pfaffen, „ parson,
der Ochs(e), des Ochsen, „ ox,
der Prinz, des Prinzen, „ prince,
der Schenk, des Schenken, „ cupbearer,
der Spatz, des Spatzen, „ sparrow,
der Thor, des Thoren, „ fool.

Der Basilist, des Basilisten, the basilisk,
der Brillant, des Brillanten, „ diamond,
der Consonant, des Consonanten, „ consonant,
der Foliant, des Folianten, „ folio,
der Komet, des Kometen, „ comet,
der Paragraph, des Paragraphen, „ paragraph,
der Planet, des Planeten, „ planet,
der Quadrant, des Quadranten, „ quadrant,
der Quotient, des Quotienten, „ quotient.

127. The words of this declension receive in all cases *singular* and *plural* -n or -en (they *never modify* the vowel).

Examples to 1.

SING.
N. Der Knabe, the boy,
G. des Knaben, of the boy,
D. dem Knaben, to the boy,
A. die Knaben, the boys,

PLUR.
die Knaben, the boys,
der Knaben, of the boys,
den Knaben, to the boys,
die Knaben, the boys;

N. der Falke, the falcon,
G. des Falken, of the falcon,
D. dem Falken, to the falcon,
A. den Falken, the falcon,

die Falken, the falcons,
der Falken, of the falcons,
den Falken, to the falcons,
die Falken, the falcons.

Example to 2.

SING.
N. Der Bär, the bear,
G. des Bären, of the bear,
D. dem Bären, to the bear,
A. den Bären, the bear,

PLUR.
die Bären, the bears,
der Bären, of the bears,
den Bären, to the bears,
die Bären, the bears.

Example to 3.

SING.
N. Der Proteſtant', the protestant,
G. des Proteſtanten, of the „
D. dem Proteſtanten, to the „
A. den Proteſtanten, the „

PLUR.
die Proteſtan'ten, the protestants,
der Proteſtanten, of the protestants,
den Proteſtanten, to the protestants,
die Proteſtanten, the protestants.

Example to 4.

SING.
N. Der Conſonant', the consonant,
G. des Conſonanten, of the „
D. dem Conſonanten, to the „
A. den Conſonanten, the „

PLUR.
die Conſonan'ten, the consonants,
der Conſonanten, of the consonants,
den Conſonanten, to the consonants,
die Conſonanten, the consonants.

The Third (or Feminine) Declension.
Die dritte (oder Feminin=)Declination.

128. The Third Declension contains all *Feminine* Nouns without exception.

129. The words of this declension receive *no inflection* in the *singular*; but add for the *plural* in all the cases -n or -en.[1]

---

1) Formerly feminine nouns ending in -e got -n in the Singular; as, die Erde, der Erden, der Erden, die Erde; this termination, however, occurs now only in poetry and in a few phrases, as, auf Erden, on earth (auf der Erde, on *the* earth), zu Schanden, to shame, von Seiten, on the part, zu Gunſten, in favour, zu Ehren, in honour, zu Weihnachten, at christmas, zu Oſtern, at easter, bei Zeiten, betimes,

Note. This obsolete inflection of certain feminine nouns has been the cause of a curious mistake which it is interesting to notice. In turning up the words for *christmas* and *easter* in a German dictionary, these will be found „Weihnachten, *plur.*", and „Oſtern, *plur.*" respectively; now the fact is that both notations are incorrect, it ought to be „Weihnacht, *fem.*, Oſter, *fem.*" The reason of this is that both words being mostly used with *prepositions* and obsolete inflection, as zu Weihnachten, *at* christmas, zu Oſtern, *at* easter, people have, as the inflection rarely occurs, in similar words, lost its sense and are actually at a loss how to express the nominative; some saying „der Weihnachten", some „die Weihnachten" (in the sense of a plural) and some correctly die Weihnacht *(fem.)*; nay there may be found all the different forms in one and the same story, as for example in the author's Reader, 1st Ed., story 50 der Weihnachtsabend by Tieck.

Similar incongruities, however, may be found in other living languages.

Examples.

SINGULAR.	PLURAL.
N. Die Blume, the flower,	die Blumen, the flowers,
G. der Blume, of the flower,	der Blumen, of the flowers,
D. der Blume, to the flower,	den Blumen, to the flowers,
A. die Blume, the flower,	die Blumen, the flowers.

Die Tugend, virtue; bie Tugenden, virtues;
die Schönheit, beauty; die Schönheiten, beauties;
die Königinn, the queen; die Königinnen, the queens.

130. *Exceptions.*

1. Die Mutter, the mother, die Tochter, the daughter, form the plural by merely[1] modifying the vowel, viz.: Mütter, Töchter.

2. Those ending in -niß which add -e instead of -en.

3. The following *Monosyllables*[2] which also take -e instead of -en and *modify* the vowel, viz.:

---

1) The dative plural, as usual, adds -n (den Müttern).

2) The following are regular, i. e. they form the plural by adding -en to the singular, viz.:

Die Au, (die Auen), Art, Bahn, Brut,
Die Bucht, (die Buchten), Burg, Cur, Fluth,
Die Fahrt, (die Fahrten), Flur, Form, Fracht,
Die Frau, (die Frauen), Frist, Gluth, Jacht,
Lift, Jagd, (Jagden), Last, Mark, Pflicht,
Pest, Post, (Posten), Pracht, Qual, Schicht,
Die Saat, (die Saaten), Schaar, Schlacht, Schlucht,
Schrift, Schuld, (Schulden), Schur, Spur, Sucht,
Stirn, That, (Thaten), Thür, Trift, Wahl,
Uhr, Welt, (Welten), Wucht, Zeit, Zahl.

Vocabulary. Au, meadow, Art, way, Bahn, path, Brut, brood, Bucht, bay, Burg, borough, castle, Cur, cure, Fluth, flood, Fahrt, drive, voyage, Flur, meadow, field, Form, form, Fracht, freight, Frau, woman, Frist, respite, Gluth, glow, Jacht, yacht, Lift, stratagem, Last, burden, Mark, mark, border, Pflicht, duty, Pest, plague, Post, post office, post chaise, Pracht, splendour, Qual, torment, Schicht, layer, Saat, seed, Schaar, host, Schlacht, battle, Schlucht, ravine, Schrift, writing, scripture, Schuld, debt, Schur, shearing, Spur, trace, Sucht, disease, Stirn(e), front, That, deed, Thür(e), door, Trift, pasture, Wahl, choice, Uhr, watch, clock, Welt, world, Wucht, weight, Zeit, time, Zahl, number.

Die Axt, (die Äxte), Bank,[1] Braut, —brunst,[2]
Die Brust, (die Brüste), Faust, —flucht,[2] Kunst,
Die Schwulst, Frucht, (Früchte), Gans, die Gruft,
Die Hand, (die Hände), Haut, Kraft, Kluft,
Die Kuh, (die Kühe), Luft, Lust, Macht,[3]
Die Magd, (die Mägde), Maus, die Nacht,
Die Naht, (die Nähte), Nuß, Schnur, —kunft,[4]
Die Stadt, (die Städte), Wand, Wurst, Zunft.

Shorter List, omitting the less common words:
Die Bank, (die Bänke), Brust, Faust, Hand,
Die Frucht, (die Früchte), Kraft, Kunst, Wand,
Die Kuh, (die Kühe), Magd, Maus, Macht,
Die Magd (die Mägde), Nuß, Stadt, Nacht.

Examples.

Die Wildniß, the wilderness.   Die Axt, the axe.
Plur. N. Die Wildnisse,   *Plur.* N. Die Äxte,
   G. der Wildnisse,   G. der Äxte,
   D. den Wildnissen,   D. den Äxten,
   A. die Wildnisse.   A. die Äxte.

Vocabulary.

die Axt, die Äxte, the axe,	die Hand, die Hände, the hand,
die Bank, die Bänke, ,, bench, form,	die Haut, die Häute, ,, hide, skin,
die Braut, die Bräute, ,, bride,	die Kluft, die Klüfte, ,, cleft,
die Brust, die Brüste, ,, breast,	die Kraft, die Kräfte, ,,strength, power,
die Faust, die Fäuste, ,, fist,	
die Frucht, die Früchte, ,, fruit,	die Kuh, die Kühe, ,, cow,
die Gans, die Gänse, ,, goose,	die Kunst, die Künste, ,, art,
die Schwulst,[5] die Schwülste, the swelling,	die Luft, die Lüfte, ,, air,
	die Lust, die Lüste, ,,pleasure,
die Gruft, die Grüfte, ,, grave,	die Macht, die Mächte, ,, might, power,

---

1) When denoting *bank* the Plural is *regular* (Banken).

2) The respective plurals of Brunst and Flucht occur only in compounds, as, Feuersbrunst, conflagration, *Plur.* Feuersbrünste, Ausflucht, evasion, *Plur.* Ausflüchte, evasions.

3) The compounds Ohnmacht, swoon, Vollmacht, full power, form the plural *regular, i. e.* in -en.

4) —kunft occurs now only in compounds; as, Einkunft, revenue, *Plur.* Einkünfte, revenues.

5) More common Geschwulst, Geschwülste.

die Magd, die Mägde, the maid, (servant),
die Maus, die Mäuse, ,, mouse,
die Nacht, die Nächte, ,, night,
die Naht, die Nähte, ,, seam,
die Nuss, die Nüsse, ,, nut,
die Schnur, die Schnüre, ,, string,
die Stadt, die Städte, the town,
die Wand, die Wände, ,, (inner) wall,
die Wurst, die Würste, ,, sausage,
die Zunft, die Zünfte, ,, corporation (of trades), guild.

Note. The following are the less common words of the same kind: die Angst, Ängste, anxiety; die Noth, Nöthe, distress (especially in Ängsten, Nöthen); die Laus, die Läuse, the louse; die Sau, die Säue or Sauen, the sow; die Zucht, die Züchten, modesty.

131. Nouns occurring in the plural only are: die Eltern, the parents; die Fasten, Lent; die Ferien, vacation; die Gebrüder, brothers; die Kosten, expenses; die Leute, people; die Masern, measles; die Molken, whey; die Ränke, tricks, intrigues.

DECLENSION OF ADJECTIVES, USED AS NOUNS.

132. As has been remarked in Rule 103 **Adjectives used substantively** *retain their peculiar adjective declension* and do not follow the rules given for the nouns. Their terminations therefore depend on, whether and what kind of *article* or *pronoun* precedes them. (Compare the declension of the adjective rules 173 etc.)

Examples of a Masculine.

SINGULAR.

N. Der Fremde, the stranger,   ein Fremder, a stranger,
G. des Fremden, of the stranger,   eines Fremden, of a stranger,
D. dem Fremden, to the stranger,   einem Fremden, to a stranger,
A. den Fremden, the stranger;   einen Fremden, a stranger;

N. Fremder, stranger,
G. Fremdes, of stranger,
D. Fremdem, to stranger,
A. Fremden, stranger;

PLURAL.

N. Fremde, strangers,   die Fremden, the strangers,
G. Fremder, of strangers,   der Fremden, of the strangers,
D. Fremden, to strangers,   den Fremden, to the strangers,
A. Fremde, strangers;   die Fremden, the strangers.

Examples of a Feminine.

SINGULAR.

N. Die Frembe,[1] the stranger, eine Frembe, a stranger (female),
G. der Fremben, of the stranger (female) einer Fremben, of a stranger „
D. der Fremben, to the stranger einer Fremben, to a stranger „
A. die Frembe, the stranger eine Frembe, a stranger (female).

Plural same as plural of masculine.

Examples of a Neuter.

SINGULAR.

N. Das Frembe, the strange (thing or matter), ein Frembes, a strange (thing or matter),
G. des Fremben, of the strange (thing or matter), eines Fremben, of a strange (thing or matter),
D. dem Fremben, to the strange (thing or matter), einem Fremben, to a strange (thing or matter),
A. das Frembe, the strange (thing or matter). ein Frembes, a strange (thing or matter).

N. Frembes, (something) strange,
G. Frembes, of „ strange,
D. Frembem, to „ strange,
A. Frembes, „ strange.

Plural as above.

Note. The examples given above may not all occur, but are given here for the sake of completeness.

---

1) The *real* noun, die Frembe, *the foreign* (land) is, of course, declined *without* inflection.

133. TABLE OF THE THREE DECLENSIONS OF THE NOUN.

The First Declension	The Second Declension	The Third Declension
contains all *Neuter* Nouns, and all *Masculine* Nouns that *do not* end now or *did not* formerly end in -e. (Rule 114.)	contains all *Masculine* Nouns that end in -e or formerly ended in -e. (Rule 126.)	contains all *Feminine* Nouns. (Rule 128.)
Singular. (Rule 115.) N. — G. —(e)s D. —(e) A. —	*Singular.* (Rule 127.) N. —(e) G. —en D. —en A. —en	*Singular.* (Rule 129.) N. G. } — D. A. } —n or —en
Plural. N. G. A. — —e D. —en *Some modify the vowel.* (Rule 118.)	*Plural.* N. —en G. —en D. —en A. —en	*Plural.* N. G. A. — D. —n

Three Classes of Exceptions.

a. N. G. A. — (Rule 121) D. —n *Some N. G. D. A.* n (Rule 122). *Some modify the vowel* (Rule 123).

b. N. G. A. —er (Rule 124 1, 2, 3). D. —ern *All modify the vowel.*

c. N. G. D. A. —n or —en (Rule 125).

Exceptions.

1. N. G. A. — (Rule 130, 1). D. —n *Both modify the vowel.*
2. N. G. A. —e (Rule 130, 2). D. —en.
3. N. G. A. —e (Rule 130, 3). D. —en *All modify the vowel.*

THE COMPOUND NOUN.
Das zusammengesetzte Hauptwort.

134. As the German language offers a great facility for the formation of Compounds their use is naturally very great and their number unlimited.

The *Compound Nouns* are formed either with two or more nouns in the *nominative*, as, Hausherr, *master of the house*, Rathhausthurm, *steeple of the townhall*; or with two or more nouns one of which is in the *genitive* and the other or others in the nominative; as, Königssohn, *son of a king*; or with a noun and verb; as, Zeichenlehrer, *drawing master*, or with a noun and adjective; as, Großvater, *grandfather*, or with nouns and any other word. The *arrangement* is generally the same as in English; as, Tischtuch, **table**cloth; Gutmüthigkeit, **good**heartedness. The emphasis lies on the *first* component.

135. *The Gender of Compound Nouns* is that of the *second* component; as, Hausfrau, **house**wife, *fem.*, because Frau is *fem*. Exceptions to this latter rule are principally the following:

Die Antwort, the answer (*fem.* though Wort *neut.*); der Abscheu, the great dislike (*masc.* though Scheu *fem.*); die Anmuth, the gracefulness, die Demuth, the humility, die Großmuth, the generosity, die Langmuth, the forbearance, die Sanftmuth, the meekness, die Schwermuth, the melancholy, die Wehmuth, the sadness (all *fem.*, though Muth *masc.*)[1].

136. *The Declension of the Compound Nouns* does not differ from that of the simple substantive; thus, der Hausherr must be declined according to the second declension, since Herr follows that declension; die Hausfrau must follow the third declension, since die Frau follows the same; das Rathhaus must follow the *first*, das Haus belonging to the first declension.

---

1) *Obs.* Other words compounded with Muth, are *masc.*; as, der Hochmuth, the haughtiness.

137. *The Spelling of Compound Nouns* varies in usage, some preferring to keep the different components separate, merely connecting them by two hyphens, others spelling them simply in one word without regard to the length; Ex.: Kreis=Gerichts=Gefängniß, *or*, Kreisgerichts=Gefängniß, *or*, Kreisgerichtsgefängniß, county-courtprison; the latter form is certainly to be preferred. However, when the different components are not joined, the hyphens are *required*, thus General=Feldmarschall, not General Feldmarschall as is the case in English; ("General Field Marshal").

138. If two or more compound nouns[1] connected by und, oder etc. have the same *second* component, this component may be only quoted *once* (viz., in the last) and indicated in the first word or words by two hyphens only; Ex.: Land= und Stadtvolk, *people of the country and town*, instead of, Landvolk und Stadtvolk; Silber= und Kupfergeld, *silver and coppercoin*, instead of, Silbergeld und Kupfergeld.

FOREIGN NOUNS.
Fremde Hauptwörter.

139. *The use of Foreign Words* in the German language was formerly frequent, but at present a good speaker or writer will make use of those foreign words only which have been altogether germanized and thus been deprived of their foreign appearance; as, Körper, body (latin *corpus*), Fenster, window (latin *fenestra*), or those words which are modern philosophical or technical expressions, such as Telegraph, Chemie, Maschinerie, etc., which by a silent consent of modern nations are universally adopted, although some modern languages are quite able to make new words for them out of

---

[1] This rule refers also to *other* compounds, *e. g.* ab= und zugehen, *to go* and *to come*.

their own roots. To use words such as Tante, Onkel, parliren, converſiren etc., where the German words Muhme, Oheim, ſprechen etc., are certainly neither worse in sound nor value, is highly objectionable, however this is frequently disregarded, especially in the terms Onkel, Tante, Couſin, Couſine.

140. Foreign Nouns have most frequently the stress on the last syllable; as, Officier, Univerſität, Philoſophie, but also on other syllables; as, Gymnaſium, Circus etc. and usually preserve the gender of the language they are taken from; as, Univerſität, f., lat. *universitas*, Gymnaſium, n., lat. *gymnasium*.

141. In their *Declension* foreign nouns generally follow the rules of the German nouns, though sometimes, especially if the word be Latin and have preserved its original inflection in the nominative the other cases may be declined as in Latin.

Example.

SING.
   N. Das Evangelium, the gospel,
   G. des Evangeliums or des Evangelii, of the gospel,
   D. dem Evangelium „ dem Evangelio, to the gospel,
   A. das Evangelium, the gospel;

PLUR.
   N. die Evangelien or die Evangelia, the gospels,
   G. der Evangelien „ (not used), of the gospels,
   D. den Evangelien „ den Evangeliis, to the gospels,
   A. die Evangelien „ die Evangelia, the gospels.

It may, however, be added, that the classical declension is looked upon as rather pedantic.

142. *Foreign Proper Names* (Fremde Eigennamen) are either declined according to their own language (especially if they are Latin) or in the German way; but the name of our Lord is always declined as in the Latin; viz.:

   N. Jeſus Chriſtus,
   G. Jeſu Chriſti,
   D. Jeſu Chriſto,
   A. Jeſum Chriſtum.
(Vocative, Chriſte, occurs only in poetry.)

PROPER NAMES.
Eigennamen.

143. *Proper Names of men, countries and places* are declined either *with* or *without* the *article;* when declined *with* the article they take no inflection in the singular, when declined *without* article, they take in the *genitive* -**s** and no other termination in the singular; formerly, however, they got -**s** or -**ns** in the *genitive*, and -**n** in the *dative* and *accusative;* these inflections which are used by Schiller and Göthe and even at the present time in conversation, *are retained by modern grammarians only for* **Feminine Proper Names** *ending in* -**e**.

Examples.

WITHOUT ARTICLE.	WITH ARTICLE.	OLD & CONVERSATIONAL.
N. Friedrich, Frederick,	der Friedrich,	Friedrich,
G. Friedrichs, of Frederick or Frederick's,	des Friedrich,	Friedrichs, or Friedrichens,
D. Friedrich, to Frederick,	dem Friedrich,	Friedrichen,
A. Friedrich, Frederick,	den Friedrich,	Friedrichen.
N. Marie, Mary,	die Marie,	but: Maria, Maria,
G. Mariens, of Mary, or Mary's,	der Marie,	Marias, of Maria, or Maria's,
D. Marien, to Mary,	der Marie,	Maria, to Maria,
A. Marie(n), Mary,	die Marie,	Maria, Maria.

Observations.

144. *Names* of *men* are, as a rule, declined *without* the article, but if any emphasis is required in those cases which, according to modern usage, receive no inflections (especially the dative), they are then often used with the *Definite Article.*

Names of *countries* are also used without the article, except they be *not neuter* (see Rule 110) which latter never occur without the article.

Names of *towns* follow the same rule.

Names of *rivers* and *mountains* are treated like *nouns.*

However, *all Proper Names* that have an epithet before them and are not used in addressing, require the article; Ex.: das große Rußland, large Russia, der arme Heinrich ist krank, poor Henry is ill; but addressing we say: Glückliches Östreich, happy Austria! or Armer Heinrich! poor Henry!

145. The **Plural** of *Names of men* is formed according to the rules of the *nouns*, so that Friedrich forms the plural Friedriche, and Marie, Marien, whilst *Names of males* ending in -a, -e, -i, -el, -en, -er, take no inflexion; as, Schiller, pl. Schiller; *names of females* in -a add -'n; as, Maria, pl. Maria'n.

FORMATION OF FEMININE TERMS.
Bildung weiblicher Ausdrücke.

146. The term for the *Female sex* may be obtained from most nouns denoting *male beings* by the addition of the syllable -in, better -inn and (generally) the modification of the radical vowel (dropping the inflection -e). Ex.:

Der Graf, the count, *fem.* die Gräfinn, the countess;
Der Bauer, the peasant, *fem.* die Bäuerinn, the peasant's wife;
Der Gatte, the husband, *fem.* die Gattinn, the spouse.

Note. For many feminine terms *original* words exist, such as, Mutter, mother, Tochter, daughter, also of animals; as, Henne, hen, Taube, dove, etc.

147. If the common term denoting human beings or animals is of the *neuter* gender, there generally exist separate expressions for the masculine and feminine. Ex.:

Das Kind, the child,
masc. der Sohn, the son, *fem.* die Tochter, the daughter.

Das Huhn, the chicken, fowl,
masc. der Hahn, the cock, *fem.* die Henne, the hen.

148. If the common word is a *Feminine*, there will be generally a separate term for the male. Ex.:

Die Katze, the cat *(fem.)*, der Kater, the cat *(male)*.
Die Taube, the pigeon *(fem.)*, der Tauber, the pigeon *(male)*.

SUBSTANTIVE DIMINUTIVES OR PETWORDS.
Diminutiv-Substantiva oder Schmeichelwörter.
a. *The Formation of Substantive Diminutives.*

149. The syllables -chen and -lein are commonly used to form the diminutives of the German language; but other terminations such as -el and -le in the south of Germany and in Switzerland, and -ing[1] in Mecklenburg are also in use; sometimes even *two* of them combined occur, as, **Gretelchen,** diminutive for Margarethchen, from Margarethe. These syllables are simply affixed to the *word*, or plural of a word, or *name*, or *part of a name*, and the radical vowel is modified,[2] if, however, the word ends in -e or -en, the termination is thrown off previously; the termination -el is only dropped, when -lein is added.

Examples.

THE SIMPLE WORD etc.	DIMINUTIVES.				
Der Sohn, the son,	Söhnchen,	Söhnlein,	Söhnel,	Söhnle,	Söhning,[3]
der Vater, the father,	Väterchen,	not used,	Väterl,	Väterle,	Vating,
die Mutter, the mother,	Mütterchen,	not used,	Mütterl,	Mütterle,	Mutting,
das Kind, the child,	Kindchen,	Kindlein,	Kindel,	Kindle,	
die Kinder, the children,	Kinderchen.				
die Taube, the pigeon,	Täubchen,	Täublein,	Täubel,	Täuble,	
der Garten, the garden,	Gärtchen,	Gärtlein,	Gärtel,	Gärtle,	
der Vogel, the bird,	Vögelchen,	Vöglein,		Vögle,	
Anna, Ann,	Ännchen or Ännchen,	Ännel,	Ännle,	Änning,	
Margarethe Margaret,	Margarethchen,	Margarethlein,	Margarethel,		

1) Pronounced like -ing in the English *ring*.
2) Frau, wife, forms its Diminutive without modification, viz.: Frauchen (not Fräuchen).
3) The diminutives in -ing might be considered more properly as belonging to the *low German* dialect.

Note. In addition to this, it is common with Proper Names of persons to drop a syllable or two in order to produce a diminutivelike term; these short forms in their turn may be connected with -chen or -lein; as:

Heinrich	short diminutive	Heinz,	from it	Heinzchen,
Friedrich	,,	,,	Fritz,	,, ,,	Fritzchen,
Johannes	,,	,,	Hans,	,, ,,	Hänschen,
Margarethe	,,	,,	Grete,	,, ,,	Gretchen, also
					Gretel and Gretelchen.

Observation. All Diminutives are *neuter* (compare Rule 109[4]).

150. The more common of the two terminations used in North Germany, is -chen, the other being reserved for words where -chen does not sound well, or in poetry; as, Büchlein, instead of Büchchen, little book.

151. Somewhat irregular are the following:

SIMPLE WORDS.   DIMINUTIVES.
die Magd, Maid: Mädchen, Mägdlein, Mädel, Mädle, maid, girl.

b. *Meaning and Application of Substantive Diminutives.*

152. *The Meaning of Diminutives.* The Diminutives are used in German to express one or more of the following qualities: *familiarity, endearment, kindness, prettiness, compassion, smallness*[1] etc.; as, Väterchen, papa, Kindchen, baby, Gärtchen, pretty little garden, Thierchen, poor little animal, Tischchen, nice little table etc.; also *to give emphasis to a negative expression*; as, *not a word*: nicht ein Wörtchen; *not a drop of water*: nicht ein Tröpfchen Wasser.

Note. Considering the variety of meanings implied in a diminutive, they may well be used with epithets having the import of one or more of the above properties; for, as it merely contri-

---

1) Diminutives are not used to express *smallness* alone; *a little garden*, that has none other of the above properties, is not „ein Gärtchen," but „ein kleiner Garten"; nay, smallness is not even a necessary condition for the use of a Diminutive, for, Väterchen (familiar term for *dear father*) does not imply *smallness*.

butes to heighten one of the qualities to which the speaker or writer wishes to give stress, it does not abolish the others; as in „ein hübſches Thierchen", a *pretty* little animal, the adjective „hübſches" gives emphasis to the property of *prettiness*, whilst the diminutive still expresses such other qualities as *smallness, affection, kindness, compassion* etc.

153. *The Application of Diminutives* in German is very extensive, but it is impossible to define their proper use, for it depends altogether on the taste and feeling of the individual: and though we hear diminutives such as, Stündchen, *hour*, Viertelſtündchen, *quarter of an hour*, Weilchen, *a little while*, Bißchen, *little bit*, we should never hear Abendeſſenchen, little supper, Spaziergängchen, little walk.[1]

THE ADJECTIVE.

Das Beiwort oder Eigenſchaftswort.

154. The Adjective is that part of speech which is used to *qualify a noun*. A great number of participles take the place of adjectives, as in English.

---

1) *Other Diminutives.* Besides Substantive Diminutives there are existing in German also Verbal and Adjective Diminutives, but these being limited to a few forms it suffices to quote the most common of them; viz.:

Lächeln, to smile, diminutive Verb of lachen, to laugh;
fächeln, to fan (fachen);
ſtreicheln, to stroke (ſtreichen);
ſchmeicheln, to flatter;
wedeln, to wag;
handeln, to deal;

ſchütteln, to shake (ſchütten);
ſäuſeln, to whisper (ſauſen);
fränkeln, to be in delicate health; etc.
röthlich, reddish, diminutive Adjective of roth, red;
bläulich, blueish (blau); etc. etc.

An Adjective can express three degrees of quality,[1] which are called Positive, Comparative and Superlative, constituting

THE COMPARISON.
Die Steigerung.

155. The Comparison of the Adjective in German is effected in the same way as is done in the English language with short adjectives, viz., by adding to *the Positive*

-er for *the Comparative*
-eſt for *the Superlative*.[2]

Ex.:	Positive.	Comparative.	Superlative.
	fein,	feiner,	feineſt,
English:	fine,	fin-*er*,	fin-*est*.

156. In addition to this, however, the superlative *must receive inflections*,[3] owing to its being subject to the same rules of declension as the positive and comparative, and the e of the inflection -eſt is dropped, if the euphony demands it; as,

der, die, das fein-ſte, instead of fein-e-ſte.

157. Monosyllabic Adjectives modify[4] the vowels a, o and u.

Ex.: alt, älter, der, die, das älteſte, *old, older, the oldest;*
groß, größer, der, die, das größeſte, or größte, *large, larger, the largest;*

---

1) Adjectives which denote a quality so definite, as not to suffer a higher or lower degree, *cannot* be compared; as, todt, dead; halb, half.

2) With adjectives ending in -ß, the superlative is usually formed by adding -t, instead of -ſt; *e. g.*, groß, *great*, superlative der, die, das größ-te, *the greatest;* with those ending in -iſch, the superlative is either avoided altogether or -t is added instead of -ſt; as, tückiſch, malicious, tückiſch-te, the most malicious.

3) The inflections given to the superlative are exemplified 188 etc.

4) The adjective *old* presents in English a similar modification in its comparison *elder, eldest.*

jung, jünger, der, die, das jüngſte, *young, younger, the youngest.*

158. Those with the diphthong **au** are not modified: as, ſchlau, ſchlauer, der, die, das ſchlauſte, *sly, slyer, the slyest.* Also in the following the vowel should not be modified:

Barſch, harsh, rough,	knapp, tight, close,	ſchal, flat, insipid,
blond, fair,	lahm, lame,	ſchlaff, slack, loose,
brav, brave, good,	laß, weary,	ſchlant, lank, slender,
bunt, motly, variegated,	los or loſe, loose,	ſchroff, ragged, steep,
dumpf, dull (of sound), damp,	matt, faint,	ſtarr, stiff,
	morſch, decayed, rotten,	ſtolz, proud,
fahl, fallow,	nackt, naked,	ſtraff, tight, strained,
falſch, false,	platt, flat,	ſtumm, dumb,
flach, flat,	plump, plump, clumsy,	ſtumpf, blunt,
froh, glad, joyful,	rar, rare,	toll, mad,
glatt, smooth,	raſch, rash, quick,	voll, full,
hohl, hollow,	roh, raw, rude,	wahr, true,
hold, lovely, well inclined,	rund, round,	wohl, well, healthy,
kahl, bald,	ſacht, slow, soft,	wund, wounded, sore,
karg, scanty, stingy,	ſanft, soft, gentle,	zahm, tame.
	ſatt, satiated, full,	

Observation.

159. It may suffice, if the learner commits to memory the following list, which excludes such of the above, as do not occur frequently in comparison, viz.:

Brav, (braver), dumpf, falſch, fahl, flach, (flacher), karg, knapp, kahl, lahm, (lahmer), matt, plump, glatt, raſch, (raſcher), ſacht, ſatt, platt, ſanft, (ſanfter), ſchlaff, ſchlant, roh, ſtolz, toll, voll, wahr, zahm, froh.

160. The following occur sometimes *with* and sometimes *without* modification of the radical vowel; viz., bange, *timid,* blaß, *pale,* geſund, *sound,* zart, *tender.*

161. The Adjective lange or lang', *long,* modifies, though consisting of two syllables; viz., länger, der, die, das längſte.

Note. Both *Comparative* and *Superlative* are declined like the positive. (See 173.)

162. The word *than* which follows the comparative is translated by **als** and (though not so frequently) by **denn**; as, er ist größer **als** ich, he is taller *than* I; er ist nicht ärmer **als** wir, he is not poorer *than* we.

163. The words *the — the*, that sometimes precede comparatives are rendered in German by **je—desto**, or **je — um so**; as, je länger ich ihn kenne, desto mehr muß ich ihn achten, or **um so** mehr etc., *the* longer I know him, *the* more I must esteem him.

164. The Superlative in its pure *adjectival* form is used almost only when an epithet, *i. e.*, when *preceding* the noun; as, **der reichste** Mann ist oft nicht so zufrieden, als **der ärmste** (Mann *understood*), *the richest man is often not so contented as the poorest*. It may, however, be used in its adjectival form, when *predicate* to the noun, provided it implies a comparison of quality belonging to different subjects; as, der reichste Mann ist nicht immer **der glücklichste**, the richest man is not always *the happiest* (compared with *other* men); yet, this is not nearly so frequent as the adverbial form „**am glücklichsten**", which peculiar form is a contraction of the preposition **an** and the dative of the superlative. Consequently the above sentence is more commonly expressed thus: Der reichste Mann ist nicht immer **am glücklichsten**. This latter form *must* be used if the comparison is made only with reference to *one* person; as, der Mensch ist **am glücklichsten**, wenn er eine gute That gethan hat, man is *happiest* when he has done a good deed; in that case the *English* superlative is used *without article*.

165. The following adjectives form their comparatives and superlatives *irregularly*:

gut, good,	**besser**, better,	der, die, das **beste**, the best;
hoch, high,	**höher**, higher,	der, „ „ **höchste**, the highest;
nah, near,[1]	**näher**, nearer,	der, „ „ **nächste**, the nearest;

---

1) Compare: *nigh, near, next*.

viel, much, **mehr,** more, der, die, das **meiſte** (rarely **mehrſte**), the most; **gering',** little, **geringer,** or **minder,** less, der, die, das **geringſte,** or **mindeſte,** the least.

166. There are some comparatives and superlatives which are derived from adverbs, but have the import of adjectives, and no direct comparison is implied in them; they are:

Adverbs.	Comparative.	Superlative.
Außen, without,	der die das } **äußere,** the outer, exterior,	der die das } **äußerſte,** the outmost, extreme;
innen, within,	„ **innere,** the inner, interior,	„ **innerſte,** the inmost;
hinten, behind,	„ **hintere,** the hinder,	„ **hinterſte,** the hindmost;
vorn, before,	„ **vordere,** the fore, anterior,	„ **vorderſte,** the foremost;
oben, above,	„ **obere,** the upper,	„ **oberſte,** the uppermost;
unten, below,	„ **untere,** the lower,	„ **unterſte,** the lowest;
mitten, amidst,	„ **mittlere,** the middle,	„ **mittelſte,** the middlemost.

Observation.

167. The two superlatives **erſt,** *first,* and **letzt,** *last,* undergo a second comparison in the words:
der, die, das **erſtere,** *the former,* der, die das **letztere,** *the latter.*

168. PARTICIPLES are only compared, when used in the pure sense of an adjective; as, dieſer Herr iſt ſehr **gebildet,** er iſt viel **gelehrter** als ſein Freund, ich kenne keinen **gelehrteren** Mann, er iſt der **gelehrteſte** Mann der Stadt; this gentleman is highly *accomplished;* he is much *more learned,* than his friend; I know no man *more learned,* he is *the most learned* man in the town. Whilst it would not be grammatically correct to say: Heinrich iſt geliebter als Ludwig, Henry is more beloved than Louis; which phrase should be expressed: Heinrich wird mehr geliebt als Ludwig, Henry is loved more than Louis.

169. The importance of the superlative may be increased by prefixing to it the genitive plural of **all,**

viz., **aller**; as, dieser Kaufmann hat die **allerschönsten** Pferde in der Stadt, this merchant has the *very finest* horses in the town. Die **allerbesten** Menschen werden oft verkannt, the *very best* (of) men are often misunderstood.

170. The superlative should never be used in German in an *absolute* sense, *adverbs* supply that want; as, er ist immer **höchst** freundlich zu uns, he is always *most* friendly to us; das ist mir **äußerst** angenehm, I am extremely (or very) glad of it.

THE DECLENSION OF THE ADJECTIVE.

171. An Adjective may be used as an *epithet*, *i. e.*, *preceding* the noun, or as an *attribute*, *i. e.*, *following* the noun in the form of the predicate.

172. When used as *predicate*, the adjective is *not* declined; as, der Vater ist **gut**, the father is good, die Mutter ist **gut**, the mother is good, das Kind ist **gut**, the child is good, die Väter — die Mütter — die Kinder sind **gut**, the fathers — the mothers — the children are good.

173. When used as an *epithet*,[1] it *is* declined and that on the following principle:

It is made to show the number, gender and case of the Noun, where that has not been done already by an Article or Pronoun; thus,

a) if preceded by an *Article* or *Pronoun* with the **strong** termination,[2] *the Adjective gets the* **weak** *termination;*

---

1) The Adjective, when an *epithet*, rarely follows the noun in German, but if it does, the noun is understood, and the adjective declined; it will be found thus sometimes in poetry.

2) Contracted forms such as **am**, **beim**, are strong; as, **am** ersten Juli.

b) if *not* preceded by an **Article** or **Pronoun** with the *strong* termination, then *the* **Adjective** *gets the* **strong** *termination.*¹

Observations.

174. a. *Two* or *more* Adjectives receive the same inflection as *one*.

b. Comparatives and Superlatives are declined in the same way as Positives.

c. Intervening adverbs do not interfere with the inflections; thus, ein guter and ein jehr guter Vater, a good *and* a very good father.

175. The **strong terminations** (die ſtarken Endungen) are those of the *definite Article*, viz.:

	SINGULAR.			PLURAL.
	Masc.	Fem.	Neut.	M. F. N.
Nom.	-er,	-e,	-es,²	-e,
Gen.	-es,	-er,	-es,	-er,
Dat.	-em,	-er,	-em,	-en,
Acc.	-en,	-e,	-es,²	-e.

Observations.

176. The strong terminations are common to *both articles and all pronouns*. The following cases, however, are altogether without inflection, viz., **ein** (a), **mein** (my), **dein** (thy), **ſein** (his, its), **kein** (no, none), **unſer** (our), **euer** (your), **ihr** (her, their).

Note. **Ich** and **du** may be added, since they require after them the adjective with the *strong termination;* as, ich unglücklicher Mann, I unhappy man, du glückliches Kind, thou happy child; whilst after the personal pronouns of the plural (wir and ihr) the adjective gets the *weak termination;* as, wir or ihr unglücklichen Leute, *we* or *you* unhappy people. Other forms, such as deſſen, need no mention, as they never occur before epithets; on the other hand, pronouns like derjenige, derſelbe are not exceptions, since they consist of an article and adjective themselves, and thus come under rule 174 a.

---

1) In two cases the Adjective must be considered as *not preceded by an Article or Pronoun with the strong termination,* viz., a) when not preceded by an Article or Pronoun *at all.*
b) when preceded by one of the ten words (Observation 176) ein, mein, dein, ſein, kein, unſer, euer, ihr, ich and du.
2) Compare Rule 47.

177. The **weak terminations** (die schwachen Endungen) to be given to the adjective are in all cases singular and plural -n or -en, excepting the *Nominative Singular* Masculine, Feminine and Neuter and the *Accusative* Singular *Feminine* and *Neuter* for which the weak termination is -e; viz.:

	SINGULAR.			PLURAL.
	Masc.	Fem.	Neut.	M. F. N.
N.	-e,	-e,	-e,	-en,
G.	-en,	-en,	-en,	-en,
D.	-en,	-en,	-en,	-en,
A.	-en,	-e,	-e,	-en.

Observations.

178. The adjective hoch drops the c and becomes hoh when declined; as,
der hohe Baum, the high tree,   ein hoher Baum, a high tree,
des hohen Baumes, of the high tree,   eines hohen Baumes, of a high tree.

179. Adjectives in -er formed from names of towns remain unchanged; as, Pariser, Parisian, Londoner, of London. Ex.:
  N. and A. Die Pariser Mode, Parisian fashion,
  G. „ D. der Pariser Mode, of and to Parisian fashion.
Some consider these adjectives nouns; this finds some confirmation in their being the only adjectives in German spelled with capital initials.

180. The Positive often *drops* its strong termination in the nominative and accusative of the neuter, as, schön Wetter, *fine weather*, instead of schönes Wetter; the Comparative *sometimes* does the same; as, ein höher Verlangen, *a higher desire*, instead of ein höheres Verlangen. The strong termination of the masculine and neuter genitive (-es) is now-a-day's often substituted by the weak termination -en, if the noun which it precedes takes an -s in the genitive; as, guten Muthes, *of good cheer*, instead of gutes Muthes.

181. TABLE FOR THE DECLENSION OF ADJECTIVES.

	SINGULAR.						PLURAL.	
	Masc.		Fem.		Neut.		M. F. N.	
	strong	weak	strong	weak	strong	weak	strong	weak
N.	er	e	e	e	es	e	e	en
G.	es	en	er	en	es	en	er	en
D.	em	en	er	en	em	en	en	en
A.	en	en	e	e	es	e	e	en

Examples.

A. Positive (gut, good).

182. The Adjective requiring the *strong* termination[1] in all cases:

Masculine.

N. Gut-er Bruder, good brother,
G. gut-es Bruders, of good brother
  (or gut-en[2] Bruders),
D. gut-em Bruder, to good brother,
A. gut-en Bruder, good brother;

Feminine.

SINGULAR.

gut-e Schwester, good sister,
gut-er Schwester, of good sister,
gut-er Schwester, to good sister,
gut-e Schwester, good sister;

Neuter.

gut-es Kind, good child,
gut-es Kindes, of good child
  (or gut-en[2] Kindes),
gut-em Kinde, to good child,
gut-es Kind, good child.

PLURAL.

N. Gut-e Brüder, Schwestern, Kinder, good brothers, sisters, children,
G. gut-er Brüder, Schwestern, Kinder, of good brothers, sisters, children,
D. gut-en Brüdern, Schwestern, Kindern, to good brothers, sisters, children,
A. gut-e Brüder, Schwestern, Kinder, good brothers, sisters, children.

183. The Adjective requiring the *weak* termination in all cases:

Masculine.

N. Der gut-e Bruder, the good brother,
G. des gut-en Bruders, of the "
D. dem gut-en Bruder, to the "
A. den gut-en Bruder, the good brother;

Feminine.

SINGULAR.

die gut-e Schwester, the good sister,
der gut-en Schwester, of the good sister,
der gut-en Schwester, to the good sister,
die gut-e Schwester, the good sister;

Neuter.

das gut-e Kind, the good child,
des gut-en Kindes, of the good child,
dem gut-en Kinde, to the good child,
das gut-e Kind, the good child.

1) As appears from Rules 173a and 175 this can only be the case, if it is not preceded by an Article and Pronoun *at all*, or by one of the forms ein, mein etc. (See Examples 184. 187, 190.)
2) See Rule 180.

PLURAL.

N. Die gut-en Brüder, Schwestern, Kinder, the good brothers, sisters, children,
G. der gut-en Brüder, Schwestern, Kinder, of the good brothers, sisters, children,
D. den gut-en Brüdern, Schwestern, Kindern, to the good brothers, sisters, children,
A. die gut-en Brüder, Schwestern, Kinder, the good brothers, sisters, children.

184. The Adjective requiring for some cases the *strong*, for the rest the *weak* termination:

N.	Ein,	mein,	dein,	sein,	unser,	euer,	ihr	gut-er Bruder,
	a,	my,	thy,	his,	our,	your,	their or her	good brother,
G.	eines,[1]	meines,	deines,	seines,	unseres,	eures,	ihres	gut-en Bruders,
	of a,	of my,	of thy,	of his,	of our,	of your,	of their or her	good brother,
D.	einem,[1]	meinem,	deinem,	seinem,	unserem,	eurem,	ihrem	gut-en Bruder,
	to a,	to my,	to thy,	to his,	to our,	to your,	to their or her	good brother,
A.	einen,[1]	meinen,	deinen,	seinen,	unseren,	euren,	ihren	gut-en Bruder,
	a,	my,	thy,	his,	our,	your,	their or her	good brother.

N. and A.	Ein,	mein,	dein,	sein,	unser,	euer,	ihr	gut-es Kind,
	a,	my,	thy,	his,	our,	your,	their or her	good child,
G.	eines,[1]	meines,	deines,	seines,	unseres,	eures,	ihres	gut-en Kindes,
	of a,	of my,	of thy,	of his,	of our,	of your,	of their or her	good child,
D.	einem,[1]	meinem,	deinem,	seinem,	unserem,	eurem,	ihrem	gut-en Kinde,
	to a,	to my,	to thy,	to his,	to our,	to your,	to their or her	good child.

---

1) As these forms have the *strong* termination, the Adjective must have the **weak**.

74

B. Comparative (beſſer, better).

185. Requiring the *strong* termination in all cases:

Masculine.

SINGULAR.

N. Beſſer-er Wein, better wine,
G. beſſer-es[1] Weines, of better wine (or beſſer-en Weines),
D. beſſer-em Weine, to better wine,
A. beſſer-en Wein, better wine;

Feminine.

N. beſſer-e Suppe, better soup,
G. beſſer-er Suppe, of better soup,
D. beſſer-er Suppe, to better soup,
A. beſſer-e Suppe, better soup;

Neuter.

beſſer-es Bier, better beer,
beſſer-es[1] Bieres, of better beer (or beſſer-en Bieres),
beſſer-em Bier, to better beer,
beſſer-es Bier, better beer.

PLURAL.

N. and A. Beſſer-e Weine, Suppen, Biere, better wines, soups, beers, etc. etc.

186. Requiring the *weak* termination in all cases:

Masculine.

N. Der beſſer-e Wein, the better wine,
G. des beſſer-en Weines, of the „ „
D. dem beſſer-en Weine, to the „ „
A. den beſſer-en Wein, the better wine;

Feminine.

SINGULAR.

die beſſer-e Suppe, the better soup,
der beſſer-en Suppe, of the „ „
der beſſer-en Suppe, to the „ „
die beſſer-e Suppe, the „ „

Neuter.

das beſſer-e Bier, the better beer,
des beſſer-en Bieres, of the „ „
dem beſſer-en Bier, to the „ „
das beſſer-e Bier, the „ „

PLURAL.

N. and A. Die beſſer-en Weine, Suppen, Biere, the better wines, soups, beers, etc. etc.

187. Requiring the *weak* in some and the *strong* in the other cases:

N. Ein, mein, dein, sein, unser, euer, ihr beſſer-er Wein,
    a,   my,   thy, his, no,   your, their or her better wine,
G. eines, meines, deines, seines, unseres, eueres, ihres beſſer-en Weines,
    of a, of my, of thy, of his, of no, of our, of your, of their or her better wine.
etc.   etc.

---

[1] See Rule 180.

C. Superlative (beſt, best).

188. Requiring the *strong* termination in all cases:

SINGULAR.

Masculine.	Feminine.	Neuter.
Beſt-er Bruder! best (dear) brother!	beſt-e Schweſter! best (dear) sister!	beſt-es Kind! best (dear) child!

PLURAL

Beſt-e Brüder, Schweſtern, Kinder! best brothers, sisters, children!
(Occurs only in the Nominative.)

189. Requiring the *weak* termination in all cases:

Masculine.	Feminine.	Neuter.
Der beſt-e Bruder, the best brother,	die beſt-e Schweſter, the best sister,	das beſt-e Kind, the best child,
des beſt-en Bruders, of the best brother; etc.	der beſt-en Schweſter, of the best sister; etc.	des beſt-en Kindes, of the best child, etc.

190. Requiring the *strong* in some, the *weak* in the *rest* of the cases:

N. Mein¹,	dein,	ſein,	unſer,	euer,	ihr	beſt-er Bruder,
my,	thy,	his,	our,	your,	their or her	best brother,
G. meines,	deines,	ſeines,	unſeres,	eures,	ihres	beſt-en Bruders,
of my,	of thy,	of his,	of our,	of your,	of their or her	best brother etc. etc.
N. and A. mein,	dein,	ſein,	unſer,	euer,	ihr	beſt-es Kind,
my,	thy,	his,	our,	your,	their or her	best child,
G. meines,	deines,	ſeines,	unſeres,	eures,	ihres	beſt-en Kindes,
of my,	of thy,	of his,	of our,	of your,	of their or her	of the best child etc. etc.

1) The Indefinite Article ein cannot be used with a Superlative.

DERIVED ADJECTIVES.
Abgeleitete Eigenschaftswörter.

191. The most common inflection of the derived adjective is -lich, next -isch; as, Glück, luck: glücklich, lucky; Vater, father: väterlich, fatherly, paternal; Bauer, peasant, boor: bäuerisch, boorish, peasant-like; Thier, animal, brute: thierisch, brutish, brutal. But a number of others occur, as, -bar, -haft, -icht, -ig, -los, -sam; as, Dank, thank: dankbar, thankful; Tugend, virtue: tugendhaft, virtuous; Milch, milk: milchicht, milklike; milchig, milky; Zweck, aim: zwecklos, aimless: Gewalt, violence: gewaltsam, violent.

192. Proper names of persons, countries, towns, etc. form their Adjectives mostly in -isch; viz.:

1. By adding it to the word itself without further change:

Ex.: Homer: homerisch; Cäsar: cäsarisch; Napoleon: napoleonisch; London: londonisch;[1] Edinburg: edinburgisch; Berlin: berlinisch.

2. By adding it to the *stem* of the word, occasionally modifying the vowel; Ex.:

Name.	Stem.	Adjective.
Gothe, Goth,	Goth-	gothisch, Gothic,
Celte, Celt,	Celt-	celtisch, Celtic,
Brite,[2] Briton,	Brit-	britisch, British,
Schotte, Scot,	Schott-	schottisch, Scottish,
Preuße, Prussian,	Preuß-	preußisch, Prussian,
Franzose, Frenchman,	Französ-	französisch, French,
Franke, Frank,	Frank-	fränkisch, Frankish,
Türke, Turk,	Türk-	türkisch, Turkish.

3. By changing -ic, -ical, -an and -can (Latin -us and -icus) into -isch; Ex.:

Latin.	English.	German Adjective.
Europaeus,	European,	europäisch,
asiaticus,	Asiatic,	asiatisch,
africanus.	African,	africanisch,

---

1) Names of towns also form an Adjective in -er; as, Londoner, Edinburger, Berliner (which are never declined, as stated in rule 179).

2) Sometimes spelled with tt.

germanus,	Germanic,	germaniſch,
gallus,	Gallic,	galliſch,
	botanical,	botaniſch.

193. Words denoting substances, such as *metals, stone, wood, leather, wool*, etc. form their adjectives in -en or -ern, occasionally modifying the vowel; as,

Noun.	Adjective.	Noun.	Adjective.
Metall, metal:	metallen, metallic,	Wolle, wool:	wollen, worsted,
Gold, gold:	golden,[1] of gold,	Seide, silk:	ſeiden, of silk,
Silber, silver:	ſilbern, of silver,	Lein, linen, or Leinen:	leinen, of linen,
Eiſen, iron:	eiſern, of iron,	Stein, stone:	ſteinern, of stone,
Stahl, steel:	ſtählern, of steel,	Holz, wood:	hölzern, wooden,
Kupfer, copper:	kupfern, of copper,	Glas, glass:	gläſern, of glass,
Blei, lead:	bleiern, of lead,	Leder, leather:	ledern, of leather.

Note. About Adjective Diminutives see note 1 to Rule 153.

194. Some peculiar adjectives are derived from Adverbs or Prepositions of *place* and *time* by the addition of the syllable -ig;[2] as:

Adv. or Prepos.	Adjectives.	Examples.
hier, here,	hieſig, of this place,	das hieſige Rathhaus, the townhall of this place;
da, there,	daſig, of that place (rare);	
dort, there,	dortig, of that place,	das dortige Theater, the theatre of that place;
diesſeit, on this side,	diesſeitig, on this side,	das diesſeitige Land, the land on this side;
jenſeit, on the other side,	jenſeitig, on the other side,	das jenſeitige Land, the land on the other side;
heute, to-day,	heutig, to-day's,	das heutige Schauſpiel, to-day's play;
geſtern, yesterday,	geſtrig, yesterday's,	die geſtrige Zeitung, yesterday's newspaper;
morgen, to-morrow,	morgend[3], or morgig to-morrow's,	das morgende, or das morgige Feſt, to-morrow's feast;
heuer, this year,	heurig, this year's,	die heurige Ernte, this year's harvest;

1) gulden and gülden are obsolete.
2) These adjectives, however, are only used as *epithets* (i. e., preceding the noun).
3) morgend is the more common form.

ehemals, vormals, formerly, before,	ehemalig, or vormalig, or vorig, former,	Der ehemalige König von Neapel, the former king of Naples;
jetzt, at present,	jetzig, present,	Der jetzige Kaiser von Frankreich, the present emperor of France;
bald, soon.	baldig, speedy,	eine baldige Rückkehr, a speedy return;
über, over,	übrig, remaining,	die übrigen Leute, the remaining people.

THE NUMERAL.
Das Zahlwort.

195. There are *Cardinal* and *Ordinal* numbers in German, the latter being derived by adding to the former up to 19 -te, thereafter -fte. Two, it will be seen, are irregular, viz., der, die, das **erste**, *the first* and der, die, das **dritte**, *the third*. The numbers are arranged in the same order as in English, excepting *that the units must always be placed before the tens*, thus, einundzwanzig, *one and twenty*, not zwanzig eins (*twenty one*).

196. THE CARDINAL NUMBERS. **197.** THE ORDINAL NUMBERS.

Die Hauptzahlen.   Die Ordnungszahlen.

0. null,
1. eins,[1]
2. zwei,[2]
3. drei,[2]
4. vier,
5. fünf,
6. sechs, (pron. zex.)

1st der, die, das **erste**,
2nd „ „ „ **zweite**,
3rd „ „ „ **dritte**,
4th „ „ „ **vierte**,
5th „ „ „ **fünfte**,
6th „ „ „ **sechste**,

---

1) See Rule 199.
2) See Rule 200.

7. sieben,	7th	der,	die,	das siebente,
8. acht,	8th	„	„	„ achte,¹
9. neun,	9th	„	„	„ neunte,
10. zehn,	10th	„	„	„ zehnte,
11. elf, (often spelled eilf),	11th	„	„	„ elfte (or eilfte),
12. zwölf,	12th	„	„	„ zwölfte,
13. dreizehn,	13th	„	„	„ dreizehnte,
14. vierzehn,²	14th	„	„	„ vierzehnte,²
15. fünfzehn (or funfzehn),	15th	„	„	„ fünfzehnte (or funfzehnte),
16. sechzehn,³	16th	„	„	„ sechzehnte,³
17. siebzehn (rarely siebenzehn),	17th	„	„	„ siebzehnte (rarely siebenzehnte),
18. achtzehn,	18th	„	„	„ achtzehnte,
19. neunzehn,	19th	„	„	„ neunzehnte,
20. zwanzig,	20th	„	„	„ zwanzigste,
21. ein und⁴ zwanzig,	21st	„	„	„ einundzwanzigste,
22. zwei und zwanzig,	22nd	„	„	„ zweiundzwanzigste,
23. drei und zwanzig,	23rd	„	„	„ dreiundzwanzigste,
24. vier und zwanzig,	24th	„	„	„ vierundzwanzigste,
25. fünf und zwanzig,	25th	„	„	„ fünfundzwanzigste,
26. sechs und zwanzig,	26th	„	„	„ sechsundzwanzigste,
27. sieben und zwanzig,	27th	„	„	„ siebenundzwanzigste,
28. acht und zwanzig,	28th	„	„	„ achtundzwanzigste,
29. neun und zwanzig,	29th	„	„	„ neunundzwanzigste,
30. dreißig,⁵	30th	„	„	„ dreißigste,
31. ein und dreißig,	31st	„	„	„ einunddreißigste,
32. zwei und dreißig,	32nd	„	„	„ zweiunddreißigste,
etc.				etc.
40. vierzig,	40th	„	„	„ vierzigste
50. fünfzig (or funfzig),	50th	„	„	„ fünfzigste (or funfzigste),
60. sechzig,³	60th	„	„	„ sechzigste,³
70. siebzig (rarely siebenzig),	70th	„	„	„ siebzigste (rarely siebenzigste),
80. achtzig,	80th	„	„	„ achtzigste,
90. neunzig.	90th	„	„	„ neunzigste,

1) Notice the spelling achte, not acht-te.
2) The vowel in vier is pronounced *long*, but in its compounds vierzehn and vierzig etc. *short*.
3) sechzehn and sechzig are pronounced and properly spelled without the s of sechs.
4) Pronounce: unn without d.
5) Observe that dreißig is spelled with ß, all other tens with z only.

100. hundert (einhundert, when emphatic),	100th der, die, das hundertste,
101. hundert(und)eins,[1]	101st „ „ „ hundert(und)erste,
102. hundert(und)zwei,	102nd „ „ „ hundert(und)zweite,
103. hundert(und)drei,	103rd „ „ „ hundert(und)dritte,
etc.	etc.
200. zweihundert,	200th „ „ „ zweihundertste,
300. dreihundert,	300th „ „ „ dreihundertste,
400. vierhundert,	400th „ „ „ vierhundertste,
500. fünfhundert,	500th „ „ „ fünfhundertste,
etc.	etc.
1000. tausend (eintausend, when emphatic),	1000th „ „ „ tausendste,
1001. tausend(und)eins,	1001st „ „ „ tausend(und)erste
1500. (ein)tausend fünfhundert or fünfzehnhundert,	1500th „ „ „ tausendfünfhundertste,
2000. zweitausend,	2000th „ „ „ zweitausendste,
10,000. zehntausend,	10,000th der, die, das zehntausendste,
100,000. hunderttausend, or einmal hunderttausend,	100,000th „ „ „ hunderttausendste,
1,000,000. (eine) Million,	1,000,000th der, die, das millionste,
1,000,000,000. eine Milliarde or tausend Millionen,	
1,000,000,000,000. (eine) Billion,	1,000,000,000,000th der, die, das billionste.

Note. From the above it will be seen that the numbers in German are arranged as in English, excepting that the *units* are always placed *before* the *tens*, thus the number 1869 may be read either achtzehnhundert (und) neun und sechzig, or (ein)tausend acht hundert (und) neun und sechzig; the number 123,456,789 must be read (ein)hundert drei und zwanzig Million, vier hundert sechs und fünfzig tausend, sieben hundert (und) neun und achtzig.

198. The monosyllabic numbers zwei, drei, vier, fünf, sechs, acht, neun, zehn, are often used with an additional -e, but only when not followed by a *noun*; viz., zweie, dreie, viere, etc.

Hundert and Tausend are also used as *nouns* with the neuter gender; as:

Was geben Sie mir für's Hundert, what will you pay me *for a hundred?*

Was wollen Sie für's Tausend, what do you charge *for a thousand?*

---

1) Words in parenthesis may be left out.

DECLENSION OF NUMERALS.

199. Ein̄s, *one*.

1. When *preceding* a *noun*, it must agree with it and is then, in its declension, *analogous to the Indefinite Article* ein, eine, ein, from which it is distinguished only by having the stress, articles never being emphatic.

Ex.: ein Mann, *one* man,   eine Frau, *one* woman, ein Kind, *one* child,

eines Mannes, of *one* man, einer Frau, of *one* woman, eines Kindes, of *one* child,

etc.   etc.   etc.

2. When *referring* to a noun it also must agree with it, but requires the *strong* terminations throughout.

Ex.: Wie viele Männer waren da? Einer! How many *men* were there? *One!*

Wie viele Frauen waren da? Eine! How many *women* were there? *One!*

Wie viele Kinder waren da? Eines (or Ein̄s)! How many *children* were there? *One!*

3. When *following* the Definite Article or a Pronoun with the force of an *Adjective*, it is, of course, declined like an adjective.

Ex.: der eine Mann, the *one* man, die eine Frau, the *one* woman, des einen Mannes, of the *one* man, der einen Frau, of the *one* woman, etc.   etc.

das eine Kind, the *one* child, des einen Kindes, of the *one* child, etc.

mein einer Fuß, my *one* foot,   meine eine Hand, my *one* hand, meines einen Fußes, of my *one* foot, meiner einen Hand, of my *one* hand, etc.   etc.

mein eines Auge, my *one* eye, meines einen Auges, of my *one* eye, etc.

200. Zwei, *two*, and drei, *three*.

1. These two numbers are sometimes declined when not preceded by an article or pronoun; viz.:

N.	Zwei(e),¹ two,	drei(e), three,
G.	zweier, of two,	dreier, of three,
D.	zweien, to two,	dreien, to three,
A.	zwei(e), two;	drei(e), three.

Ex.: Die Thaten **zweier** Könige, the deeds *of two* kings.
In **dreien** Tagen will ich wieder auferstehn, in *three* days I shall rise again. *Bible*.

2. When used *adjectively*, zwei is not so frequently employed as the plural of beides, *both*, viz., **beide**.

Ex.: Diese **beiden** Kinder haben ihre **beiden** Eltern verloren, these two children have lost both their parents.

201. All the other numbers remain uninflected, except in the dative which takes **-en** when not followed by a noun.

Ex.: Die Königinn fährt (in einem Wagen) mit Sechsen (bespannt), the queen drives in a carriage drawn by six (horses).
Das Kind läuft auf allen Vieren, the child runs on all four.

202. The ORDINAL NUMBERS are inflected like *adjectives*; as:

SINGULAR.   PLURAL.

N.	Der erste,	die erste,	das erste,	die ersten, the first,
G.	des ersten,	der ersten,	des ersten,	der ersten, of the first,
D.	dem ersten,	der ersten,	dem ersten,	den ersten, to the first,
A.	den ersten,	die erste,	das erste;	die ersten, the first.

Ex.: Die **Ersten** werden die letzten sein, the *first* (Plur.) will be the *last* (Plur).

203. *The names of Sovereigns* and *the Dates* are expressed in German as in English, viz., by means of Ordinal Numbers; Ex.:

Friedrich der Zweite, Frederick the second.
Der vierte November, the fourth (of) November.

204. When used adverbially, the Ordinal numbers may be employed in two forms, viz.,

a) with the inflection **-ens**; as, **erstens**,² firstly, **zweitens**, secondly, **drittens**, thirdly, etc.

---

1) The form zwo is *old* and *poetical*; zween is *obsolete*.
2) Instead of erstens will be found sometimes **erstlich** which is provincial.

b) with the Preposition ʒu and the definite article in the contraction ʒum followed by the dative with the weak inflection; as, ʒum erſten, ʒum ʒweiten, ʒum britten, in the first, second, third *place*, etc. The latter form is the *less* common.

205. An expression that might be termed an *Ordinal Interrogative* exists in German, signifying *what day of a month*, or *what place* or *number* in a lot? and which requires an ordinal number as answer, viz., ber, bie, baš wievielte, or wievielſte?[1]

Ex.: Der wievielte iſt heute? *what day of the month is it?* or, ben wievielſten haben wir heute?
Der wievielſte ſind Sie in der Klaſſe? *what place do you hold in your class?*

COMPOUNDS AND DERIVATIVES FORMED FROM THE NUMERALS.

206. The MULTIPLICATIVE NUMERALS (Vervielfältigungszahlen) are formed by adding to the Cardinals -fach or -fältig;[2] as,

Einfach, or einfältig, onefold, simple, plain,
zweifach, or zweifältig, or doppelt, twofold, double,
dreifach, or dreifältig, threefold, treble,
zehnfach, or zehnfältig, tenfold,
zwanzigfach, or zwanzigfältig, twentyfold,
hundertfach, or hundertfältig, a hundredfold,
tauſendfach, or tauſendfältig, a thousandfold.

Note. These numerals are declined like Adjectives.

207. REITERATIVE NUMERALS (Wiederholungszahlen) are formed both with *Cardinals* and *Ordinals* by means of the neuter substantive Mal.

Note. They may be either spelled in *one word*, as, einmal, or separately, as, ein Mal.

---

1) Compare French: *le quantième;* Latin: *quotus;* Greek: πόστος.

2) Several Adverbs are obtained in the same way; as, vielfach, or vielfältig, manifold; mannigfach, or mannigfaltig (not fältig), variegated, manifold; mehrfach, or mehrfältig, severally, manifold.

Ex.: **Einmal**[1] or ein Mal, once,   Das erste Mal, the first time,
zweimal or zwei Mal, twice,   das zweite Mal, the second time,
dreimal or drei Mal, thrice,   das dritte Mal, the third time,
viermal or vier Mal, four times, etc.   das vierte Mal, the fourth time, etc.

Zum ersten Mal, for the first time,
zum zweiten Mal, for the second time,
zum dritten Mal, for the third time,
zum vierten Mal, for the fourth time,
etc.   etc.

208. The following Adverbs which stand in connection with these numerals may be mentioned here; viz.:

Einstmals or einst, once,   oftmals often(times),
jemals or je, ever,   mehrmals, several times,
niemals or nie, never,   vielmals, many times,
manchmal, sometimes,   ehemals, formerly.

209. FRACTIONAL NUMBERS (**Bruchzahlen**) are formed by adding to the cardinal numbers up to 19 the termination **-tel**,[2] from 19 upwards **-stel** is added; as,

Ein Viertel ¹/₄   ein Sechstel ¹/₆   ein Neunzehntel ¹/₁₉
ein Fünftel ¹/₅   ein Siebentel ¹/₇   ein Zwanzigstel ¹/₂₀
      ein einundzwanzigstel ¹/₂₁.

210. Ein Eintel (¹/₁) does not occur in colloquy as *simple number*, it can occur in connection with 100 or 1000; thus ¹/₁₀₁ and ¹/₁₀₀₁ would be pronounced in German, ein Hunderteintel, ein Tausendeintel.

The same rule applies to ein **Zweitel** (¹/₂); for the proper term for *half* is **halb**, when *Adjective* or *Adverb*, and **Hälfte**, f., when *Noun*; whilst ¹/₁₀₂ or ¹/₁₀₀₂ would have to be read: ein Hundertzweitel, ein Tausendzweitel.

Ein Drittel is the form for ¹/₃ (*not* ein Dreitel).

Note. The fractional numbers are neuter, when used as nouns; *e. g.* das erste Viertel, *the first quarter.*

---

1) The Adverb of time einmal, *once upon a time*, has the stress on mal.
2) -tel is a corruption of Theil, *part*.

211. About the use of **halb** it may be proper to add the following rules:

1. It may be used *adverbially* (although not in many phrases), in which case it cannot be followed by an article or pronoun; as, halb Paris war in Bewegung, *half* Paris was in a commotion. It follows in this case the usage of ganz, *quite, whole*; as, ganz Berlin war in Aufregung, *all* Berlin was in a state of excitement.

2. It must be used *adjectively*, when in connection with *articles* or *pronouns*, contrary to English usage (*half a, half my*), etc.

Ex.: ein halber Tag, *half a* day; eine halbe Woche, *half a* week; ein halbes Jahr, *half a* year; sein halbes Vermögen, half his fortune, etc.

Thus it would be incorrect to say, halb ein Tag, halb eine Woche, etc.

3. With the Definite Article it is best to use *the Noun*, although halb *might* be used *adjectively*; as, **das halbe** Land ist schon verloren, or, **die Hälfte** des Landes ist schon verloren, half (or, the half of) the country is lost already.

4. Instead of *half past one, two*, etc. is said in German halb zwei (half two), halb drei (half three).

5. One other peculiarity of halb deserves the notice of the learner, namely, its meaning in the following expressions, the first of which especially occurs very frequently; viz.:

   anderthalb, one and a half,
   dritt(e)halb, two and a half,
   viert(e)halb, three and a half,
   fünft(e)halb, four and a half,
   sechst(e)halb, five and a half.

Ex.: Ich werde in anderthalb Stunden wieder hier sein, I shall be back in *one* hour *and a half*.

Note. It will be seen from this example that anderthalb demands the noun in the plural.

212. Variative Numerals (Artenzahlen) denoting *of — kinds* or *sorts* are formed by adding to the Cardinals **-erlei** (an obsolete feminine noun Lei signifying *kind*, preceded by the strong genitive inflection); as:

einerlei, of one kind,[1]
zweierlei, of two kinds,
dreierlei, of three kinds,
viererlei, of four kinds,
zehnerlei, of ten kinds,
zwanzigerlei, of twenty kinds.

213. *Observation.* The following words are formed in the same way; viz.:

Keinerlei, not of any kind; *e. g.*: Dabei ist **keinerlei** Gefahr, *no* danger *of any* kind is connected with it.

Beiderlei, of both kinds; *e. g.*: Personen von **beiderlei** Geschlecht, persons of *both* sexes.

Mancherlei, of various kinds; *e. g.*: Es gab da **mancherlei** zu kaufen, things of *various kinds* were to be had.

Vielerlei, of many kinds; *e. g.*: Er hatte mir **vielerlei** zu sagen, he had to tell me (things of many kinds) many things.

Allerlei, of all kinds; *e. g.*: Er spricht **allerlei** Unsinn, he speaks *all kinds* of nonsense.

Note. It will be seen from the above examples that the numerals in **-lei** are indeclinable.

214. Observe also the inflection **-weise**, expressing the manner in which a thing is done, sold, etc.; as,

paarweise, by pairs,
stückweise, by the piece,
pfundweise, by the pound,
dutzendweise, by the dozen,
glücklicherweise, happily;

further: je zwei und zwei, by (twos) pairs,
je drei und drei, by threes,
etc.

finally, the way in which *the time* is commonly expressed in German, namely by referring to the coming hour only.

---

1) Einerlei often occurs with the meaning *all the same;* as, das ist ihm einerlei, that is *all the same* to him (he does not care).

Examples.

Wie viel Uhr ist es? What time is it?

Es ist ein Uhr, or es ist eins, it is one o'clock.
Es ist in 10 Minuten ein Viertel auf zwei, it is 5 minutes past one.
Es ist in 5 Minuten ein Viertel auf zwei, it is 10 minutes past one.
Es ist ein Viertel auf zwei, it is $1/4$ past one.
Es ist in 10 Minuten halb zwei, it is 20 minutes past one.
Es ist in 5 Minuten halb zwei, it is 25 minutes past one.
Es ist halb[1] zwei, it is half past one.
Es ist in 10 Minuten drei Viertel auf zwei, it is 25 minutes to 2.
Es ist in 5 Minuten drei Viertel auf zwei, it is 20 minutes to 2.
Es ist drei Viertel auf zwei, it is $1/4$ to 2.
Es ist in 10 Minuten zwei, it is 10 minutes to 2.
Es ist in 5 Minuten zwei, it is 5 minutes to 2.
Es ist zwei Uhr or zwei, it is two o'clock.

THE VERB.

Das Zeitwort oder Verbum.

215. The Verb is that part of speech which affirms something. It may be *transitive, intransitive, reflective* or *impersonal*, the same as in English.

216. There are in German *Regular* and *Irregular* Verbs.

A. THE REGULAR VERB.
Das regelmäßige Zeitwort.

217. The Regular Verbs are divided into *strong* and *weak*.

---

[1] This expression finds its explanation in the fact that we say, when denoting the completion of a *known* hour, es ist voll, it is *full*. The Scotch student will probably know the analogous expression of *half echt*, instead of half past seven.

218. Strong Verbs (ſtarke Verba) are those that have *more than one* primitive form (commonly three, the *Infinitive* of the *Present*, the *Imperfect* and the *Perfect Participle*) **with differing radical vowels;** as:

	Infinitive.	Imperfect.	Perfect Participle.
German:	ſpringen,	ſprang,	geſprungen,
English:	to *spring*,	*sprang*,	*sprung*.

These verbs must be committed to memory; they will be found further on.

219. Weak Verbs (ſchwache Verba) are those which have *only one* primitive form (the *Infinitive* of the *Present*) and derive all their tenses and moods from this form **by the addition of inflections,** without changing the radical vowel; as:

	Infinitive.	Imperfect.	Perfect Participle.
German:	leben,	lebte,	gelebt,
English:	to *live*,	*lived*,	*living*.

All that is peculiar about these Verbs will be found in the Conjugation.

THE CO

Rules.

221. There is only *one Conjugation* in German (**Examples** on the opposite page).

222. All *simple* tenses and moods are formed from the root, *excepting those forms* of the *irregular* and *strong* verbs *that are primitive themselves* and thus cannot be *derived*, but only take the inflections which distinguish the *Persons;* viz., -(e), -eſt, (e), -en, -et, -en.

223. The **Infinitive of the Present** is the principal form; it ends in all verbs in -n or -en.

224. The **Root** is obtained from the Infinitive by dropping its inflection -n or -en.

PRELIMINARY REMARKS ON THE CONJUGATION.

220. The German Conjugation does not differ in its technical structure from that of the English language. There are the same *Moods* in both languages as well as the same Tenses; of the latter, moreover, the *same* that are *simple in English* are *simple* also *in German*, and for the formation of the other tenses *Auxiliary Verbs* are employed in both languages.

There are:
1. *five* **Moods**, viz., the *Indicative, Conjunctive* (or Subjunctive), *Conditional, Imperative* and *Infinitive* Mood;
2. *two* **Participles**, viz., the *Present* and the *Perfect* (or Past) Participle;
3. *two* **Simple Tenses**, viz., the *Present* and the *Imperfect* Tense;
4. *three* **Compound Tenses**, viz., the *Perfect, Pluperfect*, (First and Second) *Future* Tenses.

GATION.

Note. The third *Person* is always *like the first,* excepting the *Singular* of the *Present Indicative.*

The 1st and 3rd Persons Plural of the Present Indicative and Subjunctive as well as Imperative are the same as the Infinitive, except the verb ſein, to be.

Examples.

Weak Verb.	Strong Verb.
\multicolumn{2}{c}{**The Infinitive of the Present.**}	
Loben, to praise;	kommen, to come.
\multicolumn{2}{c}{**The Root.**}	
lob—	komm—

A. THE ACTIVE VOICE.
Das Activum oder die thätige Form.

225.   SIMPLE TENSES.
             Einfache Zeiten.

1. The **Present Participle** is formed by adding to the root -end;

2. The **Perfect Participle** is formed by adding to the root -(e)t[1] and prefixing to it *the Augment* ge-;[2] the Perfect Participle of *strong* verbs cannot be formed, but must be acquired by rote, as it is a primitive form.

3. The **Imperative** is formed by adding to the root:

	SINGULAR.	PLURAL.
Person 1.	—	—en,
2.	—(e),	—(e)t,
3.	—(e),	—en;

the 2nd Person Singular of certain strong verbs is *primitive*. (See Nos. 239, 240, 246b.)

4. The **Present Indicative** is formed by adding to the root:

	SINGULAR.	PLURAL.
Person 1.	—e,	—en,
2.	—(e)st,	—(e)t,
3.	—(e)t,	—en;

the 2nd and 3rd persons singular of some strong verbs are primitive forms. (See Nos. 239, 240, 241, 246b, 247.)

---

1) The *e* has in some forms been placed within brackets, because in the Perfect Participle, in the 2nd and 3rd Person Singular and 2nd Person Plural of the Imperative and in the Present and Imperfect *Indicative*, it is dropped, if the euphony allows it; that is in all cases, where the root does not end in -d, -t or -n, after which consonants the *e* is usually preserved; as, gearbeit-et, worked; arbeitet! work ye! ich arbeite, I work, du arbeitest, thou workest, er arbeitet, he works, wir arbeiten, we work, ihr arbeitet, you work, sie arbeiten, they work, ich arbeitete, I worked, du arbeitetest, thou workedst, er arbeitete, he worked, etc.

On the other hand in the *Subjunctive* mood the *e* is as a rule preserved.

2) The Augment ge- is not given: 1) to all *real compound* Verbs (see Rule 270 and 271); as, übersetzt; 2) to all Verbs ending in iren (or ieren); as, concentrirt.

THE ACTIVE VOICE.

SIMPLE TENSES.

1. Example of a **Weak Verb**.   2. Example of a **Strong Verb**.

The Present Participle.

Lobend, praising;   kommend, coming,

The Perfect Participle.

gelob(e)t, praised;   gekommen, come.

The Imperative.

Lob(e), praise (*thou*),   komm(e), come (*thou*),
lob(e) er,[1] let him praise,   komm(e) er,[1] let him come,
loben wir,[2] let us praise,   kommen wir,[2] let us come,
lob(e)t, praise (*ye* or *you*),   komm(e)t, come (*ye*),
loben sie,[3] let them praise;   kommen sie,[3] let them come.

The Present Indicative.

Ich lobe, I praise   ich komme, I come
du lob(e)st, thou praisest   du kommst, thou comest
er lob(e)t, he praises   er kommt, he comes   } or I do come
wir loben, we praise   wir kommen, we come   or I am coming.
ihr lob(e)t, you praise   ihr kommt, you come
sie loben, they praise   sie kommen, they come

or I do praise, or I am praising;

---

1) Or: er lobe, er komme; of course if there is a noun, the pronoun is dropped; as, Johann komme, let John come!

2) Or: laß, laßt or lassen Sie uns loben or kommen.

3) Conventional Imperative: loben Sie, praise! kommen Sie, come!

5. The **Present Subjunctive** is formed by adding to the root:

	SINGULAR.	PLURAL.
Person 1.	—e,	—en,
2.	—eſt,	—et,
3.	—e,	—en.

6. The **Imperfect Indicative** is formed by adding to the root:

	SINGULAR.	PLURAL.
Person 1.	—(e)te,	—(e)ten,
2.	—(e)teſt,	—(e)tet,
3.	—(e)te,	—(e)ten;

the *Imperfect of Strong Verbs* is a *primitive* form and only takes the inflections which distinguish the persons, viz., —, -(e)ſt, —, -en, -(e)t, en, as mentioned in rule 224.

7. The **Imperfect Subjunctive** is formed by adding to the root:

	SINGULAR.	PLURAL.
Person 1.	—ete,[1]	—eten,
2.	—eteſt,	—etet,
3.	—ete,	—eten;

the *Subjunctive of strong* and *irregular* Imperfects, is formed from the Indicative *by modifying the vowel and adding* -e. (Compare Rule 250.)

COMPOUND TENSES.
Zuſammengeſetzte Zeiten.

226. All the other tenses are formed by means of **Auxiliary Verbs**[2] which are joined with the **Infinitive** for *future* tenses, with the **Perfect Participle** for *past* tenses and with the **Perfect Infinitive** for *future past* tenses; viz.:

---

1) It must be noticed that the first e of the inflections is mostly dropped, even in the *Subjunctive* of the Imperfect, though never in the *Present* Subjunctive; thus, wenn ich lobte, instead of, wenn ich lobete.

2) It is a common practice with German writers in dependent clauses *to leave out* the auxiliary Verb, in cases where the tense is plain enough even without it, but especially where two Infinitives or two Participles not connected by und stand together; as, möglich, daß der Vater nun die Tyrannei des einen Rings nicht länger in seinem Hauſe dulden wollen (for hat dulden gewollt). Leſſings Nathan der Weiſe.

1. Example of a **Weak Verb**. 2. Example of a **Strong Verb**.
The Present Subjunctive.

Ich lobe, I (may) or (if) I praise,[1] ich komme, (if) I come,[1]
du lobest, thou (mayest) praise, du kommest, (if) thou comest,
er lobe, he (may) praise, er komme, (if) he come,
wir loben, we (may) praise, wir kommen, (if) we come,
ihr lobet, you (may) praise, ihr kommet, (if) you come,
sie loben, they (may) praise; sie kommen, (if) they come.

The Imperfect Indicative.

Ich lob(e)te, I praised, ich kam, I came,
du lob(e)test, thou praisedst, du kam(e)st, thou camest,
er lob(e)te, he praised, er kam, he came,
wir lob(e)ten, we praised, wir kamen, we came,
ihr lob(e)tet, you praised, ihr kam(e)t, you came,
sie lob(e)ten, they praised, sie kamen, they came,
   or, I did praise, *or* I was   *or*, I did come, *or* I was
   praising.   coming.

The Imperfect Subjunctive.

Ich lob(e)te,[2] (if) I praised, ich käme, (if) I came,
du lob(e)test, (if) thou praisedst, du kämest, (if) thou camest,
er lob(e)te, (if) he praised, er käme, (if) he came,
wir lob(e)ten, (if) we praised, wir kämen, (if) we came,
ihr lob(e)tet, (if) you praised, ihr kämet, (if) you came,
sie lob(e)ten, (if) they praised; sie kämen, (if) they came.

Note. Before proceeding to the compound tenses, the learner should first acquaint himself with the simple tenses of the auxiliary Verbs (Rules 251—253), to enable him to form the compound tenses readily.

---

1) As this mood occurs principally in indirect speech (vid. Rule 366) it has mostly to be translated by the past, thus: *I praised, I came.*

2) The Subjunctive of *weak* imperfects is always the same as the Indicative.

a. With the Perfect Participle.

227. 1. The **Perfect Infinitive** is formed by putting after the *Perfect Participle* the Infinitive of either the auxiliary Verb haben, *to have*, or sein, *to be*.

2. The **Perfect Indicative** is formed by placing before the *Perfect Participle* the Present *Indicative* of the auxiliary verbs haben or sein, viz.:

SINGULAR.	PLURAL.		SINGULAR.	PLURAL.
habe,	haben,	or	bin,	sind,
hast,	habt,		bist,	seid,
hat,	haben,		ist,	sind.

3. The **Perfect Subjunctive** is formed by placing before the *Perfect Participle* the Present *Subjunctive* of the auxiliary verbs haben or sein, viz.:

SINGULAR.	PLURAL.	SINGULAR.	PLURAL.
habe,	haben,	sei,	seien,
habest,	habet,	seiest,	seiet,
habe,	haben,	sei,	seien.

4. The **Pluperfect Indicative** is formed by placing before the *Perfect Participle* the Imperfect *Indicative* of the auxiliary verbs haben or sein, viz.:

hatte,	or	war,
hattest,		warst,
hatte,		war,
hatten,		waren,
hattet,		waret,
hatten,		waren.

5. The **Pluperfect Subjunctive** is formed by placing before the *Perfect Participle* the Imperfect *Subjunctive* of the auxiliary verbs haben or sein, viz.:

hätte,	or	wäre,
hättest,		wärest,
hätte,		wäre,
hätten,		wären,
hättet,		wäret,
hätten,		wären.

1. Example of a **Weak Verb**.   2. Example of a **Strong Verb**.

(The Perfect Participle.)
(gelobt, praised;   gekommen, come.)

The Perfect Infinitive.

Gelobt haben, to have praised;   gekommen sein, to (be) have come.

The Perfect Indicative.

Ich habe gelobt, I have praised,   ich bin gekommen, I (am) ⎫
du hast gelobt, thou hast praised,   du bist gekommen, thou (art) ⎬ have come.
er hat gelobt, he has praised,   er ist gekommen, he (is)
wir haben gelobt, we have praised,   wir sind gekommen, we (are)
ihr habt gelobt, you have praised,   ihr seid gekommen, you (are)
sie haben gelobt, they have praised;   sie sind gekommen, they (are) ⎭

The Perfect Subjunctive.

Ich habe gelobt, (if) I have[1]   ich sei gekommen, (if) I (be)[1] ⎫
du habest gelobt, (if) thou hast   du seiest gekommen, (if) thou (be)
er habe gelobt, (if) he have   ⎱praised⎰   er sei gekommen, (if) he (be) ⎬ have come.
wir haben gelobt, (if) we have   wir seien gekommen, (if) we (be)
ihr habet gelobt, (if) you have   ihr seiet gekommen, (if) you (be)
sie haben gelobt, (if) they have   sie seien gekommen, (if) they (be) ⎭

The Pluperfect Indicative.

Ich hatte gelobt, I had praised,   ich war gekommen, I (was) ⎫
du hattest gelobt, thou hadst praised,   du warst gekommen, thou (wast)
er hatte gelobt, he had praised,   er war gekommen, he (was) ⎬ had come.
wir hatten gelobt, we had praised,   wir waren gekommen, we (were)
ihr hattet gelobt, you had praised,   ihr waret gekommen, you (were)
sie hatten gelobt, they had praised;   sie waren gekommen, they (were) ⎭

The Pluperfect Subjunctive.

Ich hätte gelobt, (if) I had   ich wäre gekommen, (if) I (were) ⎫
du hättest gelobt, (if) thou hadst   du wärest gek., (if) thou (wert)
er hätte gelobt, (if) he had   ⎱praised⎰   er wäre gekommen, (if) he (were) ⎬ had come.
wir hätten gelobt, (if) we had   wir wären gek., (if) we (were)
ihr hättet gelobt, (if) you had   ihr wäret gek., (if) you (were)
sie hätten gelobt, (if) they had   sie wären gek., (if) they (were) ⎭

---

1) Or: I *had* praised, I *had* or *was* come; read Note [1] on page 93.

b. With the Present Infinitive.

228. 1. The *First* **Future Indicative** is formed by placing before the *Infinitive* the Present *Indicative* of the auxiliary verb werben, viz.:

werbe,	werben,
wirft,	werbet,
wirb,	werben.

2. The *First* **Future Subjunctive** is formed by placing before the *Infinitive* the Present *Subjunctive* of the auxiliary verb werben, viz.:

werbe,	werben,
werbeft,	werbet,
werbe,	werben.

3. The *First* **Conditional** is formed by placing before the *Infinitive* the Imperfect *Subjunctive* of the auxiliary verb werben, viz.:

würde,	würden,
würdeft,	würdet,
würde,	würden.

c. With the Perfect Infinitive.

229. 1. The *Second* **Future Indicative** is formed by placing before the *Perfect Infinitive* the Present *Indicative* of the auxiliary verb werben, viz.:

werbe,	werben,
wirft,	werbet,
wirb,	werben.

1. Example of a **Weak Verb**. 2. Example of a **Strong Verb**.
(The Present Infinitive.)
(Loben, to praise; kommen, to come.)

The First Future Indicative.

Ich werde loben, I shall praise,
du wirst loben, thou wilt praise,
er wird loben, he will praise,
wir werden loben, we shall praise,
ihr werdet loben, you will praise,
sie werden loben, they will praise;

ich werde kommen, I shall come,
du wirst kommen, thou wilt come,
er wird kommen, he will come,
wir werden kommen, we shall come,
ihr werdet kommen, you will come,
sie werden kommen, they will come.

The First Future Subjunctive.

Ich werde loben, I should[1]
du werdest loben, thou wouldst
er werde loben, he would
wir werden loben, we should
ihr werdet loben, you would
sie werden loben, they would
⎱ praise;

ich werde kommen, I should[1]
du werdest kommen, thou wdst.
er werde kommen, he would
wir werden kommen, we should
ihr werdet kommen, you would
sie werden kommen, they would
⎱ come.

The First Conditional.

Ich würde loben, I should
du würdest loben, thou wouldst
er würde loben, he would
wir würden loben, we should
ihr würdet loben, you would
sie würden loben, they would
⎱ praise;

ich würde kommen, I should
du würdest kommen, thou wdst.
er würde kommen, he would
wir würden kommen, we should
ihr würdet kommen, you would
sie würden kommen, they would
⎱ come.

(The Perfect Infinitive.)
(Gelobt haben, to have praised; gekommen sein, to be come.)

The Second Future Indicative.

Ich werde gelobt haben, I shall have praised,
du wirst gelobt haben, thou wilt have praised,
er wird gelobt haben, he will have praised,
wir werden gelobt haben, we shall have praised,
ihr werdet gelobt haben, you will have praised;
sie werden gelobt haben, they will have praised;

ich werde gekommen sein, I shall (be) have come,
du wirst gekommen sein, thou wilt (be) have come,
er wird gekommen sein, he will (be) have come,
wir werden gekommen sein, we shall (be) have come,
ihr werdet gekommen sein, you will (be) have come,
sie werden gekommen sein, they will (be) have come.

---

1) Read Note [1] page 93.

A. v. Ravensberg, German Grammar. 3rd Ed.

2. The *Second* **Future Subjunctive** is formed by placing before the *Perfect Infinitive* the Present *Subjunctive* of the auxiliary verb werden, viz.:

werde,	werden,
werdest,	werdet,
werde,	werden.

3. The *Second* **Conditional** is formed by placing before the *Perfect Infinitive* the Imperfect *Subjunctive* of the auxiliary verb werden, viz.:

würde,	würden,
würdest,	würdet,
würde,	würden.

B. THE PASSIVE VOICE.[1]
Das Passivum oder die leidende Form.

The **Passive Voice** is in all its tenses and moods formed with the help of the auxiliary Verb werden, *to become*, and the *Perfect Participle* of a Verb.

a. *With the Perfect Participle of the Active.*

230. 1. The **Present Infinitive** is formed by placing after the *Perfect Participle* of the Active the *Infinitive* „werden".

2. The **Perfect Participle** is formed by placing after the *Perfect Participle* of the Active the *Perfect Participle* of werden (without augment) viz., worden.

---
1) Compare Rule 363.

1. Example of a **Weak Verb.**   2. Example of a **Strong Verb.**

The Second Future Subjunctive.

Ich werde gelobt haben, I should[1] have praised,
du werdeſt gelobt haben, thou wouldst have praised,
er werde gelobt haben, he would have praised,
wir werden gelobt haben, we should have praised,
ihr werdet gelobt haben, you would have praised,
ſie werden gelobt haben, they would have praised;

ich werde gekommen ſein, I should[1] (be) have come,
du werdeſt gekommen ſein, thou wouldst (be) have come,
er werde gekommen ſein, he would (be) have come,
wir werden gekommen ſein, we should (be) have come,
ihr werdet gekommen ſein, you would (be) have come,
ſie werden gekommen ſein, they would (be) have come.

The Second Conditional.

Ich würde gelobt haben, I should have praised,
du würdeſt gelobt haben, thou wouldst have praised,
er würde gelobt haben, he would have praised,
wir würden gelobt haben, we should have praised,
ihr würdet gelobt haben, you would have praised,
ſie würden gelobt haben, they would have praised;

ich würde gekommen ſein, I should (be) have come,
du würdeſt gekommen ſein, thou wouldst (be) have come,
er würde gekommen ſein, he would (be) have come,
wir würden gekommen ſein, we should (be) have come,
ihr würdet gekommen ſein, you would (be) have come,
ſie würden gekommen ſein, they would (be) have come.

THE PASSIVE VOICE.

(Perfect Participle of the Active **gelobt**, *praised.)*

The Present Infinitive.
Gelobt werden, *(to) be* praised.

The Perfect Participle.
Gelobt worden, *been* praised.

---

1) Read Note [1] page 93.

3. The **Perfect Infinitive** is formed by placing after the *Perfect Participle* of the Active the *Perfect Infinitive* of werben (without augment) viz., worden sein.

4. The **Imperative** is formed by placing *before* the *Perfect Participle* of the Active the *Imperative* of werben, viz.:
SING. 1st — — 2nd werde, 3rd werde er,
PLUR. 1st werden wir, 2nd werdet, 3rd werden sie.

5. and 6. The **Present Indicative** and the **Present Subjunctive** are formed by placing before the *Perfect Participle* of the Active the *Present Indicative* of werben for the former and the *Present Subjunctive* of werben for the latter, viz..

For the Indicative.
SING. werde, PLUR. werden,
wirst, werdet,
wird, werden;

For the Subjunctive.
SING. werde, PLUR. werden,
werdest, werdet,
werde, werden.

7. and 8. The **Imperfect Indicative** and the **Imperfect Subjunctive** are formed also with the *Perfect Participle* of the Active and the *Imperfect Indicative* of werben, viz., wurde etc. for the former, but the *Imperfect Subjunctive* of werben, viz., würde etc. for the latter.

b. *With the Perfect Participle of the Passive.*

231. 1. The **Perfect Indicative.** 2. The **Perfect Subjunctive.** 3. The **Pluperfect Indicative.** 4. The **Pluperfect Subjunctive** are formed by placing before the *Perfect Participle of the Passive* the Present *Indicative* of the Auxiliary Verb sein,[1] viz., ich bin etc. for 1., the Present *Subjunctive* of it, viz., ich sei, etc. for 2, the Imperfect *Indicative*, viz., ich war etc. for 3, and the Imperfect *Subjunctive*, viz., ich wäre etc. for 4.

---

1) The Auxiliary **werben** is conjugated in its own compound tenses with the auxiliary verb sein, consequently the double compound tenses of the Passive require the same auxiliary, viz., sein.

The Perfect Infinitive.
Gelobt worden sein, *(to) have been* praised.

The Imperative Mood.

Werde gelobt, be praised (thou), werde er gelobt, let him be praised;

werden wir gelobt, let us be praised, werdet gelobt, be (ye) praised, werden sie gel., let them be praised.

The Present Indicative.

Ich werde gelobt, I am praised,
du wirst gelobt, thou art praised,
er wird gelobt, he is praised,
wir werden gelobt, we are praised,
ihr werdet gelobt, you are praised,
sie werden gelobt, they are praised;

The Present Subjunctive.

ich werde gelobt, (if) I be[1] praised,
du werdest gelobt, thou be praised,
er werde gelobt, he be praised,
wir werden gelobt, we be praised,
ihr werdet gelobt, you be praised,
sie werden gelobt, they be praised.

The Imperfect Indicative.

Ich wurde ⎫   I was   ⎫
du wurdest ⎪   thou wast   ⎪
er wurde   ⎬ gelobt, he was   ⎬ praised;
wir wurden ⎪   we were   ⎪
ihr wurdet ⎪   you were   ⎪
sie wurden ⎭   they were   ⎭

The Imperfect Subjunctive.

ich würde ⎫   I were   ⎫
du würdest ⎪   thou wert ⎪
er würde   ⎬ gelobt, he were   ⎬ praised.
wir würden ⎪   we were   ⎪
ihr würdet ⎪   you were   ⎪
sie würden ⎭   they were ⎭

(Perfect Participle of the Passive **gelobt worden**, *been praised.)*

The Perfect Indicative.

Ich bin   ⎫   I have   ⎫
du bist   ⎪   thou hast   ⎪
er ist   ⎬ gelobt worden, he has   ⎬ been praised;
wir sind ⎪   we have   ⎪
ihr seid ⎪   you have   ⎪
sie sind ⎭   they have   ⎭

The Perfect Subjunctive.

ich sei   ⎫   I have[2]   ⎫
du seiest ⎪   thou have   ⎪
er sei   ⎬ gelobt worden, he have   ⎬ been praised.
wir seien ⎪   we have   ⎪
ihr seiet ⎪   you have   ⎪
sie seien ⎭   they have   ⎭

The Pluperfect Indicative.

Ich war   ⎫   I had   ⎫
du warst ⎪   thou hadst   ⎪
er war   ⎬ gelobt worden, he had   ⎬ been praised;
wir waren ⎪   we had   ⎪
ihr waret ⎪   you had   ⎪
sie waren ⎭   they had   ⎭

The Pluperfect Subjunctive.

ich wäre   ⎫   (if) I had   ⎫
du wärest ⎪   „ thou hadst ⎪
er wäre   ⎬ gelobt worden, „ he had   ⎬ been praised.
wir wären ⎪   „ we had   ⎪
ihr wäret ⎪   „ you had   ⎪
sie wären ⎭   „ they had   ⎭

1) Or *was* etc.; read Note [1] page 93.
2) Or *had* etc.; read Note [1] page 93.

c. *With the Present Infinitive of the Passive.*

232. The *First* **Future Indicative and Subjunctive** and the *First* **Conditional** of the Passive are formed by placing before the *Present Infinitive of the Passive* the Present Indicative, the Present Subjunctive and the Imperfect Subjunctive of the Auxiliary Verb werden respectively, viz., **werde**, etc., **werde**, etc., **würde**, etc.

d. *With the Perfect Infinitive of the Passive.*

233. The *Second* **Future Indicative and Subjunctive** as well as the *Second* **Conditional** of the Passive are formed by placing before the *Perfect Infinitive of the Passive* the Present Indicative, the Present Subjunctive and the Imperfect Subjunctive of the auxiliary Verb werden respectively; viz., **werde** etc., **werde** etc., **würde** etc.

---

234. *Verbs used as Nouns* in German must stand in the *Infinitive* (not in the Present Participle as in English); as: **Das Reiten** ist eine gesunde Leibesübung, *riding* is a healthy exercise of the body; ich bin **des Scheltens** überdrüssig, I am tired *of scolding*; they are invariably *neuter*.

235. Formerly the Infinitive used to be declined; remains of the Dative ending in -**ne** are still existing, but they are generally, though erroneously, taken for Participles, since they now end in -**de** and allow of a declension; as, ein leicht **zu rathendes Räthsel**, a riddle easy *to guess*, Gen. eines leicht zu rathenden Räthsels. Der Eltern von Herzen **zu ehrende Wohlthat**, the kindness of our parents, sincerely *to be honoured*.

(*Present Infinitive* of the Passive **gelobt werden,** (to) be praised.)

First Future Ind.	First Future Subj.	First Conditional.
Ich **werde** gelobt werden, I shall be praised,	ich **werde** gelobt werden, I should[1] be praised,	ich **würde** gelobt werden, I should be praised,
du **wirst** gelobt werden, thou wilt be praised,	du **werdest** gelobt werden, thou wouldst be praised,	du **würdest** gelobt werden, thou wouldst be praised,
etc. etc.	etc. etc.	etc. etc.

(*Perfect Infinitive* of the Passive **gelobt worden sein,** (to) have been praised.)

Second Future Ind.	Second Future Subj.	Second Conditional.
Ich **werde** gelobt worden sein, I shall have been praised,	ich **werde** gelobt worden sein, I should[1] have been praised,	ich **würde** gelobt worden sein, I should have been praised,
du **wirst** gelobt worden sein, thou wilt have been praised,	du **werdest** gelobt worden sein, thou wouldst have been praised,	du **würdest** gelobt worden sein, thou wouldst have been praised,
etc. etc.	etc. etc.	etc. etc.

THE STRONG VERBS.
Die starken Verba.

236. The *strong* are the most ancient of the regular verbs; they form, as has been mentioned above, their most important tenses *by the change of the radical vowel.* They are here arranged in *twelve Classes,* according to the change of the radical vowel in the primitive tenses.

Note. The learner need only commit to memory the primitive forms; as for all the other tenses and moods he has strictly to follow the rules of the common Conjugation, with special regard to Rules 225 and 226.

---

1) Read Note [1] page 93.

THE TWELVE CLASSES OF STRONG VERBS[1].

Class I.

237. The *first Class* contains those Verbs which change the radical vowel **i** of the Infinitive into **a** *in the Imperfect Tense*, and into **u** *in the Perfect Participle*. They are:

Infinitive. (Rad. vow. i.)	Imperfect. (R. vow. a.)	Perf. Part. (Rad. vow. u).	Nouns (connected with the Verbs).
(Be)dingen, to stipulate, to bargain,	†(be)dang,[2]	(be)dungen,	Bedingung, f., condition;
binden, to bind, to tie,	band,	gebunden,	Band, m., volume, — n., tie, ribbon; Bund, m., bond, — n., bunch; Binde, f., binder;
bringen, to throng, to press,	drang,	gedrungen,	Drang, m., Gedränge, n., throng, crowd, pressure;
finden, to find,	fand,	gefunden,	Fund, m., find(ing), Finder, m., finder;
gelingen, to succeed,[3]	gelang,	gelungen,	Gelingen, n., success;
klingen, to sound, to ring,	klang,	geklungen,	Klang, m., sound, Klingel, f., bell (small);
ringen, to wrestle, to wring,	rang,	gerungen,	Ring, m., ring;
schlingen, to sling,	schlang,	geschlungen,	Schlinge, f., snare (not *sling* for throwing);
schwinden, to vanish,	schwand,	geschwunden;	
schwingen, to swing,	schwang,	geschwungen,	Schwung, m., toss, impulse; Schwinge, f., swing, van;
singen, to sing,	sang,	gesungen,	Sang or Gesang, m., song; Sänger, m., singer;
sinken, to sink,	sank,	gesunken;	

1) Some of the rarer verbs and poetical forms will be found in the alphabetical list.

2) *Observe.* Those verbs, or parts of verbs, marked with a cross (†) are used also *weak*.

3) This verb occurs only impersonally; comp. 263 b and 264.

Infinitive.	Imperfect.	Perf. Part.	Nouns (connected with the Verbs).
ſpringen, to spring,	ſprang,	geſprungen,	Sprung, m., leap, Springer, m., leaper, knight (in chess);
winden, to wind, to writhe,	wand,	gewunden,	Winde, f., windlass;
trinken, to drink,	trank,	getrunken,	Trank or Trunk, m., drink, Getränk, n., beverage;
zwingen, to compel, to force,	zwang,	gezwungen,	Zwang, m., constraint; Zwinger, m., dungeon.

Class II.

238. The *second Class* contains those Verbs which change the radical vowel **i** of the Infinitive into **a** *in the Imperfect* and **o** *in the Perfect Participle.* They are:

Infinitive. (Rad. vow. i.)	Imperfect. (Rad. vow. a.)	Perf. P. (R. vow. o.)	Nouns (connected with the Verbs).
Beginnen, to begin,	begann (Subj. also begönne),	begonnen,	Beginnen, n., doings;
gewinnen, to win,	gewann (Subj. also gewönne),	gewonnen,	Gewinn, m., gain, Gewinner, m., winner;
rinnen, to flow, to run,	rann (Subj. also rönne),	geronnen,	Rinne, f., gutter;
ſchwimmen, to swim, to float,	ſchwamm (Subj. also ſchwömme),	geſchwommen,	Schwamm, m., sponge, Schwimmer, m., swimmer;
ſinnen, to meditate,	ſann (Subj. also ſönne),	geſonnen,	Sinn, m., sense;
ſpinnen, to spin,	ſpann Subj. also ſpönne),	geſponnen,	Spinne, f., spider, Spinner(in), m., f., spinner.

Class III.

239. The *third Class* contains those Verbs which change the radical vowel **e** of the Infinitive into **a** *in the Imperfect* and **o** *in the Perfect Participle.* They also change the radical vowel **e** in the *2nd* and *3rd Person Singular* of the *Present Tense* and in the *2nd Person Singular* of the *Imperative* into **i** or **ie**, except pflegen.

Infinitive. (Rad. vow. e.)	Imperf. (R. v. a.)	Perf. Prt. (R. v. o.)	Pres. T. (R. v. i or ie).	Imp. (R. v. i or ie.)	Nouns (connected with the Verbs).
Befehlen, to command,¹	befahl(Sbj. beföhle),	befohlen,	ich befehle, du befiehlst, er befiehlt,	befiehl,	Befehl, m., command;
bergen, to hide,	barg (Sbj. also bürge),	geborgen,	ich berge, du birgst, er birgt,	birg,	Burg, f., castle, Berg, m., mountain;
bersten, to crack, to burst,	barst, and borst,	geborsten,	ich berste, du birst, er birst,	birst,	Borste, f., crack;
brechen, to break,	brāch,	gebrochen,	ich breche, du brichst, er bricht,	brich,	Bruch, m., breakage, rupture, fraction.
dreschen, to thrash, to thresh,	drasch, and drosch,	gedroschen,	ich dresche, du drischst, er drischt,	drisch,	Drescher, m., thresher;
empfehlen, to recommend,	empfahl, (Sbj. also empföhle),	empfohlen,	ich empfehle, du empfiehlst, er empfiehlt,	empfiehl,	Empfehlung, f., recommendation,
*(er)schrecken², to be frightened, to get a start.	(er)schrat,	(er)schrocken,	ich (er)schrecke, du (er)schrickst, er (er)schrickt,	(er)schrick,	Schreck(en), m., fright;
gelten, to be worth, to be at stake,	galt (Subj. also gölte),	gegolten,	ich gelte, du giltst, er gilt,	gilt,	Geld, n., money;
helfen, to help,	half (Subj. also hülfe),	geholfen,	ich helfe, du hilfst, er hilft,	hilf,	Hilfe or Hülfe, f., help, Helfer, m., helper;
nehmen, to take,	nahm,	genommen,	ich nehme, du nimmst, er nimmt,	nimm,	—nahme,³ f., taking;
pflegen⁴, to cherish, to administer,	pflag or pflog,	gepflogen,	weak,	weak,	Pflege, f., nursing;

1) The *simple* verb fehlen, *to fail, to want, to miss* is always conjugated *weak,* viz., fehlte, gefehlt.
2) All verbs marked thus * are *weak* when used *transitively.*
3) This word occurs only in Compounds; as, Einnahme, Annahme and others.
4) pflegen, *to be in the habit, to use* and *to nurse,* is *weak*

Infinitive.	Imperf.	Perf. Prt.	Pres. T.	Imp.	Nouns.
ſchelten, to scold, to chide,	ſchalt, (Sbj. also ſchölte),	geſcholten,	ich ſchelte, du ſchiltſt, er ſchilt,	ſchilt,	Scheltel, f., a scolding,
ſprechen, to speak, to talk,	ſprach,	geſprochen,	ich ſpreche, du ſprichſt, er ſpricht,	ſprich,	Sprache, f., speech, language, Spruch, m., a saying;
ſtechen, to pierce, to sting,	ſtach,	geſtochen,	ich ſteche, du ſtichſt, er ſticht,	ſtich,	Stich, m., sting, thrust;
ſtehlen, to steal,	ſtahl (Sbj. also ſtöhle)	geſtohlen,	ich ſtehle, du ſtiehlſt, er ſtiehlt,	ſtiehl,	Stehler, m., thief, Diebſtahl, m., theft;
ſterben, to die, to starve,	ſtarb (Sbj. ſtürbe),	geſtorben,	ich ſterbe, du ſtirbſt, er ſtirbt,	ſtirb;	
treffen, to hit, to meet,	traf,	getroffen,	ich treffe, du triffſt, er trifft,	triff,	Treffer, m., hit;
*verderben, to spoil,	verbarb, (Sbj. verbürbe),	verdorben,	ich verderbe, du verdirbſt, er verdirbt,	verbirb,	Verderben, n., destruction, ruin;
werben, to enlist, to sue, to woo,	warb (Sbj. würbe),	geworben,	ich werbe, du wirbſt, er wirbt,	wirb,	Werber, m., wooer, Werbung, f., enlistment, wooing;
werfen, to throw, to cast,	warf (Sbj. würfe),	geworfen,	ich werfe, du wirfſt, er wirft,	wirf,	Wurf, m., cast, throw;

Class IV.

240. The *fourth Class* contains those Verbs which change the radical vowel e of the Infinitive into a *in the Imperfect*, but remain e *in the Perfect Participle*; they also change the radical vowel e in the *2nd* and *3rd Person Singular* of the *Present Indicative* and the *2nd Person Singular* of the *Imperative* into i or ie; except geneſen which does not change its vowel. They are:

Infinitive. (R. vow. e.)	Imperf. (R. v. a.)	Perf. P. (R. v. e).	Pres. Ind. (R. vow. i or ie.)	Imper. (R. v. i or ie.)	Nouns (connected with the Verbs).
Essen, to eat,	aß,	gegessen,	ich esse, du ißt or issest, er ißt or isset,	iß,	Essen, n., food, Esser, m., eater;
fressen, to eat (immoderately, or speaking of beasts), to fret,	fraß,	gefressen,	ich fresse, du frißt, er frißt,	friß,	Fraß, m., or Fressen, n., bad food, or food for beasts;
geben, to give,	gab,	gegeben,	ich gebe, du gi(e)bst, er gi(e)bt,	gi(e)b,	Gabe, or Gift, f., gift, Geber, m., giver;
genesen, to recover (health),	genas,	genesen,	weak,	weak,	Genesung, f., recovery;
geschehen[1], to happen,	geschah,	geschehen,	es geschieht,	no Imp.;	Geschichte, f., (hi)story,
lesen, to read, to pick,	las,	gelesen,	ich lese, du liest or liesest, er liest,	lies,	Lese, f., picking, Leser, m., reader;
messen, to measure, to mete,	maß,	gemessen,	ich messe, du mißt, er mißt,	miß,	Maß, n., measure, Messer, m., metre, measurer;
sehen, to see,	sah,	gesehen,	ich sehe, du siehst, er sieht,	sieh,	Gesicht, n., face, vision, Seher, m., seer, prophet;
treten, to step, to tread,	trat,	getreten,	ich trete, du trittst, er tritt,	tritt,	Tritt, m., step, kick;
vergessen, to forget,	vergaß,	vergessen,	ich vergesse, du vergißt, or vergissest, er vergißt,	vergiß,	Vergessen, n., oblivion.

Class V.

241. The *fifth Class* contains those Verbs which change the radical vowel a of the Infinitive into u *in the Imperfect*, remaining a *in the Perfect Participle*; they

---

1) This verb occurs only *impersonally*.

also *modify the vowel* in the *2nd* and *3rd Person Singular* of the *Present Indicative*, except ſchaffen which retains its a unchanged. They are:

Infinitive. (Rad. vow. a.)	Impf. (R. v. u.)	Perf. P. (R. v. a.)	Pres. Ind. (R. v. ä.)	Nouns (connected with the Verbs).
†Baden, to bake,	buf,	gebaden,	ich bade, du bäckſt, er bäckt,	Bäcker, m., baker;
fahren,¹ to drive,	fuhr,	gefahren,	ich fahre, du fährſt, er fährt,	Fahrt, f., drive, Fuhre, f., cartload;
fragen, to ask,	frug,†	weak,	weak,	Frage, f., question,
graben, to dig,	grub,	gegraben,	ich grabe, du gräbſt, er gräbt,	Grab, n., } grave, Grube, f., } ditch; Graben, m.,
laben¹, to load, to lade, to invite,	lub,	gelaben,	ich labe, du läbſt, er läbt,	Labung, f., cargo, Labe, f., box;
ſchaffen,² to create,	ſchuf,	geſchaffen,	weak,	Schöpfung, f., creation, Schöpfer, m., creator, Geſchöpf, n., creature;
ſchlagen,³ to beat, to strike, to slay, to defeat,	ſchlug,	geſchlagen,	ich ſchlage, du ſchlägſt, er ſchlägt,	Schlag, m., stroke, Schläger, m., striker, rapier;
tragen, to carry, to bear,	trug,	getragen,	ich trage, du trägſt, er trägt,	Träger, m., porter, Trage, f., bier;
wachſen, to grow (in length), to wax,	wuchs,	gewachſen,	ich wachſe, du wächſt, er wächſt,	Wachstum, n., growth, Wuchs, m., growth, figure;
waſchen, to wash,	wuſch,	gewaſchen,	ich waſche, du wäſchſt, er wäſcht,	Wäſche, f., washing, linen.

Class VI.

242. The *sixth Class* contains those Verbs which change the radical vowel a of the Infinitive into i or ie

1) All Compounds of fahren are conjugated the same, except willfahren, *to comply*, which is *weak*.

2) ſchaffen, *to procure* and *to work*, is *weak*, also its Compounds.

3) The Compounds of ſchlagen are conjugated the same, except rathſchlagen *to consult* (intrans.), which is *weak*.

in the Imperfect, remaining **a** *in the Perfect Participle;* they also *modify the vowel* in the *2nd* and *3rd Person Singular* of the *Present Indicative*. They are:

Infinitive. (Rad. vow. **a**.)	Impf. (R. **i** or **ie**.)	Perf. P: (R. v. **a**.)	Pres. Ind. (R. v. **ä**.)	Nouns (connected with the Verbs).
Blasen, to blow,	blies,	geblasen,	ich blase, du bläst, er bläst,	Blast, m., blast;
braten, to roast,	briet,	gebraten,	ich brate, du brätst, er brät,	Braten, m., roast;
fallen, to fall,	fiel,	gefallen,	ich falle, du fällst, er fällt,	Fall, m., fall;
fangen, to catch,	fing,	gefangen,	ich fange, du fängst, er fängt,	Fang, m., catch;
halten, to hold,	hielt,	gehalten,	ich halte, du hältst, er hält,	Halt, m., hold, catch;
hangen[1], to hang,	hing,	gehangen,	ich hange, du hängst, er hängt,	Hang, m., inclination;
lassen, to let,[2] to allow to,	ließ,	gelassen,	ich lasse, du läßt or lässest, er läßt,	Gelaß, n., room;
rathen, to advise, to guess,	rieth,	gerathen,	ich rathe, du räthst, er räth,	Rath, m., advice, Räthsel, n., riddle;
schlafen, to sleep,	schlief,	geschlafen,	ich schlafe, du schläfst, er schläft,	Schlaf, m., sleep, Schläfer, m., sleeper.

Class VII.

243. The *seventh Class* contains those Verbs which change the radical vowel **ei** of the Infinitive into **i** short both *in the Imperfect* and *Perfect Participle*. They are:

---

1) The *transitive form* for this verb is, hängen, hängte, gehängt, but this distinction is not always observed by writers (compare usage in English).

2) veranlassen, is weak, being derived from Anlaß.

Infinitive. (R. v. ei.)	Impf. (R.v.i.)	Perf. P. (R. v. i.)	Nouns (connected with the Verbs).
Befleißen, sich, to apply one's self,	befliß,	beflissen,	Fleiß, m., ⎫ application; Beflissenheit, f., ⎭
beißen, to bite,	biß,	gebissen,	Biß, m., bite;
erbleichen,[1] to turn pale, to die,	ver= blich,	erblichen;	
gleichen,[2] to resemble, to be like,	glich,	geglichen,	Gleichniß, n., likeness, parable;
gleiten,[3] to glide,	glitt,	geglitten;	
greifen, to catch, to gripe,	griff,	gegriffen,	Griff, m., handle;
kneifen, to nip, to pinch,	kniff,	gekniffen,	Kniff, m., pinch, trick;
leiden,[4] to suffer,	litt,	gelitten,	Leid(en),n.,grief,sufferings;
pfeifen, to whistle, to pipe,	pfiff,	gepfiffen,	Pfiff, m., whistling, trick, Pfeife, f., pipe, Pfeifer, m., piper;
reißen, to tear, rend,	riß,	gerissen,	Riß, m., rent;
reiten, to ride,	ritt,	geritten,	Ritt, m., ride, Reiter, m., rider;
schleichen, to sneak, to slink,	schlich,	geschlichen,	Schlich, m., trick, Schleicher, m., sneak;
schleifen, to grind[5] (instruments, stones and minerals),	schliff,	geschliffen,	Schliff, m., surface of a ground (polished) instrument, Schleifer, m., grinder;
schmeißen, to throw, to smite,	schmiß,	geschmissen,	Schmiß, m., blow;
schneiden, to cut,	schnitt,	geschnitten,	Schneider,m.,tailor,cutter, Schneide, f., edge (of a sharp instrument), Schnitt, m., cut;
schreiten, to stride, to pace,	schritt,	geschritten,	Schritt, m., step, pace;
streichen, to strike,	strich,	gestrichen,	Strich, m., stroke;
streiten, to dispute, to fight,	stritt,	gestritten,	Streit, m., dispute, fight, Streiter, m., fighter, combatant;
weichen,[6] to yield, to give way,	wich,	gewichen,	Weiche, f., switch, (on railways).

1) The *simple* verb bleichen, *to bleach*, is *weak* (bleichte, gebleicht).
2) gleichen, *to make equal*, is *weak* (gleichte, gegleicht).
3) begleiten, *to accompany*, is *weak*.
4) verleiden, *to make averse to*, is *weak*.
5) schleifen, in the meaning of, *to drag*, or, *to destroy* (a fortress), is *weak*.
6) weichen, *to get soft, to steep*, is *weak*.

Class VIII.

244. The *eighth Class* contains those Verbs which change the radical vowel **ei** of the Infinitive into **ie** *both in the Imperfect* and *Perfect Participle*. They are:

Infinitive. (Rad. vow. ei.)	Imperf. (R. v. ie.)	Perf. P. (R. v. ie.)	Nouns (connected with the Verbs).
Bleiben, to stay,	blieb,	geblieben;	
gedeihen, to thrive, to succeed,	gedieh,	gediehen,	Gedeihen, n.. prosperity;
leihen, to lend,	lieh,	geliehen,	Lehn, n., Leihe, f., loan (principally in Compounds);
(ver)meiden, to avoid,	mied,	gemieden;	
preisen, to praise,	pries,	gepriesen,	Preis, m., praise, price;
reiben, to rub,	rieb,	gerieben;	
scheiden, to part,	schied,	geschieden,	Scheiden, n., parting;
scheinen, to shine, to seem,	schien,	geschienen,	Schein, m., shine, sheen, appearance;
schreiben, to write,	schrieb,	geschrieben,	Schreiben, n., letter, Schreiber, n., writer, scribe;
schreien, to cry,	schrie,*	geschrie(e)n,	Schrei, m., cry; Geschrei, n., clamour;
schweigen, to be silent,	schwieg,	geschwiegen,	Schweigen, n., silence;
speien, to spit,	spie,	gespie(e)n;	
steigen, to step, to mount,	stieg,	gestiegen,	Steig, m.. path, Stufe, f., step, Stiege, f., ladder;
treiben, to drive,	trieb,	getrieben,	Trieb, m., impulse, Treiber, m., driver, drover.
weisen, to show,	wies,	gewiesen;	
zeihen, to accuse,	zieh,	geziehen.	

Class IX.

245. The *ninth Class* contains those Verbs which change the radical vowels **ie, e, ü, au, ä** and **ö** of the Infinitive into **o** long, both *in the Imperfect* and *Perfect Participle*. They are:

Infinitive.	Imperf.	Perf. P.	Nouns (connected with the Verbs).
a) R. v. ie,	o long,	o long.	
Biegen, to bend,	bog,	gebogen,	Bug, m., bow (of vessels), Bogen, m., bow, arch;
bieten¹, to bid,	bot,	geboten,	Gebot, n., bidding, offer;
fliegen,¹ to fly,	flog,	geflogen,	Flug, m., flight; Fliege, f., fly;
fliehen, to flee,	floh,	geflohen,	Flucht, f., flight;
frieren, to freeze, to feel cold,	fror,	gefroren,	Frost, m., frost;
klieben, to cleave,	klob,	gekloben,	Klobe, f., or Kloben, m., block (of wood);
schieben, to push, to shove,	schob,	geschoben,	Schub, m., push, Schieber, m., slide;
stieben, to disperse,	stob,	gestoben,	Staub, m., dust;
verlieren, to lose,	verlor,	verloren,	Verlust, m., loss;
wiegen,² or wägen, to weigh,	wog,	gewogen,	Wucht, f., Gewicht, n., weight;
ziehen,¹ to draw, to pull, to wander, to marsh, to go,	zog,³	gezogen,	Zug, m., host, procession, draught; Zucht, f., bringing up; breeding, discipline.
b) R. v. e,	o long,	o long.	
bewegen,⁴ to induce,	bewog,	bewogen;	
heben, to lift, to heave,	hob,(hub, poet.)	gehoben,	Hebung, f., lifting, swelling;
scheren,⁵ to shear,	schor,	geschoren,	Schere, f., scissors, shears; Schur, f., shearing;
†weben, to weave,	wob,	gewoben,	Weber, m., weaver, Gewebe, n., web;

---

1) The Present and Imperative beutst, beut; beut! are poetical; the same from gebieten (compound of bieten), gebeutst, gebeut; gebeut! of fliegen, fleug! of ziehen, zeug! etc. Compare alphabetical list.

2) wiegen, *to rock, to mince, is weak.*

3) *Observe* that ziehen also changes the consonant (h) of the root into g, both in the Imperfect and Perfect Participle.

4) bewegen, *to move, is weak.*

5) bescheren, *to present, is weak.*

Infinitive.	Imperf.	Perf. P.	Nouns (connected with the Verbs).
c) R. v. ü.	o long,	o long.	
füren,[1] or fiesen, to choose,	for,	geforen,	Kurfürst, m., (prince) elector, Kur, f., election;
lügen, to lie (to tell an untruth),	log,	gelogen,	Lug, m., Lüge, f., lie, Lügner, m., liar;
trügen or triegen, to deceive,[2]	trog,-	getrogen,	Trug, m., deceit;
d) R. v. au,	o long,	o long.	
saugen,[3] to suck,	sog,	gesogen,	Sauger, m., sucker, Säugling, m., suckling;
†schnauben, to blow, to snort,	schnob,	geschnoben;	
†schrauben, to screw,	schrob,	geschroben,	Schraube, f., screw;
e) R. v. ä and ö,	o long,	o long.	
gähren, to ferment,	gohr,	gegohren;	
schwären, to suppurate,	schwor,	geschworen,	Schwären, m., sore, Geschwür, n., ulcer;
schwören, to swear,	schwor, and schwur (Subj. schwüre),	geschworen,	Schwur, m., oath.

Class X.

246. The *tenth Class* contains those Verbs which change the radical vowels ie, e, au, ö, a and i of the Infinitive into o *short* both *in the Imperfect* and *Perfect Participle;* some of these verbs also *change* or *modify* the radical vowel of the *2nd* and *3rd Person Singular* of the *Present Indicative* and *change* the *2nd Person Singular* of the *Imperative* as indicated in the list[4]. They are:

1) Generally used with the prefix er-, viz., erküren, erkor, erkoren.

2) Occurs principally as Compound, viz., betrügen, betrog, betrogen.

3) The transitive form of this verb is, säugen, säugte, gesäugt.

4) Other forms of these verbs such as du fleußt, geußt, etc. occur only in poetry and that rarely.

Infinitive.	Imperfect.	Perf. Part.	Nouns (connected with the Verbs).
a) R. v. ie,	o short,	o short.	
fließen, to flow,	floß,	geflossen,	Fluß, m., river;
genießen, to enjoy, to take (food),	genoß,	genossen,	Genuß, m., enjoyment;
gießen, to pour, to cast, to found,	goß,	gegossen,	Guß, m., cast, shower (of rain), Gosse, f., gutter, Gießer, m., founder,
kriechen, to creep,	kroch,	gekrochen;	
riechen, to smell,	roch,	gerochen,	Geruch, m., smell;
schießen, to shoot,	schoß,	geschossen,	Schuß, m., shot;
schließen, to shut, to conclude,	schloß,	geschlossen,	Schluß, m., end, conclusion, Schloß, n., lock, castle, Schließer, m., turn-key;
sieden, to boil, to seethe,	sott,	gesotten,	Suth, f., boiling-heat, Sieder, m., boiler;
sprießen, to germinate, to sprout,	sproß,	gesprossen,	Sprosse or Sprößling, m., sprout;
††triefen, to drip,	troff,	getroffen,	Traufe, f., gutter(s) (of the roof);
verdrießen, to annoy,	verdroß,	verdrossen,	Verdruß, m., annoyance;
*verwirren, to confuse,	verworr,	verworren,	Verwirrung, Wirre, f., Wirrwarr, m., confusion.

Infinitive.	Impf.	Perf. P.	Pres. T.	Imp.	Nouns.
b) R. v. e,	o short,	o short,	i	i	
fechten, to fight, to fence,	focht,	gefochten,	ich fechte, du fichst, er ficht,	†ficht,	Fechter, m., fencer; Gefecht, n., fight;
flechten, to plait,	flocht,	geflochten,	ich flechte, du flichst, er flicht,	†flicht,	Geflecht, n., wicker work;
melken, to milk,	molk,	gemolken,	ich melke, du milkst, er milkt,	†milk,	Milch, f., milk;
*quellen, to spring forth,	quoll,	gequollen,	ich quelle, du quillst, er quillt,	quill,	Quell, m., or Quelle, f., well, source;
*schmelzen, to melt, to smelt,	schmolz,	geschmolzen,	ich schmelze, du schmilzt, er schmilzt,	schmilz,	Schmelz, m., enamel;
*schwellen, to swell,	schwoll,	geschwollen,	ich schwelle, du schwillst, er schwillt,	schwill,	Schwelle, f., threshold;

8*

Infinitive.	Impf.	Perf. P.	Pres. T.	Imp.	Nouns.
c) R. v. ö, †löſchen, to extinguish, to quench,	o short, loſch,	o short, geloſchen,	i, ich löſche, bu liſcht, er liſcht,	i; liſch;	
d) R. v. au, ſaufen, to drink, (immoderately or speaking of beasts),	o short, ſoff,	o short, geſoffen,	äu; ich ſaufe, bu ſäufſt, er ſäuft,		Soff, m., or Geſöff, n., bad drink, Säufer, m., drunkard, Suppe,[1] f., soup;
e) R. v. i, glimmen, to glow, klimmen, to climb,	o short, glomm, klomm,	o short, geglommen; geklommen;			
f) R. v. a, †erſchallen,[2] to resound,	o short, erſcholl,	o short, erſchollen,			Schall, m., sound.

Class XI.

247. The *eleventh Class* contains Verbs which change the radical vowel of the Infinitive in *various* ways as indicated in the following list:

Infinitive.	Imp.	Perf. P.	Pres. T.	Nouns (connected with the Verbs).
Laufen, to run,	lief,	gelaufen,	ich laufe, bu läufſt, er läuft,	Läufer, m., runner, bishop (in chest),
kommen, to come,	kam,	gekommen,	ich komme, †bu kömmſt †er kömmt,	—kunft,[3] f.,
ſtoßen, to push, to knock,	ſtieß,	geſtoßen,	ich ſtoße, bu ſtößt, er ſtößt, weak,	Stoß, m., knock, push;
hauen, to hew, to strike,	hieb,	gehauen,		Hieb, m., blow;

1) Suppe, is derived, though perhaps indirectly, from ſupen, the low German for ſaufen.

2) ſchallen, *to sound*, is *weak*, yet sometimes, especially in the Imperfect, it is used strong, viz., ſcholl.

3) —kunft occurs only in Compounds; as, Ankunft, Abkunft etc.

Infinitive.	Imperfect.	Perf. P.	Nouns.
Heißen, to be called, to command,	hieß,	geheißen,	Geheiß, n., order;
rufen, to call,	rief,	gerufen,	Ruf, m., call, fame;
bitten, to beg,	bat,	gebeten,	Bitte, f., request;
liegen,¹ to lie, to be situated,	lag,	gelegen,	Lage, f., position, situation;
sitzen,² to sit,	saß,	gesessen,	Sitz, m., seat;
gebären, to bear,	gebar,	geboren,	Geburt, f., birth;
**gehen, to go, to walk,	ging,	gegangen,	Gang, m., walk, passage;
**stehen, to stand,	stand (Subj. also stünde),	gestanden,	Stand, m., standing, station;
**thun, to do, to make, to put,	that,	gethan,	That, f., deed; Thäter, m., doer.

Class XII.

248. The *twelfth Class* contains those Verbs which, besides changing the radical vowel of the Infinitive, take the terminations of weak verbs. They are:

Infinitive.	Imperfect.	Perf. P.	Nouns (connected with the Verbs).
**Bringen, to bring,	brachte (Sbj. ä),	gebracht,	Bringer, m., bringer, bearer;
**denken, to think,	dachte (Sbj. ä),	gedacht,	Denker, m., thinker, Gedanke, m., thought;
dünken,†† to fancy,	däuchte,	gedäucht;	
brennen, to burn,	brannte (Sbj. e),	gebrannt,	Brand, m., conflagration, brand;
kennen, to know,	kannte (Sbj. e),	gekannt,	Kenntniß, f., knowledge, Kenner, m., connaisseur;
nennen, to name,	nannte (Sbj. e),	genannt,	Name, m., name;
rennen, to run,	rannte (Sbj. e),	gerannt,	Renner, m., racer;
senden, to send,	sandte, (Sbj. sendete,	gesandt,	Sender, m., sender, Sendung, f., sending;
wenden, to turn,	wandte (Subj. wendete,	gewandt,	Wendung, f., turn.

1) Comp. the trans. legen, legte, gelegt, to lay.
2) Comp. the trans. setzen, setzte, gesetzt, to set.
**) Those five verbs of the 11th and 12th classes marked with asterisks are counted among the *Irregular* by some Grammarians.
††) This verb is used impersonally only and has besides the form es dünkt *(Present Indicative)* also es däucht.

249. *Observation.* The weak verb **mahlen**, *to grind* (corn), has in the *Perfect Participle* gemahlen, to distinguish it from **malen** *to paint* (*Perfect Participle* gemalt); the weak verb **spalten** *to split* has both gespaltet and gespalten, in the Perfect Participle, also, **salzen** *to salt* has in the Perf. Part. both gesalzt and gesalzen.

Note. It will be seen by looking at the first *eleven* classes of the *strong verbs* that the *Imperfects* of the *strong verbs* end in a **consonant**, except schrie and spie; and their *Perfect Participles* in -n; whilst, by looking back to the **weak** verbs, it will be found that their *Imperfects* and *Perfect Participles* always have a -t- in their inflection. By keeping this in mind the learner will be greatly assisted in his *German Reading.*

IRREGULAR VERBS.
Unregelmäßige Zeitwörter.

250. There are **ten** *Irregular Verbs* in the German language. The following three forms only can be irregular; the **Imperfect**, the **Perfect Participle** and the **Singular** of the **Present Indicative** (in the verb sein, *to be*, also the *Plural*); all the other moods and tenses are regular and formed according to the rules of the Conjugation (see Rules 221 etc.); except that the Subjunctive of *irregular Imperfects* is formed from its Indicative, by *modifying the vowel* and adding -e. (Compare Rule 225 [7].) They are:

a. 1 — 3 The three **Auxiliary Verbs** sein, *to be,* haben, *to have* and werden, *to become.*

b. 4 — 9 The six Auxiliary Verbs of mood dürfen, *to be allowed,* können, *to be able,* mögen, to like, müssen, *to be necessary,* sollen, *to be obliged,* wollen, *to be willing.*

c. 10. The verb wissen, *to know.*

251. a. THE AUXILIARY VERBS PROPER.[1]
Die Hülfszeitwörter.

Infinitive.	Imperfect.	Perfect Participle.
1. Sein,[2] to be,	war,	gewesen.

Present Tense.

Indicative.
ich bin, I am,
du bist, thou art,
er ist, he is,
wir sind, we are,
ihr seid, you are,
sie sind, they are;

Subjunctive.
ich sei, I be (*or* was),
du sei(e)st, thou be,
er sei(e), he be,
wir seien, we be,
ihr seiet, you be,
sie seien, they be.

Imperfect Tense.

Indicative.
Ich war, I was,
du warst, thou wast,
er war, he was,
wir waren, we were,
ihr waret, you were,
sie waren, they were;

Subjunctive.
ich wäre, I were,
du wärest, thou wert,
er wäre, he were,
wir wären, we were,
ihr wäret, you were,
sie wären, they were.

Perfect Tense.[3]

Indicative.
Ich bin gewesen, I have been,
du bist gewesen, thou hast been,
er ist gewesen, he has been,
wir sind gewesen, we have been,
ihr seid gewesen, you have been,
sie sind gewesen, they have been;

Subjunctive.
ich sei gewesen, I have (*or* had) been,
du seist gewesen, thou have been,
er sei gewesen, he have been,
wir seien gewesen, we have been,
ihr seiet gewesen, you have been,
sie seien gewesen, they have been.

---

1) To assist the learner the first of the irregular verbs has been given complete, the *irregular forms* in this and in the others are printed in black type; what is not given, must be formed according to rules 221 etc.

2) The Infinitive was formerly „wesen" of which are still in use the compound participles **anwesend**, *present*, **abwesend**, *absent*, and the noun, Wesen, n., *being*.

3) *Observation*. The verb sein is conjugated *with itself* and not with haben, though *to be* in English is conjugated with *to have*.

Pluperfect Tense.

Indicative.
Ich war gewesen, I had been,
du warst gewesen, thou hadst been,
er war gewesen, he had been,
wir waren gewesen, we had been,
ihr waret gewesen, you had been,
sie waren gewesen, they had been;

Subjunctive.
ich wäre gewesen, I had been,
du wärest gewesen, thou hadst been,
er wäre gewesen, he had been,
wir wären gewesen, we had been,
ihr wäret gewesen, you had been,
sie wären gewesen, they had been.

Future I.

Indicative.
Ich werde sein, I shall be,
du wirst sein, thou wilt be,
er wird sein, he will be,
wir werden sein, we shall be,
ihr werdet sein, you will be,
sie werden sein, they will be;

Subjunctive.
ich werde sein, I shall (*or* should) be,
du werdest sein, thou wilt be,
er werde sein, he will be,
wir werden sein, we shall be,
ihr werdet sein, you will be,
sie werden sein, they will be.

Future II.

Indicative.
Ich werde ⎫   ⎫ I shall   ⎫
du wirst   ⎪   ⎪ thou wilt   ⎪
er wird   ⎬ gewesen sein, ⎨ he will   ⎬ have been;
wir werden ⎪   ⎪ we shall   ⎪
ihr werdet ⎪   ⎪ you will   ⎪
sie werden ⎭   ⎭ they will   ⎭

Subjunctive.
ich werde ⎫   ⎫ I shall (*or* should) ⎫
du werdest ⎪   ⎪ thou wilt   ⎪
er werde   ⎬ gewesen sein, ⎨ he will   ⎬ have been.
wir werden ⎪   ⎪ we will   ⎪
ihr werdet ⎪   ⎪ you will   ⎪
sie werden ⎭   ⎭ they will   ⎭

Conditional I.

Ich würde sein, I should be,
du würdest sein, thou wouldst be,
er würde sein, he would be,
wir würden sein, we should be,
ihr würdet sein, you would be,
sie würden sein, they would be;

Conditional II.

ich würde   ⎫   ⎫ I should   ⎫
du würdest ⎪   ⎪ thou wouldst ⎪
er würde   ⎬ gewesen sein; ⎨ he would   ⎬ have been.
wir würden ⎪   ⎪ we should   ⎪
ihr würdet ⎪   ⎪ you would   ⎪
sie würden ⎭   ⎭ they would ⎭

Imperative.

Sei, be (thou),
sei er, let him be,
seien wir, ⎫
lasst uns sein, ⎬ let us be,
seid, be (ye),
seien sie, let them be.

Noun in connection with the verb:
Wesen, n., being, manner, essence.

252. Infinitive.   Imperfect.   Perfect Participle.
2. Haben, to have,   hatte,   gehabt.

Present Tense.

Indicative.
Ich habe, I have,
du hast, thou hast,
er hat, he has,
wir haben, we have,
ihr habt, you have,
sie haben, they have;

Subjunctive.
ich habe, I have (*or* had),
du habest, thou have,
er habe, he have,
wir haben, we have,
ihr habet, you have,
sie haben, they have.

Imperfect Tense.

Indicative.
Ich hatte, I had,
du hattest, thou hadst,
er hatte, he had,
wir hatten, we had,
ihr hattet, you had,
sie hatten, they had;

Subjunctive.
ich hätte, I had,
du hättest, thou hadst,
er hätte, he had,
wir hätten, we had,
ihr hättet, you had,
sie hätten, they had.

The *past tenses* of haben are formed with the same verb (haben); the Perfect therefore is „ich habe gehabt" I have had. (For the other tenses see the common Conjugation, Rule 221.)

The *Noun* in connection with this verb is Habe, f., property etc.

253. Infinitive.   Imperfect.   Perfect Participle.
3. Werden, to become,   wurde,   geworden (worden[1]).

Present Tense.

Indicative.
Ich werde, I become,
du wirst, thou becomest,
er wird, he becomes,
wir werden, we become,
ihr werdet, you become,
sie werden, they become;

Subjunctive.
ich werde, I become
du werdest, thou become
er werde, he become
wir werden, we become
ihr werdet, you become
sie werden, they become } *or* became.

---

[1] The form worden is used instead of geworden when werden takes the place of an auxiliary verb (see the past forms of the passive) and in poetry.

Imperfect Tense.

Indicative.	*Subjunctive.*
Ich wurde,[1] I became,	ich würde, I became,
du wurdest, thou becamest,	du würdest, thou becamest,
er wurde, he became,	er würde, he became,
wir wurden, we became,	wir würden, we became,
ihr wurdet, you became,	ihr würdet, you became,
sie wurden, they became;	sie würden, they became.

The *past tenses* of werden are formed with „sein, to be", (for "have" in English), thus, ich bin geworden, I *have* (am) become. (For the other tenses see The Conjugation, Rules 221-233.)

254. b. THE AUXILIARY VERBS[2] OF MOOD.

Infinitive.	**Imperfect.**	**Perf. Part.**
4. Dürfen[3], to be allowed, dare, may,	durfte,	gedurft[4].

Present Indicative: Ich darf, du darfst, er darf, wir dürfen, ihr dürft, sie dürfen, I am allowed, dare etc.

Present Subjunctive: Ich dürfe, I be (*or* was) allowed etc.

Imperfect Indicative: Ich durfte, I was allowed, dared etc.
Imperfect Subjunctive: ich dürfte, I were allowed, dared etc.

The *past Tenses* of this verb are formed with „haben", so that the *Perfect* would be „ich habe gedurft" I have been allowed. (For the rest of the tenses see the Model of Conjugation.)

Nouns connected with dürfen: Bedarf, m., requirement, and Bedürfniß, n., want.

---

1) Ich warb, du warbst, er warb, is still frequently used instead of ich wurde, du wurdest, er wurde.

2) *Obs.* The auxiliary verbs of mood are in German not defective as they are in English, but have all their Moods and Tenses, except, perhaps, the *Imperative* which could be formed, but is almost never required.

3) Dürfen implies *permission*, but besides *possibility* and *supposition*, as, darf ich gehen, may I go? wenn ich bitten darf, if I may trouble (*or* ask) you; er durfte nicht sprechen, he was not allowed to speak; es dürfte doch wahr sein, it might be true though; es dürfte nur regnen, suppose it rained, *or* it would only need to rain.

4) About the use of the Infinitive instead of the Past Participle, see 384 and 385.

255. *Infinitive.*   *Imperfect.*   *Perf. Part.*
5. **Können,**[1] to be able, can, know, **konnte,**   **gekonnt.**
    Present Tense (Ind.).   *Imperfect Tense (Ind.).*
Ich **kann,** du **kannst,** er **kann,** ich **konnte,** du konntest, er konnte,
wir können, ihr könnt, sie können, wir konnten, ihr konntet, sie konnten,
I can, thou canst, etc.;   I could, thou couldst etc.
Subj. ich könne, I can (or could) etc.   *Subj.* ich könnte, I could etc.
Past Tenses formed with haben, thus *Perfect* „ich habe gekonnt",
    I have been able.
Noun connected with können, Kunst f., art.

256. *Infinitive.*   *Imperfect.*   *Perf. Part.*
6. **Mögen,**[2] to like, may, **mochte,**   **gemocht.**
Present Indicative: Ich **mag,** du **magst,** er **mag,** wir mögen, ihr
    möget, sie mögen, I like, I may, etc.
Present Subjunctive: ich möge, I like (or liked), may (or might), etc.
Imperfect Indicative: ich **mochte,** I liked etc.
Imperfect Subjunctive: ich **möchte,** I should like, might etc.
Past Tenses formed with „haben", thus Perfect „ich habe gemocht,"
    I have liked.
Noun connected with mögen, Macht, f., might.

257. *Infinitive.*   *Imperfect.*   *Perf. Part.*
7. **Müssen,**[3] to be necessary that…, must, **mußte,**   **gemußt.**
Present Indicative: Ich **muß,** du **mußt,** er **muß,** wir müssen, ihr
    müßt, sie müssen, it is necessary that I…, I must, I have
    to, etc.

---

    1) **Können** implies *power* and *ability*, but also *possibility* and *supposition*; it, moreover, is much used elliptically; as, ich kann englisch lesen, I can *or* am able to read English; er kann deutsch, he can (speak, write, read) *or* he knows German; können Sie Ihr Gedicht (hersagen), do you know your poetry? das kann ich auswendig, I know that by heart; er kann jeden Augenblick kommen, he may come every moment; es könnte doch wahr sein, it might be true, though.

    2) **Mögen** implies *possibility* and *liking* and *likelihood*; it often is used to circumscribe the subjunctive mood; as, es möchte doch wahr sein, it might be true, though; möchten Sie mitgehen, would you like to go too? er möge kommen, for, er komme, he may *or* let him come; es möchte gehen, for, es ginge, it might do.

    3) **Müssen** implies *dependency* on *circumstances* and *necessity*; ich muß heute nach London reisen, I must *(have to)* go to London to-day (circumstances oblige me to go), comp. sollen; das muß man ihm lassen, er weiß zu leben, you must admit, he knows how to live; das muß wahr sein, that must be true, that surely is true.

Present Subjunctive: ich müsse, I must etc.
Imperfect Indicative: ich **mußte**, it was necessary that I ..., I had to.
Imperfect Subjunctive: ich müßte, it were necessary that I ..., I had to.
Past Tenses formed with „haben", thus Perfect „ich habe gemußt", it has been necessary that I ...
Noun connected with müssen, Muß, n., necessity.

258.   *Infinitive.*   *Imperfect.*   *Perf. Part.*
   8. **Sollen**, to be obliged, shall,[1]   sollte,   gesollt.

Present Indicative: Ich soll, du sollst, er soll, wir sollen, ihr sollt, sie sollen, I am obliged, I *am to*, I shall.
Present Subj.: ich solle, I be (*or* was) obliged, I shall (*or* should) etc.
Imperfect Indicative: ich sollte, I was obliged, I should (Subjunctive the same).
Past Tenses formed with „haben", thus the Perfect „ich habe gesollt", I have been obliged.

259.   *Infinitive.*   *Imperfect. Perf. Part.*
   9. **Wollen**,[2] to be willing, to want, will,   wollte,   gewollt.

Present Indicative: Ich will, du willst, er will, wir wollen, ihr wollt, sie wollen, I am willing, I will etc.
Present Subj.: ich wolle, I be (*or* was) willing, I will (*or* would) etc.
Imperfect Indicative and *Subjunctive:* ich wollte, I was willing, *and* I were willing, would.
Past Tenses formed with „haben", thus the Perfect „ich habe gewollt", I have been willing.
Noun connected with wollen, Wille(n), m., will.

---

1) Sollen implies *dependency* on the will or pleasure of *persons*; also *assertion* of *people* or *common report;* as, ich soll heute nach L. reisen, I shall *(am to)* go to L. to-day, (somebody wants me to go;) das Korn soll in diesem Jahr sehr theuer sein, the corn *is said* (or reported) to be very dear this year; der Fürst und die Fürstinn sollen krank sein, the prince and the princess are said to be ill. However, man sagt, may be used with it, or instead of it; as, man sagt, das Korn soll theuer sein, or, das Korn, sagt man, sei in diesem Jahr sehr theuer, or, es wird gesagt (passive), daß das Korn in diesem Jahr sehr theuer ist (or sei).

2) Wollen implies *will, willingness, wish;* also individual *assertion;* it is often used elliptically; willst du mit(gehen), *will* you go with me? wollen Sie ein Stück Brod (haben), *will* you have a piece of bread? das Mädchen wollte auch hinaus in den Wald, the girl also wanted to go into the wood; nehmen Sie so viel Sie wollen, take as much as you *wish* or *like;* er will es selbst gesehen haben, he *asserts* to have seen it himself; die Regentinn wollte nichts davon gehört haben (Egmont), the regent *asserted* not to have heard anything about it.

260.   *c.* THE VERB „wissen".

Infinitive.   *Imperfect.*   *Perf. Part.*
10. **Wissen**, to know,   **wußte,**   **gewußt.**

Present Indicative: ich weiß, du weißt, er weiß, wir wissen, ihr wißt, sie wissen, I know etc.
Present Subjunctive: ich wisse, I know (*or* knew) etc.
Imperfect Indicative: ich wußte, I knew etc.
Imperfect Subjunctive: ich wüßte, I knew etc.
Past Tenses formed with „haben", thus the Perfect „ich habe gewußt", I have known.
Nouns connected with wissen, Wissen, *n.*, and Wissenschaft, *f.*, knowledge.

IMPERSONAL VERBS.
Unpersönliche Zeitwörter.

261. Any German Verb in the *third* Person Singular or Plural may, in principal sentences, be used impersonally by putting it to the beginning of the phrase with the neuter Personal Pronoun es before it; as, der Vater liebt (or die Väter lieben) den Sohn, the Verb used impersonally: es liebt der Vater (or es lieben[1] die Väter) den Sohn; but there are some Verbs which occur *only* impersonally. They belong, as regards their conjugation, to the three classes of verbs, *weak*, *strong* and *irregular*.

262.   *Example of an Impersonal Verb.*

Infinitive.   *Imperfect.*   *Perfect Participle.*
Regnen, to rain,   regnete,   geregnet.

Present Indicative: es regnet, it rains; *Present Subjunctive* and *Imperative:* es regne, it may rain, let it rain, it rained.
Imperfect Indicative and *Subjunctive:* es regnete, it rained, it might rain.
Perfect Indicative: es hat geregnet, it has rained; *Subjunctive:* es habe geregnet, it may have (*or* had) rained.

---

1) It will be seen from this example that, if the Subject be in the Plural, the Verb stands in the Plural too, having the Pronoun in the Singular. Compare: There *is* only one chair in the room; es ist nur ein Stuhl im Zimmer, *but*, there *are* two chairs, etc.: es sind zwei Stühle etc.

Plup. Indicative: es hatte geregnet, it had rained, *Subjunctive:* es hätte geregnet, it might have rained.
Future I. Indicative: es wird regnen, *Subjunctive:* es werde regnen, it will (*or* would) rain.
Future II. Indicative: es wird geregnet haben, *Subjunctive:* es werde geregnet haben, it will (*or* would) have rained.
Conditional I.: es würde regnen, it would rain.
Conditional II.: es würde geregnet haben, it would have rained.

263. If the *Impersonal Verbs* are followed by a direct or indirect Object (Dative or Accusative) the personal Pronoun es may be dropped; as, instead of „es friert mich" *I am cold*, may be said „mich friert", and instead of „es gefällt mir", „mir gefällt", *I am pleased*. The following should be committed to memory, viz.:

a) with the *Accusative:*

es dürstet **mich**, } or mich dürstet, I am thirsty,
(or durstet „),

es hungert	„	„	„	hungert, I am hungry,
es friert	„	„	„	friert, I am cold,
es fröstelt	„	„	„	fröstelt, I feel chilly,
es schläfert	„	„	„	schläfert, I feel sleepy,
es verdrießt	„	„	„	verdrießt, I am annoyed,
es verlangt	„	„	„	verlangt, } I feel desirous,
es gelüstet	„	„	„	gelüstet,
es schaubert	„	„	„	schaubert, I shudder,
es reut	„	„	„	reut, I regret, repent,
es freut	„	„	„	freut, I rejoice,
es wundert	„	„	„	wundert, I wonder,
es jammert	„	„	„	jammert, I pity.

Note. Only one of the above verbs is used transitively, viz., jammern, *to pity*, it then should be followed by the Genitive; as,

mich jammert	deiner,		I pity thee,
„	„	seiner,	„	„	him *or* it,
„	„	ihrer,	„	„	her *or* them,
„	„	eurer,	„	„	you,
„	„	Ihrer,	„	„	you (polite addressing),

but in colloquial prose will be found the following construction:

du jammerst mich,			I pity thee,
er jammert	„	„	„	him,
sie „	„	„	„	her,
ihr „	„	„	„	you,
sie jammern	„	„	„	them,
Sie „	„	„	„	you (polite addressing).

b) with the *Dative:*

es gelingt **mir,** or, **mir** gelingt, I succeed,
es ahnet „ „ „ ahnet, I forebode,
es schwindelt „ „ „ schwindelt, I feel giddy,
es ist mir warm, „ „ ist warm, I am warm,
es ist mir wohl or unwohl, or, mir ist wohl or unwohl, I feel well
  (zu Muthe *understood*)   *or* unwell.
es ist mir übel, or, mir ist übel, I feel sick,
  (zu Muthe *understood*)
es ist mir bange, or, mir ist bange, I feel afraid or timid,
  (zu Muthe *understood*)
es ist mir lieb, or, **mir** ist lieb, I am glad,
es ist (or, es thut) **mir** leid, or, **mir** ist leid, I am sorry,
es thut **mir** noth,[1] I want,
es wird **mir** ohnmächtig, or, **mir** wird ohnmächtig, I feel faint,
es träumt **mir,** or, **mir** träumt, I dream,
es ekelt „ „ „ ekelt, I am disgusted,
es graut „ „ „ graut, I dread.

264. The following is the declension of this kind of verbs:

es dürstet mich, I am thirsty,   es gelingt mir, I succeed,
„ „ dich, thou art thirsty,   „ „ dir, thou succeedest,
„ „ ihn (or sie), he (or she)   „ „ ihm (or ihr), he (or
    is thirsty.   she succeeds,
„ „ uns, we are thirsty,   „ „ uns, we succeed,
„ „ euch, you „ „   „ „ euch, you „
„ „ sie, they „ „   „ „ ihnen, they „
or mich dürstet, I am thirsty,   or mir gelingt, I succeed,
  dich dürstet, thou art thirsty,   dir gelingt, thou succeedest,
      etc. etc.   etc. etc.

Notice also the declension of the transitive verb "leid thun, to be sorry".

es thut mir leid um dich,   I am sorry for thee,
„ „ „ „ „ ihn, „ „ „ „ him,
„ „ „ „ „ sie, „ „ „ „ her or them,
„ „ „ „ „ uns, „ „ „ „ us,
„ „ „ „ „ euch, „ „ „ „ you,
„ „ „ „ „ sie, „ „ „ „ them,
„ „ „ „ „ Sie, „ „ „ „ you (polite);

---

1) es thut noth, it is necessary.

or du thust mir leid,						I am sorry for thee,
er thut	„	„	„	„	„	him,
sie „	„	„	„	„	„	her,
ihr „	„	„	„	„	„	you,
sie thun,	„	„	„	„	„	them,
Sie „	„	„	„	„	„	you (polite).

REFLECTIVE VERBS.
Zurückziehende Zeitwörter.

265. The number of *Reflective Verbs* in German is pretty large and most of them are not reflective in English; they occur either with an Accusative or Dative (*i. e.*, the Reflective *Pronoun* stands either in the *Accusative* or *Dative*, for the whole verb may govern another case; as, ich erinnere mich seiner, *I remember him*, thus, erinnern governs the *Accusative* and sich erinnern the *Genitive*); the pronoun stands close after the verb (in compound tenses after the auxiliary verb), but, should the verb stand at the end, the Pronoun remains beside the subject. Ex.: ich gräme mich (verb, pron.) ich habe mich gegrämt (aux. verb., pron.); but dass ich mich über ihn gräme (verb, at the end), or dass ich mich über ihn gegrämt habe (verb, at the end, *pronoun beside the subject*).

266. a. *Example of a Reflective Verb* with the *Accusative*.

Infinitive.   *Imperfect.*   *Perf. Part.*
Sich grämen, to grieve (one's self), grämte (mich etc.), gegrämt.

Present Tense (Ind.)
Ich gräme mich, I grieve myself,
du grämst dich, thou grievest thyself,
er, sie, es, man grämt sich, he, she, it grieves him-, her-, it-, one's self,
wir grämen uns, we grieve ourselves,
ihr grämt euch, you grieve yourselves,
sie grämen sich, they grieve themselves;

Imperfect Tense (Ind.)
ich grämte mich, I grieved myself,
du grämtest dich, thou grievedst thyself,
er grämte sich, he grieved himself,
wir grämten uns, we grieved ourselves,
ihr grämtet euch, you grieved yourselves,
sie grämten sich, they grieved themselves;

Perfect Tense (Ind.).
ich habe mich gegrämt, I have grieved myself,
du hast dich gegrämt, thou hast grieved thyself,
er hat sich gegrämt, he has grieved himself,
wir haben uns gegrämt, we have grieved ourselves,
ihr habt euch gegrämt, you have grieved yourselves,
sie haben sich gegrämt, they have grieved themselves;
    etc.

Imperative.
gräme dich, grieve thyself,
gräme er sich, let him grieve himself,
grämen wir uns, let us grieve ourselves,
grämet euch, grieve yourselves,
grämen sie sich, let them grieve themselves.
    etc.

The other tenses formed in the same way.

267. b. *Example of a Reflective Verb* with the *Dative*.

Infinitive.   *Imperfect.*
Sich schmeicheln, to flatter one's self, schmeichelte (mir, etc.),
    Perf. Part.
    geschmeichelt.

Present Indicative.
Ich schmeichle mir, I flatter myself,
du schmeichelst dir, thou flatterest thyself,
er schmeichelt sich, he flatters himself,
wir schmeicheln uns, we flatter ourselves,
ihr schmeichelt euch, you flatter yourselves,
sie schmeicheln sich, they flatter themselves;

Perfect Indicative.
ich habe mir geschmeichelt, I have flattered myself,
du hast dir geschmeichelt, thou hast flattered thyself,
er hat sich geschmeichelt, he has flattered himself,
wir haben uns geschmeichelt, we have flattered ourselves,
ihr habt euch geschmeichelt, you have flattered yourselves,
sie haben sich geschmeichelt, they have flattered themselves;

The other tenses are formed in the same way[1].

268. These are the *Reflective Verbs* which need the pronoun in *the Dative*:

---

[1] *Obs.* It will be seen by comparing the two examples that the difference consists only in the 1st and 2nd Person Singular (being mich and dich and mir and dir respectively), whilst the other pronouns are the same.

Sich getrauen, to venture,
sich anmaßen, to assume,
sich einbilden, to fancy, to imagine,
sich herausnehmen, to presume,
sich schmeicheln, to flatter one's self,
sich vornehmen, to propose to one's self, to intend,
sich vorstellen, (to represent to one's mind), to comprehend,
sich verleiden, to lose the taste for something, to grow averse to,
sich zueignen, to appropriate.

COMPOUND VERBS.

269. There are two kinds of *Compound Verbs*, generally called *Inseparable* (untrennbare) and *Separable* (trennbare), but better styled *Real-* (ächte) and *Quasi-* (unächte) *Compound*.

270. a. THE REAL-COMPOUND VERBS are those which consist of *a Simple Verb* and one of the *Prepositions* hinter, wider, the *Adverb* voll, or one of the *Prefixes* be, emp, ent, er, ge, ver, zer (which latter are often called *Derived Verbs*) as *particle*. The *Real-Compound Verbs* always have the stress on the *verb* and are *never separated* from their *particle*, they are consequently conjugated like *simple* verbs, but want the augment ge- in the past participle.

Meaning of the principal prefixes.

Among other less definable meanings the following are worth noticing:

be- serves to make an otherwise intransitive verb transitive; it further is used to convey the idea of covering; as, ich lache über etwas or ich belache etwas, I laugh at something; ich gieße Wasser auf die Blumen or ich begieße die Blumen (mit Wasser), I water the flowers; beschmieren, besmear; bethauen, bedew, etc.

ent- is equivalent to *out* or *from* or *forth* and *away*; as, entſtrömen, to stream out *or* forth; entkommen, entlaufen, to get away, escape; ſich entkleiden, to undress.

er- mostly *intensifies* the meaning of the simple verb, but also expresses the result or success of the action; erſterben, erſticken, to die, choke; erfinden, erdichten, to invent; erkämpfen, to obtain by fighting; erſchwindeln, to get by swindling.

ver- is used mainly to *intensify* the meaning of a verb; as, verſinken, to sink (under); but it also represents *error, loss* and *destruction*, which latter meaning it shares with **zer-**; as, verſehen, to mistake, overlook; verlieren, verlegen, to lose, to mislay; verderben, verbrennen, to destroy, burn (up); zerbrechen, to break to pieces.

271. *Some Tenses* as an *Example* of a **Real-Compound Verb:**

Infinitive.	Imperfect.	Perf. Part.
überſetzen,¹ to translate,	überſetzte,	überſetzt.

Present Indicative.   *Perfect Indicative.*

Ich überſetze, I translate,   ich habe überſetzt, I have translated,

du überſetzt, or —ſetzeſt, thou translatest,   du haſt überſetzt, thou hast translated,

er überſetzt, he translates,   er hat überſetzt, he has translated,

wir überſetzen, we translate,   wir haben überſetzt, we have translated,

ihr überſetzt, you translate,   ihr habt überſetzt, you have translated,

ſie überſetzen, they translate;   ſie haben überſetzt, they have translated.

---

1) Compare Rule 277.

272. b. THE QUASI-COMPOUND VERBS

are those which consist of a Verb and a *Particle*. This so-called Particle may be *a noun and a preposition;* as, **in den Stand setzen**, to enable, or *a noun;* as, **stattfinden**, to take *place;* or *a verb;* as, **spazieren gehen**, to take a *walk*, or an *adjective;* as, **todtschlagen**, to kill, or a *Preposition;* as, **untergehen**, to go *down*, or an *adverb;* as, **weggehen**, to go *away;* but they are, regarding their position, all subject to the rules of the Particle.¹

These Verbs always have the *stress* on the *Particle* and are commonly spelled in *one word*,² whenever they happen to stand together in a sentence; but they must be treated, as regards their construction as **two words**,³ according to the rules laid down in the syntax of this work.

273. *Explanation.* The *Verb* (or in *compound* Tenses the *auxiliary* verb) has in *principal* sentences the *second* place, whatever be the first expression, whilst in *subordinate* phrases it stands at the *end*.

The *Particle, Participle* and *Infinitive* stand *at the end* in the order given here; so that in a *subordinate* phrase in which a simple tense of a verb, or an auxiliary verb would occur beside these three, or one or two of them, the order would be: 1) Particle; 2) Participle; 3) Infinitive; 4) Simple Tense of a verb or Aux. Verb. Now, as the Quasi-Compound Verbs consist of a *Particle* and a *Verb*, the latter would in *independent* phrases necessarily be separated from its particle, if the tense be a *simple* one (as the Particle goes to

---

1) See Rule 309.
2) This rule especially refers to such verbs, as are compounded of particles which are not *nouns* or *verbs*, the latter being generally spelled in *two* words.
3) It is necessary the learner should keep this fact in mind particularly, as it forms the easiest clue to the difficulties of these verbs.

the end and the verb holds the second place), whilst, if a *compound* tense, it would not be separated (as the Particle and Participle stand together at the end); again, if the phrase be *dependent*, the verb will not be separated from its particle either (as its place in subordinate phrases is at the *end*, *after* the *Particle*).

274. *Illustrations.* 1. Ich gehe heute mit meinem Freunde aus or heute gehe ich mit meinem Freunde aus, or mit meinem Freunde gehe ich heute aus, I go out to-day with my friend. (Because the sentence is *independent*, therefore the *Verb* has the *second* place and the *Particle* stands at the *end*).

2. Ich bin heute mit meinem Freunde ausgegangen, or heute bin ich mit meinem Freunde ausgegangen, or mit meinem Freunde bin ich heute ausgegangen, I have gone out to-day with my friend. (Because, though the sentence is still *independent*, the tense is a *compound* one, therefore the *Auxiliary Verb* has the *second* place, whilst the *Particle* stands at the *end* beside the *Participle*,[1] which is here the Verb proper).

3. Wenn ich mit meinem Freunde ausgehe[2] (because this clause is *dependent*, the Verb stands at the very *end*, where it meets the Particle); or wenn ich mit meinem Freunde ausgegangen bin,[3] or wenn ich mit meinem Freunde ausgehen werde[4]. (The phrase is still dependent, the tense, however, is now a *compound* one and therefore the *Auxiliary Verb* stands at the *end*, whilst the Particle stands before the Infinitive in its proper place).

275. Besides various Nouns, Nouns with Prepositions, Verbs, and Adjectives the following Prepositions and Adverbs are used as *Particles* in these Verbs, viz., ab, an, auf, aus, bei, dar, ein, fort, her, hin, los, mit, nach, nieder, ob, vor, weg, wieder and zu.

---

1) The same is the case if the tense is compound of an *Infinitive* and an *Auxiliary Verb*; as, ich werde heute mit meinem Freunde ausgehen.
2) if I go out with my friend.
3) if I have gone out with my friend.
4) if I shall go out with my friend.

276. A few tenses as an *Example* of a **Quasi-Compound Verb**:

Infinitive.	*Imperfect.*	*Perf. Part.*
Überſetzen,[1] to set over,	ſetzte über,	übergeſetzt,[2]

Present Indicative.
Ich ſetze über, I set over,
du ſetzt (or ſetzeſt) über, thou settest over,
er ſetzt über, he sets over,
wir ſetzen über, we set over,
ihr ſetzt über, you set over,
ſie ſetzen über, they set over;

Imperfect Indicative.
ich ſetzte über, I set over,
du ſetzteſt über, thou settest over,
er ſetzte über, he set over,
wir ſetzten über, we set over,
ihr ſetztet über, you set over,
ſie ſetzten über, they set over.

Perfect Indicative.
Ich habe übergeſetzt, I have set over,
du haſt übergeſetzt, thou hast set over,
er hat übergeſetzt, he has set over,
wir haben übergeſetzt, we have set over,
ihr habt übergeſetzt, you have set over,
ſie haben übergeſetzt, they have set over;

Future I. Indicative.
ich werde überſetzen, I shall set over,
du wirſt überſetzen, thou wilt set over,
er wird überſetzen, he will set over,
wir werden überſetzen, we shall set over,
ihr werdet überſetzen, you will set over,
ſie werden überſetzen, they will set over.

Imperative.
Setze über, set over (thou),
ſetze er über, let him set over,
ſetzen wir über, } let us set
laſſt uns überſetzen, } over,
ſetzt über, set over (ye),
ſetzen ſie über, let them set over.

etc. etc.

---

1) Compare Rule 277.

2) As we look upon these verbs as *two words*, the place of the augment **ge**, *between* the *Particle* and the *Verb*, does not require any further explanation.

277. c. REAL- AND QUASI-COMPOUND VERBS.

The Prepositions **durch, über, um** and **unter** occur both in Real- and Quasi-Compound Verbs; they are *Real Compounds*, if the Verb has *not a literal* but a *figurative meaning* and is represented in English by a *Latin or French* word *(not by a Saxon)*; as, über= ſe′ʒen, to translate, unterhal′ten, to entertain (both have a *figurative meaning* and in English a Roman representative); they are *Quasi-Compounds*, if the verb has a *literal meaning* and in English a *Saxon* representative; as, ü′berſeʒen, to set over, un′terhalten, to hold under, (both have a *literal* meaning and in English a *Saxon* representative)[1]. Hearing them pronounced, it is easy to decide whether they are the one or the other, the *Real* having the stress on the *Verb* and the *Quasi*-Compound on the *Particle*.

278. The Compound Verbs with **miß** deserve special notice, for some of them are treated in every respect like *real* compounds, viz.:

mißlingen, to be unsuccessful,   Perf. Part. mißlungen,
mißbehagen, to dislike;   „   „   mißbehagt;

whilst others have the stress on **miß** and even sometimes take the augment before miß; as,

mißbilligen, to disapprove,   Perf. Part. gemißbilligt;

still others have the stress sometimes on **miß**, sometimes on the *Verb*, and place the augment before the verb; as,

mißarten, to degenerate,   Perf. Part. mißgeartet,
{ mißhandeln, to act wrongly,   „   „   mißgehandelt,
{ mißhandeln, to illtreat;   „   „   mißhandelt;

so that one might say ich handle **miß**, I act wrongly, though it is never done.

279. *Verb diminutives.* See note to Rule 153.

---

1) Though the above rule admits of exceptions, it appears the only practical way to assist the learner.

THE ADVERB.
Das Nebenwort.

280. The Adverb is that part of speech which is used *to qualify Verbs, Adjectives, Pronouns* and words of its own kind, viz., *other Adverbs*. Besides the pure Adverbs almost all Adjectives and frequently Nouns are used adverbially.

There are distinguished:
1. Adverbs of quality or kind,
2. Adverbs of place,
3. Adverbs of time.

They may be used demonstratively, as **da**, *there;* interrogatively, as **wo?** *where?* relatively, as **wo,** *where.* This is in so far of importance, as it determines the position of the verb; if, for example, **wo?** *where?* is used *interrogatively,* the Verb must stand next to it, when used *relatively,* the Verb must stand at the end of the sentence.

1. ADVERBS OF QUALITY OR KIND.

281. This class of Adverbs is very numerous, since all Adjectives may be used as such. The most common *real* Adverbs of this class, *i. e.,* such as cannot be used as Adjectives are the following:

282. a. denoting *number, order* or *extent:*

oft, often,
selten, seldom,
wieder, again,
vorher, before,
nachher, after,
nachträglich, by way of addition, later,
zuerst, at first,

zuletzt, at last,
zugleich, at the same time,
theils, partly,
einzeln, singly,
allein, alone,
beisammen, zusammen, together,
überhaupt, altogether,
besonders, especially, etc.

as well as the numeral Adverbs in —mal, —fach, —weiſe; as, einmal, once, zweifach, double, paarweiſe, by pairs (see the rules on the Numerals).

283. b. denoting *comparison* and *estimation*:

ſo, so), as,[1]
ſowie, as,
alſo, so, thus, consequently,
folglich, consequently,
ebenſo, so, as, just as,
gleichſam, as it were,
gleichwie, like,
gleichfalls } likewise,
ebenfalls
auch, also,
doch } yet,
dennoch
gleich, like,
desgleichen, such like (referring to a *Singular*),
dergleichen, such like (referring to a *Plural*),
dergeſtalt, to such an amount,
dermaßen, to such a measure or degree,

einigermaßen, in some measure,
anders, otherwise,
ſonſt, else (means also *formerly*),
deſto[2] } so much the,
um ſo mehr
vielmehr, rather,
theils — theils, partly — partly.
bald — bald, now — then,
deſſenungeachtet, notwithstanding,
nichtsdeſtoweniger, nevertheless,
hingegen } on the contrary,
dagegen,
nämlich, namely,
daher, therefore,
deswegen
deshalb } on that account,
darum
demnach
mithin } accordingly.
ſomit

284. c. denoting *degree of strength*:

ſehr, very,
zu
allzu } too,
garzu
ganz und gar, altogether,
kaum, scarcely,
nur, only,
genug, enough,
überaus, exceedingly,
ſchier } almost,
beinahe

zumal, especially,
zuſehends, visibly,
blindlings, blindly,
jählings, precipitously,
bitterlich, bitterly,
lediglich, merely,
höchlich, highly,
ſchwerlich, hardly.
treulich, faithfully,
weislich, wisely.

---

1) The adverb ſo used to be employed analogously to the English; also instead of the Relative Pronoun, as is still to be found in the Bible and in poetry; as, von Allen, ſo da kamen.
Bürgers „Leonore".

2) Compare Rule 163.

285. d. denoting *question, relation, affirmation, negation, supposition, feeling* etc.

wann, when (?),*		wahrlich	
warum		freilich	indeed,
weswegen	why (?),*	allerdings	verily,
was		fürwahr	truly,
wie, how (?),		sicherlich	surely,
wie so, how so?		wirklich	really,
wo,¹ where (?),*		gewißlich	
wohin, whither (?),*		zwar, indeed, though,	
woher, whence (?),*		gänzlich, entirely,	
gelt	is it not?	nein	no! not at all!
nicht wahr		nein doch	
ja (sometimes jaja)		nicht, not,	
jawohl	yes!	gar nicht, not at all,	
jadoch		etwa	perhaps,
wahrscheinlich		vielleicht	
vermuthlich	probably,	hoffentlich, it is to be hoped,	
wohl		etc.	etc.

* *Note.* Those adverbs provided with an asterisk are used both interrogatively and relatively.

2. ADVERBS OF PLACE.

286. The most common Adverbs of this Class which contains few Adjectives only are the following:

hier²		überall	
hierselbst	here,	allenthalben	everywhere,
da²		allerwärts	
daselbst	there,	irgend, any,	
dort		irgendwo, anywhere,	

---

1) *Interrogative and Relative Adverbs.* The Adverb **wo** occurs frequently connected with Prepositions, instead of the Neuter of the *Interrogative* and *Relative* Pronouns; as, **wobei**, whereby, *by what? by which;* womit, wherewith, *with what? with which;* **woran**, whereon, *on what? on which;* etc. etc. Comp. Rule 84.

2) *Demonstrative Adverbs.* The Adverbs **hier** and **da** occur connected with most Prepositions instead of the Neuter of the *Personal* or *Demonstrative* Pronoun; as, **darin**, therein, *in it, in that,* **daraus**, thereout, *out of it, out of that;* hierüber, hereover, *over it, over this;* hierunter, hereunder, *under this, under that;* etc. etc. Compare page 15, note 2.

nirgend ⎫ nowhere,
nirgends ⎭
weg ⎫ away,
fort ⎭
her,¹ hither, this way,
hin,¹ thither, that way,
hierher, this way,
dorthin, that way,
rechts, to the right,
links, to the left,
gerade aus, straight on,
zurück, back,
rückwärts, backwards,
rücklings, backwards, supinely,
vorwärts, forwards,
seitwärts, sidewards,
abwärts, off the way,
anderwärts, elsewhere,
oben ⎫ above,
droben ⎭

unten, below,
innen, within,
außen ⎫ without,
draußen ⎭
hinten, behind,
vorn, in front,
mitten, in the middle,
hüben, on this side,
drüben, on the other side,
rings, all round,
bergan, up hill,
bergab, down hill;

now obsolete :   *better :*
haußen,   draußen,
dahero,   daher,
dorten,   dort,
allda,   daselbst,
allhier,   hierselbst,
fürbaß,   weiter.

3. ADVERBS OF TIME.

287. The most common pure Adverbs of this Class (which contains few Adjectives) are the following:

allezeit ⎫
stets ⎪
immer ⎬ always,
immerfort ⎪
immerwährend ⎪
immerdar ⎭
je ⎫ ever,
jemals ⎭
ewiglich, eternally,
nie ⎫
niemals ⎪
nimmer ⎬ never,
nimmermehr ⎭
schon ⎫ already,
bereits ⎭
noch, still, yet,

bis, till,
bisher, hitherto,
flugs ⎫ at once,
stracks ⎭
einstweilen ⎫
unterdessen ⎬ meanwhile,
unterdeß ⎭
indeß ⎫ meantime,
indessen ⎭
heute, to-day,
morgen, to-morrow,
übermorgen, the day after to-morrow,
gestern, yesterday,
vorgestern ⎫ the day before
ehegestern ⎭ yesterday,

1) *Adverbs expressing motion.* The Adverbs hin and her occur combined with other Adverbs or Prepositions in a large number of Adverbs and Particles, the former expressing a movement *away from* and the latter a movement *towards* the speaker or place spoken of; as, hierher, hither, dorthin, thither, herein, in, hinaus, out, etc.

heuer, this year,
sonst ⎫
ehemals ⎬ formerly,
früher ⎪
ehedem ⎭
weiland, late,
jetzt ⎫
jetzo (poetical) ⎬ now,
nun ⎫
nunmehr ⎬ now,
neulich ⎫
letzthin ⎪
jüngst ⎬ the other day,
vor Kurzem ⎪
kürzlich ⎭
vorher, before,

nachher, after,
bald, soon,
sogleich, at once,
eben, just,
einst, once,
dereinst, one day (future),
bisweilen ⎫
zuweilen ⎬ sometimes,
dann und wann, now and then,
wann, when,
fortan, henceforth,
nach gerade ⎫
nach und nach ⎬ gradually,
allmä(h)lich ⎭
gelegentlich, by and by.

288. Adverbs cannot be *declined*, but some may be *compared* and that in the same way as adjectives.

Examples.

Positive. *Comparative.* *Superlative.*
spät, late, später, later, spätest, latest;
oft, often, öfter, oftener, öftest, oftenest;

Irreg. bald, soon, eher or bälder, sooner, ehest or bäldest, soonest;[1]
gern,[2] willingly, lieber, more willingly, liebst, most willingly.

The pure form of the Superlative is used with Adverbs as little as with Adjectives, the forms am -sten, mentioned in Rule 164, or auf das -e, are used instead, when the Adverb is the predicate of the sentence, or when it qualifies *the whole phrase*; Karl liest von allen Schülern **am besten**, Charles reads of all the pupils *best*. Ich erklärte ihm die Regel **auf das genaueste**, I explained to him the rule *most minutely*.

However, when it qualifies the Verb only, the shorter form -stens is used; as, ich danke **bestens** für den guten Rath, I thank you *very much* for your good advice. Only a few Adverbs of this kind occur; viz.:

---

1) When qualifying *Verbs*, the forms ehestens and baldigst are generally used.
2) The Adverb **ungern** is compared in the regular way, viz., ungerner, ungernst.

beſtens, very much, in the best manner,
eheſtens, at the soonest,
erſtens, in the first place (see Rule 204),
frūheſtens, at the earliest, not before,
hōchſtens, at the utmost,
längſtens, at the longest,
meiſtens, for the most part,
mindeſtens, at least,
nächſtens, shortly, very soon,
ſchönſtens, in the most polite (in the finest) manner,
ſpäteſtens, at the latest, not later than,
wenigſtens, at least.

ADVERBS NOT TO BE RENDERED IN ENGLISH.

289. Where the object is represented by a whole clause, either conjunctional or infinitive, it is commonly announced, as it were, in German by an adverb, corresponding with the government of the verb, *i. e.*, by the Accusative **es**, if the verb governs that case, by **daran**, if the Verb is used by the preposition an, by **darauf**, if with the preposition auf. Ex.:

1. Ich habe **es** Ihnen ja geſagt, daſs er nicht kommen wird, did I not tell you, that he would not come (es in the first part of the sentence is intended to announce, that the object follows in the shape of a phrase, viz., daſs er nicht kommen wird).

2. Haben Sie **daran** gedacht, daſs Sie heute Ihren Oheim beſuchen ſollten, did you remember, that you were to visit your uncle to-day? (the adverb daran in the first part of the sentence again indicates that the object follows in the shape of a phrase, viz., daſs Sie heute Ihren Oheim beſuchen ſollten).

3. Können Sie ſich nicht **darauf** beſinnen, was er zu Ihnen ſagte? can you not recollect what he told you (darauf is the adverb which attracts the listener's or reader's attention to the coming phrase which is the object).

THE PREPOSITION.
Das Verhältnißwort.

—

290. Prepositions are invariable words, used with Nouns or Pronouns to indicate their relation to an action or to another person or thing. They are either *primitive* Particles, *derived* words or *compound* words, which may govern:

1. the *Genitive*, 2. the *Dative*, 3. the *Accusative*, and 4. the *Dative* and *Accusative*. The Prepositions commonly *precede* the Noun and only occasionally follow it:

291. I. PREPOSITIONS GOVERNING THE GENITIVE.

Rule.

Brauche mit dem **Genitiv**:[1]
Unweit, mittelst, kraft und **während,**
Laut, vermöge, ungeachtet,
Oberhalb und **unterhalb,**
Innerhalb und **außerhalb,**
Diesseit, jenseit, halben, wegen,
Statt, auch längs, zufolge, trotz,
Mit den letzten Drei ist auch
Oft der Dativ in Gebrauch.[2]

Note. ob, on account of, is obsolete and poetical.

292. *Meaning.* *Examples.*

Unweit (or unfern) not far. — **Unweit** der Stadt, *not far* from the town.

Mittels
mittelst } by means.
vermittelst

Man öffnete das Thor **mittels** etc. eines Brecheisens, they opened the gate *by means* of a crowbar.

---

1) Use with the *Genitive*.
2) With the last three the *Dative* may also be used.

Kraft, by virtue.	Ich verkündige Allen **kraft** meines Amtes, daß —, I announce to all *by virtue* of my office that —
Während,[1] during.	Ich lernte ihn **während** meines Aufenthaltes in Italien kennen, I made his acquaintance *during* my stay in Italy.
Laut, conformably to.	Er handelt **laut** des Gesetzes, he acts *conformably to* law.
Vermöge, by virtue.	Es ist ihm **vermöge** seiner Kraft gelungen, sich zu retten, he has succeeded *by virtue* of his strength to save himself.
Ungeachtet, notwithstanding (either *follows* or *precedes* its regimen).	**Ungeachtet** seines Alters arbeitet er den ganzen Tag, *notwithstanding* his age he works the whole day.
Oberhalb, above, **unterhalb,** below.	Wir standen **oberhalb** des Flusses und der Feind stand **unterhalb** des Hügels, we stood *above* the river and the enemy *below* the hill.
Innerhalb, within,[2] **außerhalb,** below.	Dieser Wald liegt **innerhalb** unsers Gutes und **außerhalb** des Ihrigen, this wood is situated *within* our estate and *without* yours.
Dießseit or **dießseits,** on *this* side, **jenseit** or **jenseits,** on *that* side.	Wir wohnten in Paris **dießseits** der Seine, und Sie wohnten **jenseit** des Flusses, we were lodging in Paris on *this side* of the Seine and you lived on (the other) *that side* of the river.
Halben or **halber,**[3] (always *follows* its regimen) **wegen** (either *follows* or *precedes* its regimen). **um... willen** (the case is inserted between the two words).	for the sake, on account of.
	Seiner Gesundheit **wegen** thut er Alles, seiner Bequemlichkeit **halben** wenig, **um** seiner Freunde **willen** viel, *for the sake of* his health he does everything, *on account of* his comfort little, *for the sake of* his friends much.
Statt or **anstatt,**[4] instead.	Er kam **anstatt** seines Bruders, sie ging

---

1) Occurs also as Conjunction, with the meaning of *whilst*.

2) The preposition **binnen** *within*, is only used when speaking of time and governs *the Dative;* as, **binnen** drei Tagen wird er wieder da sein, he will be back *within* three days.

3) For the combination of these Prepositions with Pronouns etc. see Rules 57, 64.

4) There is no difference between these two Prepositions.

Längs,[1] along, by the side.	**flatt ihrer Schwester,** he came *instead of his brother,* she went *instead of her sister.* **Längs des Flusses** und **längs dem Meer** stehen viel schöne Sommerhäuser, *along the river and by the side of the sea* there stand many beautiful villas.
Zufolge,[1] according (either follows or precedes its regimen).	**Zufolge des Gesetzes** und **unserem Willen zufolge** ist es recht, *according to the law and according to our will it is right.*
Trotz,[1] in spite.	Er that es **trotz** aller unserer (or unsern) Warnungen, he did it *in spite* of all our warnings.

293. II. PREPOSITIONS GOVERNING THE DATIVE.

Rule.

**Bei, binnen, gegenüber, nächst,
Mit, nach, zu, sammt, von, seit, zuwider,
Entgegen, außer, aus und nebst**
Schreib' mit dem **Dativ** nieder[2].

Observation. The Preposition **ob,** *over, on account of,* occurs only in poetry; as, **ob der holden Frühlingspracht,** *over the splendour of delightful spring.*

294. *Meaning.*   *Examples.*

Bei, by, near, with, at (the house of), in, on (denotes *nearness;* compare **mit**).	Haben Sie das **bei dem Kaufmann** gekauft? have you bought that *at (the house of)* the merchant's? Haben Sie Ihre Uhr **bei sich**? have you got your watch *with* you? Portobello liegt **bei Edinburg,** Portobello lies near Edinburgh. **Bei** schönem Wetter, in fine weather. **Bei** dieser Gelegenheit, on this occasion.
Binnen, within (used only in reference to time).	**Binnen** einer Woche werde ich wieder da sein, I shall be back *within* a week.
Gegenüber, over against (often follows its regimen, sometimes the case stands between **gegen** and **über**).	Wir wohnten in Köln **gegenüber dem Jülichsplatz,** or **dem Jülichsplatz gegenüber,** *rarely* **gegen** dem **Jülichsplatz über,** we lived in Cologne *over against* the Jülichplace.

---

1) These three Prepositions may be used either with the Genitive or Dative.
2) Use with the *Dative*.

Nächst, next to.

Er sitzt in der Schule immer **nächst seinem Bruder**, he always sits in school *next to* his brother.

Mit, with (denotes *company* and *instrumentality*; compare bei).

Ich war vor drei Jahren **mit einem Freund** in Paris, I was three years ago *with* a friend in Paris.

Ich sehe **mit vielem Vergnügen**, daß Sie so fleißig sind, I see *with* much pleasure that you are so diligent.

Nach,[1] after, according to, to (expressing a movement to a *place*; compare zu); **nach** sometimes follows its regimen.

Nach dem König folgte **nach der Sitte** des Landes der erste Minister; sie gingen zu Fuß **nach dem Schloß**, *after* the king followed *according to* the custom of the country the first minister; they walked on foot *to* the castle; **nach der Natur**, *from* nature; ihrer Natur nach, according to their nature.

Zu,[2] to, at, in, to (expressing a movement to a *person*); compare nach.

Wir gehen alle Tage **zu unserm Oheim**, welcher **zu B.** wohnt; gestern sagte ich **zu ihm**, wann kommst du **zu uns**, Oheim, we go every day *to* our uncle who lives *at* B.; yesterday I said *to* him, when are you coming *to* (see) us, uncle?

Sammt, nebst, along with, with.

Er floh **sammt Frau und Kindern**, **nebst allem**, was er hatte, he fled together *with* wife and children, *along with* everything he had.

Von, of, by, from, (*i. e.* from an *open* place, compare aus).

Er erzählte **von Ihnen**, daß Sie alle Tage ein Gedicht **von Schiller** läsen, wenn Sie **vom (von dem) Spaziergang** kämen, he said *of* you, that you read every day a poem *by* Schiller, when you were returning *from* your walk.

Seit,[3] since, for (denotes the *whole* space of time mentioned; comp. the Preposition vor, 298).

Ich habe Sie **seit acht Tagen** nicht gesehen, I have not seen you *for* (the whole space of) eight days; Mein Freund ist schon **seit vierzehn Tagen** krank, er hat **seit vier Tagen** nichts ge-

---

1) When nach *follows* the Noun it is a *Particle* and must stand at the end; as, ich **komme** dir so schnell wie (or als) möglich **nach**, I shall *follow* you as quickly as possible.
2) See Note 1 to Rule 299.
3) Occurs also as Conjunction.

Zuwider, against; **entgegen,** against, contrary to, always *follow* their regimen. **Außer,** besides, without.	geſſen, my friend has been ill *for* a fortnight, he has eaten nothing *for* four days. Das iſt **dem** Geſetze **zuwider,** that is *against* the law. Er handelt mein**em** Wunſch **entgegen,** he acts *against* my wish. **Außer** Ihr**em** Vater war Niemand zugegen, *besides* your father there was nobody present.
Aus, out of, from, (*i. e.* from an *enclosed* place or from anything *limited*, compare **von**).	**Aus** den Wolken kommt der Regen, *out of* the clouds comes rain. Eine Stelle **aus** der Bibel, a passage *from* the Bible. Wir kommen ſoeben **aus** der Schule, we are just returning *from* school.

295. The following lines of poetry illustrate these Prepositions; viz.:

Nach dir ſchmacht' ich, zu dir eil' ich, du geliebte Quelle du,
Aus dir ſchöpf' ich, bei dir weil' ich, ſeh' dem Spiel der Wellen zu,
Mit dir ſcherz' ich, von dir lern' ich heiter durch das Leben wallen,
Angelacht von Frühlingsblumen und begrüßt von Nachtigallen.

296. III. PREPOSITIONS GOVERNING THE ACCUSATIVE.

Rule.

Durch, für, ohne, um,
Sonder, gegen, wider,
Schreib' mit Accuſativ[1]
Und nie mit Dativ nieder.

297. *Meaning.*   *Examples.*

Durch, through, by.   Wir kamen auf unſerer Reiſe **durch** einen großen Wald, der **durch** den Feind war verwüſtet worden, we came on our journey *through* a great forest which had been wasted *by* the foe.

Für, for.[2]   Wollen Sie das **für** mich thun? will you do this *for* me?

---

1) Govern the Objective and never the Dative case.
2) For, referring to time, is rendered by auf with Acc.; as, for a day, **auf** einen Tag. The Conjunction *for* is in German **denn.**

Ohne **ſonder** (poetical and in a few phrases),	} without.	**Ohne den** Beiſtand ſeines Freundes wird er es nicht **ſonder** Mühe thun können, *without* the assistance of his friend he will not be able to do it *without* trouble; **ſonder Gleichen**, without equal.
Um, round, about, at, for (for the sake), (with infinitives) in order.		**Um** Mitternacht gingen wir **um das** Lager; um zwei Uhr kehrten wir wieder nach Hauſe zurück, *about* midnight we walked *round* the camp; *at* 2 o'clock we returned home; ich leibe um dich, I suffer for thee (or thy sake).
Gegen, towards *and* against.		Er iſt **gegen dich** ſehr freundlich, he is very friendly *towards* thee.
Wider, against *only*.		Ich habe nichts **gegen** (or **wider**) ihn, I have nothing *against* him.

Observation. The Preposition **gen** *towards* is used in poetry and a few phrases, such as, **gen Himmel**, *towards* heaven, gen Norden, Süden, Oſten, Weſten, *to the* north, south, east, west.

Learn also the following lines of poetry:

Philemon an ſeinen Freund.

Durch dich iſt die Welt mir ſchön, **ohne** dich würd' ich ſie haſſen,
Für dich leb' ich ganz allein, um dich will ich gern erblaſſen,
Gegen dich ſoll kein Verleumder ungeſtraft ſich je vergehn:
Wider dich kein Feind ſich waffnen — ich will dir zur Seite ſtehn.

298. IV. PREPOSITIONS GOVERNING THE DATIVE AND ACCUSATIVE.

An, auf, hinter, in and **neben, über, unter, vor** and **zwiſchen**

govern the *accusative* when a change of place[1] is implied or when they are employed figuratively (cf. note); otherwise the *dative.*

Note. **An** and **vor** require the *dative* sometimes although used in a figurative (*i. e.*, in another than *local*) sense; as, Louiſe hängt ſehr an ihrer Mutter, Louisa is very much attached (hangs on) her mother; das Kind fürchtet ſich vor **dem** Hunde, the child is afraid of the dog.

---

1) *i. e.*, if the object is to be put first *into* the place indicated.

299. *Meaning.* *Examples.*

An, on *or* at, to, in (compare **auf**). Stelle den Stuhl **an die** Wand, **an welcher** der Spiegel hängt, place the chair *to* the wall *on* which the mirror hangs; reich **an** Kindern, rich *in* children.

Auf,[1] on *or upon* (compare **an**). Legen Sie das Buch **auf den** Tisch, **auf welchem** die andern liegen, put the book *on* the table *upon* which the others are lying.
Vertrau **auf** mich, confide *in* me.

Hinter, behind. Gehen wir **hinter die** Mauer, **hinter der** wir vor dem Wind geschützt sind, let us go *behind* the wall, *behind* which we are sheltered from the wind.
Ich kann niemals **hinter** seine wahren Absichten kommen, I can never get *behind (figurative* for, I can never discover) his real intentions.
Er geht **hinter** die Schule, he plays truant.

Neben, beside, next to. Setzen Sie sich **neben** mich, wenn Sie nicht **neben** ihm sitzen wollen, sit down *beside* me, if you will not sit *next to* him.

In, in, into, at. Wir wollen **in die** Stadt gehen, **in der** gestern eine Operngesellschaft angelangt ist, let us go *into* (the) town *in* which an opera-company arrived yesterday.
Er setzt viel Vertrauen **in** sie, he puts much trust *in* them.

Über, over, above, about. Legen Sie den Mantel **über die** Stuhllehne, **über der** mein Rock liegt, put the cloak *over* the back of the chair *over* which my coat lies.
Über eine halbe Stunde war **über** diesen Wortwechsel verstrichen, *above* half an hour had been spent *over* this altercation.
Wie denken Sie **über** diese Sache, what do you think *about* this matter.

---

1) **Auf — zu,** *towards*. These two Prepositions often occur connected having the meaning of *towards,* or, *in the direction of,* governing the accusative, the case being placed between them; as, ich sah ihn **auf** mich **zu** kommen, I saw him coming *towards* me; das Mädchen ging gerade **auf** das Häuschen **zu,** the girl went straight *towards* the little house.

Unter, under *or among* (compare **zwischen**).	Er ging **unter die** Soldaten, um **unter der** Fahne des Königs zu dienen, he enlisted *among* the soldiers to serve *under* the colours of the king.
Vor, before (in front of), ago,[1] *sometimes* it also means *against*; when used with reference to time it signifies the period *before* the time mentioned (comp. **seit**).	Komm, laß uns **vor** das Thor gehen und zwar noch **vor dem** Untergang der Sonne; ich habe sie **vor** einem Jahr zum letzten Mal untergehen sehen, come, let us go (*before* the gate) out of town, *before* the setting of the sun; I have seen it set for the last time a year *ago*.
Zwischen, under *or between*.	Er drängte sich **zwischen** die beiden Freunde und zerstörte den Bund, der **zwischen** ihnen seit Jahren bestanden hatte, he intruded *between* the two friends and destroyed the union that had existed *between* them for years.

Learn also the following lines of poetry:

An den Mond.

Auf dich blicket, auf dir weilet oft mein Aug' in süßer Lust,
An dir haft' ich, an dich send' ich manch Gefühl aus froher Brust;
In dich setzet, in dir findet meine Phantasie viel Scenen,
Unter die sie gern sich träumet, **unter** denen dort die schönen
Seelen, **über** diese Erd' erhöhet, **über** Gräbern wandeln!
Vor mich tritt dann, **vor** mir steht dann der Entschluß, recht gut zu
handeln.
Zwischen diesen Sträuchern sitz' ich, **zwischen** sie stiehlt sich dein Strahl,
Neben mich sinkt, **neben** mir ruht sie, die Freundinn meiner Wahl!
Hinter mich still hingeschlichen, stand sie lachend **hinter** mir,
Und wir reden von den Sternen, unsern Lieben und von dir.

300. *Observation.* In order to give emphasis to prepositions, particles, composed of the preposition and one of the adverbs **her** or **hin**, are employed; as, die Katze lief **auf** einen Baum **hinauf**, the cat ran *up* a tree. Wir gingen gerade **durch** den Garten **hindurch**, we walked straight *through* the garden. Kommen Sie **an** den Tisch **heran**, come *up to* the table. Sie ging zur Thür **hinaus**, er schaute zum Fenster **herein**, she went *out of* the door, he looked *in at* the window.

---

1) When *ago* is used as an Adverb, it must be rendered in German by **her**; *e. g.*, Es ist sechs Monat **her**, daß ich Sie nicht gesehen habe, it is six months *ago*, that I saw you the last time; *but*, we departed six months *ago*, wir sind **vor** sechs Monat(en) abgereist.

THE CONJUNCTION.
Das Bindewort.

301. The Conjunction is that part of speech which serves to connect sentences.

302. Conjunctions may be *simple* or *compound* words, and are of course indeclinable. They are best arranged in two Classes, viz.: Conjunctions which are mere connecting links and do not influence the construction of the sentence; and Conjunctions which make the phrase *dependent* on another and in German require the Verb *at the end*. (Compare Syntax, Construction of Sentences.)

303. a. **The first Class** (those which do not influence the construction), contains the following Conjunctions:

a. **und**, *and*, **oder**, *or*, **aber**,[1] **allein**,[2] **doch**,[3] **sondern**,[4] *but*, **denn**, *for*.

---

1) **aber** may, like *autem* in Latin, follow the verb; as, es ist aber nicht recht!

2) **allein** when used adverbially, meaning *alone*, requires the Verb after it, when at the beginning of the phrase.

3) **doch** often occurs at the beginning of a sentence as an Adverb, meaning *yet* or *nevertheless* etc.; in that case it must be followed by the Verb, unless it be taken in an *exclamatory sense*, when it does not influence the construction and should be separated from the following sentence by a comma; in the latter case its character ought to be indicated in reading by a short pause.

4) **sondern** is used to translate *but*, when it introduces a sentence which is to be a correction of a negatived statement contained in the preceding, and thus marks a strong contrast; *e. g.*: Der Mann ist nicht todt, sondern er lebet, the man is *not* dead, *but* he liveth. Wir werden nicht gehen, sondern fahren, we are *not* going to walk, *but* to drive, On the other hand, however, sondern would be applied incorrectly, if connecting two sentences the first of which contains a correct statement, though in the negative; as: Dieser Schüler ist nicht sehr begabt, aber er ist sehr fleißig, this scholar is *not* very well gifted, *but* he is very diligent.

b. the following double Conjunctions also may be joined to this list; ſowohl — als auch, *as well — as*, entweder⁵ — oder, *either — or*, weder — noch, *neither — nor*, nicht — vielmehr, *not — but rather*.

b. **The second Class** contains the following Conjunctions:

a. expressing *time*: als, da, *when, as* (referring to the *past*); wenn, *when*, (whenever); indem,⁶ *while* (*not* during the time); während, *while* (during the time); nachdem, *after*⁷; ſo bald (als), ſowie, *as soon as*; ſo lange (als), *as long as*; ehe, *before*; ſeit, ſeitdem, *since*; bis, *till*.

b. expressing *purpose*: daß,⁸ *that*, damit, *in order that*.

c. expressing *cause*: weil, *because*; da, nun, *as, since*.

d. expressing *condition* or *choice*: wenn,⁹ *if*; falls, wofern, *in case*; wenn anders, *provided*; wo nicht, *if not*; (wo, *if*, as well as ſo, *if* are obsolete), ob,⁹ *if* or *whether*.

e. expressing *manner*: wie, *as* (used with a comparison of equality); als ob,⁹ als wenn,⁹ *as if*; ſo daß, *so that*.

f. expressing *concession*: obgleich,⁹ obſchon, obwohl, wiewohl, ob⁹ — (subject) auch, wenngleich,⁹ wennſchon, wenn — (subject intervening) auch, *although*; (obgleich, obſchon, wenngleich,

---

5) entweder may also be used *adverbially*. then it must be followed by the Verb.

6) indem and its Verb is often rendered in English by the *Present Participle*. (Compare the Rules about the Participles in the Syntax.)

7) nachdem should only be used for *after* and *when*, if the Verb following nachdem expresses an action already past at the time when the action mentioned in the principal sentence took place; it therefore can only be used with the Pluperfect tense; *e. g.*: Nachdem wir unſere Arbeiten beendigt hatten, gingen wir ſpazieren, *after* we had finished our tasks, we went for a walk.

8) daß may be left out, as in English, if the phrase which it is to introduce does not need emphasis; whenever it is omitted, the sentence is no longer dependent but independent as regards its construction in German, *i. e.*, the Verb takes the second place, whilst in the sentence with daß the Verb should be at the end.

9) wenn and ob may be left out (as is sometimes the case in English) and the Verb placed at the beginning of the phrase; *e. g.*: Wäreſt du hier geweſen, instead of, wenn du hier geweſen wäreſt, *hadst* thou been here, for, *if* thou hadst been here. Haſt du es gethan oder nicht, gleichviel — instead of, ob du es gethan haſt oder nicht, gleichviel, if (whether) you have done it or not, nevertheless —.

wenn ſchon, may also be used us two words, the first as Conjnnction, the second as Adverb; obgleich er nicht mehr ſehen kann —, may be expressed, **ob** er **gleich** nicht mehr ſehen kann — *although* he can see no longer; see also Note 9), **ſo — auch**, or **wie auch** ..., **ſo — doch**, *however — yet*; e. g.: **ſo ſchwer es ihm auch wurde, ſo that er es doch**, *however* difficult it was for him, *yet* he did it; **ſo viele Freunde er auch haben mag, ſo iſt er doch nicht glücklich**, *however* many friends he may have, *yet* he is not happy.

g. expressing *comparison*: **je — deſto**, or **je — um ſo**, less correct **je — je**, *the — the*; e. g., **je mehr er hat, deſto** (or **um ſo**) **mehr will er haben**, *the* more he has, *the* more he wants.

304. It must be kept in mind that, in addition to these two classes of real Conjunctions many Adverbs may be used as Conjunctions, such as, **mithin**, *consequently*, **daher**, *therefore* etc. Of all *adverbial Conjunctions*, however, only the *Adverbs* **wann**, *when*, **warum**, **weswegen**, *why*, **wie**, *how*, **wo**, *where*, **woher**, *whence*, **wohin**, *whither*, have acquired the force of Conjunctions when used in an *indirect interrogative* or *relative* sense; e. g.: **Wiſſen Sie, wie Sie das am beſten lernen können**, do you know, *how* you can learn that best? **Sagen Sie mir doch, wo Sie dieſe ſchönen Bücher gekauft haben,** tell me, please, *where* you have bought these beautiful books. **Das iſt das Haus, wo ich Sie gekauft habe,** that is the house *where* I have bought them.

In case another Conjunction precedes, as, **als wenn, als ob**, *as if*, this Conjunction keeps the first and the Verb takes the second place; e. g.: **Es iſt, als hätte Niemand etwas Anderes zu thun**, instead of: **es iſt, als ob Niemand etwas Anderes zu thun hätte**, *as if* nobody had to do any thing else. When followed by one of the Adverbs **gleich, ſchon, auch**, the same construction may be used, but the Adverb must follow the Verb; e. g., **obgleich** or **obſchon er reich iſt**, or: **wenn er auch reich iſt, ſo hat er doch keine Freunde**, may be changed into: **iſt er gleich reich**, or: **iſt er ſchon reich**, or: **iſt er auch reich, ſo hat er doch keine Freunde**, *although* he is rich, he has no friends.

THE INTERJECTION.
Das Empfindungswort.

305. The Interjection is that part of speech which expresses abruptly and shortly an emotion principally of pleasure or displeasure, or serves, when an imitation of sound, to render the sentence more expressive and natural. Interjections as well as other words used as an exclamation do not influence the construction of the sentence.

306. There are two Classes of Interjections, firstly such as express an *inner motion*, secondly such as are *imitations of sound*.

The most important of the *first class* are the following:

Used to express *joy* or *pleasure*: ah! ha! ach! hurrah! juchhe! heisa! *grief* or *sorrow*: ach! oh! o weh! *bodily pain*: au! oh! *disgust*: pfui! fi! *horror*: hu, hu! expressing the *wish for silence*: scht! st! st! used *to stop a person*: he! holla; heda! pst! halt!

307. The most important of the *second class* are the following:

Imitating *swiftness*: husch, husch! imitating a *fall*: bauz! imitating a *crack*: knacks! imitating the *report of fire arms*: piff! paff! puff! imitating the sound of a *bell*: klinglingling!

Exclamations like Wohl! *well!* Weh! *wo!* Heil! *hail!* Gottlob! *god be praised!* Bravo! *well done*, should not be called Interjections, since they express a plain, distinct idea.

THE SYNTAX. Die Satzlehre.

CONSTRUCTION OF SENTENCES.
Satzbildung.

308. The Construction of Sentences in the German language, though differing from the English, is based very much on the same principles. The subjoined rules will be found sufficient for all practical purposes.[1]

THE ORDER OF WORDS.
Wortreihenfolge.

309. The Order of words in which the Germans commonly express themselves is the same as that in which they would act; *i. e., the natural order;* a certain place therefore is assigned to each word, independent of euphony, influenced solely by emphasis. The most common expressions of a period may be arranged under *twelve* heads; the place of others depends on their character or import and is explained further on.

  a) *The order of words in an* **Independent clause** (Hauptsatz).
    1. The Subject.[2]
    2. The Verb[3] (*i. e.*, a *simple* tense or the *auxiliary* Verb in compound tenses).

---

    1) The rules on the construction of sentences as well as all the other rules of the Syntax have been restricted to as few as was compatible with a thorough explanation of the subject. In this part of the Grammar more perhaps, than in any other, practice based upon sound theory is infinitely better, than the study of an elaborate theory *without* practice. Let, however, the pupil be sure thoroughly to master the few rules given here.
    2) See Observation 310.
    3) See Observation 311.

3. The Personal Pronoun (1. Accusative. 2. Dative).[1]
4. The Adverb or adverbial expression of *time*.
5. The Personal Pronoun with a Preposition } (*Indirect Object*); if emphatic 5, 6, and 7, follow 8.
6. The Noun in the Dative
7. The Noun with a Preposition
8. The Noun in the Accusative (*Direct Object*).
9. The Adjective-Attribute to the Subject.
10. The Particle belonging to the Verb.
11. The Participle.
12. The Infinitive.

b) *The order of words in a* **Dependent clause** (Nebenſatz).
1. The Conjunction, or Relative Adverb, or Relative Pronoun.
2. The Subject.
3—12 the same as in independent clause.
13. The Verb[2] (*i. e.*, a *simple* tense or the *auxiliary* Verb in compound tenses).

Observations.

310. In **Independent sentences** *the Subject*, being usually the most important word, occupies *the first place;* however, *any* expression or even *a dependent clause* may be placed at the beginning of a period, to increase its importance and emphasis. (Compare 311).

311. *a)* As will appear from the order of words (Rule 309 *a* and *b*) **the Verb**, *i. e.*, a *simple* tense or the *Auxiliary* in compound tenses, **has the second place in independent sentences** only; this place, moreover, it must maintain, *whatever* be *the first* expression, whether it be the *Subject*, the *Object*, an *Adverb* or even a *dependent clause* (compare 312).

b) The Verb must stand **at the end in all dependent clauses;** however, if a dependent clause contains one or more Infinitives or one or more Participles not connected by und, the Verb is generally placed before them.

---

1) In dependent clauses the Pers. Pron. mostly precedes the Subst.; as, wenn ihn ſein Vater geſehen hätte; als ob ihm der Muth dazu fehlte.

c) In direct **Imperative**[1] **sentences** and in direct **Interrogative sentences** not introduced by a Pronoun or Adverb and in **Optative sentences**, the Verb stands **first**; but in all *indirect* Imperative and *indirect* Interrogative sentences it must be *last*, because they are dependent.

d) The Conjunctions mentioned in Rule 302 do not influence the order of words; such clauses are called **co-ordinate** (Beisatz).

e) The Conjunctions wenn and ob *if, whether*, may be left out, and then the Verb is placed at the *beginning* of the phrase (see note 9 to Rule 303 *d.*)

312. In **Inverted sentences**, *i. e.* in sentences in which the dependent clause precedes the independent, the Adverb so is frequently used in order to restore, to some extent, the emphasis of which the independent phrase is deprived, by being placed after the dependent.

313. a. *Adverbs* other than Adverbs *of time*, precede the word they qualify; when the whole phrase is qualified the Adverb stands last.

b. The *Negative* nicht, following the rule of other Adverbs, *precedes the word* that is *negatived*, but if the whole phrase is negatived it stands *at the end;* yet, it can never stand before the Verb Nr. 2, nor after Nrs. 9, 10, 11 and 12 in the order of words (309).

314. In dependent clauses the personal pronoun as object generally precedes the noun as subject (cf. note 1, p. 155).

315. *Incomplete phrases* or expressions that have too much emphasis and independence, to be inserted in the main clause, must be connected with the sentence by means of „und zwar" which answers to the English *and that.*

316. *Examples.*

To 309 *a) independent* sentences (verb *second*):

(1) Der Knabe (2) kauft (8) ein Buch.	The boy buys a book.
(1) Der Knabe (2) hat (8) ein Buch (11) gekauft.	The boy has bought a book.
(1) Der Knabe (2) kaufte (3) mir (4) heute (5) bei Ihnen (8) ein Buch.	The boy bought for me a book to-day at your shop.
(1) Der Knabe (2) wird (4) heute (5) für mich (7) beim Buchhändler (8) ein Buch (12) kaufen.	The boy will buy a book for me to-day at the bookseller's.

---

1) Compare Note to Rule 358.

(1) Wir (2) würden (4) gestern (5) mit euch (10) aus(11)gegangen (12) sein, wenn ꝛc.
We should have gone out with you yesterday, if etc.

(1) Der Diener (2) ist (6) seinem Herrn (9) treu.
The servant is faithful to his master.

(1) Der Diener (2) würde (R. 313) auch (4) heute (6) seinem Herrn (9) treu (11) geblieben (12) sein, wenn ꝛc.
The servant would have remained faithful to his master also to-day, if etc.

b) the same phrases as *dependent* clauses (verb *at the end*):

Wenn der Knabe ein Buch kauft.
If the boy buys a book.

Ob der Knabe ein Buch gekauft hat.
If the boy has bought a book.

Als der Knabe mir heute bei Ihnen ein Buch kaufte.
When the boy bought a book for me to-day at your shop.

Sobald (als) der Knabe heute für mich beim Buchhändler ein Buch kaufen wird.
As soon as the boy will buy for me a book at the bookseller's.

Obgleich wir gestern mit euch ausgegangen sein würden.
Although we should have gone out with you yesterday.

Ob der Diener seinem Herrn treu ist.
Whether the servant is faithful to his master.

Obwohl der Diener auch heute seinem Herrn treu geblieben sein würde.
Although the servant would have remained faithful to his master also to-day.

To 310. *Independent* phrases, showing *what expression* may be *first*.

Subject first: **Die neue Sängerin** *(Auxiliary Verb)* hat *(Adverb of time)* gestern *(Adverb qualifying Verb)* sehr schön *(Perfect Participle)* gesungen, *the new singer* sang very beautifully yesterday.

Adverb of time first: **Gestern** hat die neue Sängerin sehr schön gesungen, *yesterday* the new singer sang very beautifully.

Adverb qualifying the Verb first: **Sehr schön** hat die neue Sängerin gestern gesungen, *very beautifully* did the new singer sing yesterday.

Past Participle first: **Gesungen** hat die neue Sängerin gestern sehr schön, the new singer *sang* yesterday very beautifully.

Verb used impersonally and first: **Es hat** die neue Sängerin gestern sehr schön gesungen, the new singer *sang indeed* very beautifully yesterday.

Note. From the last example it will be seen that, to make the Verb itself emphatic, it is placed at the front with the impersonal Pronoun **es** before it. This Construction may be used, whether the Verb is in the Singular or in the Plural and is much employed by poets. (Compare Rule 261.) In prose it is more common instead to employ the Infinitive with thun for the Present, and the Past Part. with sein or haben for the Past. Compare page 176, note.

To 311a. *Independent* phrases, the Verb in the *second* place. The examples to 310 are illustrations also of this rule, since it may be seen from them, that the Verb in all variations keeps the *second place;* to illustrate a case in which the *dependent clause precedes*, it suffices to employ one instead of the Adverb, which would necessitate the Verb to stand immediately behind it; as:

Dependent clause first: Ehe die Nacht a n gebrochen war, **hat** (Verb *second* expression) die neue Sängerin sehr schön gesungen, *before the night had commenced*, the new singer sang very beautifully.

To 311b. *Dependent* phrases, Verb *at the end.*

Daß Sie es nicht absichtlich gethan **haben**, glaube ich, that you *have* not done it purposely, I believe.

Derjenige, welcher Muth und Kraft **hat**, siegt, he who *has* courage and strength, conquers.

(*Two Infinitives without* und)

Sie gab mir einen Fisch zum Abendbrod, nachdem sie ihn **hatte** zu bereiten lassen, she gave me a fish for supper, after she *had* got it prepared.

(*Two Participles without* und)

Wer weiß es nicht, daß er zu allen Zeiten **ist** von seinen Genossen beneidet worden, or, beneidet worden **ist**, who does not know (it), that he *has* ever been envied by his companions.

To 311c. *Imperative, Optative* and *Interrogative* Phrases.

Geben Sie mir ein Glas frisches Wasser, *give* me a glass of cold water!

Gehen wir nach Hause, es ist schon spät! let us go home, it is late.

Käme er doch jetzt zu uns, would he now came to see us.

Hätte ich doch eine Gelegenheit, ihm wohlzuthun, would I had an opportunity to do him good.

Wäre er doch ein wenig fleißiger, would he were a little more diligent.

Wollen Sie mir nicht ein wenig helfen, *will* you not help me a little?

Wo soll ich denn anfangen, where then *shall* I begin?

Wissen Sie noch nicht, wo Sie anfangen **sollen**, do you not yet *know* where to *begin?*

To 312. *Inverted* sentences.

Wenn das mißglücken **sollte**, so bin ich verloren, *if that should fail*, I am lost.

Wenn Sie es **sagen**, so will ich es gern glauben, *if you say so*, I will gladly *believe* it.

To 313 a. *Place of Adverbs* (not of *time*).

Es hat uns bei Ihnen **recht gut** gefallen, we have been enjoying ourselves *very well* at your house (the Verb *enjoying* is qualified).

Er hat **all** sein Geld verspielt, he has lost *all* his money (the *possessive pronoun* sein qualified).

Wir lieben unsere Freunde **sehr**, we love our friends *very much* (the *whole phrase* qualified).

b. *Place* of the *Negative* nicht.

Ich habe so viel Kniffe, sagte der Fuchs, daß die Hunde mich **nicht** fangen können, I have so many tricks, said the fox, that the hounds can*not catch* me (*catch* negatived).

Geben Sie dem Kind **nicht** so viel Zucker, do *not* give (to) the child so much sugar (*so much* negatived).

Das gefällt mir aber von Ihnen **gar nicht**, I do *not* like that of you *at all* (the *whole phrase* negatived).

To 314. Personal Pronoun as *object*, before Noun as *subject*, Wenn dich der Lehrer gelobt hätte, if the master had praised you; obgleich ihm der Schüler bekannt hatte, although the scholar had confessed to him.

AGREEMENT OF WORDS IN NUMBER, GENDER AND CASE.

317. The agreement of Articles and Pronouns with their nouns may be considered analogous in English and German, thus **Articles** and **all conjoined Pronouns** *agree* with the Nouns which they precede *in Number, Gender* and *Case.* **Disjoined Pronouns** *agree* with the Nouns to which they refer *in Gender* and *Number*, but may be in a different case; as: Der Vater, *the father* (both words *masc. nominative sing.*); dieses Mannes, *of this man* (both words *masc. genitive sing.*); jenen Weibern, *to those women* (both words *Dative plural*); but: der Mann, welchen ich kenne, the man (*masc.* nominative *sing.*) whom (*masc.* accusative *sing.*) I know.

Notice the differences in the following:

1. Any pronoun that points to a noun or pronoun in the quality of the predicate must be in the neuter, whether the predicate be in the singular or plural, but the verb agrees with the predicate in number. Ex.:

Es ist mein Vater,	*it is* my father.
Es ist meine Mutter,	*it is* my mother.
Es ist mein Buch,	*it is* my book,
Es sind unsere Väter,	*they are* our fathers.
Es sind unsere Mütter,	*they are* our mothers.
Es sind unsere Bücher,	*they are* our books.
also interrogatively, as:	
ist es mein Vater? ꝛc.	is it my father etc.?
Dies or das ist mein Vater,	*this* or *that* is my father.
Dies or das ist meine Mutter,	*this* or *that* is my mother.
Dies or das ist mein Buch,	*this* or *that* is my book.
Dies or das sind unsere Väter, Mütter, Bücher,	*these* or *those* are our fathers, mothers, books;
also interrogatively, as:	
ist dies or das mein Vater? ꝛc.	is this or that my father etc.?
Welches ist dein Vater?	which is thy father?
Welches ist deine Mutter?	which is thy mother?
Welches ist dein Buch?	which is thy book?
Welches sind eure Väter, Mütter, Bücher?	which are your fathers, mothers, books?

2. The Adjective, when an Epithet, agrees with its noun, as explained above, in rule 173.

3. The following words of quantity are used in the Singular when preceded by numbers; viz., **Fuß, Zoll, Stück, Paar, Pfund, Loth, Quart**, also **Mann** in a military sense and **Grad**, degree. Ex.: Der Feind verlor in der letzten Schlacht 5000 **Mann**, the enemy lost in the last battle 5000 *men*. Mein Freund ist 5 **Fuß**, 8 **Zoll** groß, my friend is 5 *feet* 8 *inches* in height. Gestern wurden 100 **Stück** Rindvieh ausgeschifft, yesterday 100 *heads* of cattle were disembarked. Dieses Brod wiegt 5 **Pfund** und 10 **Loth**, this loaf weighs 5 *pounds* and 5 *ounces*. Kaufen Sie mir 2 **Quart** Milch, buy 2 *quarts* of milk for me. Wir haben 10 **Grad** Kälte, there are 10 *degrees* of cold.

APPOSITION.

318. Nouns, Adjectives and Pronouns *in Apposition* must be in the same number, gender and case; as; Alexander (*nom.*) **der Große** (*nom.*) Alexander *the great*. Der Vater Friedrichs (*gen.*) **des Zweiten** (*gen.*) the father of Frederick *the* second. Die Bevölkerung der britischen Inseln besteht selbst jetzt noch aus zwei verschiedenen Racen (*dat.*), der celtischen (*dat.*), und der germanischen (*dat.*), the

population of the British Islands consists even now of two distinct races, the Celtic and Germanic. Druide soll von Drus (*dat.*) herkommen, dem griechischen Namen (*dat.*) der Eiche (*gen.*), des heiligen Baumes (*gen.*) der Celten, Druid is said to be derived from drus, *the* Greek name of the oak, the sacred tree of the Celts.

THE USE OF THE ARTICLES.

319. The Articles are employed in German nearly the same as in English. The following rules will show where they differ.

1. Nouns taken in an *abstract* and indefinite sense are used *without* an article; nouns used *concretely* and in a definite sense require the *Definite Article*.

2. Before nouns denoting *men, animals, substances* (such as metals, wood, glass, leather, stone), when strictly taken in a definite sense, the *Definite Article* is required, whilst, when taken in an indefinite sense, no article should precede it.

3. The *Definite Article* is used with Infinitives taken substantively.

4. The names of the Seasons, Months and Days require the *Definite Article*, though it is contracted with prepositions whenever a contraction is possible (see rule 48).

5. Th *Indefinite Article* which is used in English in connection with offices, professions, etc., after *to be* and *to become*, is not used in German.

Note. Compare also Rule 144.

Examples.

To 1. *a.* Nouns taken in an *abstract* sense.

Muth ist zu kühnen Unternehmungen nöthig, courage is required for bold enterprises.

Ohne Glauben ist es unmöglich Gott gefallen (*Bible*), without *faith* it is impossible to please God.

Freude hat mir Gott gegeben (*Schiller*), God has given me *joy.*

A. v. Ravensberg, German Grammar. 3rd Ed. 11

b. the same nouns taken in a *concrete* sense.

Ihm fehlt **der Muth** zu kühnen Unternehmungen, he wants (the) courage for bold enterprises.

Der Glaube ist eine gewisse Zuversicht defs, das wir hoffen *(Bible)*, *faith* is the certain expectation of things hoped for.

Die Freude ist dem Menschen Bedürfniß, *joy* is necessary to man.

c. Real *concrete* Nouns.

Der Wein erfreut des Menschen Herz, *wine* rejoices the heart of man.

Das Bier war schon den Alten bekannt, *beer* was even known to the ancients.

Die Milch ist ein gesundes Nahrungsmittel, *milk* is a wholesome food.

To 2. *a.* Names of men, animals, substances, taken in a *definite* sense.

Der Mensch lebt nicht vom Brod allein, *man* lives not by bread alone.

Der Löwe ist der König der Thiere, the *lion* is the king of animals.

Das Wasser ist eine Verbindung von Sauerstoff und Wasserstoff, *water* is a combination of oxygen and hydrogen.

Der Stickstoff, allein eingeathmet, ist tödtlich, *nitrogen* enhaled alone is fatal.

Das Eisen und **das Silber** sind nützliche Metalle, *iron* and *silver* are useful metals.

b. Same kind of nouns used *indefinitely*.

Der Gott, der Eisen wachsen ließ, — *(Arndt)*, that God who caused *iron* to grow, —

Aus **Sand** und **Asche** wird **Glas** gemacht, out of *sand* and *ashes glass* is made.

To 3. Ihm wird **das Schreiben** sehr sauer, *writing* is hard work to him.

Lassen Sie **das Lachen**, stop *laughing*.

Im Suchen nach Reichthümern verlernte er **das Arbeiten**, in *searching* for riches he unlearned how to *work*.

To 4. **Der Sonntag** ist der erste Tag der Woche, *Sunday* is the first day of the week; but: heute ist Sonntag, to-day is Sunday.

Der Januar ist der kälteste Monat im Jahre, *January* is the coldest month of the year.

Der Frühling ist die schönste Jahreszeit, *spring* is the finest season.

Im **Sommer** ist es oft sehr heiß, in *summer* it is often very hot.

Am Montag gehen wir wieder nach der Schule, on *Monday we shall go to school again*.

To 5. Was wollen Sie werden? ich will **Doctor** werden und mein Bruder wird **Soldat**, *what are you going to be? I wish to be a doctor, and my brother will be a soldier*.

320. The Definite Article is used besides instead of the *Possessive Pronoun* when the possessor is clearly understood even *without* the Pronoun: as: Setzen Sie den Hut auf, put on *your* hat. Stecken Sie die Uhr in die Tasche, put *your* watch in *your* pocket.

This is especially done where the *Verb* is *reflective*; as: Ich wasche **mir** die Hände, I wash (*myself the*) my hands.

321. The Definite Article is used lastly, where in English *a* or *per* or *each* is employed; as: Wir gehen zweimal die Woche in's Concert, we go twice *a* week to the concert. Neun Mark die Stunde, 9 mark *a* lesson. Fünfundvierzig Mark das Vierteljahr, 45 mark *per* quarter.

THE GOVERNMENT OF WORDS.

The four cases that occur in German, as has been seen in the Grammar, are the **Nominative** (also called *casus rectus*) which does not depend on another word; the **Genitive, Dative** and **Accusative** (each of them also called *casus obliquus*) which depend on another word or sentence.

I. THE NOMINATIVE.

322. The **Subject**[1] stands in the Nominative case; as, der **Mensch** (*Nom.*) lebt nicht vom Brod allein, *man does not live on bread alone*. Er (*Nom.*) liebt dich, *he loves thee*. Den Sohn liebt der **Vater** (*Nom.*) *the father loves the son*.

323. The **Nominative** should also be used in German in addressing, where in *Latin* stands the *Voca-*

---

[1] The Subject may be easily determined, since it answers to the question *who* or *what?*

tive; as: Ihnen, **mein Herr,** (*Nom.*) folgen wir gern, you, *Sir*, we gladly follow.

Likewise in *Interjections*; as: O, ihr Kleingläubigen, oh *ye* of little faith! O ich Unglücklicher, oh unfortunate man that *I* am!

324. The following *Verbs* require the Nominative: Sein, *to be*, werden,[1] *to become*, bleiben, *to remain*, heißen,[2] *to be called*, scheinen, *to appear*, as well as the *Passive* Voice of the verbs nennen, *to be named*, schelten[2] or schimpfen,[2] *to miscall*.

Examples.

325. Karl ist ein guter Junge (*Nom.*); er wird dereinst wohl auch ein guter Mann (*Nom.*) werden, Charles *is* a good boy, he *will be* one day a good man too.

Wenn Sie mein Freund (*Nom.*) bleiben, werden Sie nicht mein Feind (*Nom.*) scheinen wollen, if you *remain* my friend, you will not wish to *appear* my foe.

Du sollst mein Bruder (*Nom.*) heißen, thou shalt *be called* my brother.

Er wird von seinen Eltern lieber Sohn (*Nom.*) genannt, he is *called* by his parents dear son.

Wilhelm wird von seinen Freunden ein Narr (*Nom.*) gescholten, William is *called* by his friends foolish.

326. The verb sein *with dative* means *to have*; werden with dative *to get*; as: Es ist mir (*Dat.*) genug noch davon im Kasten des Wagens, I *have* still enough of it in the box of the carriage, *Goethe*. Dir (*Dat.*) wird dein Theil schon werden, you will *get* your share, don't fear. Observe also the use of werden with zu: Er wird noch zum Narren werden, he will eventually turn mad.

327. The Verbs heißen, gelten and schimpfen govern the *Accusative*, when used *actively*; as: Er hieß ihn einen guten Mann (*Acc.*), seinen Freund aber schalt er einen Dummkopf (*Acc.*), he *called* him a good man, but his friend he *called* a blockhead.

328. The reason why the Verb scheinen governs the Nominative, must be sought in the fact, that „sein, *to be*" is understood; as, Er scheint ein rechtschaffener Mann (*Nom.*) zu sein, he *seems* (to be) an honest man.

---

1) Compare 319 [5].
2) Compare 327.

II. THE GENITIVE.

329. The use of the Genitive is at present not so frequent as formerly; of two Nouns, standing together, one of them must be put in the Genitive *only* if possession is implied; as: Der Ring des Polykrates, the ring *of* Polykrates; das Dach des Schlosses, the roof *of the* palace; das Glück des Friedens, the blessings *of* peace; this case may be considered identical with the English Possessive; moreover, the same omission of the Article and inversion of order may be practised; as, in meines Vaters Hause sind viele Wohnungen, *in my father's house* are many mansions; which construction is practicable especially when the Noun gets § in the Genitive (see Rules 115 and 143). Besides, some verbs, adjectives and prepositions demand the Genitive, see Nos. 334—338, also 291.

330. Where there is no means of showing the genitive, a preposition (mostly von) must be used, though *possession* is implied; as, die Thaten von Kaisern und Königen, the deeds of emperors and kings; the genitives Kaiser and Könige, being the same as their nominatives, would not show the relation of these words to the preceding nominative; nor could the article be used, as it would alter the sense; however, as soon as an Adjective accompanies the noun, the genitive would at once be used; as, die Thaten großer Kaiser 2c., the deeds of great emperors etc. Die Leiber von Männern, Weibern und Kindern, the bodies of men, women and children; but, die Leiber erschlagener Männer, Weiber und Kinder, the bodies of slain men etc.

331. *Observation.* The Genitive Plural of the Personal Pronouns and of the Demonstrative das precede their Nominative or Accusative; as, es waren ihrer viele Tausend, there were many thousands *of them.*

332. *Words of quantity or measure*, such as, wenig, *little,* viel, *much,* Pfund, *pound,* Glas, *glass* etc., when not preceded by an article or pronoun, are but rarely followed by the genitive at present; as: Sie haben **wenig** Geduld, aber **viel** Muth, you have *little* patience, but *much* courage. Geben Sie mir ein **Pfund** Erdbeeren, ein **Glas** Wein und ein **wenig** Zucker, give me a *pound of* strawberries, a *glass of* wine and a *little* sugar. When, however, *preceded* by an *article* or *pronoun*, the **Genitive** or the Preposition **von** is used; as: Ein Pfund **von** diesem Obst, a *pound* of *this* fruit. Eine **Anzahl** dieser Menschen (Gen.), a *number* of *these* men. *Poetical:* Zu **viel** des Wassers hast du, arme Schwester, too *much* of water hast thou, my poor sister. *Hamlet.*

333. When the noun that follows the word of quantity, is *preceded* by an *adjective*, the **Genitive** or the **Nominative** or Accusative — if Object — may be employed; as: Holen Sie mir eine **Flasche** rothe Tinte (*Acc.*) or, rother Tinte (*Gen.*) get me a *bottle* of red ink.

Observation. From the above it will appear, that in English *of*, following words of quantity, is mostly not translated in German; it should, however, be rendered by a **Preposition** if it *refers* to a *Verb*; as, a yard *of* this cloth, *i. e.*, cut or *taken of* this cloth: eine Elle **von** diesem Tuch; a story *of* a fox, *i. e.*, a story *told* of a fox: eine Geschichte **von** einem Fuchse; whilst, when *of* refers to a *Noun* and implies possession, it is the sign of the *Genitive*; as, the house *of* your father, *i. e.*, your *father's* house: das Haus Ihres Vaters, or, Ihres Vaters Haus.

334. The number of **Verbs** which govern the **Genitive** is pretty large, the student, however, need only learn those which have been marked in the list with an asterisk, since the others have the same government in English, and for other reasons specified in the notes. They are:

335. (a.) *Neuter Verbs:*

Achten, to mind (when it signifies *to esteem*, it governs the *Accusative*),
bedürfen, to need,
begehren, to desire,
brauchen, to require,
entrathen, to dispense with,
entbehren, to do without,

erwähnen, to mention,
genießen, to enjoy,
*gedenken (or an, w. acc.), to remember,
*harren (or auf, w. acc.), to wait for,
*lachen (or über, w. acc.), to laugh at,

pflegen, to nurse,
schonen, to spare,
sein, to be *(to belong)*,
*spotten (or über, w. acc.) to mock,
verfehlen, to fail, to miss,

vergessen, to forget,
wahrnehmen ⎱ to perceive, to
gewahr werden ⎰ become aware of,
warten, to wait for.

Observation. The above Verbs are, however, used more commonly with the *Accusative*, the Genitive being rather poetical, except gedenken, harren, lachen, spotten, which require the genitive or a preposition.

Examples: Jetzt spotten Sie **seiner** (or über ihn), aber er harret **der** (or auf die) Zeit, wo er **Ihrer** (or über Sie) lachen kann; gedenken Sie **dessen** (or daran), just now you mock *at him*, but he waits *for the* time, when he can laugh *at you;* remember *that.*

336. (b.) *Reflective Verbs* having the reflective pronoun in the accusative:

*Sich a n nehmen, to interest one's self for,
 „ bedienen, to make use *of*,
* „ befleißen, to apply one's self to,
* „ begeben, to give up,
 „ bemächtigen ⎱ to take pos-
 „ bemeistern ⎰ session *of*,
* „ bescheiden, to resign, to submit,
* „ besinnen (or auf, w. acc.), to recollect, to consider,
 „ entäußern, to divest one's self *of*,
* „ enthalten, to abstain from,
* „ entschlagen, to dismiss,
* „ entsinnen, to recollect,

*sich erinnern, to remember,
* „ erbarmen (or über, w. acc.), to take pity in,
* „ erwehren, to defend one's self,
* „ freuen or erfreuen, to rejoice at (or über, w. acc.),
 „ rühmen, to boast of (or mit, w. dat.),
 „ schämen, to be ashamed of (or über, w. acc.),
* „ unterfangen ⎫
* „ unterwinden ⎬ to dare,
* „ vermessen ⎪
* „ erkühnen ⎭
* „ versehen, to expect, to be prepared for,
* „ weigern, to refuse.

Examples: Ihr Freund bedient sich unseres Beistandes, wenn sich kein Anderer seiner annimmt, your friend makes use *of* our assistance, when no one else interests himself *for* him. Seine Freunde müssen sich seiner (or über ihn) erbarmen, obgleich sie sich seiner (or über seine) Ausschweifungen schämen, his friends must take pity *on him,* although they are ashamed *of* his extravagance.

337. (c.) The following is a list of the *transitive* Verbs which govern *two* cases, one of a *person*, one of a *thing*, the former in the *Accusative* and the latter in the *Genitive;* viz.:

Anklagen, to accuse,
berauben, to bereave, to deprive,
*beschuldigen, to impute, to charge,
entbinden } to release, to deliver.
entledigen }
entblößen } to divest, to deprive,
entkleiden }
entladen, to relieve,
*entlassen, to dismiss from,
*entsetzen, to discharge, to dismiss from,
*entwöhnen, to wean, to get *off* a habit,
überführen } to convince,
überzeugen }
*überheben, to spare, to save (trouble),
versichern, to assure,
verweisen (des Landes), to banish, (the country),
*würdigen, to deign,
zeihen, to accuse.

Example: Man beschuldigte den General des Verrathes, da man ihn aber der That *(Gen.)* nicht überführen (konnte), er sich hingegen auch der Schuld nicht entladen konnte, so wurde er seines Amtes entsetzt und des Dienstes entlassen, they accused the general *of* treason, but as they could not convict him *of the* deed, and as he, on the other hand, could not relieve himself *of the* guilt, he was discharged *from* office and dismissed *(from) the* service.

338. The following adjectives and adverbs govern the *Genitive*, those marked with a cross (†) are used with the *genitive* or *accusative* indifferently; viz.:

ansichtig (werden), to get a sight of,
bedürftig } in want of,
benöthigt }
bewusst, conscious of,
eingedenk, remembering, mindful of,
fähig, capable of,
*froh (werden), to be enjoying,
†gewahr (werden), (to become) aware of,
*gewärtig, expecting,
gewiss, certain,
*gewohnt, accustomed to,
habhaft (werden), (to get) hold of,
*hinsichtlich } regarding,
*rücksichtlich }
*kundig, acquainted with, skilled in,
†los, rid,
mächtig, master of,
milde }
satt } tired of, sick of,
überdrüssig }
schuldig, guilty of,
sicher, sure, certain of,
*theilhaft } partaking in,
*theilhaftig }
verdächtig, suspected of,
*verlustig, forfeited,
†voll, full of,
*werth, worth,
würdig, worthy of.

Examples. Der Mensch wird seines Lebens selten **froh**, immer muss er des Unglücks **gewärtig** sein; nur der Weise wird des wahren Glückes **theilhaftig**, man rarely *enjoys* his life, he must ever be *expecting* misfortune, only the wise *partakes of* real happiness.

339. Though Nouns used *adverbially* stand in the *Accusative*, — the *Genitive* is used to mark the adverbial import of some Nouns, as: Des Tages or eines Tages, by *or* one day, des Nachts or eines Nachts,[1] at night *or* one night, etc.; also, stehenden Fußes, immediately;[2] meines Wissens, to my knowledge; gerades Wegs, straightways, aller Orten, everywhere etc.; comp. Rule 352.

Note. This, of course, does not prevent the use of other expressions, such as, bei Tage, bei Nacht, sogleich, überall.

III. THE DATIVE.

340. The Dative is that case which marks the person or thing *to whom* or *which* something *is given* or *done* (either beneficial or injurious); it is consequently the *indirect Object*, and may simply be designated as the *person concerned*. Although the „*person concerned*" or interested in the action is usually in the Dative in English as well as in German, yet, in the former the Possessive (v. 347) or Prepositions with the Objective Case are very common instead of the Dative in German.

Examples.

Er hat seinem Bruder das Buch gegeben, welches er Ihrem Freund genommen hatte, he has given the book to his brother (person concerned) which he had taken from your friend (person concerned).

Ich habe Ihnen *(Dat.)* ein Buch gekauft, I have bought *you* (person concerned) a book.

Er hat mir *(Dat.)* ein Geschenk gemacht, he has made *me* (person concerned) a present.

Ich werde Ihnen *(Dat.)* das machen, I will do that *for you* (person concerned).

Er hat dir was mitgebracht, he has brought something *for you*.

Es war ein Mann, dem *(Dat.)* starb seine Frau, there was a man (to him, person concerned) *whose* wife died. *Grimm.*

Sie hängte es dem armen Mädchen *(Dat.)* auf die Schulter, she hung it on the poor maiden's (person concerned) shoulder.

---

1) This expression is remarkable, since Nacht is *fem.*
2) Compare the Latin *stante pede.*

The following paragraphs (341 — 348) contain some particulars:

341. The following *Verbs* govern the *Dative:*[1]

*Antworten, to answer,
*begegnen, to meet,
behagen, to give pleasure,
*danken, to thank,
*dienen, to serve,
*drohen, to threaten,
*entfahren, to slip, as well as most other Verbs in which ent- signifies *away*,
*entsagen, to renounce,
entsprechen, to correspond to,
erliegen ⎱ to succumb,
unterliegen ⎰
*fehlen, to fail, to ail,
*fluchen, to curse,
*folgen, to follow,
*fröhnen, to indulge in,
*gefallen, to please,
*gehorchen, to obey,
*genügen, to satisfy,
glauben, to believe,
*gleichen, to resemble,
*helfen, to help,
*leuchten, to light,
nehmen, to take,
*schaden, to hurt,
*schmeicheln, to flatter,
*steuern, to steer, to put a stop to,
*trauen, to trust,
*trotzen, to defy,
*wehren, to defend, prevent,
*widersprechen, to contradict,
*widerstehen, to resist,
willfahren, to give in to, comply;

and a number of other verbs which are in English also followed by the Dative.

Examples: **Antworten** Sie (mir), und **trotzen** Sie mir nicht länger, *answer* me and *defy* me no longer. Wir sollen unsern Feinden nicht **fluchen**, sondern ihnen **helfen** und **dienen**, wo wir ihnen **begegnen**, we shall not *curse* our foes, but *help* and *serve* them, wherever we *meet* them.

342. Quasi-Compound Verbs (272), consisting of a *preposition* and a *verb*, with *emphasis* on the preposition *as particle*, generally govern the *Dative* if the same words, constituting the verb, are also used with a different meaning as *Preposition* and Verb, with emphasis on the *Verb*; as, **aufwarten**, *to wait upon*, *to call on*, governs the *Dative*; but, auf (*Preposition*) **warten**, to *wait* for: **vorstellen** *to fancy*, *to represent*, governs the Dative; but, vor (*Preposition*) **stellen**, to *place* before. *Examples:* Wir wollten gestern deinem Vater **aufwarten**,

---

1) It is recommended to learn the verbs with „einem" prefixed, as, einem antworten, to answer one, which would assist in impressing the government of each verb on the memory.

aber wie lange wir **auf** ihn warten mußten, kannst du **dir** gar nicht **vorstellen**; wir brachten **ihm** ein Geschenk **mit**, welches wir **vor** ihn **hinstellten**, we yesterday *waited on* your father, but how long we had to wait *for* him, you cannot *fancy*; we *brought with* us a present for him, which we placed *before* him.

Observe. The lists of the *Impersonal* and *Reflective Verbs* that govern the Dative, also the list of *Prepositions* with that case have been given in the Grammar (Rules 263-268 and 293); compare also 326.

343. With a few verbs sometimes the *Dative* and sometimes a *Preposition* must be used; the *dative* is required if the action expressed in the verb in any way tends or is intented to benefit, injure or interest the *person concerned*, otherwise a *preposition* is needed.

Sagen, (*to say*) *to tell*, requires the *dative*, or zu with dative.

Examples: Dein Freund sagte zu seinem Bruder Karl: „was sagte er dir in's Ohr?" er aber sagte es ihm nicht, your friend said to his brother Charles: „what did he tell you (or *say* to you) in a whisper?" but he did not tell him (not *say*).

Schicken, *to send* and **schreiben,** *to write*, require the *Dative*, or the *Prepositions* zu and an.

Examples: Ich schickte ihm einen Brief, um ihn zu trösten, I sent *to him* a letter, to comfort him (thus the letter was for the benefit of the receiver); but, ich schickte einen Boten an ihn (or zu ihm), um zu hören, wie er sich befände, I sent a messenger *to* him, to hear how he was doing (done for the information of the sender). Ich schrieb ihm einen Aufsatz, I wrote an essay *for* him, (for the *receiver's* benefit); but, ich habe an ihn geschrieben, um zu erfahren, wie ich den Aufsatz machen soll, I have written *to* him, to learn how I am to do the essay (for the *sender's* benefit).

Gehören, *to belong*, naturally when referring to a *person*, requires the *dative*, but the preposition zu is needed when referring to *a thing*.

Examples: Jenes Haus gehört meinem Freunde; dieser Garten gehört indeß nicht zu seinem Hause, sondern zu dem seines Nachbars, that house belongs *to* my friend; this garden, however, does not belong *to* his house but *to* that of his neighbour.

344. Some Verbs may be used with the *Dative* or *Accusative* indifferently; viz., heißen, *to bid, to command.* lehren[1] *to teach.* kosten *to cost.*

345. Versichern, *to assure,*[2] takes the *person* in the Dative and the *thing* in the Accusative; however, it may also be used with the person in the *Accusative* and the thing in the *Genitive*; as: Versichern Sie Ihrem Freunde meine Hochachtung (*Acc.*), or Versichern Sie Ihren Freund meiner Hochachtung (*Gen.*).

346. All *Adjectives* that refer to a *person* and allow of the question *to whom?* govern the **Dative**; as, treu, faithful *to,* gewogen, favourable *to,* etc. This class of words is very large, but does not require to be quoted here, since the same words govern the Dative in English also.

Examples: Er ist seinem Freunde treu und ergeben, dieser ist auch ihm von Herzen gewogen, he is *faithful* and *devoted* to his friend, who is *well disposed to* him in return.

Observation. These Adjectives are followed by a **Preposition** (and not by the *Dative*) if they refer to a *thing* and allow of the question *to* or *for what?* as: Dieses Papier ist nicht gut genug für mein Buch, this paper is not good enough *for* my book; but, dieses Papier ist mir nicht gut genug, this paper is not good enough *for me* (the *person concerned*). Compare 340.

347. The Dative of a Noun or Personal Pronoun is used in German frequently instead of the *Possessive Pronoun* or *Case*; as, bei dieser Nachricht entsank ihm der Muth, at this news *his* courage failed him; ich habe mir den Fuß beschädigt, I have hurt *my* foot; er fiel dem König zu Füßen, he fell to the feet *of the* king; er hat seinem Bruder das Leben gerettet, he has saved *his* brother's life.

---

1) lehren, *to teach* is used with both cases correctly only, if it is connected *with two objects,* one of the person and one of the *thing*; as: Ich lehre Sie or Ihnen die deutsche Sprache, I teach *you* the German language; it *must* be followed by the Accusative, if it has *one* only; as: Ich lehre die Kinder, I teach the children, or ich lehre die deutsche Sprache, I teach the German language.

2) versichern, *to insure,* governs the *Accusative.*

348. *Ethic Dative* (*Dativus ethicus*). **The Dative of Personal Pronouns** of the first and second persons often occurs in German in the sense of a particle, such as wohl, ja; in this character it expresses the interest, concern, fear of the speaker or an assurance to the person addressed; in this form, it naturally allows, like Particles, of manifold translations; it occurs principally in colloquial style.

Examples: Daß du mir das nicht nochmal thust, don't do that again, *I tell you.* Spielen soll sie mir am Clavier—, she shall play on the piano, *I tell you—. Goethe.*

The *Ethic Dative* is often a mere repetition, only there for the sake of euphony or emphasis; as: Und ein solcher, ich fürchte, wird Hermann immer **mir** bleiben, and such a one, *I fear*, Hermann will ever remain, *Goethe*, in which sentence **mir** is a repetition of ich fürchte.

IV. THE ACCUSATIVE.

349. The *Direct Object* of a sentence, *i. e.*, the word which answers to the question *whom?* or *what?* stands in the **Accusative** case. Ex.: Der Vater liebt den Sohn, the father loves (whom?) *the son* (*acc.*). Ich habe einen schlimmen Fuß, I have a sore foot (*acc.*).

350. All *transitive* verbs govern the **Accusative,** also all *reflective* and *impersonal* verbs, with the exception of those given in rules 263 and 268 which govern the *Dative.* Compare also 327.

351. Nouns used *adverbially* stand in the **Accusative;** as: Ich habe Sie heute den ganzen Tag noch nicht gesehen, I have not seen you *this whole day.* Diese Bank ist nur einen Fuß breit, this form is only *one foot* broad.

352. *Exceptions:* a) A few nouns stand, when used adverbially, in the *genitive* instead of the accusative (see Rule 339).

b) When nouns, used adverbially, are preceded by an adjective, a *preposition* is employed more frequently than the accusative; as: An einem heißen Tage legte sich ein Fuchs —, *on a hot* day a fox lay —. Am nächsten Morgen, or den nächsten Morgen gingen wir —, the *next* morning we went —.

Observe. The list of the *Prepositions* that govern the Accusative, and of those that govern the Accusative *and* Dative is given in the Grammar. (Rules 296 and 298.)

THE USE OF THE VERB.
A. Agreement.

353. The Verb must always *agree* in Number and Person with the noun or pronoun which precedes it; as, ich lobe, *I praise*, ich 1st pers. sing., lobe 1st pers. sing.); der Vater befiehlt, *the father commands*, (der Vater 3rd pers. sing., befiehlt 3rd pers. sing.); ihr geht, *you go*, (ihr 2nd pers. plur., geht 2nd pers plur.); meine Freunde schlafen, *my friends sleep*, (meine Freunde 3rd pers. plur., schlafen 3rd pers. plur.).

354. There are only two cases which deviate from this rule, viz.:

a) If the verb refers to *two* or *more* Nouns each of which is in the singular, it also *may* be used in the Singular: as, dein Muth und dein Vertrauen sind or ist sehr groß, thy courage and confidence *are* very great.

b) If a verb, that is not an *impersonal* proper, is used impersonally, it requires the pronoun es, but the verb must be in the *Plural* if it refers to a *plural noun*; as, die Eltern lieben ihre Kinder, construed *impersonally*: es lieben (plural) die Eltern ihre Kinder, parents love their children.

355. *Observations.*

1. Collective nouns which often in English have the verb in the *plural*, are used with the plural in German only if they themselves are in the plural; as, das Volk (Sing.) liebt (Sing.) die Freiheit, the people *love* freedom; but, die Völker (Plur.) lieben (*plur.*) die Freiheit, nations love freedom.

2. In phrases where the 1st or 2nd Person of a Personal Pronoun, is followed by a relative pronoun, the verb stands in the *third* person, agreeing with the *relative*, unless the personal pronoun be *repeated* after the relative pronoun, then the verb must agree with them also in person; e. g., ich, der das gethan hat (3rd Pers.); or, ich, der ich das gethan habe (1st Pers.), I, who have done that; du, der das gethan hat (3rd Pers.), or du, der du das gethan hast (2nd Pers.), thou who hast done that.

B. The Use of Auxiliary Verbs.

356. The Auxiliary Verb haben (*to have*), is used to express *completed action*; thus the past tenses of all transitive and reflective verbs are conjugated with it; as, ich habe gesehen, was Sie gemacht haben, I *have* seen what you *have* done; ich habe mich geirrt, I have been mistaken.

357. Sein is used as *auxiliary* with all those *intransitive* verbs which in their past[1] tenses imply a change of some kind or other, or a *coming into existence*; also with bleiben, to remain; gedeihen, to prosper and gelingen, to succeed; as, krank gewesen sein, to have been ill; reich geworden sein, to have become rich (change of state); ausgegangen sein, to have gone out; angekommen sein, to have arrived (change of place); gefallen sein, to have fallen (change of position); gestorben sein, to have died; verwelkt sein, to have withered (change of condition); geschehen sein, to have happened (coming into existence); zurück geblieben sein, to have remained behind; nicht gediehen sein, not to have prospered or flourished; gut gelungen sein, to have well succeeded. All other Verbs require haben; but compare Observation.

Observation. With some verbs implying motion, haben should be used if *action* rather than *change of place* is alluded to; as, reisen to travel, reiten to ride, e. g., dieser Mann hat viel gereist, this man *has* travelled a great deal (alluding to what he has *done*); or, ich habe den ganzen Vormittag geritten, I habe been riding this

---

1) Compare Syntax Rule 388a and 395.

whole forenoon (tells what I have *done*). Mein Vater ist heute Morgen nach Paris gereist, my father has gone to Paris this morning (*change of place*); ich bin gestern von Edinburg nach Glasgow geritten, I went on horseback from Edinburgh to Glasgow yesterday (*change of place*).

358. Werden, *to become*, is used to form the *future* tense, the *conditional* mood and the *passive* voice of all verbs, as has been exemplified in the Conjugation. The Auxiliary Verbs of Mood, dürfen, müssen, können, mögen, wollen and sollen are used in very much the same way as their equivalents in English; see 254-259.

Note. The Verb thun, *to do*, is used in German as auxiliary neither in Interrogative nor Imperative sentences; where it occurs, it is antiquated or quaint language, such as will be found in the Wallenstein's Lager of Schiller and the Faust of Göthe; however, when for the sake of emphasis an Infinitive is placed first in the sentence, the verb „thun" is, in colloquial prose, still employed as auxiliary; e. g., schreiben thut er selten, he *writes* rarely; lesen thun sie auch nur mittelmäßig, they *read* very middling. Compare also Note 2 p. 92.

C. The Use of the Voices.

359. The Active Voice is used to represent a person or thing as engaged in an *action*, or as being in a *state*; e. g., wir essen und trinken, we eat and drink; ihr lebt und seid glücklich, you live and are happy.

360. The Passive Voice is used to express that the Subject is *suffering* something from the acting of another; as, der Knabe **wird gelobt**, das Mädchen **wurde getadelt**, the boy *is* (*being*) praised; the girl *was* (*being*) blamed.

361. The passive voice, properly speaking, can be formed from transitive verbs alone, as, lieben, *to love*, loben, *to praise*, essen, *to eat*, trinken, *to drink*, (ich werde geliebt, *I am loved*; ich wurde gelobt, *I was praised*; das ist gegessen worden, *that has been eaten*; das Bier war getrunken worden, *the beer had been drunk*); but, although it does not exist with Intransitive Verbs in English, in German it often occurs with the impersonal pronoun „es" instead of the active with „man".

Examples: Es wird gelebt, for man lebt, they live, one lives; es wurde gegangen, for man ging, they walked, one walked; es ist gesprungen worden, for man hat gesprungen, they have been dancing or springing. (Compare 258 Note 1.)

362. On the other hand, the *reflective* form is sometimes used for the *passive* of the third person of transitive verbs in phrases like these: Dies Buch übersetzt sich leicht, this book *is easy to translate;* eine fremde Sprache vergißt sich leicht, wenn man sie selten spricht, a foreign language *is* easily *forgotten,* if one speaks it rarely. Das versteht sich von selbst, that is understood, *or* a matter of course.

The Verb lassen is used as auxiliary in the same way; as: Das läßt sich durchaus nicht machen, that *can not be* done at all. Das läßt sich hören, that appears reasonable.

363. *Note.* The student requires to be particularly careful in distinguishing between the Neuter Verb *to be* and the Passive voice; *to be* must be translated by the Passive only if the Verb expresses *action* and if the sentence may be turned into the active construction; as, the dog *is* punished, because he bit the child; *i. e., they punish* the dog etc.; in German, der Hund wird gestraft, weil er das Kind gebissen hat; whilst, when it merely expresses a **state,** *i. e.,* attributes a quality to the subject, it is the *neuter* verb and must be rendered in German by sein; as, dieser Mann ist bestraft, this man is punished, *i. e.*, a punished man.

D. The Use of the Moods.

364. The Indicative is used in German to express *reality, certainty, belief,* both affirmatively und negatively.

365. The Subjunctive is used:

1) To express *uncertainty, probability, supposition, doubt, unbelief, wish* etc.

2) In phrases with *Imperfect* or *Pluperfect* tenses governed by the Conjunctions wenn and ob, *if, whether;*

however, when the tense is purely narrative, the Indicative should be used.

3) In indirect speech.

366. *Observation.* Indirect Speech requires the Verb in the Subjunctive of *that* tense which would be used, if the quotation were *direct*, except that form of the Subjunctive were the same as that of the Indicative; as, habe, haben, werden, in which case the corresponding *past* Tense must be used, *i. e.*, hätte, hätten, würden. It must, however, be remarked, that the corresponding *past tenses* are occasionally used by Germans for *those* Subjunctive forms which *are different* from the Indicative.

Examples.

To 364.—Wahrheitsliebe zeigt sich darin, daſs man überall das Gute zu finden und zu schätzen weiſs.

Das Beste, was wir von der Geschichte haben ist der Enthusiasmus, den sie erregt.

Der Aberglaube gehört zum Wesen des Menschen und flüchtet sich, wenn man ihn ganz und gar zu verdrängen denkt, in die wunderlichsten Ecken und Winkel, von wo er auf einmal, wenn er einigermaſsen sicher zu sein glaubt, wieder hervortritt.

Love of truth shows itself in this that one knows how to find and to appreciate everywhere the good (*i. e.*, what is good).

The greatest good we have from history is the enthusiasm which it stirs up.

Superstition forms part of the nature of man and when one fancies that one drives it out wholly, it takes refuge in the oddest nooks and corners, from whence, if it believes itself to be but tolerably safe, it all of a sudden makes its appearance again.

To 365 (1).—Unbedingte Thätigkeit, von welcher Art sie sei, macht zuletzt bankerott.

Gewisse Bücher scheinen geschrieben zu sein, nicht damit man daraus lerne, sondern damit man wisse, daſs der Verfasser etwas gewuſst hat.

Dem thätigen Menschen kommt es darauf an, daſs er das Rechte thue; ob das Rechte geschehe, soll ihn nicht kümmern.

Es käme Niemand mit der Brille auf der Nase in ein ver-

Unrestricted activity of whatever kind it be ends in bankruptcy.

Certain books seem to be written not that we may learn from them, but that we may know that the author knew something.

It concerns an active man that he do the right thing; whether the right thing happen is not to concern him.

Nobody would enter a '*boudoir*', with spectacles on his nose,

trauliches Gemach, wenn er wüßte, daß den Frauen sogleich die Luſt vergeht, ihn anzuſehen und ſich mit ihm zu unterhalten.

Kant hat uns aufmerkſam gemacht, daß es eine Kritik der Vernunft gebe, daß dieſes höchſte Vermögen, was¹ (sic) der Menſch beſitzt, Urſache habe, über ſich ſelbſt zu wachen. Wie großen Vortheil uns dieſe Stimme gebracht, möge Jeder an ſich ſelbſt geprüft haben. Ich aber möchte in eben dem Sinne die Aufgabe ſtellen, daß eine Kritik der Sinne nöthig ſei, wenn die Kunſt überhaupt, beſonders die deutſche, irgend wieder ſich erholen und in einem erfreulichen Lebensſchritt vorwärts gehen ſolle.

Autorität, daß nämlich etwas ſchon einmal geſchehen, geſagt oder entſchieden worden ſei, hat großen Werth, aber nur der Pedant fordert überall Autorität.

Gehen wir in die Geſchichte zurück, ſo finden wir überall Perſönlichkeiten, mit denen wir uns vertrügen, andere, mit denen wir uns gewiß in Widerſtreit befänden.

To 365 (2). — P.: Wenn Sie mir vorhergeſagt hätten, daß es dem Grafen das Leben koſten werde — Nein, nein! und wenn es mir ſelbſt das Leben gekoſtet hätte!

M.: Wenn ich Ihnen vorhergeſagt hätte? Als ob ſein Tod in meinem Plane geweſen wäre! Ich hatte es dem Angelo auf die Seele gebunden, zu verhüten, daß Niemandem Leides geſchähe. Es würde auch ohne die geringſte Gewaltthätigkeit abgelaufen ſein, wenn ſich der Graf nicht die erſte erlaubt

if he knew that ladies at once lose the desire to look at and converse with him.

Kant has drawn our attention to the fact that there is a critique of reason, that this, the highest faculty man possesses, has cause to watch over itself. How great a gain this voice has brought us, everyone may have tested in himself. I, however, should like, in the very same sense, to put the proposition that a critique of the senses is necessary if art altogether, especially German art, is at all to recover again and to advance in a gratifying spirited step.

An authority for a certain thing having been done, said or decided already, is very valuable, but the pedant alone demands an authority in every instance.

If we look back into history we find everywhere characters with whom we should agree, others with whom we should certainly be in antagonism.

P.: If you had told me before that it would cost the count his life — no, no! and if it had cost my own life!

M.: If I had told you before? As if his death had entered into my plan! I had strictly enjoined Angelo to prevent that harm should befal anybody. And indeed, it would have passed off without the least act of violence, had not the count committed the first. He shot

---

1) Correct form das or welches.

hätte. Er schoß Knall und Fall den einen nieder.

P.: Wahrlich, er hätte sollen Spaß verstehen.

O daß er noch lebte! Alles in der Welt wollte ich darum geben.

Und wenn er es nicht selbst verrathen hätte? — Traun! ich möchte doch wissen, aus welcher meiner Anstalten Mutter oder Tochter den geringsten Argwohn gegen ihn schöpfen könnte? Ah, wenn Sie wüßten, wie ich .... von ihm beleidigt worden bin, Sie könnten, Sie würden Ihre eigne Beleidigung darüber vergessen. Lessing.

To 365 (3) and 366. — Der König Lysimachus (sagten sie) habe ihnen sechs Städte und ein Gebiet von vielen Meilen dafür angeboten; aber sie hätten sich nicht entschließen können, ein so herrliches Stück hinzugeben, zumal da es — gerade die Höhe und Breite habe, um eine ganze Seite der Rathsstube einzunehmen; und überdies habe einer ihrer Kunstrichter in einem weitläufigen, mit großer Gelehrsamkeit angefüllten Werke die Beziehung des allegorischen Sinnes dieser Schilderei auf den Platz, wo sie stehe, sehr scharfsichtig darrgethan. — Wieland.

Der Gesandte meldet unserm Bruder: Clavigo habe ihn peinlich angeklagt, als sei er unter einem falschen Namen in sein Haus geschlichen, habe ihm im Bett die Pistole vorgehalten, und habe ihn gezwungen, eine schimpfliche Erklärung zu unterschreiben. Goethe.

one of the fellows down without ado.

P.; Really, he ought to have understood a joke. Oh, would that he lived still! I would give anything for it.

And if he himself had not betrayed it? Faith! I should rather like to know from which of my arrangements mother or daughter might entertain the least suspicion toward him? Ah, if you knew how I .... have been insulted by him, it could, it would cause you to forget your *own* insult.

King Lysimachos (they said) had offered them for it six towns and territory of many miles, but that they had not been able to make up their minds to part with so splendid a piece, particularly as it — possessed exactly the hight and breadth to occupy a whole side of the council-chamber, moreover that one of their critics in a voluminous work, replete with great learning, had very ingeniously shown the relation of the allegorical meaning of this picture to the place where it stood.

The ambassador informs our brother, that Clavigo had accused him of the crime of having stolen into his house under a false name, of having presented a pistol to him while in bed and that he had compelled him to sign an ignominious declaration.

367. The Imperative mood is in its use quite analogous to the English Imperative, viz., it expresses a command; likewise the use of the auxiliary Verbs ſollen, *shall,* wollen, *will,* mögen, *may* and laſſen *let,* with the Imperative, is the same as in English.

Examples.

Komm mit nach der Stadt (Pure Imp.), come ⎫ with me
Du ſollſt mit nach der Stadt kommen, you shall come ⎬ to
Du magſt mit nach der Stadt kommen, you may come ⎭ town.

Gehen wir in den Garten (Pure Imp.), go we (obs.) ⎫
Wir wollen in den Garten gehn, we will go ⎬ into the
Laß uns (or laßt uns, or laſſen Sie uns) in den Garten ⎭ garden.
gehen, let us go

368. The Conditional mood is used to express a *condition;* see Rule 398.

Examples. Wenn Ludwig fleißig ſein würde, würde ich ihn belohnen, if Louis would be diligent, I should reward him. Du würdeſt ihm glauben, wenn du ihn kennteſt, thou wouldst believe him, if thou knewest him.

369. *Observation.* The first Conditional is often substituted by the *Imperfect Subjunctive,* and the second Conditional by the *Pluperfect Subjunctive.*

Examples. Thäten Sie es wohl, wenn ich es auch thäte, instead of, würden Sie es wohl thun, wenn ich es auch thun würde, *would you do it, if I should do it.* Hätten Sie das geglaubt, wenn man es Ihnen vorhergeſagt hätte, instead of, würden Sie das geglaubt haben, wenn man es Ihnen vorhergeſagt haben würde, *would you have believed it, if they had predicted it to you.*

This form is often preferable to the Conditional, especially in sentences like the above, where two occur in one period, one of them, at least, should be converted into the Imperfect Subjunctive.

370. The Infinitive mood is used in all cases in which it occurs in English, thus principally to form the Future Tenses and Conditional Mood, also, where in English the Inf. *or* Pres. Partc. may be used; as, I see him *come* or *coming,* ich ſehe ihn kommen; in addition it is used in German:

371. a) Instead of the English Present Participle, when used *substantively*; as, das Reiten und Fechten ſind geſunde Leibesübungen, **riding** and **fencing** are healthy exercises; consequently also *when preceded by a Pre-*

position; in that case, however, the German Infinitive requires the Preposition zu before it; as, ſie kämpften ohne auf die Gefahr zu achten, they fought *without heeding* the danger; alle Hoffnung, die Mannſchaft zu retten, war nun verſchwunden, all hopes *of saving* the crew had now vanished.

372. b) Instead of the *Imperative* (though rarely), which property it shares with the Perfect Participle; as, trinken! *drink!* kommen! *come;* (It would appear, that in those cases the auxiliary Verb ſollen is understood, viz., du ſollſt trinken, kommen etc., *thou shalt drink, come* etc.; compare 383 *b*).

Note. About the Declension of the Infinitive comp. Rule 235.

Accusative with Infinitive.
Accusativus cum Infinitivo.

373. This construction, so familiar to English, is entirely foreign to the German language, a conjunctional construction always requiring to be substituted for it; as, everybody allows him *to be the best man,* German construction: *everybody allows, that he the best man is:* Jedermann giebt zu, daß er der beſte Menſch iſt. I believe *them to have learnt* a great deal, German construction: I believe that they a great deal learnt have: ich glaube, daß ſie viel gelernt haben.

374. The Infinitive may be used *with* and *without* the Preposition zu; this construction is analogous to the English use of *to,* except in the following cases:

375. *a)* Where the Infinitive is quoted *alone* the English language requires the Preposition *to* prefixed, for the sake of indicating the Mood; whilst in German it has the Inflection -n or -en and does not need the preposition for that purpose; as, ſpielen, *to* play; lachen, *to* laugh.

376. *b)* Where in English a *neuter* Verb and in German an *auxiliary* precedes the Infinitive; as, ich

kann deutsch lesen, „*I am able*" to read German. Johann will nicht kommen, John „*does not want*" to come. If, however, in English an auxiliary be employed instead of the neuter Verb, *to* is not used, as in German; viz., *I can read* German; John *will* not *come*.

377. *c)* The Preposition zu is not used with the following Verbs: lassen, (to) *let, to allow to, to cause to be;* helfen, *to help;* hören, *to hear;* lehren, *to teach;* lernen, *to learn;* fühlen, *to feel,* sehen, *to see,* and others which do not need to be quoted, since there is no difference between them and their English equivalents in this respect. To this latter class must be reckoned the Auxiliary Verbs of Mood; as, mögen, *may,* dürfen, *dare*.

378. *Observation.* Although in English after the Adverb *so* the Adverb *as* is required invariably after the Adjective, even in phrases where *as* is used to connect an Infinitive sentence conveying a *request* with an Interrogative phrase containing *so*: in German the latter construction is rendered either by und *and an Infinitive without* zu, or by *the Infinitive with* zu without und. *Ex.*: Will you be *so* kind, *as* to tell me what o'clock it is: Wollen Sie so gut sein und mir sagen, wieviel Uhr es ist, or, wollen Sie so gut sein, mir zu sagen etc.; for the English idiom *I don't know what to do, to say* etc., the German demands *what I shall do, say* etc.; viz., ich weiß nicht, was ich thun (or sagen) soll.

379. *If a purpose* is to be indicated with special precision, the Infinitive clause ought to be introduced by the Preposition um (in English *in order* with *Infinitive*). *Examples:* Das Gitter des Fensters war zu dicht für ihn, um mit dem Körper durchzukommen, the bars of the window were too close for him, *in order to* get through with his body. Ich komme, um Abschied von Ihnen zu nehmen, I am come, *in order to* take leave of you.

380. If the Verb, however, is taken *substantively*, *i. e.*, if it does not imply action, but *a state* or *fact*, the Infinitive is connected with zum, a contraction of zu and the Arte. dem (in English *for* with *Pres. Partc.*).

Examples: Die Stäbe waren zu stark **zum Zerbrechen**, the bars were too strong to break (*for breaking*). Das ist kein Gegenstand **zum Lachen**, that is no subject to laugh at (*for laughing* or laughter).

E. The Use of the Participles.

381. The Present Participle is used in its *verbal* character (*i. e.*, expressing *action*) almost only in elevated language. Its *Adjective and Adverbial* uses, on the other hand, are rather extensive, as in English. (Compare Rule 386.)

Examples. Der **lächelnde Knabe**, the smiling boy; der **schwatzende Bach**, the talkative brook. Er kann das **spielend** machen, he can do that *playingly*.

382. The Perfect (or Past) Participle is used principally for the formation of the *past compound* tenses of the active voice, and for the formation of the passive voice (see the Rules of the Conjugation).

When used without auxiliaries it is, in its *verbal* character, subject to the same restrictions as the *Present* Participle. (Compare Rule 386.)

Examples. Mein **geliebtes Kind**, my beloved child; ein **befriedigter Mensch**, a satisfied man.

383. The Perfect Participle is besides used in German in these peculiar cases:

a) Instead of the English Present Participle in certain phrases; as, er kam in großer Eile **gelaufen**, he came *running* in great haste.

b) Instead of the Imperative, in abrupt, encouraging, commanding and also in coarse language; as: Stille **gestanden**! *stand still!* Wohl auf, Kameraden, auf's Pferd, auf's Pferd, in's Feld in die Freiheit **geflogen**, arise ye comrades, mount your steeds, *fly* out to the field, to freedom! *Schiller.* (Such Participles must be looked upon as the *Passive Imperative* having the Auxiliary Verb *understood*; thus, es werbe gestanden, es werbe geflogen, would be the complete forms.)

384. The Perfect Participle of the following Verbs is *replaced by the Infinitive* when preceded by a Verb in the Infinitive, viz., dürfen, können, lassen, mögen, müssen, sollen, wollen, helfen, hören, lehren, lernen, sehen and fühlen; as, kommen **dürfen** instead of kommen geburft; gehen **können**, instead of gehen gekonnt.

If the sentence is *dependent*, the Verb or Auxiliary should *precede* these Infinitives, contrary to the general Rule (311. *b.*); as, **hat** kommen **dürfen**, instead of, kommen geburft hat; **hat** gehen **können**, instead of, gehen gekonnt hat; some authors in this combination frequently drop the auxiliary.

Examples. Man hat den Gefangenen entkommen **lassen** (instead of gelassen), they *have allowed* the prisoner *to escape*. Nachdem sie den Fisch auf den glühenden Kohlen halb **hatte** röften **lassen** (instead of röften gelassen hatte) — after she *had caused* the fish *to be half broiled* on the embers —. Haben Sie Ihren Freund abreisen **sehen** (instead of gesehen), have you *seen* your friend depart?

385. *Note.* This peculiarity can be accounted for only by supposing that originally it was the Perfect Participle without the augment „ge" that was used after Infinitives; since, however, this form is with several Verbs the same as the Infinitive, as, gelassen without augment lassen, gesehen without augment sehen, Infinitives of other Verbs of which the Perf. Partc. without augment does not represent the Infinitive, were, by analogy, used in the same way.

386. The English Participles, when not used adjectively, or when not forming part of a compound tense, must be rendered in German by a *Conjunction or Relative Pronoun and a tense.* *Examples:*[1] Having to preach before the clergy — must be changed into: *when he had to preach,* **als** er vor der Geiftlichkeit zu **predigen hatte.** *Having* separated the leaves, he sewed them up again — must be changed into: *after he had separated* the leaves etc., **nachdem** er die Blätter **getrennt hatte,** nähte er sie wieder **zusammen.** The Delft, one of the Dutch ships *taken* at the battle of Camperdown,— must be changed into: *which were taken* etc., **das Schiff Delft,** eines der holländischen, **welche** in der Schlacht bei Camperduin **genommen wurden.** Cæsar describes the

---

1) In order to become thoroughly familiar with this important rule, the pupil should at once find many more examples in English and change them into the German construction.

Celtes as fighting on horseback etc. German: Cæsar describes, that the Celtes on horseback etc. fought; Cäsar erzählt, daß die Celten zu Pferde etc. kämpften. (See also Rule 371 about the use of the *Infinitive* instead of the Present Participle.)

Observation. The learner should keep in mind that it will be a *correct* change of a participial construction only if the sentence, so changed, makes also good English.

F. The Use of the Tenses.

387. **The Present Tense** is used in German *principally* to express an act or state, going-on at the time; *e. g.*, **ich schreibe**, I write, I am writing, I do write; **ich werde gelobt**, I am (being) praised.

388. In addition *the Present* is used:

a) To express a *continued action or state* of the past, where the Perfect tense is used in English; as; Wie lange sind Sie schon in dieser Stadt (or an diesem Orte), how long *have* you *been* in this place? Wie lange ist Ihr Vater schon krank, how long *has* your father been ill? whilst, when the action or state is *past* and no longer going on, the *past* tense must be used in German as well as in English; thus the above sentences with the Perfect: wie lange sind Sie an diesem (rather jenem) Orte gewesen, how long were you in that place; wie lange ist Ihr Vater krank gewesen, how long was your father ill, imply, that the person is *no longer* in that place, is *no longer* ill.

389. b) *Instead of the Future*, to give greater *precision, promptness, certainty* etc. to the Verb; *e. g.*: Wir **gehen** heute Nachmittag auf's Land, *we shall go* to the country this afternoon. Mein Vater **kommt** morgen von der Reise zurück, my father *will return* to-morrow from his journey. (This is often the case in English too.)

390. c) *Instead of the Imperfect* in narrative, to give greater *vivacity* to it; as: Sobald der Knabe fort

war, **hängt** sich der Kaiser einen Mantel um, **begiebt** sich nach dem Hause der kranken Frau—, as soon as the boy was gone, the emperor *put* on a cloak, *went* to the house of the sick woman —.

391. d) *Instead of the Imperative*, to increase its force; as: Du kommst mit, nnd er bleibt da, *come* you with me, and *let him remain* here.

392. The Imperfect Tense is used, as in English, principally in *narration*; e. g., ich schrieb, I wrote, I was writing, I did write; ich wurde gelobt, I was (being) praised.

393. The Imperfect is also used:

a) To make a statement *which has reference to another occurrence*. Ex.:

Wir machten unsere Aufgaben, als Sie eintraten, we were doing our exercises, *when you entered*. (Compare Rule 395.)

394. b) When relating anything *of which the narrator was an eyewitness*. Ex.:

Es ereignete sich gestern ein Eisenbahnunfall, a railway-accident happened yesterday. (Compare Rule 395.)

395. The Perfect Tense is used:

1. To express an act or to make a statement of the past that has no reference to another.

2. To relate a thing of which the narrator has *not* been an eyewitness (see the previous rule), in which case in English the Imperfect, or in questions the Imperfect of the auxiliary Verb *to do* is used.

Examples to 1: Wir haben gestern einem großen Feste beigewohnt, we *were* present yesterday at a great festivity. Der König ist vor acht Tagen gekrönt worden, the king *was crowned* a week ago.

Examples to 2: Wie ich höre, hat gestern ein Ball im Gesellschaftshause stattgefunden, I understand there *was* a ball yesterday in the club. Haben Sie auch getanzt? *did* you dance too?

396. The Pluperfect Tense is used only to denote an occurrence of the *past* that was past before the other, referred to, took place.

Examples. Nachdem sie die Burg **erstürmt hatten**, wurde sie den Flammen **übergeben**, after they *had stormed* the castle, it was given over to the flames.

Wenn Sie mir **gefolgt wären**, wäre das nicht **geschehen**, if you *had followed* me, that would not have happened.

Obgleich sie meilenweit **verfolgt worden waren**, **hatten** sie doch Zeit genug **gehabt**, sich zu retten, although they *had been* pursued for many miles, yet they *had (had)* time enough to save themselves.

397. The Future Tense is used only to express an act or state of *futurity; to be going* may be substituted for **shall** and **will** in that case. Ex.:

Ich **werde** morgen eine Reise nach Deutschland **unternehmen**, *I shall (I am going to) set out* for Germany to-morrow. **Wird** Ihr Bruder **mitgehen?** *Will* your brother *go* likewise? Wann **werden** Sie mit Ihrer Arbeit fertig **sein**, when *will* you be ready with your work?

398. *Observation.* Before translating shall, should, will, would, it is necessary first to consider their import, since those forms are used in English not only for the Future Tense and Conditional Mood, but also as auxiliaries of mood; different Auxiliary Verbs, however, are required in German for each different import; thus the Auxiliary **werde** etc. can be employed only to render *shall* and *will* if *futurity* is expressed; **würde** etc. only renders *should* and *would* if a *condition* is implied; but *will* and *would* ought to be rendered by the Verb **wollen**, if denoting a *will*, a *wish, willingness* etc., and if in English *to be willing* can be substituted; on the other hand, *shall* and *should* ought to be rendered by the Verb **sollen**, if *dependency, obligation, supposition* is implied, or if in English *to be obliged, in case*, may be said instead. Ex.: **Wollen** Sie mir einen großen Gefallen thun, *will* you (are *you willing* to) do me a great favour. Er soll heute noch all seine Arbeiten fertig machen, he *shall* (is *obliged* to) finish to-day all his tasks yet. **Sollten** Sie um halb Vier nicht hier sein, so **werden** wir ohne Sie gehen, *should* you not be (*in case* you are not) here at half past three, we *shall* (we are *going* to) start without you. Examples of the old future (formed as in English) are not wanting; as, was will ich (dagegen) machen, what shall I do? Compare the use of *will* in Scotland, such as, *will* I go, for *shall* I go.

PUNCTUATION.

399. It is necessary, in conclusion, to give a few hints about punctuation.

On the whole the usage of punctuation is analogous in English and German; it therefore suffices to notice the principal differences.

1) The *Commas* which in English separate adverbs from the rest of the sentence, such as »however«, »of course« are not used in German.

2) All *dependent* (including *relative*) clauses should in German be separated from the independent clause by a *comma* which is not *always* done in English.

3) All *Infinitive* clauses, however short, ought to be separated from the preceding clause by a *comma*, contrary to usage in English.

4) Before unb a *comma* should be put only if the two clauses which it connects have different subjects.

400. *Example.* About sunset(,) however(,) as I was preparing to pass the night in this manner(,) and had turned my horse loose, that it might graze at liberty, a negro-woman returning from the labours of the field(,) stopped to observe me(,) and perceiving that I was weary and dejected(,) inquired into my situation *(Mungo Park)*: Gegen Sonnenuntergang jedoch(,) als ich mich anschickte(,) die Nacht in dieser Weise zuzubringen und mein Pferd los gelassen hatte(,) damit es nach Gefallen grasen möchte(,) blieb eine Negerin(,) die von der Feldarbeit zurückkehrte(,) stehen(,) um mich zu betrachten; und da sie bemerkte(,) daß ich ermüdet und niedergeschlagen war(,) forschte sie nach meiner Lage.

ALPHABETICAL LIST OF STRONG AND IRREGULAR VERBS.

Those marked * are irregular, those marked † weak *or* strong and those marked †† are weak when used *transitively.*

Infinitive.	Imperfect.	Perf. Part.	Present.	Imp.
baden, to bake,	but,	gebacken,	ich bade, du bäckſt, er bäckt.	
bebingen, stipulate,	bedang,	bedungen.		
befehlen, command,	befahl, (Sj.) befähle,	befohlen,	ich befehle, du befiehlſt, er befiehlt,	befiehl.
befleißen, apply,	befliſs,	befliſſen.		
beginnen, begin,	begann,	begonnen.		
beißen, bite,	biſs,	gebiſſen.		
bergen, hide,	barg,	geborgen,	ich berge, du birgſt, er birgt,	birg.
berſten, burst,	barſt, and borſt,	geborſten,	ich berſte, du birſt(eſt)†, er birſtt,	birſtt.
bewegen, induce,	bewog,	bewogen.		
biegen, bend,	bog,	gebogen,	old: du beugſt, er beugt.	
bieten, bid,	bot,	geboten,	old: du beutſt, er beut.	
binden, bind,	band,	gebunden.		
bitten, pray, ask,	bat,	gebeten.		
blaſen, blow,	blies,	geblaſen,	ich blaſe, du bläſt, er bläſt.	
bleiben, remain,	blieb,	geblieben.		
††bleichen, turn pale,	blich,	geblichen.		
braten, roast,	briet,	gebraten,	ich brate, du brätſt, er brät.	
brechen, break,	brach,	gebrochen,	ich breche, du brichſt, er bricht,	brich.
brennen, burn,	brannte(Sj.) brennete,	gebrannt.		
bringen, bring,	brachte,	gebracht.		
denken, think,	dachte,	gedacht.		
dreſchen, thresh,	draſch, and droſch,	gedroſchen,	ich dreſche, du driſch(eſ)t, er driſcht,	driſch.
dringen, throng,	drang,	gedrungen.		
dünken, think,	däuchte,	gedäucht,	mich dünkt, methinks.	
*dürfen, dare, be allowed,	durfte,	gedurft,	ich darf, du darfſt, er darf.	
empfehlen, recommend, v. befehlen.				
eſſen, eat,	aß,	gegeſſen,	ich eſſe, du iſſ(eſ)t, er iſſt,	iſs.

Infinitive.	Imperfect.	Perf. Part.	Present.	Imp.
fahren, drive,	fuhr,	gefahren,	ich fahre, du fährst, er fährt.	
fallen, fall,	fiel,	gefallen,	ich falle, du fällst, er fällt.	
fangen, catch,	fing,	gefangen,	ich fange, du fängst, er fängt.	
fechten, fight,	focht,	gefochten,	ich fechte, du fichst, er ficht.	
finden, find,	fand,	gefunden.		
flechten, plait,	flocht,	geflochten,	ich flechte, du flichst, er flicht,	flicht.
fliegen, fly,	flog,	geflogen,	old: du fleugst, er fleugt,	fleug.
fliehen, flee,	floh,	geflohen,	old: du fleuchst, er fleucht,	fleuch.
fließen, flow,	floß,	geflossen,	old: du fleußt, er fleußt,	fleuß.
fressen, devoure,	fraß,	gefressen,	ich fresse, du friss(es)t, er frißt,	friß.
frieren, freeze,	fror,	gefroren.		
gähren, ferment,	gohr,	gegohren.		
gebären, bear,	gebar,	geboren,	ich gebäre, du gebierst†, er gebiert†,	gebier†.
geben, give,	gab,	gegeben,	ich gebe, du gi(e)bst, er gi(e)bt,	gi(e)b.
gedeihen, prosper,	gedieh,	gediehen.		
gehen, go,	ging,	gegangen.		
gelingen, succeed,	gelang,	gelungen,	es gelingt mir, I succeed.	
gelten, be worth,	galt,	gegolten,	ich gelte, du giltst, er gilt,	gilt.
genesen, recover health,	genaß,	genesen.		
genießen, enjoy,	genoß,	genossen.		
geschehen, happen,	geschah,	geschehen,	es geschieht.	
gewinnen, win,	gewann, (Sj. also) gewönne,	gewonnen.		
gießen, pour,	goß,	gegossen,	old: du geuß(es)t, er geußt,	geuß.
†gleichen, be like,	glich,	geglichen.		
gleiten, glide,	glitt,	geglitten.		
†glimmen, glow,	glomm,	geglommen.		
graben, dig,	grub,	gegraben,	ich grabe, du gräbst, er gräbt.	
greifen, seize,	griff,	gegriffen.		
haben, have,	hatte,	gehabt,	ich habe, du hast, er hat.	
halten, hold,	hielt,	gehalten,	ich halte, du hältst, er hält.	
hangen, hang,	hing,	gehangen,	ich hange, du hängst, er hängt.	
hauen, hew,	hieb,	gehauen.		
heben, lift, heave,	hob, and hub,	gehoben.		
heißen, be called bid,	hieß,	geheißen.		

Infinitive.	Imperfect.	Perf. Part.	Present.	Imp.
helfen, help,	half, (Sj. also) hülfe,	geholfen,	ich helfe, du hilfst, er hilft,	hilf.
kennen, know,	kannte, (Sj.) kenn(e)te,	gekannt.		
†klimmen, climb,	klomm,	geklommen.		
klingen, sound,	klang,	geklungen.		
kneifen, nip,	kniff,	gekniffen.		
kommen, come,	kam,	gekommen,	ich komme, du kömmst†, er kömmt†	
*können, can, be able,	konnte,	gekonnt,	ich kann, du kannst, er kann.	
kriechen, creep,	kroch,	gekrochen.		
küren, choose,	kor,	gekoren.		
laden, load, invite†,	lud,	geladen,	ich lade, du lädst, er lädt.	
lassen, let, cause to,	ließ,	gelassen,	ich lasse, du läßt, or lässest, er läßt.	
laufen, run,	lief,	gelaufen,	ich laufe, du läufst, er läuft.	
leiden, suffer,	litt,	gelitten.		
leihen, lend,	lieh,	geliehen.		
lesen, read, pick,	las,	gelesen,	ich lese, du liest or liesest, er liest.	lies.
liegen, lie,	lag,	gelegen.		
löschen††, quench,	losch,	geloschen,	ich lösche, du lischt, er lischt,	lisch.
lügen, lie, tell a lie,	log,	gelogen.		
mahlen, grind (corn),	mahlte,	gemahlen.		
meiden, avoid,	mied,	gemieden.		
melken, milk,	molk,	gemolken,	ich melke, du milkst†, er milkt†,	milkt.
messen, measure,	maß,	gemessen,	ich messe, du miss(es)t, er mißt,	miß.
*mögen, may, be possible,	mochte,	gemocht,	ich mag, du magst, er mag.	
†müssen, must, have to,	mußte,	gemußt,	ich muß, du mußt, er muß.	
nehmen, take,	nahm,	genommen,	ich nehme, du nimmst, er nimmt,	nimm.
nennen, name,	nannte,(Sj.) nenn(e)te,	genannt.		
pfeifen, whistle,	pfiff,	gepfiffen.		
pflegen, cherish,	pflag,	gepflogen.		
preisen, praise,	pries,	gepriesen.		
quellen, spring forth,	quoll,	gequollen,	ich quelle, du quillst, er quillt.	

Infinitive.	Imperfect.	Perf. Part.	Present.	Imp.
†rächen, revenge,	roch,	gerochen.		
rathen, guess, advise,	rieth,	gerathen,	ich rathe, du räthst, er räth.	
reiben, rub,	rieb,	gerieben.		
reißen, tear,	riß,	gerissen.		
reiten, ride,	ritt,	geritten.		
rennen, run,	rannte, Sj. renn(e)te,	gerannt.		
riechen, smell,	roch,	gerochen,	old: du reuchst, er reucht,	reuch.
ringen, wring, wrestle,	rang,	gerungen.		
rinnen, flow, run,	rann, s. also rönne,	geronnen.		
rufen, call, cry,	rief,	gerufen.		
salzen, salt,	salzte,	gesalzent.		
saufen, drink,	soff,	gesoffen,	ich saufe, du säufst, er säuft.	
saugen, suck,	sog,	gesogen.		
schaffen, create,	schuf,	geschaffen.		
scheiden, separate,	schied,	geschieden.		
scheinen, shine, seem,	schien,	geschienen.		
schelten, chide,	schalt, Sj. schölte,	gescholten,	ich schelte, du schiltst, er schilt,	schilt.
scheren, shear,	schor,	geschoren,	ich schere, du schierst, er schiert,	schiert.
schieben, push, shove,	schob,	geschoben.		
schießen, shoot,	schoß,	geschossen.		
schinden, flay,	schand,	geschunden.		
schlafen, sleep,	schlief,	geschlafen,	ich schlafe, du schläfst, er schläft.	
schlagen, strike,	schlug,	geschlagen,	ich schlage, du schlägst, er schlägt.	
schleichen, slink,	schlich,	geschlichen.		
schleifen, grind,	schliff,	geschliffen.		
schleißen, slit,	schliß,	geschlissen.		
schließen, shut,	schloß,	geschlossen,	old: du schleußest, er schleußt,	schleuß.
schlingen, twine, swallow,	schlang,	geschlungen.		
schmeißen, throw, smite,	schmiß,	geschmissen.		
††schmelzen, smelt, melt,	schmolz,	geschmolzen,	ich schmelze, du schmilz(es)t, er schmilzt,	schmilz.
schneiden, cut,	schnitt,	geschnitten.		
schnieben, snort,	schnob,	geschnoben.		
schraubent, screw,	schrob,	geschroben.		

Infinitive.	Imperfect.	Perf. Part.	Present.	Imp.
††schrecken, startle,	schrak,	geschrocken,	ich schrecke, du schrickst, er schrickt,	schrick.
schreiben, write,	schrieb,	geschrieben.		
schreien, cry,	schrie,	geschrie(e)n.		
schreiten, stride,	schritt,	geschritten.		
schwären, suppurate,	schwor,	geschworen,	old: du schwierst, er schwiert.	
schweigen, be silent,	schwieg,	geschwiegen.		
††schwellen, swell,	schwoll,	geschwollen.		
schwimmen, swim,	schwamm, Sj. also schwömme,	geschwommen.		
schwinden, vanish,	schwand,	geschwunden.		
schwingen, swing,	schwang,	geschwungen.		
schwören, swear,	schwor and schwur,	geschworen.		
sehen, see,	sah,	gesehen,	ich sehe, du siehst, er sieht,	sieh, old: siehe.
*sein, be,	war,	gewesen,	ich bin, du bist, er ist, wir sind, ihr seid, sie sind, .	sei, pl. seid.
senden†, send,	sandte, Sj. sendete,	gesandt.		
sieden, seethe,	sott,	gesotten.		
singen, sing,	sang,	gesungen.		
sinken, sink,	sank,	gesunken.		
sinnen, meditate,	sann Sj. also sönne,	gesonnen.		
sitzen, sit,	saß,	gesessen.		
*sollen, shall, be obliged,	sollte,	gesollt,	ich soll, du sollst, er soll.	
speien, spit,	spie,	gespie(e)n.		
spinnen, spin,	spann, Sj. also spönne,	gesponnen.		
spleißen, split,	spliß,	gespliffen.		
sprechen, speak,	sprach,	gesprochen,	ich spreche, du sprichst, er spricht,	sprich.
sprießen, sprout,	sproß,	gesprossen.		
springen, spring,	sprang,	gesprungen.		
stechen, pierce,	stach,	gestochen,	ich steche, du stichst, er sticht,	stich.
stehen, stand,	stand (old: stund),	gestanden.		

Infinitive.	Imperfect.	Perf. Part.	Present.	Imp.
ſtehlen, steal,	ſtahl Sj. also ſtöhle,	geſtohlen,	ich ſtehle, du ſtiehlſt, er ſtiehlt,	ſtiehl.
ſteigen, mount,	ſtieg,	geſtiegen.		
ſterben, die,	ſtarb, Sj. ſtürbe,	geſtorben,	ich ſterbe, du ſtirbſt, er ſtirbt,	ſtirb.
ſtieben, disperse,	ſtob,	geſtoben.		
ſtinken, stink,	ſtank,	geſtunken.		
ſtoßen, push,	ſtieß,	geſtoßen,	ich ſtoße, du ſtöß(eſ)t, er ſtößt.	
ſtreichen, strike,	ſtrich,	geſtrichen.		
ſtreiten, strive, dispute,	ſtritt,	geſtritten.		
thun, do,	that,	gethan.		
tragen, carry,	trug,	getragen,	ich trage, du trägſt, er trägt.	
treffen, hit,	traf,	getroffen,	ich treffe, du triffſt, er trifft,	triff.
treiben, drive,	trieb,	getrieben.		
treten, tread,	trat,	getreten,	ich trete, du trittſt, er tritt,	tritt.
triefen, drip,	troff,	getroffen,	old: du treuffſt, er treuft.	treuf.
triegen or trügen, deceive,	trog,	getrogen.		
trinken, drink,	trank,	getrunken.		
†verderben, spoil,	verdarb, Sj. verdürbe,	verdorben,	ich verderbe, du verdirbſt, er verdirbt,	verdirb.
verdrießen, annoy,	verdroſs,	verdroſſen,	es verdrießt, (old verdreußt), mich etc.	
vergeſſen, forget,	vergaß,	vergeſſen,	ich vergeſſe, du vergiſſ(eſ)t, er vergiſſt,	vergiß.
verlieren, lose,	verlor,	verloren.		
wachſen, grow,	wuchs,	gewachſen,	ich wachſe, du wäch(ſe)ſt, er wächſt.	
wägen or wiegen, weigh,	wog,	gewogen.		
waſchen, wash,	wuſch,	gewaſchen,	ich waſche, du wäſch(eſ)t, er wäſcht.	
weben†, weave,	wob,	gewoben.		
weichen, yield,	wich,	gewichen.		
weiſen, old†, show,	wies,	gewieſen.		
wenden†, turn,	wandte, Sj. wendete,	gewandt.		
werben, woe, sue,	warb Sj. würbe,	geworben,	ich werbe, du wirbſt, er wirbt,	wirb.
*werden, become,	ward or wurde, pl. wurden, Sj. würde,	geworden,	ich werde, du wirſt, er wird.	
werfen, throw,	warf,	geworfen,	ich werfe, du wirfſt, er wirft,	wirf.
winden, wind,	wand,	gewunden.		
*wiſſen, know,	wuſste,	gewuſſt,	ich weiß, du weißt, er weiß.	
*wollen, will, be willing,	wollte,	gewollt,	ich will, du willſt, er will.	

zeihen, accuse, sich, | geziehen.
ziehen, draw, go, zog, | gezogen, | old: bu zeugst, er zeugt. | zeug.
zwingen, force, zwang, | gezwungen.

SECOND PART.

CONVERSATIONAL EXERCISES, DIALOGUES AND IDIOMATIC EXPRESSIONS.

Note. The Exercises should be used as follows. The Rules of the Grammar referred to at the head of each Vocabulary should be explained in order to be learnt by heart for the next lesson-day. The vocabulary of words should also be committed to memory. Many words are inserted which do not occur in the following exercise, in order to give the pupil an opportunity of acquiring a large stock of words, which will be of future use. Some are even entered twice for the sake of contrast with some other word.

When the pupil is thoroughly acquainted with the rules and the vocabulary, he may proceed to read the Exercise aloud in German, following the sense; after which he must give it in English without looking at the German; both sentence by sentence. The pupil may then translate at sight (as far as practicable) the English sentences into German, which must be continued until perfect fluency is attained, *after which* he may write them. Should there not be time for the teacher to do this, he should recommend this method to his pupils, as the numerous errors which too often occur in exercises are caused from writing them before the study of them is completed.

After the 100 Exercises are mastered, more difficult ones should be used, such as the author's "Exercises on Syntax",[1] or "English into German".[2]

The phrases and idioms at the end are intended to be learnt by heart, a few each day.

In conclusion the author would wish to impress on teachers the great necessity of revisal or repetition, for what is once learnt, should never be forgotten and it can only be impressed on the

---

1) James Thin, Edinburgh.
2) Williams & Norgate, London and Edinburgh.

memory by constant repetition. He recommends this the more, feeling sure that the pupil gets a much greater mastery over the language by learning each time a limited portion of fresh matter and repeating a much larger one of what he has already learnt, than if he went rapidly through the book without doing so.

CONVERSATIONAL EXERCISES
ON THE ACCIDENCE OF THE GRAMMAR.

FIRST LESSON.
Learn Rules 45 and 115.

Ich-bin',[1] I am,	Bin ich? am I?
du-bist', thou art,	bist du? art thou?
er-ist', he is,	ist er? is he?
sie'-ist, she is,	ist sie? is she?
es'-ist, it is,	ist es? is it?
man'-ist, one is (people are),	ist man? is one (are people)?
wir-sind', we are (pr. *zint*),	sind wir? are we?
ihr-seid', you are (» *zite*),	seid ihr? are you?
sie-sind', they are.	sind sie? are they?

1. *Note.* The hyphens and accents have been introduced to teach the pupil correct accentuation, they are, of course, to be omitted in writing.

Der-Va'ter, the father,	das-Gold', the gold,
die-Mut'ter, the mother,	das-Haus', the house,
das-Eis', the ice,	das-Licht', the light, candle,
das-Feu'er, the fire,	das-Recht', the right,[1]
das-Glas', the glass,	das-Un'recht, the wrong.

1) Recht and Unrecht are used as Nouns in German when signifying that *people are right*, just as in English words like *courage*; therefore they must be connected with the auxiliary „haben" instead of the English *to be*; as: Ich habe Unrecht, Sie haben Recht, I am wrong, you are right; similar to the English "you have courage"

Alt, old, aged, ancient,   gesund, sound, healthy,
jung, young,   wholesome, well,
neu, new,   krank, ill,
arm, poor, reich, rich,   wohl, well,
lang, long, kurz, short, curt,   ja, yes! nein, no!
                   und, and.

Note. Interrogative sentences should be answered by the pupil in German.

1st *Exercise.*

1. Das-Haus des-Vaters ist alt. 2. Die-Mutter ist krank. 3. Ist der-Vater reich? 4. Er-ist arm. 5. Sind-wir jung? 6. Du-bist gesund, sie-ist krank. 7. Das-Haus ist lang. 8. Die-Mutter ist arm. 9. Sind-sie reich? 10. Ist das-Haus neu?

2nd *Exercise.*

1. The mother is well. 2. The father is ill. 3. The house of the father is new. 4. Are you rich? 5. We are poor, thou art rich. 6. Is she young? 7. Are we old? 8. Is it the father? 9. Is she the mother? 10. It is the father's house.

SECOND LESSON.
Learn Rule 49 and read 349.

Ich-ha'be, I have,   Hab' ich? have I?
du-hast', thou hast,   hast du? hast thou?
er-hat', he has,   hat er? has he?
wir-ha'ben, we have,   haben wir? have we?
ihr-habt', you have,   habt ihr? have you?
sie-ha'ben, they have.   haben sie? have they?

Der-Bru'der, the brother,   das-Au'ge, the eye,
die-Schwe'ster, the sister,   das-Haar', the hair,
das-Kind', the child,   das-Ohr', the ear.

Braun, brown,
grau, grey,
faul, lazy, rotten, foul,
groß, large, tall, big, great,
klein, little, short, small,
gut, good,
treu, faithful, true.

3rd Exercise.

1. Ich-habe einen-Bruder und eine-Schwester. 2. Haben-sie ein-Haus? 3. Das-Haar des-Vaters ist grau. 4. Ein-Bruder ist einer-Schwester treu. 5. Das-Auge des-Kindes ist groß. 6. Hat-er einen-Bruder? 7. Das-Haus der-Schwester ist klein. 8. Braun ist das-Haar des-Kindes. 9. Reich ist der-Vater, arm ist die-Mutter. 10. Ein-Kind ist einer-Mutter treu.

4th Exercise.

1. The brother has a house. 2. The mother has a child. 3. A sister is faithful¹ to a brother. 4. Has the child a brother? 5. The mother and the sister have a house. 6. The brother's hair is brown. 7. The eye of the sister is grey. 8. Have you a brother? 9. Has she a sister? 10. He is a brother of the child.

1. Compare sentence 4th of exercise 3rd.

THIRD LESSON.
Revise the previous Rules.

Ich-wer'de,¹ I become³,
du-wirst',² th. becomest,
er-wird',² he becomes,
wir-wer'den,¹ we become,
ihr-wer'det,¹ you become,
sie-wer'den,¹ they bec.,
} wax, grow, fall. {
Werd(e) ich? become I
wirst du? becomest thou
wird er? becomes he
werden wir? become we
werdet ihr? become you
werden sie? become they
} or, do I become? etc.

1. Pronounce with a long vowel.
2. Pronounce with a short vowel.
3. werde is used also as auxiliary for the Future and Passive.

Der-Sohn', the son,
die-Toch'ter, the daughter,
das-Fräu'lein, the young lady, miss,
die-Magd',[1] the maid or servant,
das-Mäd'chen, the girl,
das-Metall', the metal,

der-Schuh'macher, the shoemaker,
das-Thier', the animal,
das-Pferd',[1] the horse,
das-Brod', (or, Brot), the bread, the loaf (of bread),
das-Mes'ser, the knife,
das-Fen'ster, the window.

1. Pronounce with a long vowel.

Gekommen, come,
gegangen, gone,
gefunden, found,
verloren, lost,

gegessen, eaten,
getrunken, drunk,
gekauft, bought,
verkauft, sold.

Observe. The **Perfect Participle** stands at the end of the sentence (compare Rule 309).

5th Exercise.

1. Die-Magd hat ein-Messer verloren. 2. Habt-ihr es gefunden? 3. Das-Kind-des-Schuhmachers hat ein-Brod gekauft. 4. Hast-du es gegessen? 5. Der-Sohn hat ein-Pferd verkauft. 6. Die-Magd hat einen-Bruder verloren. 7. Das-Fräulein hat eine-Magd. 8. Der-Bruder-des-Mädchens ist faul. 9. Haben-wir gegessen und getrunken? 10. Hat die-Magd ein-Licht gekauft?

6th Exercise.

1. Is the father of the girl come? 2. The maid of the young lady is gone. 3. Hast thou lost[1] a knife? 4. I have found[1] a knife. 5. The hair of the animal is grey. 6. Is the shoemaker poor? 7. Have you bought[1] a (loaf of) bread? 8. The father has a son and a daughter. 9. The servant of the daughter is a sister of the shoemaker. 10. Has[2] the shoemaker's son come?

1. At the end. 2. Transl. *is*.

FOURTH LESSON.

Learn Rules 61, 62 and 105.

Der-Früh'ling, the spring,
der-Som'mer, the summer,
der-Herbst', the autumn,
der-Win'ter, the winter,
der-Ball', the ball,
der-Fall', the fall,
der-Mann', the man, husband,
der-Jüng'ling,[1] the youth,
der-Sper'ling, the sparrow,
der-Hund', the hound, dog,
der-Fund', the find, treasure,
der-Klang', the sound,
der-Sang', the song,
der-Trank', (or Trunk), the drink,
der-Sprung', the spring, leap,
das-Horn', the horn, bugle.

1. Words in -ling, properly diminutives, have an e elided before ling, so that soft vowels preceding that termination retain their natural character, thus Jüngling pronounced: Jüng'ling.

Gehört, heard, belonged, belongs,
gegeben, given,
gemacht, made,
gethan, done,
gesehen, seen,
schön, beautiful, nice, fine,
frisch, fresh,
kalt, cold,
warm, warm,
für (*Acc.*), for,
oft, often,
oder, or.

7th Exercise.

1. Dieser-Frühling ist schön und warm. 2. Jener-Vater hat einen-Fall gethan (got). 3. Hat-er den-Fund jenes-Jünglings gesehen? 4. Wir-haben den-Klang dieses-Hornes gehört. 5. Dieses-Kind hat jenen-Ball gefunden. 6. Er-gehört jenem-Mädchen. 7. Hast-du jenen-Sang gemacht? 8. Dieser-Winter ist kalt. 9. Hat-sie dem-Vater diesen-Trank gemacht? 10. Dieser-Mann hat jenen-Hund gekauft.

8th Exercise.

1. (The)[1] autumn is often beautiful. 2. (The) spring is often fresh and cold. 3. (The) winter is

long and cold. 4. This youth has bought that² child a ball. 5. Have you heard the sound of that horn? 6. Has he seen the fall of this house? 7. We have bought this horse and that [one].³ 8. Is that animal old or young? 9. That young lady has made this² child a ball. 10. That drink is fresh and good.

1. Words in parenthesis should be translated when not belonging to the English. 2. Dative. 3. Words in this kind of parenthesis are not to be translated.

FIFTH LESSON.

Learn Rules 70, 71 and 106; read also Observation 55.

Karl, Charles,
der-Wein', the wine,
die-Milch', the milk,
das-Waſſer, the water,
das-Bier', the beer,
der-Freund', the friend (*male*),
der-Gar'ten, the garden,

das-Buch', the book,
das-Wet'ter, the weather,
ſchlecht, bad,
ſauer, sour,
ſüß, sweet,
bitter, bitter,
viel, much.

Nicht, not,
nichts, nothing,
noch, yet, still,
noch nicht, not yet,
immer, always,
ſchon, already,
ſo, so.

ſehr, very,
wenig, little,
aber, but,
als, as,
auch, also, even,
denn, for (*Conjunction*),

9th Exercise.

1. Ihr-Bier iſt ſauer, aber mein-Wein iſt ſüß. 2. Unſere-Milch iſt ſehr gut, aber unſer-Waſſer iſt ſchlecht. 3. Mein-Vater hat viel-Wein gekauft; er-iſt ſehr-gut. 4. Haben-Sie ſchon ein - Glas - Milch getrunken? ſie - iſt warm - und - ſüß. 5. Unſers - Vaters - Bruder hat - immer Wein - und - Bier im-Hauſe. 6. Haben - Sie ſeinem - Bruder ein - wenig - Brod

gegeben? er-ift fehr-arm. 7. Mein-Bier ift bitter, aber dein-Wein ift fauer. 8. Ich-habe mein-Glas-Wein schon getrunken; er-ift fehr-schön. 9. Ihr-Bruder hat viel-Milch getrunken; er-hat-auch unfer-Brod gegessen. 10. Hat Ihr-Vater das-Pferd-meines-Bruders gekauft, oder nicht?

10th Exercise.

1. My brother has bought[1] the horse of your father. 2. Our servant has made[1] the milk sweet. 3. His beer is very cold and bitter. 4. I have already drunk[1] my glass [of] wine, but he has not[2] yet eaten his bread. 5. Have you found[1] my knife? 6. Our father is very rich, he has a house and a horse. 7. This girl is very dutiful (treu)[1] to her father. 8. Their brother has not[1] heard[1] the prohibition. 9. Your beer turns[3] sour even in (im) winter. 10. That is my castle, I have bought it.

1. At the end. 2. Say: *yet not*. 3. Transl. *becomes*.

SIXTH LESSON.

Learn Rules 83, 107, 128 and 129.

Die-Frau', the woman, wife,
die-Katze, the cat,
die-Lippe, the lip,
die-Tinte, the ink,
die-Heimat, the home,
die-Abtei',[1] the abbey,

die-Freiheit, liberty, freedom,
die-Schönheit, beauty,
die-Dankbarkeit, thankfulness, gratitude,
die-Freundschaft, friendship,
die-Hoffnung, hope.

Geben-Sie! give!
geben-Sie? do you give?
Sie-geben, you give,
nehmen-Sie! take!

gehen-Sie! go!
kommen-Sie! come!
sagen-Sie! say, tell me!
Sie-sagen, you say.

In[2] (*Dat.* and *Acc.*), in, into,
mit (*Dat.*), with,

von (*Dat.*), from, of,
zu (*Dat.*), to,

1. *Observe.* All nouns ending in -ei have the stress on the last syllable. 2. See Rule 298.

wo, where?
da, there, then,
werth, worth, valuable,

kein, keine, kein, no (none), declined like the ind. Art. ein, eine, ein.

11th Exercise.

1. Wo-ist Ihre-Heimat? 2. Wem-ist die-Freiheit nicht-werth? 3. Was-ist mit-seiner-Lippe? 4. Wem hat-er seine-Freiheit verkauft? 5. Was haben-Sie in-dem-Haus gesehen? 6. Was hat-er in-der-Abtei gemacht? 7. Wessen ist das-Schloss? 8. Wer hat-nicht Hoffnung? 9. Wen haben-Sie gesehen? 10. Von-wem haben-Sie das gehört?

12th Exercise.

1. Whose gratitude is so great as[1] your friend's? 2. Who has no hope? 3. With whom is he gone [in]to[2] his home? 4. To whom (do) you give that book? 5. From whom have you bought this ink? 6. To whom have you sold your house? 7. In whom is [there] no hope? 8. Who is that[3] in your father's garden? 9. Whom have you seen in your sister's house? 10. What is that[3] in the water?

1. als. 2. in, Acc. 3. das da.

SEVENTH LESSON.

Learn Rules 87 and 108, revise Rule 107.

Der Tag, the day,
(der) Sonntag, Sunday,
(der) Montag, Monday,
(der) Dinstag, Tuesday,
(der) Mittwoch, Wednesday,
(der) Donnerstag, Thursday,
(der) Freitag, Friday,
(der) Samstag ⎫
(der) Sonnabend[1] ⎭ Saturday,
das Land, the land, country,
der Norden, the north,
der Süden, the south,
der Osten, the east,
der Westen, the west,

1. Sonnabend is more commonly used than Samstag.

der Wind, the wind,
der Nordwind, the north wind,
Heute,¹ to-day,
gestern, yesterday,
geschrieben, written,
der Südwind, the southwind,
der Südwestwind, the southwestwind.
findet, finds,
aus (*Dat.*), out of, from,
an (*Dat. & Acc.*), on, at, to.

13th Exercise.

1. Welcher von diesen-Männern¹ ist aus-dem-Norden? 3. Welchen-Tag haben-wir-heute, ist-es Donnerstag oder Freitag? 3. Welches-Kind hat keine-Dankbarkeit? 4. In welchem-Haus haben-Sie meinen-Bruder gefunden? 5. Mit-welcher-Schwester ist-er heute gekommen? 6. Welchem-Mann gehört jenes-Schloss? 7. Mit-welcher-Tinte haben-Sie dies geschrieben? 8. Welches-Land ist seine-Heimath? 9. Welches von-diesen-Pferden² hat Ihr-Vater gekauft? 10. Welches ist Ihr-Bruder-Karl?

1. men. 2. horses.

14th Exercise.

1. To which man does this house belong¹? 2. Which man is your friend? 3. To which girl have you written? 4. Which day of the week is this²? 5. With which horse [do] you come on³ Monday? 6. Which wind is very cold in this country? It is the eastwind. 7. In which country is your home? 8. To what⁴ child have you given the ball? 9. Which house is the abbey? 10. In which glass is the drink?

1. Transl.: To which man belongs this house? 2. Transl.: Which day have we to-day? 3. am. 4. Transl.: to which.

EIGHTH LESSON.

Learn Rules 90—92 and 109; read also Rule 317.

Das Gold, the gold,
das Silber, the silver,
das Eisen, the iron,
das Kupfer, the copper,
das Blei, the lead,
das Zinn, the tin,

das Neusilber, the German (or nickel) silver,
der Stahl, the steel.
Großbritannien, Great Britain,
England, England,
Schottland, Scotland,
Irland, Ireland;
Deutschland, Germany,

Das Schicksal, the fate,
das Christentum, the Christendom, christianity,
der Brief, the letter,
die Insel } the island,
das Eiland }

Weich, soft,
hart, hard,
theuer, dear,

Preußen, Prussia,
Sachsen, Saxony,
Baiern, Bavaria,
Hessen, Hesse;
Östreich[1], Austria,
Frankreich, France,
Rußland or Reußen, Russia,
Polen, Poland,
Holland, Holland.

1. Rarely Österreich.

das Volk, the people, folk,
das Räthsel, the riddle,
das Heiligtum, the sanctuary, holy thing, palladium.

jedermann, every body,
mehr, more, anymore,
herrscht, reigns, rules, prevails.

Observe. In **dependent** clauses the Verb (*i. e.*, a simple tense or auxiliary) stands at the end of the sentence, after Infinitives and Participles.

15th Exercise.

1. Deutschland ist ein-Land, welches (or das) reich an[1] Silber, Eisen, Kupfer, Blei und Zinn ist. 2. Das-Gold ist ein-Metall, welches (or das) sehr-weich ist. 3. Ist Schottland ein-Land, welches (or das) viel-Eisen hat? 4. Haben-Sie Stahl, welcher (or der) in-Preußen gemacht-ist? 5. Ist-dies ein-Land, in-welchem (or dem) das-Christenthum herrscht? 6. Welches ist die-Insel,[2] die (or welche) zu-Großbritannien gehört? 7. Östreich ist ein-Land, welches (or das) nicht-mehr

(no longer) zu-Deutschland gehört. 8. Das-ist ein-Schicksal, welches (or das) mir³ ein-Räthsel ist. 9. Die-Freiheit ist ein-Heiligtum, welches (or das) jedem⁴ Volk gehört. 10. Am-Sonnabend ist mein-Bruder von-Frankreich gekommen, wo-er in-Paris einen-Freund hat.

1. in. 2. isle. 3. to me. 4. each.

16th Exercise.

1. Is this the land, which is[1] so rich in[2] iron? 2. Prussia is the country, which rules[1] in Germany. 3. Have you seen the youth, who is[1] come from England with my brother? 4. Which is the land, in which liberty rules? 5. Charles has lost the letter, which his father had[3] written to a friend. 6. Which is the mother, who has[1] lost her child? 7. This is the boy, whose father is[1] in Ireland. 8. Come with [me] to[4] the castle, in which is[1] the sanctuary of the people. 9. It is his friendship, which Charles has[1] lost. 10. This is the country, in which[5] every man finds[1] a home.

1. Verb *at the end.* 2. an. 3. *had,* hatte, at the end. 4. to, nach, with Dative. 5. *or,* where.

NINTH LESSON.

Learn Rules 89 and 110, revise 109.

Der Mensch, man (*male* and *female*),
der Mann, the man (*male* only), husband,
die Frau, the woman, wife,
der Freund, the friend (*male*),
die Freundinn, or Freundin, the friend (*female*),
der Kaiser, the emperor,
die Kaiserinn, the empress,
der König, the king,
die Königinn, the queen,
der Sultan, the sultan,
die Sulta'ninn, the sultana,
der Gemahl, the consort, husband,
die Gemahlinn, the spouse, wife,

das Geschlecht, the sex, gender,
die Flasche, the bottle,
die Tintenflasche, the inkbottle,
männlich, masculine, manly,
weiblich, feminine, womanly,
sächlich, neuter,
sehen Sie? do you see?

17th Exercise.

1. Was-für-ein Land ist die Krim, und-wem gehört-es? 2. Wer-herrscht in-der-Schweiz, ein-Kaiser oder ein-König? 3. Was das für-ein-Irrtum ist, or, was-für-ein-Irrtum das ist! 4. Stahl und Zink sind männlichen-Geschlechts, Platina ist weiblichen-Geschlechts. 5. Was-für-ein-Geschlecht hat-Eisen? 6. Welch-eine-Schönheit das ist! sehen-Sie sie? 7. Welch-ein-Mensch ist-das! 8. Was-für-ein-Stöpsel ist-das, gehört-er zu-der-Tintenflasche? 9. Was-für-einen-Reichtum sein-Vater-hat! 10. Was-für-ein-Geschlecht haben Stahl, Eisen, Christentum, Irrtum, Weib und Frauenzimmer? Sind-sie alle sächlich?

18th Exercise.

1. What kind of a man is the sultan of Turkey? 2. What kind of a country is Switzerland? 3. What an emperor he is! 4. What liberty rules[1] in this country! 5. With what kind of ink have you written the letter? 6. Of what kind of metal is this knife, is it of iron or of steel? 7. What kind of an animal is the lion? 8. What a fate has this man! 9. What kind of a man is the emperor of Russia, is he tall or little? 10. Have you seen his wife, the empress? Is she young and beautiful?

1. Insert nicht.

TENTH LESSON.

Learn Rule 95 and of 112 what is in black type, read also 111.

Ich sei,[1] I be (was)
ich habe, I have (had) } Pres. Subj.
ich werde, I become (became)

(Each declined with the regular inflections, *i. e.*, (e), eſt, (e), en, et, en).

1. The Pres. Subj. is used principally in Indirect speech *(oratio obliqua)* and translatable mostly by the *past*.

Der Stein, the stone,   der Meer'ſchaum, the meer-
der Diamant', the diamond,   ſchaum,
der Granit', the granite,   der Sand, the sand,
der Mar'mor, the marble,   die Erde, the earth,
                das Jahr, the year.

Offen, open,   läſſt, leaves,
bezahlt, pays, paid,   liegt, lies,
                kennt, knows,

19th Exercise.

1. Geben-Sie-mir den-Band, in-welchem das-Band liegt! 2. Dies-iſt der-Bauer, der das-Bauer gemacht-hat. 3. Jemand hat auf-der-Heide einen-Hut gefunden. 4. Hat Niemand mein-Meſſer geſehen? 5. Jedermann hat einen-Gasmeſſer in-ſeinem-Hauſe. 6. Was-für-ein-Thor dieſer-Menſch iſt! er-läſſt das-Thor immer offen. 7. Dieſer-Kunde bezahlt ſchlecht? von-wem haben-Sie dieſe-Kunde? 8. Er-iſt Jedermanns-Freund, das-iſt ſein-Verdienſt. 9. Das-Verdienſt ſeines-Vaters iſt ſehr-groß, aber der-Verdienſt ſeines-Vaters iſt klein. 10. Ein-Theil-jenes-Erbes gehört dieſem-Menſchen.

20th Exercise.

1. The sea is great and beautiful, but the lake in[1] my country[2] is also very fine. 2. Take you the helm,

what a wind there³ is! 3. My share of⁴ the gain is not very large; but my merit is not great either.⁵ 4. Somebody has lost his tie, has nobody found it? 5. One has given to my brother a shield and a knife. 6. Oh thou fool[ish man], who (thou) hast lost the friendship of thy brother! 7. Everybody does not pay⁶ so well⁷ as⁸ this customer. 8. Has anybody found the hat, which I have lost on⁹ the heath? 9. Does nobody know¹⁰ the heir¹¹ of this peasant, who is so very rich? 10. The want in that country is great this year.

1. in, Dat. 2. Heimat, f. 3. Transl.: *it is*. 4. an, Dat. 5. auch, before *not*. 6. Transl.: *pays not*. 7. gut. 8. wie or als. 9. auf, Dat. 10. Transl.: *knows nobody*. 11. Acc., den Erben.

ELEVENTH LESSON.

Study Rules 155—164; learn 159 and 165.

Friedrich, Frederick,
Heinrich, Henry,

Friedrike, Fredrica,
Henriette, rare Heinrike, Henrietta,

Johann' or Johan'nes, John,
Karl, Charles,
Ludwig (pr. Lud'wig), Louis,
Wilhelm, William,

Johan'na or Johanne, Jane,
Karoli'ne, Caroline,
Luise, rare Ludewike, Louisa,
Wilhelmi'ne, Wilhelmina.

artig, well-behaved,
un'artig, naughty,
edel, noble, precious,
un'edel, ignoble,
glücklich, lucky, happy, fortunate,
un'glücklich, unlucky, unhappy, unfortunate,

zufrieden, contented, satisfied, pleased,
un'zufrieden, dissatisfied,
fleißig, diligent,
faul, lazy, rotten, foul,
gestern, yesterday,
gestrig, of yesterday,
heute, to-day,

heutig, of to-day,
morgen, to-morrow,
morgend, to-morrow's,

als, as, than,
der Knabe, the boy,
die Klasse, the class,
das Geld, the money.

aller, alle, alles, all
jeder, jede, jedes, each, every
mancher, manche, manches, many a (*plur.* some)
solcher, solche, solches, such (a)

} have the import of Pronouns in German when preceding nouns or adjectives and are declined like dieser, e, es.

21st Exercise.

1. Ist Ihre-Schwester-Louise jünger, als-Sie? 2. Ludwig-ist das-kleinste-Kind meines-Freundes-Heinrich. 3. Sein-Bruder-Johann ist-viel-älter, als-er. 4. Ich-bin mit-Karl immer-zufriedener, als-mit-Ludwig. 5. Er-ist der-fleißigste-Sohn meines-Freundes-Johann. 6. Mancher-Knabe ist-größer und-fleißiger[1] und-doch[2] jünger, als sein-Bruder. 7. Meine-Schwester-Johanna ist artiger,[3] als-manches-Mädchen, das-älter-ist, als-sie. 8. Alles-Gold der-Erde macht nicht[4] zufried'ner und glücklicher, als-die-Freiheit und-Freundschaft. 9. Welcher-Knabe ist-wohl[5] fauler, als-Heinrich; er-ist der-faulste-Mensch[6] in-der-Klasse. 10. Du-bist-heute artiger,[3] als-gestern.

1. Pronounce: *flise-yer*. 2. yet. 3. Pronounce: *art'yer*. 4. does not make one. 5. can possibly be. 6. fellow.

22nd Exercise.

1. Not every boy is so diligent as my friend's son John, he is the best behaved and most diligent boy in the class. 2. My sister Henrietta is older and taller than your sister Caroline. 3. Charles has lost all [the] money which his father has given him[1]. 4. On[2] Monday* it was[3] much colder than to-day. 5. Many a

*) The Verb (*i. e.*, a simple tense or the auxiliary in compound tenses) in *independent* sentences must have the **second** place, whatever be the first expression, even a dependent clause occupying the first place in the period, is reckoned as such and must be followed by the verb.

wine is sweeter than this, but not more generous (edel). 6. January[4] is in the north of Germany the coldest month[5] of the year (or, in the year). 7. Give me[6] a bottle [of] beer which is not so bitter as this. 8. This milk is much sweeter than that. 9. John is older than his brother Louis, but the latter[7] is taller and more diligent than the former[8]. 10. [9]Gold is the most precious and finest metal; it is, however[10], not so rare[11] as [9]platina.

1. ihm. 2. am. 3. war. 4. der Januar. 5. der Monat. 6. mir. 7. or *this*. 8. or *that*. 9. Use the Def. Art. 10. aber. 11. rar or selten.

TWELFTH LESSON.

Learn Rules 114 and 115; study 171—181.

(Der) Januar', January,
» Februar', February,
» März, March,
» April', April,
» Mai, May,
» Ju'ni or Junius, June,

(der) Ju'li or Julius, July,
» August', August,
» September, September,
» October, October,
» November, November,
» Dezember, December.

Das Jahr, the year,
der Monat, the month,
die Woche, the week,
der Tag, the day,
die Stunde, the hour,
die Minu'te, the minute,

die Secun'de, the second;
der Anfang, the beginning,
die Freude, the joy,
das Herz, the heart,
das Stück, the piece,
die Welt, the world.

Geschenkt, presented,
lieb, dear (*not* expensive),
theuer, dear *and* expensive,
nächst, next,

stark, strong,
trocken, dry,
würdig, worthy,
wie, how,
doch, please, do.

23rd Exercise.

1. Lieber Freund, kommen Sie doch zu Anfang nächsten[1] Monats nach Berlin. 2. Er ist ein großer Freund von warmem Wetter. 3. Karoline ist ein artiges Kind, sie macht[2] ihrem guten Vater viel(e) Freude. 4. Unser alter Vater hat gestern seinen liebsten Bruder verloren. 5. Der März ist in Deutschland ein kalter Monat. 6. Ich habe gehört, ein guter Freund Ihres jüngsten Bruders hat ein schönes, neues Haus gekauft. 7. Das ist ja[3] sehr schönes Brod, wo haben Sie es gekauft? 8. Du faules Kind, du bist nicht deines hohen Namens werth[4]. 9. Ein reicher Mann hat Johanns altem Vater schönen Wein und starkes Bier geschenkt. 10. Ein zufrieb'nes Herz ist besser als aller Reichtum der Welt.

1. See Rule 180. 2. gives. 3. I say. 4. worthy.

24th Exercise.

1. Give me[1] a small glass [of] fresh milk and a large piece [of] dry[2] bread. 2. Good wine is dear, and bad [wine] is worth nothing. 3. What a well-behaved child that is! Is it the youngest son of this good man? 4. What a long name that is! Is it the name of this new book? 5. She has given me her name and the name of her friend. 6. He has no strong faith and also[4] no right peace. 7. He is not worthy[5] of the name of his great father. 8. The strong wind has done great damage[6] to our new house. 9. He has a noble heart; he is a worthy man. 10. Our strong beer is more wholesome than your sour wine.

1. mir. 2. See Rule 180. 3. nichts werth. 4. auch. 5. werth, at the end. 6. Dative before Accusative, thus: *to our house great damage.*

THIRTEENTH LESSON.
Learn Rules 126, 1. 2. and 127.

Ich hatte, I had,	wir hatten, we had,
du hattest, thou hadst,	ihr hattet, you had,
er hatte, he had,	sie hatten, they had.

Die Geschichte, the story, history,
die Thür(e), the door.

das Loos, the lot, fate,
die Schöpfung, the creation,

Bezwingt, conquers,
gebunden, bound,
gelesen, read,
ich sah, I saw (regularly inflected),
steht, stands,

gerecht, just, right,
weise, wise,
wild, wild,
wundervoll, wonderful,
gegen (*Acc.*), towards, against,
je, ever.

25th Exercise.

1. Des Menschen Loos auf¹ dieser schönen Welt liegt nicht in seiner Hand. 2. Die wundervolle Geschichte eines großen Helden steht in diesem schön gebundenen Buch. 3. Dieser ed'le Fürst ist gerecht gegen jeden Menschen, auch² den ärmsten. 4. Wir haben gestern einen wilden Bären gesehen, er gehört dem Grafen X. 5. Haben Sie schon das neue Buch vom Prinzen N. gelesen? 6. Hast du je einen solchen Gecken gesehen? 7. Wer hat den Menschen zum Herrn der Schöpfung gemacht? 8. Der Löwe ist das stärkste Thier, aber der Mensch bezwingt auch² den Löwen. 9. Ich sah gestern einen kleinen Knaben mit einem schönen Falken auf³ der rechten Hand. 10. Er hatte einen alten Mohren zum Genossen.

1. in. 2. even. 3. upon.

26th Exercise.

1. Did you see¹ the young prince yesterday in the house of the noble count? 2. His happy companion was the youngest son of a great hero. 3. We have an old herd, who is² a very wise man. 4. The good king has made the worthy count a³ prince. 5. Who has made this poor negro a³ christian? 6. He is very faithful to his noble master. 7. I have written a long letter to old Mr. W. 8. To which boy belongs this beautiful ball? 9. Whose is that large new

house with the high door? 10. We have lost our good companion.

1. Transl. *Have you — seen.* 2. Verb at the end. 3. zum, Dat.

FOURTEENTH LESSON.
Learn Rules 128 and 129.

Ich war, I was,
du warst, thou wast,
er war, he was,

wir waren, we were,
ihr war(e)t, you were,
sie waren, they were.

Die Aufgabe, the task,
die Stadt, the town,
die Ader, the vein,
die Achsel[1] }
die Schulter } the shoulder,
die Brust, the breast,
die Hand, the hand,
die Haut, the skin, hide,

die Lunge, the lungs,
die Kehle, the throat,
die Leber, the liver,
die Nase, the nose,
die Sehne, the sinew,
die Stirn(e), the forehead,
die Zehe, the toe,
die Zunge, the tongue.

Sprechen, to speak,
sprechen Sie! speak!
laut, loud,
rein, pure, clean,
schlimm, sore,
selten, seldom, rare,

ich stand,[2] I stood,
deshalb, therefore,
da (*Conjunction*), as, since,
da (*Adverb*), there, then,
zu, too, to.

1. Pronounce Axel. 2. Declined like ich war.

27th Exercise.

1. Wir haben heute Morgen Zunge gegessen, sie war sehr schön und weich. 2. Louise hat eine schöne, hohe Stirn und eine kleine Nase. 3. Er stand da, die rechte Hand auf der Brust. 4. Johann hat eine sehr gute Lunge. 5. Eine

kleinere Hand hab' ich selten gesehen. 6. Er hat eine schlimme Kehle. 7. Wer¹ ein reines Herz in der Brust hat, ist glücklich. 8. Wilhelm hat eine größere Hand als sein jüngerer Bruder, er hat die größte Hand von Allen. 9. Die liebe Freundinn seiner guten Mutter war die beste Frau von der Welt, eine bessere Frau sah ich nie. 10. Diese schöne Blume ist aus dem schönen Haar einer jungen Königinn.

1. He who.

28th Exercise.

1. I had yesterday a sore hand and therefore I have¹ not written my exercise of to-day. 2. Take your² hand from your² forehead. 3. John was a good child, he had a pure heart in his² breast. 4. You have very good lungs³, speak louder! 5. I have a sore throat, I can (kann) not speak⁴ louder. 6. He has done a better exercise than his elder brother. 7. Have you read the new book of your youngest sister? 8. Give your dear mother⁵ this beautiful flower⁶, it is the sweetest flower of my little garden. 9. Have you seen the youngest daughter of our noble queen? 10. Have you ever seen a more beautiful town?

1. Transl. *have I*. 2. Transl. *the*. 3. Transl. *a very good lung*. 4. sprechen, at the end. 5. Dat. 6. Acc.

FIFTEENTH LESSON.

Learn Rules 117 and 196; read 198—201.

Ich wurde (or ward), I be-   wir wurden, we became,
came,¹

du wurdest (or wardst), thou   ihr wurdet, you became,
becamest,

er wurde (or ward), he be-   sie wurden, they became.
came,

1. Used also for the Impf. Passive instead of English *was*.

Der Arzt, the physician,
der Doc'tor, the doctor,
der Apothe'ker, the apothecary,
der Barbier', the barber,
der Schmied, the smith,
die Leute¹ (*Plur.* noun), the people,
das Korn, the corn,
der Schirm, the screen,
der Regenschirm, the umbrella,
der Sonnenschirm, the parasol,
das Pfund, the pound,
der Schilling, the shilling,
der Thaler, the dollar,
die Mark, mark (one shilling),
der Groschen, the groat,
der Pfennig, the penny,
die Krone, the crown,
das Schiff, the ship,
der Tisch, the table.

1. The Sing. das Leut, the person, is now obsolete, it occurs however still in the Southern Dialects.

Angekommen, arrived,
abgereist, departed,
erhalten, to get, got, to receive, received,
kosten, to cost, taste,
ich sehe, I see,
es giebt (*Acc.*), there is, there are, or *there exists*,
es gab, there was, there were,
nennen Sie! name!
geherrscht, ruled,
englisch, English,
deutsch, German,
schwarz, black,
ander, other,
zusammen, together,
für (*Acc.*), for,
vor (*Dat. & Acc.*), before, ago,
seit (*Dat.*), since,
nur, only,
so — als, as — as,
als, as, when.

29th Exercise.

1. Vor acht Tagen ist unser alter Freund der Doctor angekommen; er war viele Jahre in der Türkei. 2. Wie viele Tische sind in diesem Zimmer? Ich sehe nur zwei, einen großen und einen kleinen. 3. Es giebt in diesem Land viel reiche Leute, aber auch sehr viel arme. 4. Ich habe heute

zwei sehr schöne Pferde gekauft, das eine ist braun und das andere ist schwarz; das schwarze ist am theuersten,[1] ich habe 1450 Mark dafür[2] bezahlt. 5. Meine Freunde Karl und Ludwig haben von ihrem Vater zwei Bote erhalten, jeder eines, welche zusammen 1110 Mark und 50 Pfennige kosten. 6. Das Jahr hat zwölf Monate, nennen Sie sie mir! 7. Nennen Sie mir auch die sieben Tage der Woche! 8. Er wurde ein Freund aller guten Leute, als er alt war. 9. Geben Sie den neuen Pferden schönes, reines Korn! 10. Ferdinands Schwester hat schwarze Haare, eine kleine Nase und eine hohe Stirn.

Read the following figures in German: 87. 329. 1,157. 1,268. 1,640. 1,024. 2,009. 31,554. 573,420. 3,892,732.

1. Read Rule 164. 2. for it.

30th Exercise.

1. I saw yesterday on[1] the open sea 16 large vessels and about (an) 70 large and small boats. 2. Have you many faithful friends? 3. The young man has given to your new horses beautiful corn and pure fresh water. 4. I have paid for these beautiful brown horses 2577 marks and 50 pfennig; is it too much? 5. Name the year in which the great revolution (Revolution, f.) in France began (anfing); 1789. 6. Our good friends have[2] departed a fortnight ago[3]. 7. How many kings have ruled in England from[4] the year 1400 to[5] the year 1500? 8. There are three great kings in[6] history, Alexander, Cæsar and Frederick the Great. 9. One [German] mark has 100 pence and is equal to one English shilling, therefore one sovereign is equal to 20 marks, one crown equal to 5 marks and 6 pence[7] equal to 50 [German] pence. 10. What[8] are the names of the 7 days of the week and what do you call the 12 months of the year?

1. auf, Dat. 2. Transl. are. 3. Transl. before [vor, Dat.]

14 *days.* 4. from the: vom. 5. to the: bis zum. 6. Use the Def. Art. 7. Say Pence. 8. What are the names of: Wie heißen.

SIXTEENTH LESSON.

Learn Rules 118, 119 and 197; read also 195, 202—204.

Der Hals, die Hälse, the neck,
der Kopf, die Köpfe, the head,
der Fuß, die Füße, the foot,
der Mund, die Münde, the mouth,
der Zahn, die Zähne, the tooth,
der Hut, die Hüte, the hat, bonnet,
der Rock, die Röcke, the coat, frock,
der Stock, die Stöcke, the stick, cane,
der Strumpf, die Strümpfe, the stocking,
das Stück, the piece,
Wachsen,[1] to grow, to wax,
getödtet, killed,
beginnt, commences, begins,
ich saß, I sat ⎫ all declined
ich stand, I stood ⎬ with the regular inflections.
ich lag, I lay ⎭

der Fluß, die Flüsse, the river,
der Satz, die Sätze, the sentence,
der Stuhl, die Stühle, the chair,
der Schrank, die Schränke, the press,
der Fisch, the fish,
die Wand, the wall (of the inner house),
der Wandschrank, the press (in the wall), cupboard,
das Holz, the wood,
die Schule, the school,
das Zimmer, the room,
die Prinzessinn, the princess.
scharf, sharp,
golden, golden,
königlich, kingly, royal,
unter (*Dat.* and *Acc.*), under,
und so weiter (u. s. w.), and so on, etc.

1. Pronounce: *vaxen.*

31st *Exercise.*

1. Der Mensch hat 32 Zähne; die ersten acht kommen im ersten Jahr, bis zum[1] Ende des zweiten Jahres wachsen

zwölf neue; die letzten vier, die Weisheitszähne,² wachsen erst vom³ zwanzigsten bis⁴ dreißigsten Jahr. 2. Die Hydra der Alten hatte neun Köpfe. 3. In Norddeutschland hat man nicht oft Wandschränke im Hause. 4. Die meisten Schränke, in denen man Röcke, Hüte u. s. w. aufbewahrt⁵, sind von Holz. 5. Es waren im großen Zimmer zwölf Stühle, auf dem ersten saß der neue König, auf dem zweiten die junge Königinn und auf den andern die Prinzen und Prinzessinnen des königlichen Hauses. 6. Ein jedes von diesen deutschen und englischen Stücken hat zehn Sätze. 7. Mein Freund S. ist mit all seinen Söhnen auf das Land⁶ gegangen. 8. Seine ältesten Söhne waren in der Schule immer die ersten. 9. Es giebt oder gab in den Flüssen von Deutschland viel(e) Aale und Lachse und andere Fische. 10. Geben Sie mir meine Schuhe und Strümpfe.

1. up to the. 2. wisdom teeth. 3. not before the. 4. to the. 5. keeps. 6. to the country.

32nd Exercise.

1. I saw in the beautiful palaces of the new king many dukes, great generals and worthy bishops. 2. They stood at the¹ foot of the golden thrones of the new king and the young queen. 3. There are in Holland many large and small canals. 4. With sharp daggers they² have killed the unhappy man. 5. He lay under³ the hoofs of his horses. 6. ⁴Spring commences on the¹ 21st [of] March, ⁴summer on the¹ 21st [of] June, ⁴autumn on the¹ 23d [of] September and ⁴winter on the¹ 22nd [of] December. 7. Mr. N. is the first of all our young physicians. 8. Has the English shoemaker made your new shoes? 9. Who sat on⁵ the three first chairs? 10. How many moons has the planet⁷ Jupiter?

1. am. 2. Transl. *have they.* 3. Dat. 4. Insert the Def. Art. 5. auf, Dat. 6. der Planet.

SEVENTEENTH LESSON.

Learn Rules 121 and 206.

Ich wäre, I were (Impf. Subjunctive),
ich hätte, I had   do.,
ich würde, I became do.

(Each declined with the regular inflections.)

Der Schneider, die Schneider[1], the tailor,
der Tischler, the joiner,
der Hutmacher, the hatter,
der Glaser, the glazier,
der Handwerker, the artisan,
der Händler, the dealer,
der Weinhändler, the wine-merchant,
der Buchhändler, the bookseller,
der Lederhändler, the leather-merchant,
der Krämer, the grocer,
der Engländer, the Englishman,
der Spanier, the Spaniard,
der Italiener, the Italian,
der Amerikaner, the American,
der Spiegel, the mirror,
der Stiefel, the boot,
der Finger, the finger,
das Fenster, the window,
die Sohle, the sole,
der Sturm, the storm.

1. Supply with each noun the Plural.

Erhalten, to get *and* got,
versucht, tried,
gehabt, had,
erlitten, suffered,
geheirathet, married,
thun, to do, to put,
legen, to put, to lay,
hiesig, here, of this place.

kennen, to know, to be acquainted with,
zurück, back,
wieder, again,
wieder zurück, back again,
da, since, as,
nach (*Dat.*), after,

33rd Exercise.

1. Ich habe es schon mit vielen Schneidern versucht, aber keiner hat mir einen einfachen[1] Rock gut gemacht. 2. Es giebt im Norden von Deutschland viel große und kleine Häuser[2] mit zweifachen (or doppelten) Fenstern. 3. Die hiesigen Glaser haben nach dem großen Sturme viel zu thun gehabt, da die meisten Fenster vielfachen Schaden erlitten hatten. 4. Legen Sie dreifache Sohlen unter meine neuen Stiefel! 5. Die fleißigen Krämer und Händler werden oft reich. 6. Die Hüte der Londoner und Pariser Hutmacher sind am besten. 7. Es giebt in dieser großen Stadt sehr viel reiche Buchhändler. 8. Kennen Sie den würdigen Vater dieser jungen Amerikaner? er ist einer der reichsten Händler in New-York. 9. Die glücklichen Italiener haben die schönen Schwestern zweier reicher Engländer geheirathet. 10. Was haben Sie mit diesen unglücklichen Spaniern zu thun?

1. ordinary. 2. houses. 3. Read Rule 179.

34th Exercise.

1. How many fingers has man on[1] each hand? 2. Have your boots single or double soles? 3. The sons of these poor grocers are[2] going to be artisans. 4. This[3] is the best of all [the] hatters in the new town. 5. These rich winemerchants are the faithful friends of those poor Americans. 6. Give back[4] to the dealers the mirrors which you have bought from them[5]. 7. Have you tried[6] these tailors? 8. Come with [me] to[7] those artisans! 9. Do you know the eldest sons of these rich booksellers? 10. Give that back[8] to the grocers from whom you have got it!

1. an, Dat. 2. Transl. *become*. 3. Read Rule 317, 1. 4. *back*, stands at the end of the sentence, after *mirrors*. 5. ihnen. 6. Insert: *it with*. 7. zu, Dat. 8. *back*, stands at the end, after *grocers*.

EIGHTEENTH LESSON.

Learn Rules 122, 123, 207 and 208.

Ich besaß, I possessed, ich fand, I found.

(Each declined with the regular inflections.)

Das Mittagessen, the dinner,
eingekauft, purchased,
eisern, (of) iron (Rule 193),
gesprochen, spoken,
gewöhnlich, generall(y), common(ly),
hangen, to hang (intr. verb),
hängen, to hang (trans. verb),
lang, long (speaking of *space*),
lange or lang', long (Adverb of *time*),
umgeben, surrounded,
tief, deep,
vergessen, forgotten,
todt, dead,
verkaufen, to sell,
verstorben, deceased, late,
nach Hause, home,
von Hause, from home,
zu Hause, at home, in,
wohl, perhaps, probably,
bei (*Dat.*), with, at the house of, at,

35th Exercise.

1. Geben Sie diese schönen Äpfel Ihren jüngern Brüdern! 2. Die alten Klöster besaßen gewöhnlich große Gärten. 3. Sie waren mit tiefen Gräben umgeben. 4. Es giebt wohl in keinem Land so viel gute Häfen als in England. 5. Wie lang die rothen Schnäbel dieser kleinen Vögel sind! 6. Unsere reichen Vettern haben die schönsten Äcker von der Welt. 7. Ihre verstorbenen Väter waren arme Bauern. 8. Heute habe ich zum ersten Mal in diesen neuen Läden eingekauft. 9. Fünf mal sechs ist dreißig, und wie viel macht sieben mal neun? 10. Ist das nicht das zweite Mal, daß Ihre kleinen Vettern ihre warmen Mäntel vergessen haben?

36th Exercise.

1. The poor fathers of these old cloisters are[1] long dead. 2. How [do] you sell these beautiful apples

per pound²? 3. My good brothers have forgotten the bad defects of these little gardens, they have bought them. 4. Did you see³ my young cousins twice yesterday? 5. We were to-day for the first time at the house of your dear cousins. 6. How much is 3 times 80? 7. I was three times at the house of the good peasants, the first time they⁴ were on⁵ their fine fields, the second time they⁴ were at their dinner, but the third time I⁶ have seen and spoken [to] them. 8. Have you forgotten the ancient story of the wicked birds with the iron beaks? 9. Hang your new cloaks on⁷ the strong nails in the wall behind⁸ the iron stoves, where the old saddles [are] hang[ing] already! 10. What beautiful shops the artisans in this large town have!

1. Insert ſchon. 2. Transl. *how sell you the pound of these beautiful apples.* 3. Transl. *have you — seen.* 4. Transl. *were they.* 5. auf, Dat. 6. Transl. *have I.* 7. an, Acc. 8. hinter, Dat.

NINETEENTH LESSON.

Learn Rules 124, 1. 2, (masculines only), 209 and 210.

Perfect Participle.

Geweſen, been, gehabt, had, geworden, become.

Perfect Tense.

Ich bin geweſen, I have been (Ind.),
ich ſei geweſen, I have been (Subj.);
ich habe gehabt, I have had (Ind.),
ich habe gehabt, I have had (Subj.);

ich bin geworden, I have become (Ind.),
ich ſei geworden, I have become (Subj.).

Die Anzahl } the multitude,
die Menge } great number, many,

der Bruch, the fraction, the breach,

der Einwohner, the inhabitant,
das Königreich (*concrete*), das

Leben, to live,
lesen, to read,
nützen, to avail,
verehren, to honour, to worship,
folgend, following,

Königthum (*abstract*), the kingdom,
das Leben, the life,
der Morgen, the morning,
großartig, grand, great,
grün, green,
seltsam, strange,
früher } formerly.
ehemals }

37th Exercise.

1. Was nützen dem Menschen alle Reichtümer der Welt, wenn er nicht zufrieden ist? 2. Die Würmer leben unter Sträuchern, auch in Wäldern. 3. Die Geister dieser Männer waren großartig. 4. Die alten Germanen (Germans) verehrten mehrere Götter. 5. Kennen Sie die Namen der Götter, die bei (with) den Griechen (Greeks) die größten waren? 6. Diese Männer haben nicht ein Viertel von den Reichtümern ihrer Väter gehabt und sind doch (yet) glücklich gewesen. 7. Lesen Sie die folgenden Brüche: $2/3$, $3/5$, $6/8$, $7/9$, $1/100$, $2/101$, $1/10,000$. 8. Der Mond ist im ersten Viertel. 9. Wo sind Sie diesen Morgen mit jenen Männern gewesen? 10. Wie viele Örter kennen Sie in Schottland, die mehr als 10,000 Einwohner haben?

38th Exercise.

1. Those young men have been in the large woods of your dear father. 2. Who has seen all (the) large places in Scotland? 3. (Do) you know the German names of these strange worms? 4. Are there many tall men in Switzerland[1]? 5. Are there people in Europe (Europa) who worship several gods? 6. How (do) those poor men live in the large woods? 7. Have your elder brothers had formerly great riches? 8. How

many kingdoms are there in Europe? 9. We have found these rare worms under the green shrubs. 10. What a number (of) errors are in that new book!

1. Compare Rule 110.

TWENTIETH LESSON.

Learn Rules 124, 2 (neuters), 212—214.

Sein, to be, haben, to have, werden, to become.

Future.

Ich werde sein[1], I shall be,
ich werde haben, I shall have,
ich werde werden, I shall become.

Pluperfect Indicative.

Ich war gewesen, I had been,
ich hatte gehabt, I had had,
ich war geworden, I had become.

1. The Infinitive stands at the end of the phrase; in dependent clauses the Verb (*i. e.*, a simple tense or auxiliary) follows it.

The Future Tense of all German Verbs is formed by means of ich werde (vid. 253) and an Infinitive; as, Ind.: ich werde, du wirst, er wird gehen, I shall go; Subj.: ich werde, du werdest, er werde sehen, I shall (*or* should) see.

Die Mandel, a lot of fifteen,
das Schock, a lot of sixty,
die Einheit, Einzahl, the singular,

die Mehrheit, Mehrzahl, the plural,
das Stroh, the straw.

Bauen, to build, to cultivate,
bilden, to form, educate,
geben, to give,
gehen, to go,
liegen, to lie,
stehen, to stand,

sehen, to see,
aussehen, to look,
anführen, to mention,
führen Sie — an, mention!
zwischen (*Dat. & Acc.*), between, among,
also, thus.

39th Exercise.

1. Wer hat den Kindern dieser Weiber meine neuen Bücher gegeben? 2. Was sehen Sie in Dörfern? Hühner, Kälber, Lämmer, Rinder u. s. w.¹ 3. Wir werden heute nach den Schlössern des Königs gehen. 4. Sehen Sie nur (just), wie schön die Felder in jenen Thälern stehen! 5. Die Vögel bauen ihre Nester in den Löchern unter den Dächern der Häuser, auch zwischen den Blättern der Bäume und Sträucher. 6. Die Thiere haben Mäuler, die Menschen haben Münde. 7. Haben Sie schon die schönen Bilder in diesen Büchern gesehen? 8. Wir haben heute viererlei Bänder gekauft, auch zweierlei Gläser und mancherlei Kräuter. 9. Verkaufen Sie diese Tücher stückweise oder dutzendweise? 10. Die Eier verkauft man (they sell) in Deutschland mandelweise und schockweise; eine Mandel hat fünfzehn und ein Schock sechzig Stück, also ist ein Schock gleich (equal to) vier Mandeln.

1. Read: und so weiter, *and so on* (etc.).

40th Exercise.

1. The great¹ (people) have the high² offices. 2. A contented heart is better than all (the) possessions of this world. 3. (Do) you sell these eggs by the dozen? 4. Mention such names of animals (in German), as³ form the plural in (auf) -er. 5. In these graves (there) lie the bodies of (von) men, women and children. 6. The most roofs in these villages are thatched⁴. 7. How many words of (the) neuter gender form the plural in (auf) -er? 8. (Do) you know (any) German songs? 9. On⁵ the green fields (there) grow herbs and grasses, on the high trees grow green leaves. 10. The princes are the heads of the peoples⁶.

1. Adjectives used substantively require a capital initial. 2. Compare Rule 178. 3. Transl. *which*. 4. Transl. *are of straw*. 5. auf, Dat. 6. Use the plural.

TWENTY-FIRST LESSON.
Learn Rules 124, 3. and 214.

Conditional I.

Ich würde sein, I should be,
ich würde haben, I should have,
ich würde werden, I should become.

Pluperfect Subjunctive.

ich wäre gewesen, I had been,
ich hätte gehabt, I had had,
ich wäre geworden, I had become.

Abmarschiren, to march away,	offen, open,
abmarschirt, marched away,	zahlreich, numerous,
ausgehen, to go out,	gefälligst¹, if you please,
sagen, to say, to tell,	gerade, just, straight,
er giebt, he gives,	hier, here,
fertig gemacht haben, (to) have finished,	wann, when (of time)?
	wenn, if, ob, if *or* whether,
berühmt, famous,	als ob, as if,
folgend, following,	bis, to, till, until,
häßlich, ugly,	je or jemals, ever,
hübsch, pretty,	nie or niemals, never,
	um (*Acc.*), about, at.

1. gefälligst precedes the Acc.; as, geben Sie mir gefälligst ein Buch, give me a book, if you please!

Note. 1. The Verb in **dependent phrases** stands *at the end*; if the dependent phrase precedes the independent (*Inverted construction*), the verb of the latter must stand before the subject. (See Rules 309—312.)

Note. 2. The **Subjunctive Mood** must be used after wenn and ob, if the Verb is in the *Imperfect* or *Pluperfect* tense and not purely narrative.

41st Exercise.

1. Die drei Regimenter Infanterie würden heute um drei Viertel (auf) zwei abmarschirt sein, wenn das Wetter besser gewesen wäre. *Inverted*: Wenn das Wetter besser gewesen wäre, würden die drei Regimenter.... 2. Würden Sie mir wohl sagen, wie viel Uhr es ist? 3. Ich würde um halb drei (Uhr) mit dem jungen Doctor nach den Hospitälern gegangen sein, wenn er nicht krank geworden wäre. *Inverted*: Wenn der junge Doctor nicht krank geworden wäre, würde ich mit ihm um.... 4. Die Gemächer in diesen Schlössern sind von ein Viertel auf eins bis um vier Uhr offen. 5. Wenn Sie um halb acht bei mir (at my house) gewesen wären, [1]hätten Sie die neuen Gewänder gesehen. (*Inverted*). 6. Nennen Sie mir einmal (please) die Geschlechter der folgenden Wörter: Kind, Mann, Weib, Mädchen, Haus. 7. Dieser Mann giebt seinen Freunden oft Gastmähler, als ob er sehr reich wäre. 8. Kommen Sie zu den neuen Denkmälern! 9. Ich habe nie in meinem Leben solche häßlichen Gesichter gesehen. 10. Wie viel Uhr ist es? Es ist gerade in zehn Minuten drei Viertel auf zwölf.

1. See Rule 369.

42nd Exercise.

1. If you had been here at half past four[1], we should[2] have seen the high castles of the king and all their beautiful apartments. 2. If the tailor had not[3] become ill, he would have finished[4] our new garments. 3. When have[5] the famous regiments marched away, was it at a quarter to eight? 4. The pretty monuments and fine hospitals of this great nation are very numerous. 5. We should go out[6] at 12 o'clock, if the weather were better. 6. Have you ever seen in pictures such beautiful faces? 7. In the first of the fine hospitals are the men, in the second, which is the largest, are the women, and in the third are the children. 8. Give, if you please, the genders of the following words[7]: England, Eisen, Glas, Wein, Bier, Milch

and Waſſer. 9. At what o'clock have you been in the woods? 10. Take the two candles and follow me (mir) to⁸ my apartments.

    1. Arrange so that *the time* (at half past four) stands before *the place* (here) and *the Verb* (been had) *last*. 2. Construe *should we....seen have*. 3. The negative stands before *ill*. 4. fertig ge= macht haben, at the end. 5. Transl. *are* instead of *have*. 6. Infinitive (go out) *last*. 7. Insert an. 8. auf, Acc.

TWENTY-SECOND LESSON.
Learn Rules 125 and 205.

Perfect Infinitive.

Geweſen ſein, to have been, gehabt haben, to have had, geworden ſein, to have become.

Future II.

Ich werde geweſen ſein, I shall have been,
ich werde gehabt haben, I shall have had,
ich werde geworden ſein, I shall have become.

Die Arbeit, the labour, work,
der Arbeiter, the labourer, working man,
die Feder, the feather, pen,
die Mühe, the trouble,
der Werth, the value.

der Reiter, the rider, horseman,
die Sonne, the sun,
die Weiſe ⎫ the air, melody,
die Melodie¹ ⎭

    1. Silent -e.

Dringen, to penetrate,
finden, to find,
reiſen, to travel,
ab reiſen, to leave, to go away,
tragen, to carry, to wear,
wiſſen, to know, *i. e.*, to

have a *thorough* knowledge, be conscious of,
zahlen, to pay,
bezahlen, to pay for,
geliehen, lent,
zerriſſen, torn;
an (*Dat.* and *Acc.*), on *or* at,

auf (*Dat.* and *Acc.*), on or upon,
durch (*Acc.*), through,
für (*Acc.*), for,
über (*Dat.* and *Acc.*), over,
blau, blue,
dicht, tight, close, dense,
eigen, own,
schlimm, sore,
schlimmer, worse,
silbern, of silver.
traurig, dreary, sad,
wie? how?
wenn? when?
und zwar, and that.

43rd Exercise.

1. Haben Sie nicht am zweiten October meine Nachbarn in der Stadt gesehen? 2. Wir werden diesen Sommer nach den schönen Seen in Cumberland reisen, und zwar am ersten Juli. 3. Die Dornen an den dichten Sträuchern haben ihm seine neuen Kleider zerrissen und ihm viel(e) Schmerzen gemacht. 4. Kennen Sie den Werth dieser Diamanten? 5. Die Strahlen der Sonne dringen nicht durch diese dichten Forsten. 6. Die armen Unterthanen in diesen Staaten zahlen hohe Zinsen. 7. Der Mensch hat zwei Augen und zwei Ohren; Insekten haben oft mehr als zwei Augen. 8. Wie finden Sie die deutschen Weisen dieser Psalmen? 9. In Frankreich tragen die Arbeiter über den Kleidern blaue Hemden, die sie Blousen nennen. 10. Der Quell seiner großen Schmerzen liegt in seinem kranken Herzen.[1]

1. Compare Rule 116.

44th Exercise.

1. I shall give you (Ihnen) the silver spurs, when you will have become a good horseman. 2. He will have had much trouble to get the interest (Plur.) from your own neighbours for the money (Sing. *or* Plur.), which you have lent them (ihnen). 3. The value of [the] feathers and beds is not so great in Germany as in England. 4. If you have read the sad history of our unhappy ancestors, you will know, how many bitter sufferings they had. 5. Who has found the

sources of the Nile (Nil, m.)? 6. His eyes will have turned¹ worse, therefore he did² not come. 7. I have heard with (my) own ears, that those states will not pay their interest (Plur.). 8. What day of the month is it? 9. I shall go away on the (am) 15th (of) January, if you will not come with me to³ the lakes in Switzerland⁴. 10. The high masts of these great ships are made from⁵ trees from⁵ those green forests.

1. Transl. *become*. 2. Transl. *is he*, instead of, he did. 3. nach, Dat. 4. Compare Rule 110. 5. aus, Dat.

TWENTY-THIRD LESSON.

Learn Rules 126, 3. 4. and 127.

Conditional II.

Ich würde gewesen sein, I should have been,
ich würde gehabt haben, I should have had,
ich würde geworden sein, I should have become.

Der Protestant', the protestant,
der Katholik', the catholic,
der Jesuit', the jesuit,
der Philosoph', the philosopher,
der Lithograph', the lithographer,
der Student', the student,
der Regent', the regent,
der Adjutant', the adjutant,
der Soldat', the soldier,

Es giebt (*Acc.*), there is, there are,

die Aussprache, the pronunciation,
der Degen, the sword,
die Familie, the family,
der Führer, the leader,
die Klasse, the class,
die Klugheit, the cleverness, prudence,
der Krieg, the war,
der Ring, the ring,
der Ursprung, the origin,
die Weisheit, wisdom.

es gab, there was, there were,

halten für (*Acc.*), to take for, think, consider,
hielten für (*Impf.*), took for, etc.,
lernen, to learn,

Bekannt, known,
unbekannt, unknown,
wohlbekannt, well known,
geschickt, clever, skilful, able,
ungeschickt, awkward,
gelehrt, learned,
herrlich, lordly, glorious, splendid,
kostbar, costly, precious,
letzt, last,

umgeben, to surround *and* surrounded,
verehren (*Dat.*), to present, (*Acc.*), to honour, adore,
das Son'nensystem', the solar system.

nützlich, useful,
tapfer, gallant,
unheilbringend, disastrous,
selb, same, self,
derselbe ⎫
dieselbe ⎬ the same,
dasselbe ⎭
genug, enough,
mehr, more,
mehrere, several.

45th Exercise.

1. Wie viel(e) Planeten gehören zu unserm Sonnensystem? 2. Vor noch nicht sehr langer Zeit hielten die Leute die Kometen für unheilbringend. 3. Kennen Sie den Ursprung des Namens Protestant? 4. Wer war der große Führer der Protestanten zur Zeit der Reformation in Deutschland? 5. Das Volk wird dem glücklichen Führer der Soldaten im letzten Krieg einen kostbaren Degen verehren. 6. Vor mehreren hundert Jahren gab es in den Wäldern von Deutschland noch braune Bären. 7. Mein jüngerer Bruder würde auch Soldat geworden sein, wenn er stark genug gewesen wäre. 8. Der letzte Krieg würde nicht so unheilbringend gewesen sein, wenn die Führer der Soldaten geschicktere Männer gewesen wären. 9. Was für einen schönen Brillanten haben Sie da in Ihrem Ringe! 10. Die Klugheit der Elephanten ist Jedermann bekannt.

46th Exercise.

1. Our glorious sun is surrounded by[1] large and small planets. 2. In this costly ring (there) are brilliants of[1] great value. 3. Would more German catholics have become protestants, if the emperor of Germany had become (a) protestant[2]? 4. Wouldst thou have become (a) soldier[2], if thou hadst been strong? 5. Henry and Louis would not have been the last of all (the) boys in the class, if they had been more diligent. 6. How many paragraphs of your German lesson have you to learn for to-morrow? 7. The pronunciation of several consonants is the same in (im) German and English. 8. The noble ancestors of these young princes were counts of[3] a well known family. 9. The learned professors present at the end[4] of the year to the most diligent students useful books. 10. Give that costly sword with splendid diamonds to the most gallant soldier!

1. von, Dat. 2. Nom. 3. aus, Dat. 4. am Schluſſe or am Ende.

TWENTY-FOURTH LESSON.

Learn Rules 129 and 130, also 54, 55 and 58.

Imperative.

Sei, be (thou),   habe, have (thou),
seid, be (ye *or* you),   habet or habt, have (ye *or* you),
seien Sie, be (polite form)!   haben Sie, have (polite form)!

werde, become (thou),
werdet, become (ye *or* you),
werden Sie, become (polite form)!

Die Beſchreibung, the description,
der Fremde, the stranger,

die Güte, the kindness,
das Leder, the leather,
die Taſche, the pocket.

Bringen, to bring,
fliegen, to fly,
irren, to err, to wander,
irrten, erred, wandered (Impf.),
machen, to make,

Beide, both, two,
böse (*Dat.*), angry,
einige[1], some (*a few*),
gaſtlich, hospitable,
nett, nice, pretty,

man macht, one makes, people make, is *or* are made,
rücken, to move (without lifting or rising),
zerbrechen, to break (to pieces),
zerbrochen, broken (to pieces).

woher, whence,
wohin, whither,
zuſammen, together,
aus (*Dat.*), out of, from,
daſs (*Conjunction*), that.

1. The Singular occurs rarely, etwas being used instead.

Remember, the Verb, *i. e.*, a simple tense or auxiliary, stands at the end in dependent phrases.

47th Exercise.

1. Sei gaſtlich gegen den Fremden, gieb ihm von den Früchten deines Feldes und Gartens. 2. Geben Sie ſich die Hände, meine lieben Freunde. 3. Haben Sie die Güte, den Mägden zu ſagen, daſs ſie uns einige Nüſſe bringen. 4. In dieſen Häuſern giebt es viel(e) Mäuſe, woher kommt das[1]? 5. Aus den Häuten der Kühe und Ochſen macht man Leder. 6. In Deutſchland macht man ſehr ſchöne Würſte. 7. Rücken Sie dieſe beiden Bänke[2] an jene beiden Wände. 8. Väter, Mütter, Söhne, Töchter irrten in den Wildniſſen. 9. Haben Sie die Güte, mir eine Beſchreibung von den Städten zu machen, welche wir dieſen Sommer geſehen haben. 10. Die Wände haben Ohren.

1. woher kommt das: what is the cause of that. 2. Compare the second plural of Bank in Rule 112.

48th Exercise.

1. Tell the pretty daughters¹ of² Mr. N., that I have bought them¹ (some) beautiful nuts. 2. Give us a few of³ these sweet fruits, if you please! 3. Take your⁴ hands out of your⁴ pockets. 4. The short descriptions of these German towns are very faithful. 5. I say⁵, our awkward servants have broken several of your beautiful glasses, but (do) not become angry with them! 6. Give me some of these splendid flowers, if you please! 7. The wild geese fly high in the air⁶. 8. Be good and give him some of³ these fine nuts. 9. Have you done⁷ your English lessons with him⁸? 10. These poor women⁹ have each several nice daughters, take one or two of³ them as¹⁰ servants into¹¹ your house!

1. Dat. 2. des. 3. von. 4. Transl. *the*. 5. Hören Sie, or wissen Sie schon. 6. Sing. or Plur. 7. Transl. *made*. 8. Insert: *together*. 9. Use Frau. 10. als. 11. in, Acc.

TWENTY-FIFTH LESSON.

Learn Rules 65—67 and 132.

Deutsch, German,
der Deutsche, the German ⎫ *made, fem.*
ein Deutscher, a German ⎭
die Deutsche, the German ⎫
eine Deutsche, a German ⎭
das Deutsche, the German (*thing*),

bedient, served,
der Bediente,¹ the man-servant, footman,
ein Bedienter, a servant,
der Beamte,¹ the official, officer,
ein Beamter, an official;

fremd, strange, foreign,
der Fremde, the stranger ⎫ *made.*
ein Fremder, a stranger ⎭

die Fremde, the stranger ⎫ *fem.*
eine Fremde, a stranger ⎭
das Fremde, the strange (*thing*);

gesandt, sent,
der Gesandte,[1] the ambassador,
ein Gesandter, an ambassador.

1. Those three words, Bediente, Beamte, Gesandte, and similar ones are now as frequently used as nouns that follow the 2nd declension.

Der Hof, the court,
die Hauptstadt, the capital,
die Treue, faithfulness,
die Pflicht, the duty,
die Last, the burden,
das Vertrauen, the confidence,
das Bad, the watering-place.

Auszeichnen, to distinguish,
a u s gezeichnet, distinguished,
sich betragen, to behave,
sich irren, to be mistaken,
erhalten, to receive,
nutzen, nützen, to use,
man nutzt, nützt, one uses,
schicken, to send,
thut, does,
aufmerksam, attentive,
königlich, royal,
vorig, former, last,
am meisten, most,
während (*Gen.*), during.

49th Exercise.

1. Der Deutsche ist derjenige unter den Völkern Europas, welcher sich schon immer durch große Treue ausgezeichnet hat. 2. Schicken Sie mir denjenigen von Ihren alten Bedienten, zu dem Sie das größte Vertrauen haben. 3. Diejenigen sind gute Beamte, welche ihre Pflicht thun. 4. Dieser fremde Herr ist spanischer Gesandter am königlichen Hofe. 5. Er ist der treue Freund desjenigen (or dessen, *not* des), welcher seine Pflicht thut. 6. Sie sprechen von demjenigen (or dem) Hause, welches unser junger Freund gestern gekauft hat. 7. Geben Sie uns von denjenigen (or den, *not* denen) Früchten, von welchen diese reichen Fremden gekauft haben. 8. Ich liebe denjenigen (or den) Schüler am meisten, welcher fleißig und aufmerksam ist. 9. Kennen Sie jene Fremde? Ja! es ist dieselbe junge Frau, welche wir voriges Jahr in der französischen Hauptstadt gesehen haben. 10. Ich werde (I shall) dieses hübsche Buch demjenigen (or dem) geben, welcher sich während des ganzen Jahres am besten betragen hat.

50th Exercise.

1. I give the highest¹ wages to that servant who does his duty most faithfully. 2. This is not your French book, it is that of the young stranger. 3. Do you know that tall German? it is the same man whom we saw last year in the foreign watering place. 4. We have the greatest confidence in² that servant who has distinguished himself by³ his fidelity. 5. These two beautiful horses belong to the French ambassador; you are mistaken, they (es) are those of the royal officer. 6. Those pupils who behave well during the whole year, receive at the end of it⁴ a useful book. 7. Are you speaking of that young stranger (*fem.*)? 8. That which one does not use, is a great burden. 9. He is the friend of that young man who is the most attentive and most diligent of all. 10. He who distinguishes himself most this year shall (soll) receive this beautiful penknife.

1. Transl. *the most.* 2. zu, Dat. 3. durch, Acc. 4. Transl. *of the same.*

TWENTY-SIXTH LESSON.

Learn Rule 225 1—3 and revise 68.

Das Buch, the book,
der Buchbinder, the bookbinder,
der Buchhändler, the bookseller;
das Blei, the lead,
der Stift, the peg,
der Bleistift, the lead-pencil;
der Stahl, the steel,
die Feder, the feather, the pen, the plume,

die Stahlfeder, the steel-pen,
der Halter, the holder,
der Stahlfederhalter, the penholder;
die Tinte, the ink,
das Faß, the barrel, the vessel,
das Tintenfaß, the inkbottle;
das Schreibzeug, the inkstand.

(Ich) bitte, (I) pray,
binden (*st. v.*), to bind, to tie,
halten (*st. v.*), to hold,
zeigen (*w. v.*), to show.

handeln (*w. v.*), to deal, to act,
lesen (*st. v.*), to read,
schreiben (*st. v.*), to write,

Wissen, to know (facts),
ich weiß, du weißt, er weiß,
I know, thou knowest,
he knows,

wollen (*irr. v.*), (will) to wish, to want,
ich will, du willst, er will,
I will, thou wilt, he will.

Ausländisch, outlandish, foreign,
liebend, loving,
reizend, charming,
sehenswürdig, worthy (of being seen) of notice,
steif, stiff,
still, still,

unterhaltend, interesting,
wahr, true,
wahrscheinlich, probable;
einmal, mal, just, please,
neulich, the other day,
recht, right, very,
nach (*Dat.*), to (see *places*),
zu (*Dat.*), to (see *persons*).

51st *Exercise*.

1. Gehen Sie mal zum ausländischen Buchhändler und bezahlen Sie das deutsche Buch, welches ich neulich gekauft habe. 2. Was reizend ist, ist nicht immer gut. 3. Halten Sie die Feder nicht so steif! 4. Seine liebende Mutter thut oft für ihn, was nur eine Mutter thun würde. 5. Wem diese neue Stahlfeder gehört, der sage es! 6. Wer von mir ein unterhaltendes Buch zum Lesen haben will, der sei recht fleißig! 7. Gehen wir zum englischen Buchbinder und geben ihm dies reizende Buch zum Binden! 8. Schreiben Sie, wem Sie wollen und was Sie wollen! 9. Was Sie da sagen, ist nicht sehr wahrscheinlich. 10. Wer diesen langen Brief geschrieben hat, der lese ihn auch!

52nd Exercise.

1. A loving mother does everything for her dear children. 2. What you¹ say is very true. 3. Give me that new book and that pen, if you please, I will write an English letter. 4. I know to² whom you write that long letter. 5. Bring me the new inkstand with some³ fresh ink in one bottle, if you please! 6. Come, Henry, let us read this beautiful book together! 7. Show me that charming picture! where have you bought it? 8. Hold your⁴ hands still! 9. Let us go together to the royal castle, we have not yet seen all (that is) worthy of notice in the same. 10. Act, as⁵ your good old father has acted and you will⁶ act right.

1. Insert: da. 2. an, Acc. 3. some: etwas. 4. Transl. *the* instead of *your*. 5. wie. 6. Future.

TWENTY-SEVENTH LESSON.

Learn Rules 75—81 and 225, 4.

Arbeiten,	to work,	sagen,	to say,
beten,	to pray,	spielen,	to play,
hören,	to hear,	strafen	
leben,	to live,	bestrafen	} to punish,
lieben,	to love,	wohnen,	to dwell, to live,
loben,	to praise,	tadeln,	to blame,
lohnen	} to reward,	zahlen,	to pay,
belohnen		bezahlen,	to pay for,

denken (*st. v.*), to think.

Die Bank, the form, bench,   der Stuhl, the chair,
die Tafel, the (long) table,   der Schemel, the stool,
   slate, (black) board,   der Morgen, the morning,
der Tisch, the table,   der Vormittag, the forenoon,

der Mittag, the mid-day, noon,
der Nachmittag, the afternoon;
der Abend, the evening;
die Nacht, the night,
die Mitternacht, the midnight;
die Rechnung, the bill.

Fromm, pious,
halb, half,
nicht wahr, is n't it? don't you? etc.
jetzt, now,
noch, yet,
bei (*Dat.*), with, at, at the house of.

53rd *Exercise.*

1. Ich arbeite alle Tage eine Stunde in meinem eignen Garten und eine halbe Stunde in dem seinigen (or dem seinen, or seinem). 2. Du liebst denjenigen Schüler, der seine eignen Aufgaben macht und die deinigen (or die deinen, or deine), nicht wahr? 3. Jetzt wohnt er in seinem eignen Hause, vor einem Jahr aber in dem Ihrigen (or dem Ihren, or Ihrem). 4. Wir leben glücklich mit unsern lieben Freunden und mit den ihrigen (or den ihren, or ihren). 5. Ihr bezahlt eure neuen Tische und Stühle und auch die unsrigen (or die unseren, or unsere), nicht wahr? 6. Die frommen Menschen beten jeden Morgen und jeden Abend. 7. Belohnen Sie die fleißigen Schüler, die ihre deutschen und französischen Arbeiten gut machen? 8. Gehen Sie zu seinem Freunde oder zu dem Ihrigen (or dem Ihren, or Ihrem)? 9. Hört er nicht, was man von seinem armen Vater sagt, oder denkt er, man sagt es nur von dem meinigen (or dem meinen, or meinem)? 10. Wenn Sie diese Woche Ihre letzte Rechnung bezahlen, so bezahlen Sie auch die meinige (or die meine, or meine), ich gebe Ihnen das Geld noch heute.

54th *Exercise.*

1. [Do] I hear right, you [do] not live in your own house, but[1] in his? 2. Thou sayest, thou workest the[2] whole day? then[3] thou[4] workest too much. 3. Does he play every evening in his own small room

or in yours? 4. We reward John; he always does his German exercises, but we punish William, for he does not [do] his. 5. Tell [me], [do] you buy your pens and pencils at my bookseller's or at yours? 6. How many of these German exercises do you [do] in a year in your class; does he [do] more in his? 7. He does indeed[5] more, but we do ours much better than he [does] his. 8. We know your worthy father very well; we also know his, he is a friend of mine (*i. e.*, of my father). 9. I [do] not love that boy who does not do his work[6] diligently. 10. We write at[7] school [in] the forenoon[8] on our slate(s), and we only read [in] the afternoon[8].

1. fondern; read Note 4 to Rule 303. 2. Read 351. 3. then: denn. 4. Verb *second*; thus, then workest thou. 5. indeed: zwar. 6. work; Arbeit, f., use the plural. 7. Transl. *in the*. 8. in the forenoon, *Genitive* (compare Rule 339).

TWENTY-EIGHTH LESSON.

Learn Rules 88, 225, 6. 7. and 237 (first half).

fragen, to ask,
glauben, to believe,
klopfen, to knock,
öffnen, to open,
stecken or thun, to put,
hängen, to put *or* hang,
legen, to put *or* lay,
setzen, to put *or* set,
stellen, to put *or* place,

ziehen, to put *or* pull,
anziehen, to put *or* pull on,
ausziehen, to take *or* pull off,
ruhen } to rest,
sich ausruhen }
spazieren, to walk,
wünschen, to wish,
zeigen, to show.

Der Keller, the cellar,
die Noth, the need, distress,
die Sehenswürdigkeit, the place of interest,
die Uhr, the clock, watch,

das Knie, the knee,
das Zimmer }
die Stube } the room.
das Gemach }

Als, as, when (referring to one occurrence of the *past*),
bis, till, to,
da, as, since (*time* and *reason*),
dann, then, warum, why?
natürlich, of course.

55th *Exercise.*

1. Als wir in Berlin wohnten, zeigten wir unsern Freunden immer die vielen Sehenswürdigkeiten der Stadt, wenn welche es wünschten. 2. Sie legten Ihrem Freunde was in die rechte Hand, was war es? 3. Sie wünschten neulich mal meine deutschen Bücher zu sehen, da Sie keine,[1] ich aber welche habe. 4. Wenn noch weißer Wein im Keller ist, so bringen Sie welchen herauf. 5. Warum stellten Sie die Flasche mit Bier nicht auf den Tisch, es war ja (you know) noch welches darin (in it)? 6. Wünschte er nicht, Ihrem Freunde was zu sagen? 7. Meine Freunde spazierten diesen Vormittag bis zwölf Uhr, und dann ruhten sie sich etwas aus. 8. Wir klopften an die Thüre, aber man öffnete nicht, und doch waren welche im Zimmer. 9. In dieser großen Noth beteten alle Leute auf den Knien. 10. Sie sagten Ihrem Freunde doch (I hope), wo wir wohnten?

1. haben understood.

56th *Exercise.*

1. Did he say[1] anything, when he showed you his rare books? 2. He asked me, if[2] I wished [to have] some. 3. We placed the new chairs in[3] the room which you showed us, but, I believe, there were already some in it[4]. 4. He walked last year[5] every morning [for] an hour. 5. What did you [do] when I knocked at[6] the door, did you pay[7] your bill? 6. Thou didst not open, although[8] there were some [people]. 7. If [there] is still beer in the barrel, put some on[9] the table. 8. Henry showed your German friends this morning the places of interest of this town, as some wished to see them. 9. We have here very

beautiful pens, do you wish any? 10. They asked me, if I punished the boy, who did not [do] his tasks; I said, of course! — 1. Transl. *said he.* 2. if or *whether*: ob. 3. in, Acc. 4. darin. 5. Nouns used adverbially commonly stand in the Accusative. 6. an, Acc. 7. Transl. *paid you.* 8. obgleich. 9. auf, Acc.

TWENTY-NINTH LESSON.

Learn Rules 227, 1—3. and 237 (second half).

Die Welt, the world,
die Erde, the earth,
der Himmel, the sky, heaven.
die Sonne, the sun.
der Mond, the moon,
der Stern, the star,
das Land, the land,
das Wasser, the water,
die See } das Meer } the sea.
die Luft, the air,
der Nebel, the fog, mist,
die Wolke, the cloud,
der Wind, the wind,
der Sturm, the gale,
das Gewitter, the thunderstorm,

der Blitz, the lightning,
blitzen, to lighten,
der Donner, the thunder,
donnern, to thunder,
der Hagel, the hail,
hageln, to hail,
der Regen, the rain,
regnen, to rain,
der Schnee, the snow,
schneien, to snow,
der Thau, the dew,
das Thauwetter, the thaw,
thauen, to thaw, dew fall(s),
das Eis, the ice,
das Wetter, the weather, storm,
die Sitte, the custom, the manner.

Bereisen (*Acc.*), to travel *in*,
bedecken (*Acc.*), to cover,

Ganz, whole,
hell, bright, light,
klar, clear,

vermehren, to increase,
wehen, to blow, wave.

sonderbar, strange,
stark, strong, heavy,
umher, about.

57th Exercise.

1. Habt ihr gestern das starke Gewitter gehört? 2. Wir haben wohl¹ den hellen Blitz gesehen, aber keinen lauten Donner gehört. 3. Dieser weise Mann ist viel in der Welt umher gewesen, er hat viel fremde Länder gesehen und von ihren Sitten gelernt. 4. Der Nordwind, welcher gestern so stark wehte, hat sich heute noch vermehrt und ist zum Sturm geworden. 5. Gestern hat den ganzen Tag ein dichter Nebel über unserer Stadt gestanden, heute ist die Luft klar. 6. Was für ein heller Stern war das, den Sie gestern am südlichen Himmel gesehen haben? 7. Was für fremde Länder haben Sie bereist, was für große Städte haben Sie gesehen? 8. Was für große Männer haben Sie kennen gelernt? 9. Was ist das für ein starker Regen! so hat es lange nicht geregnet. 10. Welch ein sonderbares Land wir voriges Jahr bereist haben!

1. indeed.

58th Exercise.

1. Have you learned the names of the greatest stars in the (am) heavens¹? 2. What beautiful weather we have had all this week²! 3. What a strong wind has blown this whole day³! 4. Heavy clouds have covered the whole sky, we have not seen the moon and the stars this whole night⁴. 5. My worthy friend has travelled in many countries of the world; he has even⁵ been in Australia⁶. 6. He has learned (to) know the manners of many peoples. 7. Let us ask your old friend, if he has also been in China⁷, and what kind of people the Chinese⁸ are? 8. What a bright lightning was that, did you see it⁹? 9. What a clear sky we have had all this week¹⁰! 10. We have not had any snow (yet) this whole winter¹¹.

1. Sing. 2. Transl. *already the whole week*. 3. Transl. *already the whole day*. 4. Transl. *the whole night* and put it after stars. 5. selbst. 6. Australien. 7. China. 8. Chinese, m. 9. Transl. *have you it seen*. 10. Transl. *already the whole week*. 11. Transl. *the whole winter* (Acc.) *yet no snow had*.

THIRTIETH LESSON.

Learn Rules 227, 4. 5. and 238; read 134—137.

Das Tuch, the cloth,
das Tischtuch, the tablecloth;
der Teller, the plate,
das Tellertuch, the napkin;
die Hand, the hand,
das Handtuch, the towel;
der Hals, the neck,
das Halstuch, the necktie;
die Tasche, the pocket,
das Taschentuch, the pocket-handkerchief;
die Uhr, the watch, *or* clock,
die Taschenuhr, the watch (only),
der Löffel, the spoon,
der Eßlöffel, the tablespoon,
der Theelöffel, the teaspoon;
das Messer, the knife,
das Federmesser, the penknife,
das Brodmesser, the breadknife,
das Bratenmesser, the carvingknife,
das Gartenmesser, the gardener's knife;
die Gabel, the fork,
die Heugabel, the hayfork;
die Suppe, the soup,
die Fleischsuppe, the broth,
der Braten, the roast,
der Rinderbraten, the roastbeef;
die Arbeit, the work,
die Schularbeit, the lesson;
das Gedicht, the poetry,
das Gesicht, the face,
das Landhaus, the villa.

Beschenken, to present,
angekommen, arrived,
besuchen, to visit,
vorig, last, former,
nachdem (*conj.*), after,
da (*conj.*), as,
mit (*Dat.*), with,
ohne (*Acc.*), without,
darauf, thereupon, upon it.

59th *Exercise.*

1. Als er das gesagt hatte, bedeckte er das Gesicht mit den Händen. 2. Nachdem man die Fleischsuppe gegessen hatte, kam der Rinderbraten auf den Tisch. 3. Da sie ihr Gedicht

nicht gelernt hatten, bestrafte sie der Lehrer. 4. Als wir in London bei unserm Vater angekommen waren, beschenkte er uns mit schönen Hals= und Taschentüchern. 5. Meine Freunde waren gestern ausgegangen, als wir sie in ihrem Landhaus besuchten. 6. Wo warst du gewesen, mein Kind, als ich dich ohne Halstuch in den Garten kommen sah? 7. Hatte er schon seine Taschenuhr verloren, als sein Vater ihn danach (after it) fragte? 8. Nachdem er seine Schularbeiten gemacht hatte, besuchte er seine Freunde. 9. Wohin waren Sie ge= gangen, als ich gestern mit meinem Bruder zu Ihnen kam? 10. Die Magd hatte den Tisch gedeckt und die Teller und Tellertücher darauf (on it) gelegt.

60th Exercise.

1. Had you already done your English tasks yesterday, when my young friend visited you with his father? 2. We had not yet learned our long poetry. 3. Had he been in his new villa, when we saw him the other day? 4. Henry had lost his gold[1] watch in[2] the country, when he visited me to-day. 5. They were all gone out, when we came to learn our lessons with them. 6. Had the wind increased,[3] when you heard the first thunder? 7. What had he done thee[4], when thou wouldst[5] not walk with him yesterday? 8. Had your German friend become rich already, when we knew[6] him first?[7] 9. After she had put the tablecloth, the napkins, (the) plates, spoons, knives and forks on[8] the table, she brought[9] the soup. 10. After we had done our lessons, we always visited our dear friends, when we lived in our countryhouse last year.

1. golden. 2. auf, Dat. 3. Compare fourth sentence of exercise 57. 4. Dat. 5. wolltest. 6. kannten. 7. zuerst. 8. auf, Acc. 8. brachte.

THIRTY-FIRST LESSON.

Learn Rules 228, 1. 2. and 239 (first six verbs); read 139—141, also Observation 398.

Das Essen, the food,
das Mittagessen or Mittagbrod, the dinner,
das Abendessen or Abendbrod, the supper,
das Frühstück, the breakfast,
das zweite Frühstück, the luncheon.
der Kaffe, the coffee,
der Thee, the tea,
das Brod, the bread, the loaf of bread,
das Fleisch, the flesh, meat,
das Gemüse (*Plur.* die Gemüse), the vegetables,
die Kartoffel, to potatoe,
der Kohl, the cabbage,
der Käse, the cheese,
der Schinken, the ham,

der Wein, the wine,
das Bier, the beer,
die Milch, the milk,
das Wasser, the water,
die Sahne, the cream,
die Butter, the butter,
der Zucker, the sugar,
das Salz, the salt.
der Pfeffer, the pepper,
der Senf, the mustard,
die Schale | the cup and
die Tasse | saucer,
die Philosophie', philosophy,
die Theologie', divinity,
die Maschinerie', the machinery,
die Medicin', medicine,
der Photograph', the photographer.

Essen, to eat, to dine,
trinken, to drink,
bekommen, to get,
verlassen, to leave,
studiren, to study;

tapfer, gallant,
hiesig, of this place,
salzig, salt (*Adjective*),
wacker, brave,
sobald (als), as soon as,

genug, enough.

61st *Exercise.*

1. Wann werden wir heute essen? Sobald Sie vom Gymnasium kommen. 2. Werden Sie uns heute zum Mittagessen besuchen? 3. Du wirst heute zum zweiten Frühstück Brod und Käse und ein Glas Milch oder Bier bekommen. 4. Er wird morgen bei seinem alten Freunde Thee trinken. 5. Zum Abendessen wird es kaltes Fleisch und warme Kartoffeln, aber keinen Wein geben; ich werde ein Glas Bier oder Wasser trinken. 6. Wenn Sie sich so viel Pfeffer zu Ihrem Kohl nehmen, wird er Ihnen zu stark sein. 7. Du wirst dir nicht zu viel Salz nehmen, mein liebes Kind, nicht wahr? 8. Ich werde dir eine Schale süße Milch und Sahne geben, wenn du mal trinken willst. 9. Wird er in's Wasser gehen, wenn wir am Meere wohnen werden? 10. Werden Sie ihn mit einer goldenen oder silbernen Taschenuhr beschenken, wenn er seine Aufgaben in der Chemie immer gut gelernt hat?

62nd *Exercise.*

1. We shall attend[1] the university of this place, when we leave the Grammar School. 2. Wilt thou take tea to-morrow with[2] my father? 3. The dinner, which the brave officers give to their gallant general, will be[3] very grand. 4. We shall[4] not[5] take any[5] mustard to our cold meat, if you [do] not want it. 5. Take[6] a little[7] salt, you will not find it salt enough. 6. What are you going to study[8] at[9] the university, philosophy or theology? 7. I am going to study[8] chemistry and medicine. 8. We shall go to-morrow to the new circus, will[8] you go with [us]? 9. They are going to see[8] to-morrow the whole machinery of the telegraph of this place, their father will[10] show them. 10. He is going to be[11] [a] photographer and not, as[12] you thought, [a] lithographer.

1. besuchen. 2. with: bei, Dat. 3. Transl. *become.* 4. Ins. uns. 5. not any: kein. 6. Ins. sich. 7. ein wenig. 8. Fut. 9. at, auf, Dat. 10. Ins. *it.* 11. Fut. of werden. 12. as: wie.

THIRTY-SECOND LESSON.

Learn Rules 228, 3. and 239 (first 12); read 142–145; revise the names in the 11th lesson.

Die Hoffnung, the hope,   das Vermögen, the fortune
der Muth, the courage,   (money *or* property),
Wien, Vienna.

Ausgehen, to go out,   verbinden, to oblige,
ging aus, went out,   anziehend, interesting,
erlauben, to allow,   hungrig, hungry,
helfen, to assist, to help,   durstig, thirsty,
hälfe or hülfe, Impf. Subj.   traurig, dreary, sad, me-
of helfen,   lancholy,
bald, soon.

Remember, after the Conjunctions wenn, if, and ob, if *or* whether, the Verb must stand in the Subjunctive mood, if in the Imperfect or Pluperfect tense and not purely narrative.

63rd *Exercise.*

1. Sie würden mich sehr verbinden, wenn Sie Friedrichen (or Friedrich, or dem Friedrich) nicht bei seinen Schularbeiten hälfen. 2. Ich würde Friederiken dieses schöne Buch geben, wenn sie in der Schule fleißiger wäre. 3. Würdest du mit dem kleinen Karl ausgehen, wenn dein Vater es dir erlaubte? 4. Wenn die arme Johanna nicht so krank wäre, würde ihr guter Vater nicht so traurig sein. 5. Louisens ältester Bruder würde reicher sein, wenn er nicht seinen armen Freunden so oft mit Geld aus der Noth hülfe. 6. Würden wir recht thun, wenn wir ohne Heinrichs jüngsten Bruder ausgingen? 7. Was würden Sie sagen, wenn Ihr Herr Vater jetzt käme? 8. Würde er Sie wohl[1] beschenken, wenn ich ihm sagte, wie faul Sie sind? 9. Ihr würdet mit Karln (or dem Karl, or Karl) studiren, wenn ich es euch erlaubte. 10. Ich würde nicht essen, wenn ich nicht hungrig wäre.

1. do you think.

64th Exercise.

1. Would you tell[1] me who has written this German exercise, if I allowed[1] you to go home? 2. Thou wouldst give[1] thy little brother John of thy bread and milk, if he were hungry; wouldst thou not? 3. If he were here to-day, he would help[1] us with[2] our work, I know.[3] 4. We should go to the great circus to-morrow, if Frederick's poor father were not so ill. 5. I should give you a glass [of] wine or beer, if you were thirsty and wished to drink. 6. My good cousins would give[1] this interesting book to little Louisa, if their dear mother would allow it. 7. Would you believe that Henrietta's father is [a] minister[4] in France? 8. We should go this summer to Vienna, the capital of Austria, if Henry's poor father had not lost all his fortune. 9. Wouldst thou be very unhappy, if thou hadst lost so much money? 10. I know William very well, he would not lose (the) courage and (the) hope.

1. Followed by the Dative. 2. bei, Dat. 3. Transl. *so much is certain*, gewiß. 4. Minister, m.

THIRTY-THIRD LESSON.

Learn Rules 229, 1. 2. and 239 (the rest); read 146.

Der Freund, the friend, *m.*,
bie Freundinn, the friend, *f.*;
ber Fürst, the prince,
bie Fürstinn, the princess;
ber Herr, the master,
bie Herrinn, the mistress;
ber Gatte, the husband,
bie Gattinn, the wife;
ber Koch, the cook,
bie Köchinn, the female cook;
ber Schneider, the tailor,
bie Schneiberinn, the dressmaker;
bie Nähterinn, the seamstress;
bie Putzmacherinn, the milliner;
bie Wäscherinn, the laundress.

Die Nachricht, the news,
bie Oper, the opera,
mittheilen, to communicate,
nützen, to be of use, to avail,

erreichen, to reach,
tadeln, to blame,
kurzsichtig, shortsighted.
fertig, done *or* ready,
alle, done *or* finished.
schnell, quick,
liebenswürdig, amiable, kind,
glauben Sie, do you think,
ausführlich, minute,

hoffentlich (*Adv.*), I hope, *or* it is to be hoped,
todt, pron. *toat*, dead,
nach Hause ⎱
heim   ⎰ home,
schon längst, long ago,
da, since,
ehe (*Conjunction*), before,
weil, because,
wohl, I think, probably.

65th *Exercise.*

1. Der Kaiser wird die junge Kaiserinn nicht gesehen haben, weil er kurzsichtig ist. 2. Ich werde zwei lange Briefe an die edle Fürstinn geschrieben haben, ehe deine lieben Freundinnen mit ihren kurzen an die Näherinn fertig sind. 3. Du wirst schon längst durch den Telegraphen die traurige Nachricht von dem erhalten haben, welches ich dir in diesem Brief ausführlicher mittheile. 4. Hoffentlich werden Sie das anziehende Buch von der unglücklichen Königinn erhalten haben. 5. Was[1] wird die fleißige Wäscherinn nicht alles gethan haben, ehe die langsame Putzmacherinn mit ihrer Arbeit fertig ist! 6. Wenn du nicht schnell gehst, so wird die geschickte Schneiderinn ausgegangen sein, eh' du ihr Haus erreichst. 7. Die junge Gräfinn wird zum letzten Mal bei der alten Herzoginn gewesen sein, wenn Sie ihr diese schlimme Nachricht mittheilen. 8. Die liebenswürdige Königinn wird nicht auf den Ball Ihrer Herrinn gekommen sein, weil sie nicht ganz wohl ist. 9. Wird er die anziehende Geschichte von dieser großen Heldinn wohl schon gelesen haben? 10. Ihr werdet der armen Bäuerinn wohl ausführliche Nachricht von ihrem unglücklichen Sohn gegeben haben.

1. Was nicht alles: how many things!

66th *Exercise.*

1. What will poor Henry have told his young wife, when he saw her again yesterday! 2. Your little friend

Amalia will have¹ gone to the seamstress, before you are done with your dinner. 3. She will not have seen the noble duchess, I think,² because she is so short-sighted. 4. Do you think, that we shall have read the interesting story of this unfortunate princess, before our dear mother comes home from that French milliner? 5. I hope, he won't have lost the fortune of his poor wife. 6. He will have¹ gone to the opera, I think, with his young wife. 7. You will probably have received more minute news, long before you receive this short letter. 8. She won't have blamed the poor cook³ much,⁴ when she saw that she was so ill. 9. Of what use will that have been⁵ to the unfortunate empress, since her beloved husband is dead? 10. He will have gone home with the gallant brother of the noble countess, I think.²

1. Transl.: gone be; to, zu, Dat. 2. Put wohl after *will*.
3. female. 4. sehr. 5. Construe: *what will that....have availed*.

THIRTY-FOURTH LESSON.

Learn Rules 229, 3. and 240 (first half); read also 147—148.

Der Oheim, the uncle,
die Muhme, the aunt,
der Vetter, the cousin (*male*),
die Base, the cousin (*female*),
der Neffe, the nephew,
die Nichte, the niece,
der Knecht, the servant, groom,
die Magd, the servant, maid,
der Diener, the footman,
das Mädchen, the girl,

der Kammerdiener, the valet, chamberlain,
die Zofe, the chambermaid,
das Glück, (good) luck, fortune, happiness,
das Unglück, bad luck, misfortune, accident,
der Gefallen, the favour,
die Rückkehr, the return,
die Sache, the thing, affair,
der Zustand, the state.

Heirathen, to marry,
geheirathet, married,

zustoßen, to happen,
zugestoßen, happened,

gebrauchen, to use, to require.	französisch, French,
verkaufen, to sell.	schottisch, Scotch,
sich beeilen, to hurry, to be quick,	früh, early, soon,
	redlich, honest,
entlassen, to dismiss.	klug, prudent,
enterben, to disinherit.	wohin, whither,
gewußt, known,	woher, whence.

67th Exercise.

1. Würden Sie Ihrem reichen Oheim die Sache mitgetheilt haben, wenn Sie ihn so recht[1] gekannt hätten? 2. Würde Ihr armer Vater nicht noch einen[2] Knecht genommen haben, wenn ihm nicht dieses Unglück zugestoßen wäre? 3. Ich würde meinem lieben Vetter dieses schöne Pferd nicht verkauft haben, wenn ich nicht Geld gebraucht hätte. 4. Würde Ihre gute Muhme Ihre kleine Base sehr getadelt haben, wenn sie mit ihrer Freundinn ausgegangen wäre? 5. Wenn Heinrich seine Schularbeiten fertig gehabt hätte, würde er mit uns zusammen ausgegangen sein. 6. Würdet ihr mir wohl[3] diesen Gefallen gethan haben, wenn ich euch früher was davon[4] gesagt hätte? 7. Würde Emilie den redlichen Kammerdiener der Gräfinn geheirathet haben, wenn ihre Mutter es ihr erlaubt hätte? 8. Was würden Ihr Oheim und Ihre Muhme gesagt haben, wenn sie bei ihrer Rückkehr die neue Zofe nicht zu Hause gefunden hätten? 9. Wenn Ihr Herr Neffe sich nicht beeilt hätte, würde ihm mein lieber Vetter sein nettes Haus nicht mehr verkauft haben. 10. Was würde Base Henriette gesagt haben, wenn sie Sie bei uns gesehen hätte.

1. so recht: thoroughly. 2. noch einen: another. 3. wohl: do you think. 4. davon: of it.

68th Exercise.

1. Would you have gone out with your old uncle, if you had known, where[1] he was going to[2]? 2. Would your good cousin have dismissed her French chambermaid, if you had told her that she is not faithful?

3. You would have lost all³ your fortune, if you had not been so prudent. 4. My prudent friend would have disinherited his young nephew, if he had known him well.⁴ 5. Would your good cousin have done me the favour, if I had allowed him to use my French books? 6. If Henry had been prudent, he would not have sold his beautiful horse. 7. I should have allowed you to take a walk this afternoon, if you had done your French tasks better. 8. We should not have dismissed our Scotch footman, if we had known what a great misfortune has happened to him. 9. The French groom would not have sold the grey horses, if he had been faithful to his good master. 10. They would not have required more money, if no misfortune had happened to them.

1. where *or* whither: woher; where *or* whence: wohin. 2. gehen wollte. 3. Transl. *your whole fortune* or *all your fortune.* 4. so recht.

THIRTY-FIFTH LESSON.

Learn Rule 240 (second half); read also Rules 149—152, and 365, 366.

Bitten (*Acc.*), to beg,
bat, begged,
gebeten, begged;
bleiben, to stay,
blieb, staid,
geblieben, staid;
geben, to give,
gab, gave,
gegeben, given;
geschehen, to happen,
geschah, happened,
geschehen, happened;

können, (can) to be able,
konnte, (could) was able,
gekonnt, been able;
mögen, (may) to be possible, to like,
mochte, (might) was possible,
möchte, Impf. Subj. (*should like*),
gemocht, been possible;
singen, to sing,
sang, sang,
gesungen, sung;

thun, to do,	trinken, to drink,	wissen, to know,
that, did,	trank, drank,	wußte, knew,
gethan, done;	getrunken, drunk;	gewußt, known.

meinen (*w. v.*), to mean, to think, to say.
fehlen (*w., imp. Verb*), to fail, to be the matter.

Das Concert', the concert,	An'genehm, pleasant,
das Thea'ter, the theatre,	gefährlich, dangerous, serious,
die Gele'genheit, the opportunity,	herüber, over,
das Geschenk, the present,	jetzt, just now,
die Krankheit, the malady,	gern, willingly, gladly.
das Lied, the song.	

69th *Exercise.*

1. Was meintest[1] du, liebes Väterchen, wenn wir heute Abend in's französische Theater gingen[1]? 2. Wenn du das thätest, liebes Kindchen, würde ich dich belohnen. 3. Johann erzählte mir gestern, sein Vater habe ein nettes Häuschen und ein Gärtchen am Meere gekauft; das ist recht gut für die artigen Töchterchen. 4. Er thäte es wohl, wenn Sie es wünschten. 5. Ich hörte gestern, in der nahen Stadt sei ein großes Unglück geschehen. 6. Als ich Ihren alten Freund fragte, ob er uns diese Woche besuchen werde, sagte er, er könne noch nicht wissen, ob das geschehen werde. 7. Er käme wohl auf (for) ein Stündchen herüber, wenn er nur wüßte, ob es uns angenehm wäre. 8. Was gäben Sie mir, wenn ich Ihnen sagte, was Sie gern wissen möchten? 9. Ich wünschte,[1] Sie blieben noch ein Weilchen hier und tränken Thee mit uns. 10. Was meintest[1] du, liebes Brüderchen, wenn du uns ein nettes Liedchen sängest?

1. Imperfect Subjunctive.

70th Exercise.

1. People¹ say, the new king and the young queen have arrived² yesterday with the youngest prince. 2. Wouldst thou do* me this small favour, if I gave* thee this beautiful book? 3. Would he sing* us a nice song just now,³ if I went* with him to the concert tomorrow? 4. If your good father knew* what you have done with your new books, he would punish* you. 5. What a pretty little dog you have there! your eldest brother says it came† from Germany. 6. Oh, [would] I had⁴ an opportunity to do him good! 7. What would you⁵ say,* if I made* your young friend a present of⁶ this pretty little stick? 8. Our little daughter is ill, the doctor thinks the malady is† not serious. 9. [Would] he⁷ came* now with our new little horse! it is such a nice opportunity. 10. Dear mother, could* I⁸ go to my friend John this afternoon, he begged [of] me to come?

*Use the Impf. Subj. †Use the Pres. Subj. 1. man, Sing. 2. The verb anfommen is conjugated with sein, thus say as it were *be arrived*. 3. Insert wohl. 4. Commence with the Verb *had*,* oh, had I (insert doch). 5. Insert dazu. 6. Transl. mit, Dat. 7. Commence with the verb *came* — came he (insert doch). 8. Insert wohl.

THIRTY-SIXTH LESSON.

Learn Rules 230 and 241; revise 237.

Anklagen, to accuse, angeklagt, accused;	lieben, to love,
begleiten, to accompany, begleitet, accompanied;	hassen, to hate, befehlen, to command, bezahlen, to pay for,
bewundern, to admire, bewundert, admired;	ermorden, to murder, scheinen, to shine, to seem.

Die Asche (*Sing.*), the ashes,
das Feuer, the fire,
die Flamme, the flame,
die Kohle, the coal,
der Feind, the enemy,
das Festland, the continent,
die Glocke, the bell,
das Leben, the life,
der Sand, the sand,
die Schuld, the debt,
der Wagen, the waggon, carriage.

Bewaffnet, armed,
fürchterlich, dreadful,
gewiß, certain, surely,
grausam, cruel,
lustig, merry,
seltsam, strange,
vernünftig, sensible,
dazu, to it,
sehr viel, a great deal of,
weit, wide,
dicht, thight, thick,
fern, far, distant.

71st *Exercise*.

1. Der Klang der neuen Glocken wird von allen vernünftigen Leuten bewundert. 2. Wenn es deinen grausamen Feinden gelingt, dich zu finden, so wirst du auf[1] Tod und Leben angeklagt (werden), das ist gewiß. 3. Der Wagen der Königinn wurde jedesmal von bewaffneten Soldaten begleitet. 4. Wißt ihr schon,[2] daß ihr sehr bewundert wurdet? 5. Wenn du nicht thust, was ich dir befehle, so wirst du dazu gezwungen (werden). 6. Diese neuen Gesänge werden nur ganz langsam gesungen. 7. Er sprang auf's Pferd und verschwand im dichtesten Gedränge. 8. Die grausamen Feinde zwangen uns dazu (v. Rule 289), sie in die ferne Stadt zu begleiten. 9. Findest[3] du es seltsam, daß sie von Jedermann gehaßt werden? 10. Man ist hier sehr lustig, wie ich sehe, es wird gesungen und gesprungen, auch getrunken, wie's scheint.

1. auf Tod und Leben: of capital crime. 2. And do you know. 3. Do you think it?

72nd *Exercise*.

1. Out of[1] sand and ashes is made glass. 2. He said shortly[2] before his death, I was loved by my friends and have few or[3] no enemies, I am satisfied.

3. The English glass is paid for in Germany very dear. 4. They were admired even⁴ by their worst enemies. 5. A⁵ great deal of fine coal⁶ is found in England⁵, but on⁷ the continent is⁶ also much acquired⁸. 6. If it is certain, that they are not [to be] punished by you, then⁹ we¹⁰ are satisfied. 7. The high flames of this dreadful fire were seen very far. 8. What are they doing there¹¹? 9. He was accused by his enemies that he did not pay his debts; but now he is forced to pay them. 10. Thou art loved and admired by all thy numerous friends, how happy that must¹² make thee!

1. Aus. 2. kurz. 3. Insert gar. 4. selbst. 5. Commence the phrase with: *In England*. 6. Use the *plural*. 7. auf, Dat. 8. Transl.: *won*. 9. so. 10. The Verb must have the second place in the period, thus *are we*. 11. Transl.: *what is there made*. 12. muß second *or* last.

THIRTY-SECOND LESSON.

Learn Rules 242 and 261—263, a. and revise 238.

Blühen, to bloom, to blow,
scheinen, to seem, to shine,
es scheint, it seems,
frieren, to freeze,
fror, froze,
gefroren, frozen,

schneien, to snow,
trocken, dry,
trocknen, to dry,
draußen, outside,
breit, broad,
herrlich, lordly, splendid.

Der Baum, the tree, beam,
die Frucht, the fruit,
das Obst, (orchard) fruit,
der Apfel, the apple,
die Birne, the pear,
die Feige, the fig,

die Kirsche, the cherry,
die Nuß, the nut,
die Haselnuß, the hazelnut,
die Wallnuß, the walnut,
die Pflaume, the plum.

Die Beere, the berry,
die Erdbeere, the strawberry,

die Stachelbeere, the gooseberry,

die Apfelsi'ne, the orange,
die Citro'ne, the lemon,
die Mandel, the almond,
die Rosine, the raisin,
die Weintraube, the bunch of grapes,
das Spiel, the game, play,
die Wolle, the wool.

73rd Exercise.

1. Es freut mich sehr zu sehen, daß die herrlichen Bäume in Ihrem großartigen Garten so voll blühen. 2. Es scheint, wir werden in diesem Jahr viel(e) schöne Äpfel und Birnen haben. 3. Die süßen Nüsse beginnen schon reif zu werden. 4. Wenn es heute Nacht friert, werden wir in diesem Jahr wohl¹ keine schönen Erdbeeren gewinnen. 5. Es hat ihn sehr gewundert, daß Sie Ihre schwere Arbeit noch nicht begonnen hatten. 6. Es hungert mich, geben Sie mir doch² ein paar von jenen getrockneten Feigen, sie scheinen sehr schön zu sein. 7. Es hat heute den ganzen Tag geregnet, aber jetzt beginnt es zu frieren. 8. Können Sie spinnen? früher spannen fast alle fleißigen Frauen. 9. Es hat mich heute schon den ganzen Tag gefroren, wie es scheint, ist es draußen sehr kalt. 10. Es verlangt mich sehr zu wissen, wer gewonnen hat.

1. probably. 2. please.

74th Exercise.

1. I am thirsty, give me something to drink. 2. Will you [have] some of¹ these beautiful cherries? I am sorry that I have nothing but² fruit in the house. 3. Who has spun this fine wool? 4. I am very sorry to see, that we shall not³ win many strawberries this year. 5. I am glad to hear, that you have won the last game. 6. I feel desirous to buy a few of those fine almonds and raisins. 7. It rained yesterday the whole day and to-day, it seems, it will snow. 8. It annoyed me, that you commenced to talk, when⁴ I was⁵ going to do my French exercises. 9. Henry is a fine⁶ swimmer, he swam yesterday over the broad river. 10. It seems, that you would give him all [the] nuts, if he gained⁷ this game.

1. von, Dat. 2. but: als. 3. Put *not* before *many strawberries*. 4. when: als. 5. Transl.: 1 — *make would*. 6. fine: gut. 7. Impf. Subj.

THIRTY-EIGHTH LESSON.
Learn Rule 243 (first half) and 263, b.; revise Rule 239.

Vernehmen, to hear,
bekommen, to get.

Das Thier, the animal,
das Pferd, the horse,
der Esel, the ass,
der Hund, the dog,
die Katze, the cat,
die Maus, the mouse,
die Ratte, the rat,
das Rind, the cattle,
der Ochs(e), the ox,
die Kuh, the cow,
das Schaf, the sheep,
das Lamm, the lamb,
der Hammel, the wether (wedder),

das Schwein, the pig,
der Affe, the ape,
der Hase, the hare,
der Löwe, the lion,
der Bär, the bear,
der Fuchs, the fox,
der Wolf, the wolf,
der Tiger, the tiger,
der Elephant', the elephant,
das Kameel', the camel,
der Käfig, the cage,
die Kugel, the ball, bullet,
die Nachricht, the news,
der Preis, the price, prize.

Schrecklich, dreadful,
besonders, especially,
gleich, alike, equal,
weit, far.

sogleich, immediately,
vielleicht, perhaps,
unschuldig, innocent,

75th Exercise.

1. Mein lieber Vater hat mir befohlen, die neuen Pferde besonders zu pflegen. 2. Es ist mir lieb, daß dein großer Bruder seinen wilden Hund nicht mitgenommen hat. 3. Man sprach davon, daß neulich ein böser Tiger aus seinem eisernen Käfig ausgebrochen sei. 4. Die armen Leute in der ganzen Stadt waren sehr erschrocken, als sie die schreckliche Nachricht

vernahmen. 5. Es hat uns Jemand gestern unsere schwarze Katze gestohlen, vielleicht gelingt es dir, sie wiederzubekommen. 6. Sprichst du von den wilden Thieren, die wir heute gesehen haben? 7. Wer hat dir bei deinen deutschen Arbeiten geholfen, ich empfehle dir, sie allein zu machen. 8. Ist Ihnen nicht wohl? Mir ist nur sehr warm. 9. Es ist meinem guten Vater nicht lieb, daß du meiner jüngsten Schwester bei ihrer leichten Arbeit geholfen hast. 10. Thut es Ihnen nicht leid, daß Sie uns das unschuldige Vergnügen verdorben haben?

76th Exercise.

1. If you succeeded to throw this heavy ball as far as young Henry, I would give you this pretty little stick. 2. I am afraid that you will spoil your new horse, if you [do] not nurse it better. 3. The doctor says, that John would die, if he did not take[1] what he has recommended him. 4. Take[2] the brown bread and break[2] it into two equal pieces. 5. I forebode that[3] he will not succeed in this difficult work. 6. If you helped him,[4] he would gain the splendid prize. 7. Do you believe, the fox would die, if the bullet hit him in the head? 8. The new master scolded little William, because he talked continually[5] with his two neighbours. 9. Who has stolen my fine dog? 10. I wish you would succeed[6] to hide your poor friend in your house.

1. einnehmen. 2. Sing. 3. Transl.: *that him* (Dat.) *his difficult work not succeed will.* 4. Dat. 5. immerwährend. 6. Transl.: *If you but* (doch) *succeeded.*

THIRTY-NINTH LESSON.

Learn Rules 243 (second half), 265 and 266 and revise 240.

Sich baden, to bathe,
sich begnügen, to be satisfied,
sich erinnern, to remember,
sich irren, to be mistaken,
sich messen, to compete, to measure one's self,
sich waschen, to wash.

Der Vogel, the bird,
das Huhn, the fowl, hen,
der Hahn, the cock,
die Henne, the hen,
die Ente, the duck,
die Gans, the goose,
die Krähe, the crow,
der Kukuk, the cuckoo,
die Lerche, the lark,

das Küchlein, the chicken,
die Nachtigall, the nightingale,
der Rabe, the raven,
die Schwalbe, the swallow,
der Schwan, the swan,
der Sperling, the sparrow,
der Storch, the stork,
die Taube, the dove, pigeon.

Weder—noch, neither—nor,
fett, fat,

zahm, tame,
gebraten, roast(ed).

77th Exercise.

1. Die arme Nachtigall grämt sich sehr in ihrem engen Käfig, sie kann nicht vergessen, daß sie gefangen ist. 2. Siehst du, wie sich jene kleine Schwalbe da wäscht und badet? 3. Die Lerche kann sich nicht mit der Nachtigall im Singen messen. 4. Was issest du da? Es ist eine gelbe Birne, die ich im Garten aufgelesen habe. 5. Heinrich hat sich viele Mühe mit seinen kranken Vögeln gegeben, aber sie werden doch wohl nicht genesen. 6. Können Sie mir sagen, was die zahmen Schwäne fressen? 7. Diese Gans frißt gern[2] frische Fische, aber sie begnügt sich auch mit grünem Gras. 8. Was ist Ihnen geschehen, daß Sie weder essen noch trinken? 9. Irrte ich mich, oder sah ich da eben Ihren großen Bruder in's Haus treten? es ist lange her,[2] daß wir uns nicht gesehen haben. 10. Du vergissest dich, mein lieber Sohn, siehst du nicht, mit wem du sprichst?

1. frißt gern: likes to eat. 2. ago.

78th Exercise.

1. Do not[1] give yourself any[1] trouble, I shall not give you[2] the tame bird. 2. Are you not mistaken in believing[3], that he has forgotten, what you have

promised him? 3. Take⁴ a little of this fowl, I shall give thee a small piece. 4. What dost thou [do] with these young crows, dost thou eat them? 5. Hast thou forgotten all [the] trouble I⁵ have taken with thee? 6. [Do] not eat too much of this roast goose! it is too fat. 7. I have seen to-day the first swallow, she began already to build⁶ her nest. 8. We [do] not remember, where we saw your amiable friend. 9. I was not mistaken, it was William who stepped into the open garden with a tall stranger. 10. What did you give to your tame pigeons, when they were ill?

1. not any, equal to *no*: tein, teine, tein. 2. *I give you* (Dat.) yet (doch) *not*. 3. Instead of *in believing* translate: *to believe*. 4. Transl.: *eat* (sing.). 5. Transl.: *which I me* (Dat.) *with thee given have*. 6. Transl.: *herself* (Dat.) *her nest* (Acc.) *to build*.

FORTIETH LESSON.

Learn Rules 244, 232, 233 and revise 241.

Quälen, to torment,
Der Fisch, the fish,
der Aal, the eel,
der Lachs ⎫
der Salm ⎭ the salmon,
die Forelle, the trout,
der Hecht, the pike,
der Hering, the herring,
der Karpfen, the carp,
der Krebs, crayfish, crawfish,
der Schellfisch, ⎫
der Caubeljau ⎭ the cod,
die Krabbe, the crab,
der Hummer, the lobster,
die Auster, the oyster,
das Insect, the insect,

schmecken, to taste.
die Biene, the bee,
die Fliege, the fly,
der Frosch, the frog,
die Motte, the moth,
die Mücke, the midge,
die Schlange, the serpent,
der Schmetterling, the butterfly,
die Spinne, the spider,
der Wurm, the worm,
die Wespe, the wasp,
bunt, motly, spotted, varigated,
schmackhaft, tasty, nice,
streng, strict.

79th Exercise.

1. Der unartige Knabe würde nicht geschlagen worden sein, wenn er nicht den armen Schmetterling gequält hätte. 2. Das kleine Kind wird von der starken Magd getragen werden, wenn es nicht mehr gehen kann. 3. Diese Würmer würden nicht ausgegraben worden sein, wenn ich nicht schmackhafte Fische fangen wollte. 4. Ihr guter Freund würde auch geladen worden sein, wenn Sie mich gefragt hätten. 5. Die frischen Heringe werden gebraten werden, ehe sie auf den Tisch getragen werden. 6. Wir fuhren gestern in einem offnen Boot auf dem Meer, wo wir viel große Fische gefangen haben. 7. Glauben Sie nicht, daß er von seinem strengen Vater wird gefragt werden, wohin er heute gefahren ist? 8. Wir würden sicher gefragt werden, wenn wir spät nach Hause führen. 9. Diese bunten Forellen sind zwar[1] klein, aber sie werden noch wachsen. 10. Wenn diese frischen Fische gebacken wären, so würden sie viel besser schmecken.

1. zwar: it is true.

80th Exercise.

1. The little boat would have been carried away[1], if we had[2] sailed[3] only a little farther out[4]. 2. Big John struck your little brother, because he would not carry the spotted trout [5]he had caught to-day. 3. Thou askest me, if these fresh crabs taste well; I tell thee, take[6] one of them,[7] and thou wilt[8] see[9] [thy]self. 4. We should not have been invited,[10] if we had not brought[11] him these fresh oysters. 5. No insect, worm or any other[12] animal was created in order[13] to be tormented. 6. Carry this big salmon and the fresh herrings into that green house. 7. How much[14] you are grown, since I saw you last[15], I should not have known[16] you again. 8. When[17] you drive to (the) town to-day, will you ask the old doctor, if I can eat fresh salmon now? 9. It seems to me, as if he grew much more than his elder brothers. 10. If you carried these varigated butterflies [for] me (*Dat.*), I would show you[18] what I have caught to-day.

1. hinweg. 2. Transl.: *were*. 3. fahren. 4. hinaus. 5. Insert the Relative Pronoun *which*. 6. Transl.: *eat*. 7. of them: davon. 8. Insert *it*. 9. erfahren. 10. laden. 11. brought: gebracht. 12. any other: irgend ein. 13. in order: um. 14. much: sehr. 15. Transl.: *since I have not seen you*. 16. known: gekannt or erkannt. 17. Transl.: *will you* (Wollen Sie) .... *ask, if* (or, *whether*) *I* .... *now, when you to-day to* (nach).... 18. Dat., stands after *I*.

FORTY-FIRST LESSON.
Learn Rule 250, learn Rules 245 (first 7 verbs), 254—260 and revise 242.

Trauen (*Dat.*), to trust,
verlassen, to abandon,

bedürfen (*Acc.* and *Gen.*), to require.

Die Seele, the soul,
der Sinn, the sense,
das Gefühl, the feeling,
das Gehör, the hearing,
der Geruch, the smell,
der Geschmack, the taste,
das Gesicht, the sight,

das Gedächtniß, the memory,
die Sprache, the language,
die Stimme, the voice, vote,
die Vernunft, the reason,
der Verstand, the understanding, the sense,
die Ruhe, the peace, rest.

Sonst, else,

leicht, light, easy,

passend, suitable.

81st *Exercise.*

1. Kannst du rathen, was für eine Stimme das ist? 2. Ich muß dich halten, sonst fällst du. 3. Wenn man schläft, schlafen auch die Sinne mehr oder weniger. 4. Ich weiß nicht, was ich von ihm halten soll, mein Verstand räth mir, ihm nicht zu trauen. 5. Darf ich fragen, ob dieser Braten nach Ihrem Geschmack ist? 6. Ich wollte Sie bitten, mir doch Ihre Stimme zu geben. 7. Wenn er nicht schliefe, könnten Sie ein wenig auf Ihrem neuen Horn blasen. 8. Möchten Sie die französische Sprache lernen? 9. Was Sie für ein gutes Gedächtniß haben! Wenn ich solch ein gutes Gedächtniß hätte, so sollte Niemand mehr wissen und

können als ich. 10. Wenn Ihr Verstand es Ihnen räth, so lassen Sie sich nicht davon abhalten, es zu thun.

82nd Exercise.

1. Guess the easy riddle which I have given¹ you, if you can. 2. If he had not slept too little yesterday, he would not require rest now. 3. They would not have caught him, if he had² not fallen. 4. Will you not advise me³? where shall I find suitable words⁴ to express⁵ my feelings? 5. Will you roast us this piece [of] meat? 6. My memory forsakes me and I can no longer trust my sight. 7. If you like⁶, you may⁷ know now, what you must know one day⁸ at any rate⁹. 8. He said he was not allowed¹⁰ to learn that difficult language, else he would certainly do it. 9. What shall we think¹¹ of her voice? 10. Her voice may be all very¹² good, but to¹³ my taste it is not.

1. given: aufgegeben. 2. Transl.: *were* (Subjunctive). 3. Dat. 4. Find the proper plural in Rule 112. 5. to express: ausjudrücken. 6. Transl.: *will*. 7. Transl.: *can*. 8. Gen. 9. ja doch. 10. he was allowed to: *Present Subj.* of dürfen. 11. halten. 12. all very: zwar ganz. 13. nach, Dat.

FORTY-SECOND LESSON.

Learn Rules 245 (first 14 verbs); revise Rules 230 and 243.

Entweichen, to escape,
ergreifen, to seize,
angreifen, to attack,
angegriffen, attacked,
bestreiten, to dispute, to assert the contrary.

Die Erbse, the pea,
die Bohne, the bean,
der Kohl, the cabbage,
der Blumenkohl, the cauliflower,
das Korn, the corn,
der Weizen, the wheat,
der Roggen, the rye,
der Hafer, the oats,
die Gerste, the barley,
die Grütze, the groats,
die Hafergrütze, the oatmeal,
der Mais, or türkische Weizen, Turkish corn,

der Reis, the rice,
der Flachs, the flax,
der Hanf, the hemp,
der Hanfsamen, hempseed,
die Sichel, the sickle.
die Hirse, millet,
der Kanariensamen, canary-seed,
die Linse, lentil (lense),

Die Stelle, the place, situation.
das Gefängniß, the prison,
der Dieb, the thief,
der Räuber, the robber.

Mitten durch, straight through,
reif, ripe,
schlau, sly, clever,
tapfer, brave,
ab, off.
toll, mad,
zufällig, by chance,
eben, soeben, just now,
gerade, just,
weg,[1] away,

1. weg, pronounced exceptionally *reck*.

83rd Exercise.

1. Ende August wurde im vorigen Jahr der erste Hafer geschnitten, er hatte sehr durch den vielen Regen gelitten. 2. Warum wurde hier gestritten (see Rule 361)? Oh, man stritt sich hier darüber, ob der Blumenkohl dem Kohl gliche. 3. Wer hat mit den Erbsen geschmissen? 4. Die bösen Kinder haben mir meine schönen rothen Bohnen aus der Erde gerissen. 5. Hätte ich dem bösen Hunde nicht gepfiffen, so würde der kleine Knabe jetzt von ihm gebissen. 6. Ich litte das nicht, wenn ich an Ihrer Stelle wäre; auch[1] wäre ich ihm nicht[1] gewichen. 7. Er ritt gestern mit seinen Freunden mitten durch das Land, aber sie wurden von den Leuten ergriffen und in das Gefängniß geworfen. 8. Es wurde (see 361) hier eben gepfiffen; wer ist es gewesen? 9. Die schlauen Räuber waren aus dem festen Gefängniß entwichen, aber wie (as) sie sich aus der Stadt schlichen, wurden sie gesehen und von einigen bewaffneten Soldaten in's Gefängniß zurück-

begleitet. 10. Als ich ihn eben besuchte, schliff er gerade die Sichel, um morgen den reifen Weizen zu schneiden.

1. auch nicht, neither.

84th Exercise.

1. The wicked robbers wanted[1] to slink away,[1] but it was not suffered by the gallant soldiers. 2. When was the poor boy bitten by[2] the mad dog? to-day! he bid him in[3] the right hand. 3. The yellow corn was being cut this morning, when I strode through[4] the field. 4. (The) little Charles tore up[5] yesterday your pretty beans and peas; it was seen by[6] nobody, except[7] me. 5. My new brown horse was ridden on[8] Monday by your little cousin Louis. 6. Poor Fred[9] was thrown off[10] and suffered great pain[s]. 7. The clever thief would have escaped[11], if they[12] had[13] not seized him by chance. 8. I was told to-day[14], that little Henry[9] had resembled his poor father[15] very [much]; is that true? 9. It was never yet disputed by [any] one, as far as[16] I know. 10. The foreign soldiers were attacked, but they fought so bravely that the enemy soon gave way.

1. Transl.: *would* themselves *away slink*. 2. von, Dat. 3. in, Acc. 4. durch, Acc. 5. aus, at the end. 6. von, Dat. 7. außer, Dat. 8. am. 9. Read Rule 144. 10. ab. 11. Pluperf. Subj. 12. man. 13. Transl.: *it was* me (*Dat.*) *to-day told*. 14. Dat. 15. Transl.: *as* [so] *much*.

FORTY-THIRD LESSON.

Learn Rules 231 and 245 (rest); revise 244.

Verzeihen (*Dat.*), to excuse, pardon,
vertreiben, to drive away,
verleihen, to grant, to bestow upon,

siegen (intrans. verb), to conquer, to vanquish,
besiegen (trans. verb), to conquer,
bewässern, to water.

Die Blume, the flower,
die Lilie, the lily,
die Rose, the rose,
die Tulpe, the tulip,
die Hyacin'the, the hyacinth,
die Narcis'se, the narcissus,
der (Gold)lack, wallflower,

das Maiblümchen, the lily of the valley,
die Rese'da, mignonette,
das Schneeglöckchen, snowdrop,
das Stiefmütterchen, pansy,
das Veilchen, the violet,
das Vergißmeinnicht, the forgetmenot.

Der Hügel, the hill,
der Kampf, the battle.
der Orden, the order,

Wegen (*Gen.*), on account of,
duftig, fragrant,
fest, fast, fortified,
hinaus, out (*Adv.*).

kühl, cool,
roh, rude, rough,
verschieden, various,

85th Exercise.

1. Ich bin dazu¹ getrieben worden, ihnen meine rothen Rosen und weißen Lilien zu weisen. 2. Du bist sehr wegen deiner schönen Hyacinthen und Tulpen gepriesen worden; sind auch die Narcissen in diesem Jahr gediehen? 3. Nachdem die duftige Reseda von dem gelben Goldlack war geschieden worden, gediehen beide besser. 4. Es schien mir, als ob ihm von seinem guten Vater sei verziehen worden. 5. Wir blieben noch eine Weile im kühlen Zimmer, aber er trieb uns hinaus in den duftigen Garten, seine schönen Blumen zu sehen. 6. Besonders seine bunten Stiefmütterchen mußten wir ihm preisen. 7. Was nützt Ihnen das Schreien, es wäre besser, Sie schwiegen. 8. Meinem Freunde Karl ist vom König ein hoher Orden verliehen worden; er ist schon hoch gestiegen und kann noch höher steigen. 9. Gestern sind die rohen Barbaren von den Christen nach kurzem Kampfe besiegt worden. 10. Bleiben Sie doch noch ein wenig, bis ich meinen zweiten Brief geschrieben habe.

1. Read Rule 289.

86th Exercise.

1. Is it true, that an order has been bestowed upon your dear father by the good king?¹ 2. After the enemy had been driven out of the fortified town, they ascended² the high hills. 3. Joseph wrote to me yesterday, that his last work had been praised very [much] by the people. 4. These sweet violets and this fragrant wallflower seemed so fresh, when I bought them, and now they [do] not succeed in the open garden. 5. Stay a little longer and write a short letter for me, if you please. 6. After the various flowers had been watered, the roses soon seemed to thrive. 7. We have pardoned him³ and⁴ parted as good friends. 8. He cried as⁵ loud [as] he could, but nobody seemed to hear him. 9. My beautiful tulips and hyacinths, but especially my sweet narcissi, succeeded well in the room last winter. 10. If you are not silent, the other pupils cannot write their difficult exercises.

1. Compare the eighth sentence of the previous exercise. 2. to ascend: hinaufsteigen. 3. Dat. 4. Insert: *are*. 5. so.

FORTY-FOURTH LESSON.

Learn Rule 246 (first half); revise 245.

Die Hoffnung, the hope,
die Verzweiflung, the despair,
die Achtung, the respect,
die Verachtung, the contempt,
die Rettung, the safety, deliverance,
die Angst, the anxiety,
die Furcht, the fear,
die Sorge, the sorrow,

der Ärger, the vexation, annoyance,
der Zorn, the wrath, anger,
die Liebe, the love,
der Haß, the hatred,
die Freundschaft, the friendship,
die Feindschaft, the enmity,
die Tugend, the virtue,

das Laster, the vice,   das Schauspiel, the play,
der Wunsch, the wish,   die Stelle, place, situation.

Anbieten, to offer,   gern, willingly,
verwandeln, to change,   lieber, more willingly. rather,
entfernt, distant, remote,   am liebsten, most willingly,
wenn auch, although.

How to translate *to like*:

1. By mögen, or stronger gern mögen, it may be translated pretty safely in *any* connection, although this is not the most common way.
2. By gern haben, or, ein Freund von.... sein, } when expressing *generality*, as:

   Haben Sie gern Blumen und Gemälde, or, sind Sie ein Freund von Blumen und Gemälden? } Do you like (or are you fond of) flowers and pictures (in general)?
3. By gern essen, gern trinken, gern sehen, gern hören, gern lesen, gern machen etc., when the liking refers to one of the senses and expresses the liking of the thing *in general*, not of a *special* one; as: Ich esse gern Schinken, du trinkst gern Wein, er sieht gern Gemälde, wir hören gern Musik, ihr leset gern Gedichte, sie machen gern Lärm, I like (to eat) ham, thou likest (to drink) wine, he likes (to see) pictures, we like (to hear) music, you like (to read) poetry, they like (to make) noise.
4. By gefallen, when expressing liking for a thing defined by an article or pronoun, and by schmecken, if such thing can be tasted; as: Mir schmeckt dieser Schinken, dir schmeckt der Wein, ihm gefallen seine Gemälde, uns gefällt jene Musik, euch gefallen ihre Gedichte, ihnen gefällt der Lärm, I like *this* ham, thou likest *the* wine, he likes *his* pictures, we like *that* music, you like *her* poems, they like *the* noise.
5. To like *people* may be rendered by any verb expressing liking; e. g., ich mag diesen jungen Mann, ich habe diesen jungen Mann gern, dieser junge Mann gefällt mir, ich kann diesen jungen Mann leiden. The liking or loving of abstract ideas is mostly rendered by lieben.

87th Exercise.

1. Ich flöhe gern mit Ihnen, wenn ich nur die entfernteste Hoffnung auf Rettung hätte. 2. Möchtest du mit

mir nach dem warmen Süden ziehen? Mich zieht es nach Italien fort, ich kann nicht in diesem Lande bleiben. 3. Wie gefällt Ihnen dieser Wunsch, glauben Sie, daß er erfüllt werden wird? 4. Sehen Sie gern Bilder? Nun (well), ich werde Ihnen eins zeigen, das Ihnen gewiß gefallen wird. 5. Furcht und Verzweiflung ergriff den Feind, er floh in wilder Unordnung. 6. Was hat Sie dazu bewogen, Ihre große Liebe zu ihm in bittern Haß zu verwandeln? 7. Er schwor dem Fürsten ewige Freundschaft, und er wird ihn nicht betrügen. 8. Wer einmal lügt, dem glaubt man nicht, und wenn er auch die Wahrheit spricht. 9. Essen Sie gern Obst? Ich biete Ihnen dieses Körbchen voll an, nehmen Sie's mir zu Liebe (to please me). 10. Hören Sie gern Musik? Ich höre zwar gern Musik, aber diese Musik gefällt mir nicht.

1. Long S.

88th *Exercise.*

1. I [do] not like this young man; I shun[1] him, as[2] vice.[3] 2. [Do] you like French wine? Yes, I like French wine, but I prefer Rhenish.[4] 3. Tell [me], how does your brother like his new situation, has he hope, to please his master? 4. I [do] not know,[5] but it seems he would not like to lose it. 5. Dost thou like plays? Yes, I like[6] plays, but I [do] not like this piece. 6. If it should freeze this night, the hope[7] of the husbandman[8] would be deceived[9] again. 7. Shun [3]vice, [do] not lie and deceive nobody. 8. What have you lost? I offer you my help to seek it. 9. [Do] not be induced by your anger to swear enmity to him, you should rather forgive him. 10. The one pulled, the second pushed and the third lifted.

1. Transl.: *flee.* 2. wie. 3. Insert the Def. Artc. 4. Rheinwein. 5. Insert *it.* 6. Insert zwar. 7. Plur. 8. Landmann. 9. Insert wohl.

FORTY-FIFTH LESSON.

Learn Rules 246 (complete) and 270.

Beschießen, to fire at,
beschließen, to resolve, deliberate,
überlassen, to leave (over),
umgeben, to surround,
unternehmen, to undertake,
sich unterhalten, to converse, to entertain,

verlassen, to leave, to forsake, to abandon,
vollbringen, to perform, to execute,
vollenden, to accomplish,
widerlegen, to refute,
widersprechen, to contradict.

Der Schwiegervater, the father-in-law,
der Stiefvater, the stepfather,
der Schwager, the brother-in-law,
die Schwägerinn, the sister-in-law,
die Jungfrau, the maiden,
der Vormund, the guardian.

der Jüngling[1], the youth,
die Jugend, youth,
der Greis, the old man,
die Greisinn, the old woman (*or* lady),
das Alter, old age,
der Wittwer, the widower,
die Wittwe, the widow,
die Waise, the orphan,

1. Pron.: Jüng'ling.

Der Kranz, the wreath,
die Jagd, the hunting, chase,
das Glied, the limb, the rank;
weshalb, why.

schnell, quick,
endlich, at last,
hinfort, henceforth,

89th Exercise.

1. Es hat mich sehr verdrossen, daß ich meinen guten Schwager heute nicht getroffen[1] habe. 2. Weshalb widersprach der thörichte Jüngling dem klugen Greise, er konnte ihn doch nicht widerlegen. 3. Die edle Greisinn war von ihren untreuen Söhnen und Töchtern verlassen, von ihren Schwieger=

söhnen und Schwiegertöchtern. 4. Ich war gestern mit meinem Vormund auf der Jagd; wir haben oft geschossen, aber daß wir viel getroffen hätten, könnte ich gerade nicht sagen. 5. Hat Sie das nicht sehr verdrossen? O nein, ich habe das Vergnügen doch genossen. 6. Diese Eier sind zu hart gesotten, sieden Sie zwei andere. 7. Die tapfern Soldaten wurden von allen Seiten beschossen, aber es gelang ihnen dennoch, ihre Glieder zu schließen und endlich das harte Gefecht zu gewinnen. 8. Die schnelle Jugend unternimmt, das bedächtige[2] Alter beschließt gern. 9. Dieses arme Kind hat Vater und Mutter verloren, nun ist es ganz verlassen und zur Waise geworden. 10. Mein guter Vater hat beschlossen, sein Vormund zu sein.

1. Perf. Part. of treffen. 2. wary, prudent.

90th Exercise.

1. The old man was surrounded by his faithful sons and (by his) daughters-in-law. 2. What[1] are the noble youth and the maiden conversing about[1], have they had annoyance? 3. What did they resolve yesterday, will they undertake the difficult task or leave it to your prudent brother-in-law? 4. It annoys you very [much], I suppose[2], that they will not leave it to you. 5. The broad river is swelling, because the snow is fast melting[3]. 6. Who has boiled these eggs? The girl! she has allowed[4] them to boil too long. 7. My brother-in-law and my sister have wound[5] for the old lady a beautiful wreath. 8. John's stepfather has resolved to leave the large business to him henceforth. 9. When the last snow is melted, the fragrant flowers will soon sprout. 10. Why dost thou not extinguish the fire?

1. What..about: wovon. 2. I suppose: wohl, put before *very*. 3. is fast melting: ist im schnellen Schmelzen. 4. allowed to: lassen (read 384). 5. flechten or winden.

FORTY-SIXTH LESSON.
Learn Rules 247 and 272.

Ankommen, to arrive,
ausrufen, to cry out, to exclaim,
aufrufen, to call (a roll),
ausgehen, to go out,
weggehen, to go away,
spazieren gehen, to take a walk,
aufstehen, to get up,

niederliegen, to lie down,
sich **niederlegen,** to lie down,
sich **niedersetzen,** to sit down,
niedersitzen, to be seated,
ausstehen, to stand, to endure,
heimkommen, to return, to come home,
vorkommen (*Dat.*), to appear,
weglaufen, to run away,
mittheilen, to communicate.

Die Arbeit, the work, labour,
die Erlaubniß, the permission,
die Gefahr, the danger,
das Glück, the happiness,
das Unglück, the misfortune,
das Schicksal, the fate, adventure,
die Armut, poverty, the poor,

der Reichtum, the riches, wealth,
der Schlaf, the sleep,
der Traum, the dream,
die Vergangenheit, the past,
die Gegenwart, the presence, present,
die Zukunft, the future,
die Wohlthat, the benefit, blessing.

Besonder, special,
wohlthätig, beneficent,
schattig, shady,
erst, only (used of time).

91st *Exercise.*

1. Wer hat dir (or dich) geheißen, ohne meine besondere Erlaubniß wegzugehen? 2. Ich bat ihn, mir seine ganze Vergangenheit mitzutheilen; aber er wollte es nicht thun. 3. Steh' auf und geh an die Arbeit. 4. Was nützt uns

aller Reichtum, wenn wir nicht wohlthätig sind und der Armut von unserm Glück mittheilen? 5. Jetzt gehen wir fort von hier und wissen nicht, ob uns die Zukunft Glück oder Unglück bringen wird. 6. Sie saßen unter einem schattigen Baum nieder, und dort hat ihnen der Fremde all seine Schicksale erzählt, welche Gefahren er ausgestanden[1] und wie ihm seine Vergangenheit jetzt wie ein Traum vorkomme. 7. Ich rief, so laut ich konnte, seinen Namen aus; aber er kam nicht zurück, sondern lief fort. 8. Es war (die) Sitte in unserer Schule, daß, wenn der Rector in die Klasse kam, alle Schüler aufstanden. 9. Oft gingen wir bei schönem Wetter spazieren, besuchten die schattigen Wälder und die nächsten Dörfer und kamen erst spät wieder heim. 10. Ich würde gern mitgegangen sein, wenn ich nur von meinem Vater die Erlaubniß dazu erhalten hätte.

1. habe, understood.

92nd Exercise.

1. [Do] not run away from your work now! when you have done[1] all your tasks, we shall take a long walk together. 2. It appears to me, that you have done right[2] to communicate your great misfortune to your old friend. 3. Let us sit down under this beautiful tree, or let us lie down, if you like. 4. Why did you go away yesterday, before I had called out[3] your name? 5. You [can]not believe, how much we have endured in former[4] years. 6. I had yesterday a bad[5] dream and when I rose [from my bed], it was already very late. 7. My father has given me (the) permission to take a walk with my friend, but not to come home too late. 8. I cannot leave[6] my work, I have still so much to do. 9. Come with [me], we ask for[7] your father's permission. 10. He rose, took his books and went home, without saying a word[8].

1. Transl. *made*. 2. Insert daran. 3. *out*, rendered here auf. 4. früher. 5. böse. 6. Transl. *go away from*. 7. bitten um. 8. Change into: *without a word to say*.

FORTY-SEVENTH LESSON.
Learn Rules 248 and 277.

Darbringen, to offer,
einernten, to earn, win,
beeinflussen, to influence,
verdenken, to find fault with, to blame,
verkennen (trans. verb), to mistake,
Durchlaufen, to run *through*,
durchlaufen, to cross, traverse,
Durchlesen, to read *through*,
durchlesen, to peruse,
übergeben, to hand over, deliver,
überführen, to lead *over*,
überführen, to convict, to convince (governs the Acc. of the *person*, and Gen. of the *thing*),
übergehen, to go over, cross,
übergehen, to pass over,
übersetzen, to set *over*,
übersetzen, to translate,
unterhalten, to hold *under*,
sich unterhalten, to entertain, to converse,
sich wenden (an, *Acc.*), to apply (to),
warten, to wait.

Die Ehre, honour,
die Schande, disgrace,
der Muth, courage,
der Ruhm, glory,
der Stolz, pride,
die Geduld, patience,
der Glaube, faith,
die Güte, kindness,
die Lüge, the lie,
das Mitleid, pity, compassion,
die Wahrheit, truth,
die Menschheit, mankind,
die Bedeutung, the meaning,
die Handlung[1], the action,
die Eisenbahn, the railway,
der Zug, the train,
der Eisenbahnzug, the railwaytrain,
der Krieg, war,
der Rücken, the back, rear.

1. Pron. Hand'lung.

Leicht, easy, light,
schwer, difficult, heavy, grave,
letzt, last, late,
wörtlich, word for word, literally,
beinahe, almost,
soeben, just now,
was — auch, whatever.

93rd Exercise.

1. Man kann es diesem Manne nicht verdenken, daß er beinahe den Glauben an die Menschheit verloren hat. 2. Was er auch unternimmt, so erntet er Ehre und Ruhm dabei ein. 3. Wenn Sie sich ihm übergeben haben, so haben Sie sich an den Rechten gewandt. 4. Die Einwohner des Landes brachten dem fremden König selt'ne Früchte auf gold'nen Tellern dar; er aber übergab sie der Königinn. 5. Wir unterhielten uns gestern mit Ihrem Bruder über die Bedeutung von Ruhm und Ehre. 6. Es ist oft sehr schwer, einen Satz wörtlich zu übersetzen. 7. Ich habe dir einen Brief von der Post mitgebracht, hast du ihn schon durchgelesen? 8. Er hat die ganze Stadt durchlaufen, hat aber keinen Arzt finden können. 9. Wenn sie mir die Wahrheit sagt, will ich ihr gern vergeben. 10. Die Feinde umringen den Wald, um uns in den Rücken zu fallen.

94th Exercise.

1. Were you conversing just now about the late war? 2. Are you going to translate[1] that difficult book into (the) English, when you have read it through? 3. To tell [you] the truth, I have undertaken that difficult task already. 4. The railwaytrain crosses the whole country in 24 hour from north to[2] south. 5. I cannot understand, how you can have so much patience with him. 6. You mistake my poor friend, it is not pride, it is honour which[3] influences his actions. 7. Think[4] of his former kindness and [do] not turn (yourself) away from him. 8. He has lost all patience, he will not wait any longer.[5] 9. What a great blessing it is to[6] suffering mankind, that he has given over his arm to the good cause. 10. After they had convicted him of his terrible lies, they led him over[7] the river to the brave general.

1. Fut. 2. nach. 3. *which* refers to the whole phrase *not to honour,* hence: was (v. Rule 93). 4. Gedenken Sie (gen.). 5. länger mehr. 6. Transl.: *for the.* 7. Acc.

FORTY-EIGHTH LESSON.
Learn Rules 290—292; revise 54—68.

Aussteigen, to get out (of a carriage),
anhalten, to stop (hold on), continue, (keep on).
einstecken, to put in.
sich befreunden, to make friends,
nachgeben, to give in, to yield.

Die Reise, the journey,
der Reisende, the traveller,
der Koffer, the box,
der Mantelsack, the portmanteau,
das Gebirge, the mountain-range,
die Hitze, the heat,
die Sicherheit, safety,
das Pistol / die Pistole } the pistol,
der Degen / der Säbel / das Schwert } the sword.

Streng, strict,
öffentlich, public,
vorwärts, forwards,
rückwärts, backwards.
gerade aus, straight along,
rechts, to the right,
links, to the left,
indessen, indeß, however, but.

95th Exercise.

1. Schreiben Sie meinem alten Freunde, ich könnte einer kleinen Reise wegen nicht zu ihm kommen; ich würde indeß innerhalb weniger Tage (or binnen wenigen Tagen) wieder da sein. 2. Wo ist mein treuer Bedienter? sagen Sie ihm, er soll meinen Mantelsack und den seinigen packen, auch soll er nicht vergessen, der Sicherheit halber die Pistolen einzustecken. 3. Jenseits des Gebirges hält der Zug auf einen Augenblick an, dann werden wir aussteigen und trotz der Hitze etwas Warmes genießen. 4. Im vorigen Jahr haben wir unweit der neuen Stadt ein großes Haus gebaut. 5. Im Sommer wohnen wir gern außerhalb der Stadt, da es innerhalb der Stadt zu warm ist. 6. Nehmen Sie anstatt des

alten Mantelsacks den neuen Koffer mit auf die lange Reise.
7. Ihretwegen, mein Lieber, werde ich Alles thun. 8. Den neuesten Nachrichten zufolge hat das arme Volk nachgegeben.
9. Sie hat ihre deutschen Aufgaben gemacht und ungeachtet meines strengen Verbotes auch die seinigen, ist das recht?
10. Würden Sie ihm helfen, wenn Sie wüßten, daß er es um seiner lieben Eltern willen thut.

96th Exercise.

1. Which is my eldest brother's sword and which is yours? 2. If the foreign traveller has forgotten his good pistols, lend him mine for the sake of his safety! 3. Do you think, [1]this uncommon heat will continue during the whole summer? 4. If you show me your new books, Charles, I shall also show you mine. 5. Do you know,[2] Henry, that (the) good uncle John is going to build a large house[3] on the other side of the broad river, outside of the old town? 6. According to the latest news we shall have to make a long journey. 7. On account of the war all public schools have been closed in our town, [4]I hear they will soon be closed in yours too. 8. If you have forgotten your own portmanteau, I will lend you mine. 9. Shall we live in Vienna with your German friends or with mine? 10. You do not[5] know my family,[6] if you knew them, you would seek to make friends with them.

1. Insert *that*, daß. 2. Insert schon. 3. Insert und zwar. 4. Insert *as*, wie. 5. Insert nur. 6. Read Rule 81.

FORTY-NINTH LESSON.

Learn Rules 293—297; revise 70—89.

Sich betragen, to behave, conduct one's self,

fortreisen } to set out,
abreisen } depart,

zurückkehren, to return,
verlangen, to wish, want, demand.

Die Abwesenheit, absence,
die Beschäftigung, the occupation,
das Bedürfniß, want, need,
der Mangel, want, distress,
der Grundsatz, the principle,
der Schatz, the treasure,

das Gut, the property, estate, *plur. also:* goods,
die Kirche, the church, kirk,
die Nothwendigkeit, the necessity,
der Überfluß, abundance,
der Zustand, the state.

Freundlich, friendly, kind, unfreundlich, unfriendly, etc.

97th Exercise.

1. Derjenige, welcher immer im Überfluß lebt, hat selten Mitleid mit dem, der Mangel leidet. 2. Was kann ich ohne dich machen, da ich außer dir niemand kenne. 3. Was Sie von mir verlangen, ist gegen meinen Grundsatz. 4. Meine Muhme wird sammt Kindern und Mägden auf einen Monat nach ihrem Gute reisen. 5. Ich habe sie seit einem vollen Jahr nicht gesehen. 6. Vor drei Tagen ist mein Vater von der Reise zurückgekehrt; wissen Sie auch,[1] was er mir mitgebracht hat? 7. Als er vor sechs Wochen nebst meiner Mutter abreiste, sagte er noch, er werde demjenigen das Beste mitbringen, der sich während seiner Abwesenheit am besten betragen werde. 8. Kommen Sie, wir wollen dem Mann entgegengehen, der all unsern Grundsätzen entgegen ist. 9. Derjenige, der nie ohne nützliche Beschäftigung ist, wird selten vom Mangel zu leiden haben. 10. Von wem kommen Sie? sind Sie bei dem Arzt gewesen?

1. *and* do you know.

98th Exercise.

1. He desires, that you return immediately from (the) town to him. 2. Give back the great treasure to him, who had lost it. 3. Are you still[1] living

opposite the new church? 4. I cannot live without a suitable occupation. 5. About the twelfth hour it was, when he departed along with his faithful spouse and their child. 6. Come to [see] us this evening and bring your young friend with you. 7. I have not seen him for² many months; you never speak of him. 8. Why are you always so unkind towards him, is not his state bad³ enough without that? 9. For you I should do anything, but do not desire from me that I do the same for him, who dislikes me so much.⁴ 10. Do not speak of (that) what he said to you, he was beside himself at the time.

1. noch immer. 2. Transl.: *since*. 3. schlimm. 4. Transl.: *to whom* I so much (sehr) against (zuwider) am.

FIFTIETH LESSON.
Learn Rules 298 and 299; revise 90—102.

Aufmachen, to open,
zu machen, to shut,
gebrauchen, to use, require,
klopfen, to knock,

Die Brücke, the bridge,
der Celte, the Celt,
die Commode, or das Schränk=chen, the cabinet,
die Eltern (*pl. n.*), the parents,
das Geschwister, brother or sister,
der Germane, or Deutsche, the German,

Fern, far,
französisch, French,

lachen, to laugh,
rechnen, to count, to reckon,
sich stellen, to place one's self,

der Obstbaum, the fruit-tree,
die Sache, the affair, matter,
der Schatten, the shade,
das Sofa, the sofa,
der Schlüssel, the key,
die Seelenwanderung, the transmigration of souls,
das Thor, the gate,
die Wand, the wall.

hoffentlich, I hope,
rund, round,
wenigstens, at least.

99th Exercise.

1. Wer klopft an die Stubenthür, geh' und mach' auf. 2. Ich weiß nicht, wo der Schlüssel ist; hängt er noch an der linken Wand? 3. Du wirst ihn auf dem runden Tisch finden, auf den ich ihn erst vor einer Stunde gelegt habe. 4. Wen sehe ich da mit Ihrem alten Freunde über die lange Brücke kommen, ist es nicht der junge Graf? 5. Wessen Messer ist das, welches ich hier hinter der Hausthür gefunden habe? 6. Es gehört dem kleinen Knaben, welcher neben mir auf der Schulbank sitzt. 7. Woran denken Sie soeben? Ich denke an meine fernen Eltern und Geschwister. 8. Haben Sie nicht erst vor wenigen Tagen einen langen Brief von ihnen erhalten? 9. Stellen Sie sich nicht zwischen mich und Ihren Bruder. 10. Ich muß mich sehr über Ihr schlechtes Betragen wundern.

100th Exercise.

1. In which room do you [do] your schoolwork?[1] 2. Does John sit below or above you in (the) French. 3. We [will] go into the green wood this afternoon; who would like to go with [us]? 4. Did[2] the ancient Celts and Germans believe[2] in the transmigration of souls? 5. Yes! at least we have read so[3] in the new history, which we use in (the) school. 6. Can I count upon you in this matter? 7. Did[2] you see[2] where the ball fell? I believe, it[4] fell behind the cabinet; oh no, it[4] lies beside the sofa, I see it.[4] 8. Let us go out of town,[5] I have not been on the hills [for a] long [time]. 9. He lay[6] down among the grass under the shadow of the fruit-trees. 10. At[7] whom do you laugh? I hope you are not laughing at my friend.

1. Use the plural. 2. Use Imperfect. 3. Transl.: read *it*. 4. Masculine, referring to Ball, *masc*. 5. Transl.: *before the gate*. 6. to lie down: sich niederlegen. 7. at: über (acc.).

THIRD PART.

Nützliche Gespräche. — **Useful Dialogues.**

I.

Begrüßung und Höflichkeits= formeln.	Salutation and forms of politeness.
Gehorsamer Diener (oder: Ihr Diener).	Your obedient servant.
Guten Morgen.	Good morning, Sir.
Ich wünsche Ihnen einen guten Morgen.	I wish you a good morning.
Guten Tag.	Good day.
Gesegnete Mahlzeit.	(In rising after dinner.)
Ich empfehle mich (Ihnen). (polite form).	Good bye. (I recommend myself to you.)
Guten Abend; gute Nacht.	Good evening; good night.
Schlafen Sie wohl.	Sleep well.
Ich wünsche Ihnen angenehme Ruhe.	I wish you a good night's rest.
Lebewohl, lebet wohl, leben Sie wohl; adieu! [Fahr(e) wohl, only poetical].	Farewell, good bye!
Auf Wiedersehen!	May we meet again (*au revoir*)!
Adieu unterdeß.	Good bye just now.
Wie haben Sie geschlafen?	How did you sleep?
Haben Sie gut geschlafen?	Did you sleep well?
Haben Sie ausgeschlafen?	Have you had a good night's rest?
Danke, sehr gut.	Thank you, very well.
Ich konnte lange nicht ein= schlafen.	I could not sleep for a long time.

Nicht besonders.	Not particularly.
Ich habe die Zeit verschlafen.	I have overslept myself.
Wie geht es Ihnen? (polite).	How are you?
Wie befinden Sie sich? (formal).	How do you do?
Danke, sehr wohl (oder: sehr gut).	Thank you, very well.
Und Sie, wie geht es Ihnen?	And you, how do you do?
Was machen Sie? oder: wie geht's? (familiar).	How are you?
Ich war vergangene Nacht ein wenig unwohl (unwell).	I was a little indisposed last night.
Wie geht es Ihrem (Herrn) Bruder?	How is your brother?
Wie befindet sich Ihre Frau Gemahlinn? Was macht Ihre Frau, (fam.)	How does your lady do?
Wie geht's mit Ihrer Gesundheit?	How is it with your health?
Ich dank(e) Ihnen, ich fühle mich sehr wohl (not sehr gut).	(I) thank you, I myself feel very well.
Ihre Familie befindet sich doch wohl?	I hope your family are well?
Danke, alle sind wohl, ausgenommen meine Frau, welche sehr an Kopfweh leidet.	Thank you, all are well; except my wife, who suffers much from head-ache.
O! das thut mir sehr leid.	Oh, I am very sorry for it.
Auch Ihre Familie ist hoffentlich wohl?	And your family are well too, I hope?
Danke, sie sind alle sehr wohl.	Thank you, they are all well.
Das freut mich sehr zu hören.	I am very glad to hear it.
Empfehlen Sie mich Ihrer Frau Gemahlinn, wenn ich bitten darf.	Present my compliments to your good lady, if you please.
Grüßen Sie Ihren (Herrn) Bruder (von mir).	Remember me to your brother.
Erlauben Sie mir, Ihnen Herrn B. vorzustellen.	Allow me to introduce to you Mr. B.
Wollen Sie die Güte haben, mich jener Dame vorzustellen?	Will you have the kindness to introduce me to that lady?

Soll ich Sie bei dieser Familie einführen?	Shall I introduce you to that family (at their house)?
Ja, bitte, führen Sie mich bei ihnen ein.	Yes, please, introduce me to them.
Mit dem größten Vergnügen.	With the greatest pleasure.
Ich bitte um Entschuldigung (oder Verzeihung).	I beg your pardon.
Wie beliebt?	I beg your pardon?
Verzeihen Sie.	Pardon me.
Entschuldigen Sie.	Excuse.
Es hat nichts zu sagen (ob.: bitte).	Don't mention.
Nicht Ursache.	No occasion.
Sehr gern.	Willingly.
Herzlich gern (oder: von Herzen gern).	Most willingly.
Von ganzem Herzen.	With all my heart.
Haben Sie die Güte, oder seien Sie so gut, mir zu sagen...	Have the kindness, or be so kind as to tell me...
Darf ich Sie bitten?	May I trouble you?
Wenn ich bitten darf, oder: wenn's beliebt.	If you please!
Wenn es Ihnen nicht zu viel Umstände macht.	If it is not too much trouble for you.
Durchaus nicht.	Not at all.
Machen Sie meinetwegen keine Umstände, wenn ich bitten darf.	Don't trouble yourself on my account, if you please.
Nehmen Sie Platz.	Take a seat.
Ich bin so frei.	Thank you!
Wollen Sie noch eine Tasse Kaffee? Ich danke; wenn ich bitten darf.	Will you have another cup of coffee? No, thank you; thank you.

II.

Die Zeit.   The Time.

Den wievielsten haben wir heute? oder: Der wievielste ist heute?	What day of the month is it?
Welches Datum haben wir heute?	What date is it?

Wir haben heute den dritten April.	It is to-day the third of April.
Heute ist der siebenundzwanzigste October.	To-day is the 27th of October.
Welches Jahr schreiben wir?	What year are we in?
Was für einen Tag haben wir heute?	What day of the week is it to-day?
Heute ist Sonntag.	To-day is Sunday.
Morgen.	To-morrow.
Übermorgen.	The day after to-morrow.
Gestern.	Yesterday.
Gestern Morgen.	Yesterday morning.
Gestern Abend.	Last night (yesterday evening).
Vorgestern.	The day before yesterday.
Heute Morgen.	This morning.
Morgen früh.	To-morrow morning.
Heute Abend.	This evening.
Heute Nacht.	To-night (after 10 p.m.)
In drei Tagen.	In three days.
(Heut) über acht Tage.	This day week.
Vor acht Tagen.	A week ago.
Über vierzehn Tage (oder: In vierzehn Tagen).	This day fortnight.
Vor vierzehn Tagen.	A fortnight ago.
Vorige, oder: vergangene Woche.	Last week.
Vorigen, oder: vergangenen Monat.	Last month.
Nächstes Jahr.	Next year.
Neujahr (oder: Neujahrstag).	New Year's day.
Zu Ostern.	At Easter.
Johannis (zu Johanni).	Midsummer (at Mid.).
Michaelis (zu Michaeli).	Michaelmas (at Mich.).
Zu Weihnachten.	At Christmas.
Erkundigen Sie sich, wie viel Uhr es ist.	Ask or inquire what time it is.
Können Sie mir sagen, wie viel Uhr es ist?	Can you tell me what time it is?
Sehr gern.	Most willingly.

Es thut mir leid, meine Uhr geht nicht (oder: steht).	I am sorry, my watch does not go.
Es ist drei Uhr.	It is three o'clock.
Es ist fünf Minuten nach (oder: über) vier (oder: viere).	It is 5 minutes past four.
Es ist zehn Minuten nach sechs (oder: sechse).	It is 10 minutes past six.
Es ist ein Viertel auf zehn.	It is a quarter past nine.
Es ist in zehn Minuten halb zehn.	It is 20 minutes past nine.
Es ist halb eins.	It is half-past twelve.
Es ist drei Viertel auf zwei.	It is a quarter to two.
Es ist in zehn Minuten zwei.	It is 10 minutes to two.
Es ist Schlag zwölf Uhr.	It is exactly twelve o'clock.
Hat es schon geschlagen?	Has it already struck?
Es wird gleich schlagen.	It is going to strike.
Es hat eben zwei geschlagen.	It has just struck two.
Die Uhr ist abgelaufen.	The clock has run out.
Die Uhr ist stehen geblieben.	The clock has stopped.
Ziehen Sie die Uhr auf.	Wind up the clock.
Sie geht vor, soll ich sie zurückstellen?	It is fast, shall I put it back?
Nein, sie geht nach, stellen Sie sie vor.	No, it is behind. put it forward.
Wie Sie befehlen.	As you desire.
Sehr wohl; schön; gut.	All right, very well.

III.

Die Eisenbahn.   The Railway.

Die Pferdeeisenbahn oder: Pferdebahn.	The tramway.
Fahren Sie nach dem Kölner Eisenbahnhof (oder Bahnhof).	Drive to the Cologne Railway station.
Nehmen Sie meine Sachen, und kommen Sie mit.	Take my luggage and come.

Bleiben Sie bei meinem Gepäck, bis ich zurückkomme.	Take care of my luggage till I come back.
Wo ist die Billetexpedition.	Where is the booking-office?
Wo werden die Billets verkauft?	Where are the tickets sold?
Auf der andern Seite.	On the other side.
Am Schalter in der Vorhalle.	At the office in the lobly.
Ein Billet zweiter Klasse nach Berlin.	A ticket, second-class, for Berlin.
Wie viel kostet es?	How much is it?
Fünfundzwanzig Mark[1].	Twenty five Marks.
Wie viel Fracht hab' ich für mein Gepäck zu zahlen.	How much carriage is to pay for the luggage?
Sie haben keine Überfracht zu zahlen.	You have to pay no overfreight. (There is no extra-charge.)
Können Sie dies wechseln?	Can you change this piece?
Geldwechsler.	Money-changer.
Wie viel gilt es (oder: ist es werth)?	What is its value?
Vorgesehen!	Take care! look out!
Schaffner, wo ist der Wagen zweiter Klasse für Berlin?	Guard, where is the carriage for Berlin, second class?
Träger, wie viel bekommen Sie?	Porter, how much have you to ask (for your services)?
Für jedes Stück fünf und zwanzig Pfennige, also für vier Stück eine Mark.	Each packet 25 Pfennigs that is one mark for four.
Einsteigen!	Take your seats!
Die Billets, meine Herren!	Tickets, Gentlemen!
Müssen wir den Wagen wechseln (oder: umsteigen), oder bringt uns derselbe Zug nach Berlin?	Have we to change, or does the same train take us to Berlin?
Dieser Zug geht bis Berlin.	This train goes as far as Berlin.
Umsteigen!	Change carriages!
Ist es erlaubt, hier zu rauchen?	Is one allowed to smoke here?
So viel Sie wollen (oder: So viel Sie Lust haben).	As much as ever you like!

---

1) 20 mark nominally, but really 3 or 4 d. less = £ 1.

Was steht auf jenem Zettel?	What does that placard say?
Vor Taschendieben wird gewarnt.	Beware of pickpockets.
Darf ich Sie um etwas Feuer bitten?	May I trouble you for a light?
Wie lange hält der Zug auf der nächsten Station an?	How long does the train stop at the next station?
Nur fünf Minuten.	Only 5 minutes.
Auf der Hauptstation hält er zehn Minuten oder eine Viertelstunde an.	At the principal station it stays 10 minutes or $1/4$ of an hour.
Da wird man Zeit zum Mittagessen haben.	There will be time for us to take dinner.
Wann werden wir in B. ankommen?	What time shall we arrive at B.?
In einer halben Stunde.	In half an hour.
Um Mittag.	At noon.
Gegen Mitternacht.	Towards midnight.
Sind wir jetzt da?	Are we there now?
Wie heißt jene Stadt?	How is that town called?
Was für eine herrliche Aussicht!	What a beautiful view!
Wie gefällt es Ihnen hier zu Lande?	How do you like our country?
Sehr gut.	Very well.
Ich bin schon einmal hier gewesen.	I have been here before.
Jetzt sind wir da.	Now we are arrived.
Träger, besorgen Sie mir eine Droschke.	Porter, get me a cab.
Wohin wollen Sie?	Where do you want to go to?
Hôtel de Rome, Friedrichstraße Nr.[1] 144.	Hôtel de Rome, 144 Frederick street.
Was (oder: wie viel) hab' ich zu bezahlen?	What have I to pay?
Wie viel (oder: was) kostet es?	What does it cost?

---

1) Numero or Nummer.

Der Steuerbeamte.	The Custom-house officer.
Am Thore der Stadt.	At the gate of the city.
St. Haben Sie etwas Steuerbares?	C. Have you anything subject to custom?
Passagier, or Fahrgast.	Passenger.
P. Nein, ich denke nicht (oder: Nicht, daß ich wüßte).	P. No, nothing, I think.
St. Was enthält dieser Koffer?	C. What does this box contain?
P. Kleidungsstücke und Wäsche.	P. Clothes and linen.
St. Haben Sie kein Fleisch, Brod, oder Mehl?	C. Have you any meat, bread, or flour?
P. Nein, ich habe nichts dergleichen.	P. No, nothing of that kind.
St. Öffnen Sie Ihre Koffer!	C. Open your boxes!
St. Kann passiren.	C. All right, it may pass.

Schutzmann, Constabler, or Polizist.	The Policeman.
Haben Sie einen Paß, mein Herr?	Have you a passport, Sir?
Ja, hier ist er.	Yes, here it is.
Nein, ich habe keinen.	No, I have none.
Wie können Sie sich legitimiren?	How can you identify yourself?
Der britische Gesandte kennt mich.	The British ambassador knows me.
Ah so! Ja so!	Ah, I see!
Wo gedenken Sie abzusteigen (oder: zu logiren)?	Where do you intend to take up your lodgings?
Hier ist meine Karte, ich werde im Hôtel de Rome absteigen (oder: logiren).	Here is my card, I shall lodge in the Hôtel de Rome.

IV.

Der Gasthof.	**The Hôtel.**
Der Wirth, die Wirthinn, der Kellner (oder: Aufwärter).	Host, hostess, waiter.
Kellner! ein Zimmer mit Kabinet'.	Waiter! a sitting-room with closet.
Wünschen Sie eins oben oder unten?	Would you like one up- or downstairs?
Eine Treppe hoch (oder: Im ersten Stock).	First floor.
Dort sind alle Zimmer besetzt.	All the rooms there are occupied.
Dann zwei Treppen hoch (oder: im zweiten Stock).	Well, second floor, then.
Kellner, sprechen Sie englisch?	Waiter, do you speak English?
Nein, mein Herr, aber ich werde Ihnen meinen Colle'gen senden, der spricht englisch und auch französisch.	No, Sir, but I will send you my comrade, he speaks English and French too.
Wohnen gegenwärtig hier Engländer (oder: Logiren bei Ihnen zur Zeit Engländer)?	Are there at present any Englishmen residing here?
Spricht hier Niemand etwas englisch?	Is there nobody who talks a little English?
Ich bedaure sehr, aber unser Kellner, der englisch spricht, ist gegenwärtig krank.	I am very sorry, but our waiter who speaks English is ill at present.
So müssen wir wohl ohne ihn fertig werden.	Well then, we must do without him.
Sie sprechen sehr gut deutsch.	You speak German very well.
So? verstehen Sie denn, was ich sage?	Indeed? Do you understand what I say?
Ich kann wohl sagen, ich verstehe jedes Wort.	I dare say I understand every word.
Das freut mich.	I am glad of it.

Wo sind meine Sachen?	Where are my boxes?
Im Nebenzimmer.	In the next room.
Öffnen Sie meinen Koffer (oder: Machen Sie meinen Koffer auf) und nehmen Sie reine Wäsche heraus.	Open my trunk and take out fresh linen.
Wann ißt man hier gewöhnlich zu Mittag?	When do you generally dine here?
Um vier Uhr table d'hôte, und à la carte zu jeder Zeit (oder: wann Sie wünschen).	Table d'hôte at four o'clock, and à la carte at any time.
Ich werde heute auf meinem Zimmer essen.	I shall dine to-day in my own room.
Bringen Sie mir die Speisekarte!	Get me the bill of fare!
Sollte Jemand nach mir fragen, so bringen Sie ihn zu mir.	If any one should ask for me, bring him here.
Schön, oder: sehr wohl, mein Herr.	Very good, Sir.

V.

Das Dampfboot. — The Steamboat.

Wo ist das Dampfschiffs-Comptoir?[1]	Where is the steamboat-office?
Wollen Sie so gut sein, mir ein Billet' für das Dampfboot nach Hamburg zu besorgen?	Will you be kind enough to get me a ticket for the steamboat for Hamburg?
Wann geht das Schiff ab?	When does the vessel start?
Es wird bald abgehen.	She will soon start.
Sie müssen in einer Viertelstunde an Bord sein.	You must be on board in a quarter of an hour.
Wie lange glauben Sie, daß die Fahrt dauern wird?	How long do you think it will take us to go to L.?
Matrose.	Sailor.

---

1) Pronounce: *contor'*.

Ja, sehen Sie, je nach dem der Wind ist, vielleicht 10, 20, vielleicht auch 25 Stunden.	Well, Sir, according to the wind, it may take us 10, 20, or 25 hours.
Stuart.	Steward.
Geben Sie mir eine Flasche Soda- oder Potasch- oder Selters-wasser.	I want a glass of soda or potash- or selters-water.
Augenblicklich (oder: im Augenblick, oder: gleich).	Presently, Sir.
Mir ist sehr übel, bringen Sie mir ein Glas Wasser.	I feel very ill, bring me a glass of water.
Ich fürchte, ich werde mich übergeben müssen.	I fear I shall be sick.
Gehen Sie ein wenig an die frische Luft, es wird bald vorübergehen.	Go a little into the open air, Sir, it will soon be over.
Wünschen Sie etwas?	Do you want anything?
Ja, ich denke eine Flasche Limonade möchte nichts schaden.	Yes, a bottle of lemonade, I think, would be very good.
Nehmen Sie ein Brausepulver!	Take a soda-powder!
Ich befinde mich nun besser, ich hoffe, daß ich nicht werde seekrank werden.	I feel better now, I hope I shall not be sea-sick.
Die Seekrankheit ist sehr unangenehm, aber (man sagt,) es soll gesund sein, sie zu haben.	Sea-sickness is very disagreeable, but it is said to be healthy to get it.
Kommen Sie an Deck!	Come on deck!
Wie gefallen Ihnen die Ufer dieses Flusses?	How do you like the banks of this river?
Sehen Sie dort jene Insel? Das ist Helgoland.	Do you see that island there? That is Heligoland.
Wie weit ist sie von hier entfernt?	How far off is it from here?
Acht Meilen.	Eight miles.
Die See geht sehr hoch.	The sea runs very high.
Wir haben eine feine Brise.	There is a fine breeze.
Der Himmel ist so dunkel, ich	The sky is so dark, I am

fürchte, wir werden einen Sturm bekommen.	afraid we shall have a storm.
Hören Sie das Rollen des Donners in der Ferne?	Do you hear the roaring of the thunder in the distance?
Da blitzt es schon.	There it lightens already.
Und nun beginnt es zu gießen.	And now it commences to pour.
Lassen Sie uns in die Kajüte gehen.	Let us go into the cabin.
Ich bleibe lieber an Deck, ich sehe gern dem Aufruhr der Elemente zu.	I had rather remain on deck, I like to see the uproar of the elements.
Fürchten Sie sich nicht vor dem Regen?	Are you not afraid of the rain?
Ich mache mir nichts daraus.	I don't mind it.
Das schadet nichts.	Never mind.
Aber Sie werden ganz naß werden.	But yon will get quite wet.
Das ist mir gleichgültig (ob: egal).	I don't mind.
Meinetwegen.	(On my account) All right.
Das Gewitter ist vorüber.	The thunderstorm is past.
Das Wetter klärt sich auf.	The weather is clearing up.
Ich muß meine Kleider wechseln (ob.: Ich muß mich umziehen).	I must change my clothes.
Wollen wir eine Partie Schach spielen (ob.: Wollen Sie Schach mit mir spielen)?	Would you like a game at chess?
Lassen Sie uns eine Partie Karten machen (oder: Wollen Sie Karten mit mir spielen)?	Let us have a game at cards.
Was für ein Spiel wollen Sie spielen?	At what game do you wish to play?
Ich spiele gern Whist.	I like to play at whist.
Das Boot hält an, wir sind am Ort.	The boat stops, we are arrived.
Adieu (oder: Leben Sie wohl), meine Herren, es hat mich sehr gefreut, Ihre Bekantschaft zu machen.	Good bye, gentlemen, I am very happy to have made your acquaintance.

VI.

Vor dem Schlafengehen.	Before going to Bed.
Es beginnt zu dunkeln.	It is growing dark.
Es ist Dämmerung (oder: die Schlummerstunde).	It is twilight.
Die Nacht bricht an.	Night comes on.
Ist es schon sehr spät?	Is it already very late?
Nein, es ist erst elf Uhr.	No, it is but eleven.
Es ist Zeit zum Schlafengehen.	It is time to go to bed.
Ich gehe zeitig zu Bett.	I go early to bed.
Das Bett ist feucht und kalt.	The bed is damp and cold.
Lassen Sie es wärmen.	Get it warmed.
Ist mein Bett gemacht?	Is my bed made?
Es ist sehr schlecht gemacht.	It is made very badly.
Machen Sie es noch einmal.	Make it up again.
Geben Sie mir meine Nachtmütze (oder: Schlafmütze).	Give me my night-cap.
Helfen Sie mir meine Kleider, Schuhe und Strümpfe ausziehen.	Help me to pull off my clothes, shoes, and stockings.
Helfen Sie mir beim Auskleiden.	Help me to undress.
Wollen Sie die Jacke anbehalten?	Will you keep on that jacket?
Sie haben noch Ihre Stiefel an.	You have still your boots on.
Wünschen Sie den Stiefelknecht?	Do you want the boot-jack?
Nein, ich danke, ich brauche ihn nicht.	No, thank you, I can do without it.
Sind Sie fertig?	Are you ready?
Sind Sie mit dem Ausziehen fertig?	Have you done undressing?
Ja, ich bin ausgezogen.	Yes, I am undressed.
Soll ich das Licht hier lassen?	Shall I leave the candle?
Kommen Sie und holen es nach einer Weile.	Come by and by to fetch it.
Geben Sie mir mein Gebetbuch!	Give me my prayer-book!
Ich lese gern im Bett.	I like to read in bed.
Löschen Sie das Licht aus!	Put out the candle!

Laſſen Sie das Gas ein wenig brennen!	Leave the gas burning a little!
Wecken Sie mich morgen früh um acht Uhr!	Call me to-morrow morning at eight o'clock!
Ich ſtehe gern früh auf.	I like to rise early.
Verſäumen Sie nicht, mich zu wecken.	Do not fail to waken me.
Ich muß beim Anbruch des Tages (or Tagesanbruch) aufſtehen.	I must rise at break of day.
Ich werde mit dem erſten Zug abreiſen.	I shall go away with the first train.
Gute Nacht, ſchlafen Sie wohl!	Good night, sleep well.
Ich wünſche Ihnen eine angenehme Ruhe.	I wish you a good night's rest.

VII.

Aufſtehen und ſich Anziehen des Morgens.
Rising and Dressing in the morning.

Es klopft.	There is a knock.
Herein!	Come in!
Es klopft Jemand an die Thüre.	Someone knocks at the door.
Wer iſt da?	Who is there?
Sind Sie noch im Bett?	Are you still in bed?
Sind Sie wach (oder: munter)?	Are you awake?
Nun, es iſt wohl Zeit aufzuſtehen?	Well, I think it is time to rise.
Ich werde im Augenblick aufſtehen.	I will be up immediately.
Kann ich hineinkommen?	May I come in?
Kommen Sie nur herein!	Just come in.
Guten Morgen, Herr B.	Good morning, Sir.
Wie haben Sie geſchlafen?	How did you sleep?
Haben Sie ausgeſchlafen?	Did you rest well?
Danke, ich habe ſehr gut geſchlafen.	Thank you, I slept very well.

Ich war in Folge der Reise übermüdet und konnte lange nicht schlafen.	I was over-tired in consequence of the journey, and could not sleep for a long time.
War das Bett nach Ihrem Geschmack?	Was the bed to your mind?
Es ist zu schwer, ich bin an wollene Decken gewöhnt.	It is too heavy, I am accustomed to blankets.
Ich werde Ihnen welche besorgen, wenn Sie es wünschen.	I shall get you some, if you like.
Ich bitte darum, wenn es Ihnen nicht zu viel(e) Umstände macht.	Please do so, if it is not too much trouble for you.
O nein, durchaus nicht.	Oh no, not at all.
Wünschen Sie sich jetzt anzukleiden?	Do you want to dress just now?
Ja, bringen Sie mir meine Kleider (oder: mein Zeug)!	Yes, bring my clothes!
Sind meine Stiefel gereinigt?	Are my boots cleaned?
Ja, sie sind gut geputzt.	Yes, they are well polished.
Geben Sie mir meine Schlafschuhe (oder: Pantoffel) und Beinkleider (oder: Hosen)!	Give me my slippers and trousers!
Soll ich Ihnen warmes Wasser zum Waschen besorgen?	Shall I fetch you some warm water for washing?
Nicht zum Waschen, nur ein Glas warmes Wasser.	Not for washing, only a glass of warm water.
Ich wasche mich gern in kaltem Wasser, und deßhalb bringen Sie mir ein großes Becken voll.	I like to wash in cold water, and therefore get me a large basin full.
Geben Sie mir das Handtuch!	Give me the towel!
Machen Sie mir das Haar (oder: Frisiren Sie mich)!	Dress my hair!
Ja, gnädige Frau.	Yes, my lady.
Welches Kleid wünschen Sie heute anzuziehen, das grüne oder schwarze?	What dress would you like to put on to-day, the green or the black one?
Geben Sie mir das hellseidene,	Give me the light silk one,

ich habe heute einen Besuch zu machen.	I have to pay a visit.
Sitzt mein Kopfputz schief?	Is my head-dress awry?
Nein, es ist alles in Ordnung.	No, it is all right.
Sage dem Kutscher, er soll anspannen!	Go and bid the coachman put the horses to the carriage.
Der Wagen ist bereit, er steht vor der Thür.	The carriage is ready, it is before the door.
Satteln Sie mein Pferd! ich will ausreiten.	Saddle my horse, I will have a ride.
Wo ist meine Reitpeitsche?	Where is my riding-whip?
Das Pferd ist gesattelt.	The horse is saddled.
Legen Sie meine Sachen weg, und räumen Sie ordentlich auf!	Put by all my things, and put everything in order.

VIII.

Essen und Trinken.	Eating and Drinking.
Das Frühstück.	Breakfast.
Frühstücken.	To breakfast.
Das zweite Frühstück (oder: Gabelfrühstück).	Lunch.
Haben Sie schon gefrühstückt?	Have you had your breakfast?
Das Mittagessen (oder: Mittagbrod).	Dinner.
Zu Mittag essen oder speisen.	To dine.
Der Thee.	Tea.
Thee trinken.	To take tea.
Das Abendessen (oder: Abendbrod).	Supper.
Zu Abend essen.	To sup.
Sind Sie hungrig (oder: Haben Sie Hunger)?	Are you hungry?
Nein, ich bin nicht hungrig, aber ich habe starken Appetit.	No, I am not hungry, but I have a good appetite.
Ich bin noch nüchtern.	I have not broken fast yet.

Wünschen Sie etwas zu essen?	Do you want something to eat?
Sind Sie durstig (oder: Haben Sie Durst)?	Are you thirsty?
O ja! sehr.	Yes, very.
Ich vergehe vor Durst.	I am dying of thirst.
Wollen Sie ein Glas Wasser?	Do you want a glass of water?
Nein, geben Sie mir lieber ein Glas Bier.	No, I prefer a glass of beer.
Trinken Sie gern Bier?	Do you like beer?
Wie schmeckt Ihnen dieser Wein?	How do you like this wine?
Vortrefflich.	Very much.
Ich esse gern Käse zu Wein.	I like cheese with my wine.
Ich esse lieber Nüsse dazu.	I like nuts better with it.
Wann frühstücken Sie gewöhnlich?	When do you generally breakfast?
Ich trinke um acht eine Tasse Kaffe.	At eight I have a cup of coffee.
Wann nehmen Sie Ihr zweites Frühstück ein?	When do you take lunch?
Ich frühstücke nicht zweimal.	I don't take lunch.
Wir essen um fünf Uhr zu Mittag.	We dine at five o'clock.
Haben Sie schon gespeist?	Have you already dined?
Ist das Abendbrod fertig?	Is supper ready?
Wollen Sie Thee oder Kaffe?	Do you want tea or coffee?
Ich bitte um eine Tasse Thee.	I'll trouble you for a cup of tea.
Ist Ihnen noch eine Tasse gefällig?	May I help you to another cup.
Wenn ich bitten darf[1].	If you please, *or* thank you!
Geben Sie mir eine Tasse Kaffe, wenn ich bitten darf.	Please give me a cup of coffee.
Trinken Sie den Kaffe bitter?	Do you take your coffee without sugar?
Ja, ich trinke ihn bitter und schwarz.	Yes, I take it without sugar and cream.
Soll ich Ihnen noch eine Tasse einschänken.	Shall I help you to another cup?
Ich danke Ihnen, ich habe zur Genüge.	No, thank you, I have had enough.

1) Not „danke", because „(ich) danke" means *no*, thanks.

Langen Sie zu (oder: Bedienen Sie sich).	Help yourself!
Ohne Umstände (oder: Lassen Sie sich nicht nöthigen).	Without ceremony.
Wollen Sie so gut sein, mir das Salz zu reichen? Wollen Sie mir gefälligst das Salz zukommen lassen!	Will you be so kind as to pass me the salt?
Darf ich Sie um den Senf (or Mostrich) bitten.	May I trouble you for the mustard?
Essen Sie etwas von diesem Schinken!	Take some of this ham!
Er sieht sehr gut aus.	It looks very nice.
Kann ich Ihnen noch mit irgend etwas aufwarten?	Can I help you to anything else?
Ich danke.	No, thank you!
Räumen Sie ab!	Clear the table!

Mittagessen und Abendessen. — **Dinner and Supper.**

Halten Sie mein Mittagessen um vier Uhr bereit!	Have my dinner ready at 4 o'clock!
Ist der Tisch gedeckt?	Is the cloth laid?
Für wie viele haben Sie gedeckt?	How many covers did you lay?
Ich habe sechs Gedecke gelegt.	I laid 6 covers.
Nehmen Sie Platz, meine Herren!	Sit down, Gentlemen.
Bringen Sie die Suppe.	Bring the soup.
Der Wein steht vor Ihnen, weißer und rother, bedienen Sie sich nach Gefallen (oder: Belieben).	The wine is before you, white and red, take which you like best.
Johann, zieh' diesen Kork heraus (oder: Entkorke diese Flasche).	John, draw the cork!
Hier ist der Korkzieher.	Here is the cork-screw.
Wechseln Sie die Teller!	Change the plates!
Bringen Sie das Gemüse und die Cotelets!	Bring vegetables and cutlets!

Sind Ihnen einige Schoten gefällig, Fräulein?	Shall I help you to some of these green pease, Miss?
Geben Sie mir gefälligst einige grüne Bohnen!	Give me some French beans, please.
Ich esse Gemüse sehr gern.	I am very fond of vegetables.
Sie auch?	You too?
Ich esse lieber Fleisch.	I prefer meat.
Das Fleisch ist nicht gahr.	The meat is underdone.
So! meinen Sie?	Do you think so?
Ich finde es zu gahr.	I find it too much done.
Befehlen Sie etwas von diesem Eingemachten?	Do you wish some of these pickles?
Ich esse sehr gern englische Mixpickel.	I like the English pickles very much.
Mir sind sie zu scharf.	I find them too sharp.
Aber Sie trinken ja nicht, meine Herrschaften; schänken Sie den Damen noch ein Glas Wein ein.	But you don't drink, ladies and gentlemen; help the ladies to some more wine.
Bitte, schänken Sie mir nicht mehr ein, ich kann nicht mehr als ein Glas Wein trinken (oder: vertragen).	Don't give me any more, please, I can't take more than one glass.
Kellner, bringen Sie den Braten.	Waiter, bring the roast.
Wollen Sie mir erlauben, den Braten zu zerlegen (oder: vorzuschneiden)?	Will you allow me to carve the roast?
O, bemühen Sie sich nicht.	Oh, don't trouble.
Es macht mir durchaus keine Mühe, sondern vielmehr Vergnügen.	It is no trouble to me, it rather gives me pleasure.
Sie sind wirklich sehr freundlich.	You are very kind, indeed.
Nehmen Sie sich einige Kartoffeln.	Take some potatoes.
Lassen Sie uns nun Burgunder trinken.	Let us now have some Burgundy.
Ich habe die Ehre, auf die Ge-	I have the honour to drink

sundheit unserer liebenswürdigen Wirthinn zu trinken.	the health of our amiable hostess.
Meine Herren, ich schlage vor, auf das Wohl der jungen Damen zu trinken.	Gentlemen, I propose to drink the health of the young ladies.
Ihr Wohlsein, mein Fräulein.	To your health, Miss.
Lassen Sie uns auf ein fröhliches Wiedersehen anstoßen.	Let us drink to another happy meeting.
Meine Herrschaften, ich danke Ihnen für die Ehre Ihres Besuches und hoffe Sie bald wiederzusehen.	Ladies and gentlemen, I thank you for the honour of your visit, and hope to see you soon again.
So lassen Sie uns denn aufstehen.	Well, let us rise then.
Ich denke, es ist Zeit aufzubrechen (oder: nach Hause zu gehen).	I think it is time to go home now.

IX.

Vergnügungen.	Amusements.

(a)

Auf einem Ball.	**At a Ball.**
Haben Sie schon Ihre Damen engagirt?	Have you already engaged your ladies?
Ich habe für die Polonaise Fräulein A., für die Polka Frau R., für den Walzer Fräulein D., für den Contre-Tanz Fräulein E. und für die Polka-Mazurka Fräulein F. engagirt.	I have engaged for Polonaise Miss A., Polka Mrs. R., Waltz Miss D., Contredance Miss C., Polka-Mazurka Miss F.
Kennen Sie jene Dame?	Do you know that lady?
Ja, ich kenne sie von Ansehen.	Yes, I know her by sight.
Ich kenne sie nur dem Namen nach.	I know her only by name.
Sie würden mich sehr verpflichten (oder: verbinden), wenn Sie mich ihr vorstellten.	You would oblige me very much if you would introduce me to her.

Mein Fräulein, erlauben Sie mir, Ihnen Herrn F. vorzustellen.	Miss B., I have the honour to introduce to you Mr. F.
Ich habe die Ehre, Ihnen Fräulein A. vorzustellen.	Allow me to introduce Miss A. to you.
Es freut mich sehr, Ihre Bekanntschaft zu machen.	I am very happy to make your acquaintance.
Darf ich Sie um die Ehre für den nächsten Tanz bitten?	May I have the honour of engaging you for the next dance?
Es thut mir leid, ich bin schon engagirt.	I am sorry, I am already engaged.
Es ist hier sehr heiß, wünschen Sie ein wenig auszuruhen?	It is very hot here, do you wish to rest a little?
Darf ich Ihnen mit einer Erfrischung aufwarten?	May I help you to some refreshment?
Ich bitte (Sie) um ein Glas Limonade.	I'll trouble you for a glass of lemonade.
Tanzen Sie gern Walzer?	Do you like waltzes?
Ich tanze lieber Polka-Mazurka.	I like Polka-Mazurka better.
Kann ich die Ehre haben, Sie nach Hause zu begleiten?	May I have the honour to accompany you home?
Ich danke Ihnen, Sie sind wirklich sehr freundlich, jedoch mein Wagen erwartet mich.	No, thank you, you are very kind, indeed, but my carriage is waiting.
Ich nehme Ihr freundliches Anerbieten mit dem größten Dank an.	I accept your kind offer with many thanks.
Wann befehlen Sie Ihren Wagen?	At what time do you desire your carriage?
Um Mitternacht, wenn ich bitten darf.	At midnight, please.
Der Ball wird bald zu Ende sein.	The ball will soon be at an end.
Ich hoffe, Sie haben sich gut gefallen.	I hope you enjoyed yourself.
O ja, ich danke, sehr gut.	O yes, thank you, very much.

(b)

Concert.	**Concert.**
Wollen Sie mich heute Abend nach dem (or ins) Concert' begleiten?	Will you accompany me to-night to the concert?
Wird es im Freien oder im Saal stattfinden?	Will it be in the open air or in the hall?
Wer dirigirt' das Concert'?	Who conducts the concert?
Geben Sie mir ein Programm'.	I want a programme.
Wie gefällt Ihnen das Stück?	How do you like this piece?
Es gefällt mir sehr, von wem ist es geschrieben, wenn ich fragen darf?	I like it very much, by whom is it written, may I ask?
Es ist eine der besten Compositionen Jos. Gungl's.	It is one of Joseph Gungl's best pieces.
Lassen Sie uns da capo rufen.	Let us call *encore*.
Glauben Sie, man wird es noch einmal spielen?	Do you think they will play it again?
O sicher!	O, certainly!
Nun, was sagte ich Ihnen?	Well, what did I tell you?
Ich hätte es nicht gedacht.	I should not have believed it.
Das nächste Stück ist die Ouvertüre zum Freischütz.	The next piece is the overture to „Der Freischütz".
O! die kenne ich.	I know it very well.

(c)

Theater; Schauspiel.	**Theatre.**
Morgen wird Shakespeare's Hamlet gegeben. Werden Sie hingehen?	To-morrow there will be performed Shakespeare's „Hamlet". Are you going?
Wer gibt den Hamlet?	Who performs the part of Hamlet?
Besorgen Sie die Billete!	Get you the tickets!
Er spielt ganz ausgezeichnet.	He plays excellently (or first rate).

Sind Sie gestern im Opernhaus gewesen?	Were you in the opera-house yesterday?
Nein, weshalb?	No, why?
Fräulein Kramer sang wunderschön, sie gab die Lucia in „Lucia von Lammermoor".	Miss Kramer sang beautifully, she played Lucia in ‚Lucia de Lammermoor'.
Hören Sie gern Opern?	Do you like operas?
Ich höre zwar gern Opern, aber sehe doch lieber ein Trauerspiel.	I like them well enough, but I prefer a tragedy.
Da haben Sie eine gute Gelegenheit, da morgen Abend Goethe's Faust im Schauspielhaus aufgeführt wird.	Then you will have a good opportunity, as to-morrow night Goethe's Faust will be performed in the playhouse.

(d)

Spiele.	Games.
Spielen Sie Schach?	Do you play at chess?
Wenn Sie mich nicht zu schnell matt machen wollen, will ich schon eine Partie spielen (oder: ein Spiel machen).	If you don't check-mate me too soon, I will play you a game.
Ich spiele nicht gern Karten.	I don't like playing at cards.
Spielen Sie ein Stückchen am Klavier', bitte!	Give us a tune on the piano, please.
Es thut mir leid, ich spiele gar nicht Klavier'.	I am sorry, I don't play the piano at all.
So singen Sie denn ein Lied!	Will you give us a song then?
Herzlich gern.	Most willingly.

X.

Redensarten.	Idiomatic Phrases.
Einen hinaus gehen heißen.	Order one out.
Wie heißt das auf Deutsch?	What is that (called) in German?

20*

Wie heißen Sie?	What is your name?
Wie heißen Sie mit Vornamen?	What is your Christian name?
Was soll das heißen!	What do you mean?
Wahrhaftig!	I declare.
Obendrein.	Into the bargain.
Wecken Sie mich morgen früh um sechs Uhr!	Will you call me to-morrow morning at six o'clock?
Besuchen Sie uns, wenn Sie vorübergehen!	Give us a call, when you pass.
Ich war gestern bei Ihnen, aber Sie waren nicht zu Hause.	I called on you yesterday, but you were not in.
Wenn Sie mich heute Abend besuchen wollen, so werden Sie mich zu Hause finden.	If you call to-night, you will find me at home.
Ist Herr B. zu Hause?	Is Mr. B. in?
Ja, er ist allein.	Yes, Sir, he is alone.
Ich werde Sie abholen.	I will come for you.
Wollen Sie es holen lassen?	Will you send for it?
Es ist nicht der Mühe werth (es lohnt nicht).	It is not worth while.
Ich will meinen Freund besuchen.	I will go and see my friend.
Ich wünsche Herrn S. zu sprechen.	I want to see (speak to) Mr. S.
Mit dem größten Vergnügen.	I shall be most happy.
Er besucht uns dann und wann.	He calls upon us now and then.
Laß (oder: lassen Sie) mich zufrieden.	Let me alone.
Laß mich in Ruh'.	Don't bother me.
Das schadet nichts.	Never mind.
Es ist lange her, daß ich Sie nicht gesehen habe.	It is a long time since I saw you.
Das hat nichts zu sagen.	Don't mention it.
Leisten Sie mir Gesellschaft!	Keep me company?
Wie Schade!	What a pity!
Halten Sie den Mund!	Hold your tongue!
Seien Sie ruhig (oder schweigen Sie)!	Be silent!
Ruhe!	Silence!

Schämen Sie sich!	You ought to be ashamed of yourself.
Ohne Zweifel; natürlich; sicher.	Of course.
Ich kann den Menschen nicht leiden.	I don't like that man. (I cannot bear him).
Das begreife ich nicht, ich mag ihn sehr gern (leiden).	I don't understand that; I like him very much.
Mich friert.	I am cold.
Mich friert an die Füße.	My feet are cold.
Wärmen Sie sich die Hände.	Warm your hands.
Ich habe mich erkältet.	I have caught cold.
Ich habe den Schnupfen.	I have caught cold in the head.
Schnupfen Sie?	Do you take snuff?
Was giebt es Neues?	What news is there?
Sie gehen mit mir, nicht wahr?	You go with me, don't you?
Er hat es Ihnen gesagt, nicht wahr?	He told it you, didn't he?
Er ist ein unartiger Knabe, nicht wahr?	He is a bad boy, isn't he?
Das ist genug (oder: so wird's gehen).	That will do.
Das wird nicht gehen (oder: das kann nicht so bleiben).	That will never do.
Sind Sie böse mit mir?	Are you angry with me?
Bist du mir gut?	Dost thou love me?
Das ist mir gleichgültig (oder: egal). Meinetwegen.	I don't care.
Er macht sich nichts daraus.	He does not care.
Ich kann nichts dafür.	It is not my fault, I can't help it.
Ihretwillen.	For your sake.
Um Gotteswillen.	For God's sake.
Auf mein Ehrenwort (oder: Ich gebe Ihnen mein Ehrenwort).	Upon my word.
Scherz bei Seite.	Joking apart.
Sie werden sehen, es ist kein wahres Wort daran.	You will see there is nothing in it.
Es ist erfunden (oder: es ist eine Ente).	It is an invention.

Was wird Ihnen das nützen?	What good will it do you?
Wo möglich.	If possible.
Des Nachts.	At night.
Rede stehen.	To answer.
Was hat's gegeben?	What has been the matter?
Es wird mir nachgesetzt.	I am being pursued.
Frisch!	Quick!
Es geht nicht.	It won't do. (It can't be done.)
Ich bin (ein Kind) des Todes.	I am a dead man.
Heinrich läßt Sie grüßen.	Henry sends his compliments.
Auf seine eigene Hand.	On his own account.
Ich seh' es ihm an.	I see it by his looks.
Der erste beste.	The first that comes (any one whosoever).
Wer zuerst kommt, mahlt zuerst.	First come, first served.
Er weiß sich nicht zu rathen und zu helfen.	He is in a great dilemma.
Wir werden ihm einen Strich durch die Rechnung machen.	We shall thwart him.
So manchen schönen Thaler.	Many a nice piece of money.
Ich hatte es ihm auf die Seele gebunden.	I had enjoined him strictly.
Er hätte Spaß verstehen sollen.	He ought not to have taken it in earnest.
Jedermann würde es ihm auf den Kopf zusagen.	Every one would charge him with it openly.
Das will ich nicht hoffen.	I hope not.
Wir sind geschiedene Leute.	We are done with one another.
Hören Sie mal!	I say!
Ich verbitte mir das.	Do not offer to do that again.
Immer zu!	Just you go on!
Wie schön dir das steht!	How nicely that suits you!
Laß das sein!	Leave that alone!
Geh' mir aus den Augen!	Go out of my sight!
Nebenbei gesagt (oder: da fällt mir ein).	By the bye.

Was wollen Sie damit sagen (oder: was soll das heißen)?	What do you mean?
Was Sie und Ihren Freund anbelangt (oder: anbetrifft, ob. : betrifft) —	As to you and your friend —
Der Verstand steht mir still.	My mind misgives me.
Darum handelt es sich nicht.	That's not the thing.
So heißt es.	So they say.
Gebt euch mit denen nicht ab!	Don't have anything to do with them.
Das läßt sich hören.	I agree to that.
Er lebt in den Tag hinein.	He lives thoughtlessly.
Unter freiem Himmel.	In the open air.
Halten zu Gnade!	I beg your humble pardon.
Er lebt aus der Hand in den Mund.	He lives from hand to mouth.
Es geht um's Leben.	Life is at stake.
Sie verstehen sich auf Juwelen, wie?	You are a judge of jewels, are you not?
Was Sie sagen!	You don't say!
Wenn er's zu toll macht —	If he carries it on too rashly —
Einerlei.	All the same.
Es dürfte ihm schwer werden.	It might turn out a difficult task for him.
Ich bin darüber noch nicht im Klaren.	I have not yet settled my mind about it.
Ich könnte das nicht über's Herz bringen.	I could not bring my mind to do that.

Observe also the following characteristic sayings of the Germans in which the speaker wishes to express either gratitude to the creator, or pity with the being to which he applies such a term; they convey in their simplicity a greater meaning than the reader might suppose.

Der liebe Gott; die liebe Sonne; das liebe Brod; die liebe Einfalt; meine liebe Noth and others. .

The following are specimens of old alliterations still in use:

Keine Ruh' und Rast.	No peace.
Bei Nacht und Nebel.	By night and mist.

Mit Zittern und Zagen.	With fear and trembling.
Mit Mann und Maus untergegangen.	Foundered with all hands.
Haus und Hof.	All (his etc.) property.
Müd und matt.	Faint and weary.
Zu beißen und zu brechen.	To bite and to break.
Kind und Kegel.	Kith and Kin.
Über Stock und Stein.	Over stock and stone (at full speed).
Land und Leute.	Land and people.
Mit Haut und Haar.	With skin and hair.
Roß und Reiter.	Horse and rider.
Mit Sing und Sang.	With songs.
Mit Kling und Klang.	With music.
Bei Wind und Wetter.	In wind and weather.
Leib und Leben.	Body and life.

Observe also the following rhymes and rhymed proverbs:

Knall und Fall.	Suddenly.
Rath und That.	Advice and help.
Saus und Braus.	Revelry.
Gut und Blut.	Property and life.
Wie gewonnen, so zerronnen.	Lightly come, lightly go.
Aufgeschoben ist nicht aufgehoben.	Omittance is no quittance, *or*, Forbearance is no acquittance.
Eile mit Weile! (*Festina lente!*)	Fair and softly goes far in a day.
Der Hehler ist wie der Stehler.	The receiver is as bad as the thief.
Heute mir, morgen dir.	To-day is ours, to-morrow may be yours; *or*, to-day me, to-morrow thee.
Heute roth, morgen todt.	To-day a man, to-morrow a mouse; *or*, to-day on a throne, to-morrow in a dungeon.

Borgen macht Sorgen.	He that goes a-borrowing goes a-sorrowing.
Träume sind Schäume.	Dreams are lies.
Wie die Alten sungen, so zwit= schern die Jungen.	As the old cock crows so crows the young.
Unverhofft kommt oft.	Something unexpected often turns up.
Mit gefangen, mit gehangen.	Bad company puts a bad end.

FOURTH PART.

VOCABULARY
FOR REFERENCE AND REVISAL.

I.
ENGLISH-GERMAN.

a.

a, Ind. Art.	ein, vid. R. 49.	act, to,	handeln (w. v..)		
abandon, to,	verlassen (st. v.).	action, the,	die Handlung.		
abbey, the,	die Abtei.	adjutant, the,	der Adjutant.		
able, to be (can),	können (irr. v.).	admire, to,	bewundern (w. v.).		
able, been (could),	gekonnt.	affair, the,	die Sache.		
able, was (could),	konnte.	after, Prep.,	nach (Dat.).		
about, Adv.,	umher.	after, Conj.,	nachdem.		
about, Prep.,	um (Acc.).	after, Adv.,	nachher, hernach.		
absence, the,	die Abwesenheit.	afternoon, the,	der Nachmittag.		
abundance, the,	der Überfluss.	again, Adv.,	wieder.		
accident, the,	das Unglück.	against, Prep.,	gegen (Acc.).		
accompanied, P. Part.,	begleitet.	ago, Prep.,	vor (Dat. and Acc.).		
accompany, to,	begleiten (w. v.).	ago, Adv.,	her.		
accomplish, to,	vollenden (w. v.).	air, the (melody),	die Melodie, die Weise.		
accuse, to,	anklagen (w. v.).	air, the,	die Luft.		
accused, P. Part.,	angeklagt.	alike, Adv.,	gleich.		

all, Adv.,	all.	attacked, P. Part.,	angegriffen.
all, Pron.,	aller, -e, -es.	attentive, Adj.,	aufmerksam.
all, Adj.,	ganz.	August,	der August.
allow, to,	erlauben (w. v.).	Austria,	Östreich, n.
almond, the,	die Mandel.	aunt, the,	die Muhme.
almost, Adv.,	beinahe, fast.	autumn, the,	der Herbst.
already, Adv.,	schon.	avail, to,	nützen (w. v.).
also,	auch.	away, Adv.,	weg.
although, Conj.,	wenn auch.	awkward, Adj.,	ungeschickt.
always, Adv.,	immer.	axe, the,	die Axt.
ambassador, the,	der Gesandte.		
american, the,	der Amerikaner.	**b.**	
amiable, Adj.,	liebenswürdig.	back, the,	der Rücken.
an, vid. a.,	ein, etc.	back, Adv.,	zurück.
ancestor, the,	der Ahn, Vorfahr.	backward, Adv.,	rückwärts.
and, Conj.,	und.	bad, Adj.,	schlecht.
and that,	und zwar.	ball, the,	der Ball, die Kugel.
angry, Adj.,	böse.		
animal, the,	das Thier.	banquet, the,	das Gastmahl.
animating, Adj.,	belebend.	barber, the,	der Barbier.
anxiety, the,	die Angst.	barrel, the,	das Faß.
ape, the,	der Affe.	bath, the,	das Bad.
apothecary, the,	der Apotheker.	bathe, to,	baden (w. v.).
appear, to,	vorkommen (st. v. Dat.).	battle, the,	der Kampf.
		Bavaria, n., —n, m.	Baiern, n., der Baier.
apple, the,	der Apfel.		
April,	der April.	be, to,	sein (irr. v.).
approach, to,	sich nähern (w.v.).	be (thou)!	sei.
armed, Adj.,	bewaffnet.	be (ye or you);	seid.
arrive, to,	ankommen (st. v.).	bean, the,	die Bohne.
		bear, the,	der Bär.
arrived, P. Part.,	angekommen.	beautiful, Adj.,	schön.
art, the,	die Kunst.	beauty, the,	die Schönheit.
artisan, the,	der Handwerker.	because, Conj.,	weil.
as (so), Adv.,	so.	become, to,	werden (irr. v.).
as — as, Conj.,	so — wie.	become, P. Part.,	geworden.
as (than), Conj.,	als.	become (thou)!	werde!
as (when), Conj.,	da.	become(ye or you)!	werdet!
as soon as, Conj.,	sobald (als).	become (polite address)!	werden Sie!
ashes, the,	die Asche (sing.).		
ask, to,	fragen (mixed verb).	bed, the,	das Bett.
		bee, the,	die Biene.
ass, the,	der Esel.	been, P. Part.,	gewesen.
assist, to,	helfen (st. v.).	beer, the,	das Bier.
at last, Adv.,	endlich.	before, Conj.,	ehe.
at, Prep.,	bei, zu (Dat.).	before, Prep.,	vor (Dat. and Acc.).
attack, to,	angreifen (st. v.).		

beg, to,	bitten (st. v.).	bridge, the,	die Brücke.
begged, Impf.,	bat.	bright,	hell.
begged, P. Part.,	gebeten.	bring, to,	bringen (st. v.).
behave, to,	sich betragen (st. v.).	broad, Adj.,	breit.
		broken, (to pieces),	zerbrochen.
believe, to,	glauben (w. v.).	broth, the,	die Suppe, die Brühe.
bell, the,	die Glocke.		
belongs,	gehört.	brother, the,	der Bruder.
belonged, P. Part.,	gehört.	brother-in-law, the,	der Schwager.
benefit, the,	die Wohlthat.		
benevolent, Adj.,	wohlthätig.	brother and sister,	das Geschwister (sing.).
berry, the,	die Beere.		
between,	zwischen (Dat and Acc.).	brown, Adj.,	braun.
		bugle, the,	das Horn.
big, Adj.,	groß.	build, to,	bauen (w. v.).
bill, the,	die Rechnung.	bullet, the,	die Kugel.
bind, to,	binden (st. v.).	burden, the,	die Last.
bird, the,	der Vogel.	but, Conj.,	aber, sondern.
bitter, Adj.,	bitter.	butter, the,	die Butter.
black, Adj.,	schwarz.	butterfly, the,	der Schmetterling.
blame, to,	tadeln (w. v.); verdenken (st. v.).		
		by, Prep.,	bei, von (Dat.), durch (Acc.).
bloom, blow, to,	blühen (w. v.).		
blow, to,	wehen (w. v.).	by chance, Adv.,	zufällig.
blue, Adj.,	blau.		
board, the,	das Brett.		**C.**
boat, the,	das Boot.		
bonnet, the,	der Hut.	cabbage, the,	der Kohl.
book, the,	das Buch.	cabinet, the,	der Schrank.
bookbinder, the,	der Buchbinder.	cage, the,	der Käfig, das Bauer.
bookseller, the,	der Buchhändler.		
boot, the,	der Stiefel.	calf, the,	das Kalb.
both, Adj.,	beide.	camel, the,	das Kameel.
bottle, the,	die Flasche.	can (to be able),	können (irr. v.).
bought, P. Part.,	gekauft.	canary-seed, the,	der Kanariensamen.
bound, Part.,	gebunden.		
box, the,	der Koffer.	candle, the,	das Licht.
boy, the,	der Knabe.	cane, the,	der Stock.
brave, Adj.,	tapfer.	capital, the,	die Hauptstadt.
breach, the,	der Bruch.	Caroline,	Karoline, f.
bread, the (loaf of bread),	das Brod.	carp, the,	der Karpfen.
		carriage, the,	der Wagen.
break, to (to pieces),	zerbrechen (st. v.).	carry, to,	tragen (st. v.).
		castle, the,	das Schloss, die Burg.
breakfast, the,	das Frühstück.		
breast, the,	die Brust.	cat, the,	die Katze.
bride, the,	die Braut.	catholic, the,	der Katholik.

cattle, the,	das Rind.	commencement,	der Anfang.
cauliflower, the,	der Blumenkohl.	communicate, to,	mittheilen (w. v.).
cause, the,	die Sache.	compartment, the,	das Fach.
cellar, the,	der Keller.	companion, the,	der Genosse, Ge=
certain, Adj.,	gewiß.		selle.
chair, the,	der Stuhl.	compassion, the,	{das Mitgefühl,
chambermaid, the,	die Jose.		{das Mitleid.
change, to,	verwandeln, wech=	compete, to,	sich messen.
	seln (w. v.).	concert, the,	das Concert.
Charles,	Karl, m.	confidence, the,	das Vertrauen.
charming, Pres.	reizend.	conquer, to,	siegen, besiegen.
Part.,		conquers, Pres.	bezwingt.
cheese, the,	der Käse.	Ind.,	
cherry, the,	die Kirsche.	consort, the,	das Gemahl.
chicken, the,	das Küchlein or	consort, the *(m)*,	der Gemahl.
	Küchen.	consort, the *(f)*,	die Gemahlin.
child, the,	das Kind.	contempt, the,	die Verachtung.
Christendom,	das Christen=	contented, Adj.,	zufrieden.
	thum.	continent, the,	das Festland.
christian, the;	der Christ; christ=	converse, to,	sich unterhalten,
— Adj.,	lich.		(st. v.).
christianity,	das Christen=	convict, to,	überführen
	thum.		(w. v.).
church, the,	die Kirche.	continue, to,	anhalten (w. v.).
class, the,	die Klasse.	contradict, to,	widersprechen
clean, Adj.,	rein.		(st. v.).
clear, Adj.,	klar.	cook, the, *(male)*,	der Koch, die
cleft, the,	die Kluft.	*(female)*,	Köchinn.
clever, Adj.,	geschickt.	cool, Adj.,	kühl.
cleverness,	die Klugheit.	copper, the,	das Kupfer.
clock, the,	die Uhr, die	corn, the,	das Korn.
	Wanduhr.	— Turkish, the,	Mais oder der
close, Adj.,	dicht.		türkische Wei=
cloth, the,	das Tuch.		zen.
cloud, the,	die Wolke.	cord, the,	die Schnur.
coal, the,	die Kohle.	costly, Adj.,	kostbar.
coat, the	der Rock.	could (was able),	konnte.
cock, the,	der Hahn.	could (been able),	gekonnt.
cod, the,	{der Schellfisch,	count, to,	rechnen (w. v.).
	{der Cabeljau.	count, the,	der Graf.
coffee, the,	der Kaffee.	country, the,	das Land.
cold, Adj.	kalt.	courage, the,	der Muth.
come, P. Part.	gekommen.	court, the,	der Hof.
come, to,	kommen (st. v.).	cousin, the *(male)*,	der Vetter.
come!	kommen Sie!	cousin, the *(fem.)*,	die Base.
command, to,	befehlen (st. v.).	cover, to,	bedecken (w. v.).
commences,	beginnt.	cow, the,	die Kuh.

crayfish,	der Krebs.	diligent, Adj.,	fleißig.
crab,	die Krabbe.	dine, to,	essen (st. v.), speisen (w. v.).
cream, the,	die Sahne.		
creation, the,	die Schöpfung.	drink, to,	trinken (st. v.).
cross, to, (run through),	durchlaufen (st. v.).	dinner, the,	das Mittagsessen.
		disgrace, the,	die Schande.
go over,	übergehen.	disinherit, to,	enterben (w. v.).
crow, the,	die Krähe.	dismiss, to,	entlassen (st. v.).
cruel, Adj.,	grausam.	dispute, to,	bestreiten (st. v.).
cry out, to,	ausrufen (st. v.).	dissatisfied, Adj.,	unzufrieden.
cuckoo, the,	der Kuckuk.	distinguish, to,	auszeichnen (w. v.).
cultivate, to,	bauen (w. v.).		
cup and saucer, the,	die Tasse, die Schale.	distinguished, P. Part.,	ausgezeichnet.
custom, the,	die Sitte.	distress, the,	der Mangel.
		divinity, the,	die Theologie.
d.		do, to,	thun (st. v.).
		doctor, the,	der Doktor.
dagger, the,	der Dolch.	dog, the,	der Hund.
dale, the,	das Thal.	dollar, the,	der Thaler.
danger, the,	die Gefahr.	done, P. Part.,	gethan.
daughter, the,	die Tochter.	done (ready), Adj.,	fertig.
day, the,	der Tag.	door, the,	die Thüre.
day, of to-, Adj.,	heutig.	dotard, the,	der Geck.
day, the other, Adv.,	neulich.	dove, the,	die Taube.
		drank, Impf.,	trank.
dead, Adj.,	todt.	draw, to,	ziehen (st. v.).
deal, to,	handeln (w. v.).	dreadful, Adj.,	fürchterlich, schrecklich.
dealer, the,	der Händler.		
dear (expensive), Adj.,	theuer.	dream, the,	der Traum.
		dreary, Adj.,	traurig.
dear (affectionate), Adj.,	lieb, theuer.	dress, the,	das Kleid.
		dressmaker, the,	die Schneiderin.
death, the,	der Tod.	drink, the,	der Trank.
debt, the,	die Schuld.	drink, to,	trinken (st. v.).
deceased, Adj.,	verstorben.	drive away, to,	vertreiben (st. v.).
December,	der Dezember.	drunk, P. Part.,	getrunken.
deep, Adj.,	tief.	dry, Adj.,	trocken.
dense, Adj.,	dicht.	dry, to,	trocknen (w. v.).
departed, P. Part.,	abgereist.	duck, the,	die Ente.
description, the,	die Beschreibung.	during, Prep.,	während (Gen.).
despair, the,	die Verzweiflung.	duty, the,	die Pflicht.
dew, the,	der Thau.	dwell, to,	wohnen (w. v.).
diamond, the,	der Diamant.		
did, Impf.,	that.	**e.**	
difficult, Adj.,	schwer.	each, Pron.,	jeder, -e, -es.
		eal, the,	der Aal.

ear, the,	das Ohr.	faithful, Adj.,	treu.
early, Adj. & Adv.,	früh.	faithfulness, the,	die Treue.
earn, to,	einernten (w. v.).	fall, the,	der Fall.
earth, the,	die Erde.	family, the,	die Familie.
east,	der Osten.	famous, Adj.,	berühmt.
easy, Adj.,	leicht.	far, Adj. & Adv.,	fern, weit.
eat, to,	essen (st. v.).	fast, Adj.,	fest, schnell.
eaten, P. Part.,	gegessen.	fat, Adj.,	fett.
egg, the,	das Ei.	fate, the,	das Loos.
elephant, the,	der Elephant.		das Schicksal.
else, Adv.,	sonst.	father, the,	der Vater.
emperor, the,	der Kaiser.	favour, the,	der Gefallen.
empress, the,	die Kaiserin.	fear, the,	die Furcht.
end, the,	das End(e).	feather, the,	die Feder.
endure, to,	ausstehen (st. v.).	February,	der Februar.
		feeling, the,	das Gefühl.
enemy, the,	der Feind.	fellow, the,	der Gesell,
England,	England, n.		Bursche.
Englishman, the,	der Engländer.	feminine,	weiblich.
English, Adj.,	englisch.	fifteen (lot of),	die Mandel.
enmity, the,	die Feindschaft.	field, the,	das Feld.
enough, Adv.,	genug.	fig, the,	die Feige.
entertain, to,	sich unterhalten.	finch, the,	der Fink.
equal, Adj.,	gleich.	find, the,	der Fund.
err, to,	irren (w. v.).	find, to,	finden (st. v.).
escape, to,	entweichen (st.v.).	finds, Pres. Ind.,	findet.
especially, Adj.,	besonders.	find fault with, to,	verdenken (st. v.).
estate, the,	das Gut, das Eigenthum.	fine, Adj. & Adv.,	schön, fein.
		finger, the,	der Finger.
evening, the,	der Abend.	finish, to,	fertig machen.
ever, Adv.,	je, or, jemals.	fire, the,	das Feuer.
every, Pron.,	jeder, -e, -es, vid. Rule 101.	fire at, to	beschießen (st. v.).
		fish, the,	der Fisch.
everybody, Pron.,	jedermanns, vid. Rule 95.	fist, the,	die Faust.
		flame, the,	die Flamme.
exclaim, to,	ausrufen.	flax, the,	der Flachs.
exercise, the,	die Aufgabe, die Übung, die Übungsaufgabe.	flesh, the,	das Fleisch.
		flower, the,	die Blume.
		fly, the,	die Fliege.
		fly, to,	fliegen (st. v.).
eye, the,	das Auge.	food, the,	das Essen.
		fog, the,	der Nebel.
f.		following,	folgend.
		fool, the,	der Narr, der Thor.
face, the,	das Gesicht.		
fail, to,	fehlen (w. v.).	foot, the,	der Fuß.
faith, the,	der Glaube.	footman, the,	der Diener.

for, Prep.,	für (Acc.).		
for, Conj.	benn.	gale, the,	der Sturm.
forehead, the,	die Stirne.	gallant, Adj.,	tapfer.
forenoon, the,	der Vormittag.	game, the,	das Spiel.
forest, the,	der Forst.	garden, the,	der Garten.
forget, to,	vergessen (st. v.).	garment, the,	das Gewand.
forgetmenot, the,	das Vergißmein= nicht.	gate, the, gave, Impf.,	das Thor. gab.
forgotten,	vergessen.	gender, the,	das Geschlecht.
fork, the,	die Gabel.	generally, Adj. & Adv.,	gewöhnlich.
form, the,	die Bank.		
form, to,	bilden (w. v.).	gentleman, the,	der Herr.
former, Adj.,	vorig.	German, (ancient), Adj.,	deutsch, germanisch.
formerly, Adv.,	früher, ehemals.		
fortified, Adj.,	fest.	German, the (male)	der Deutsche, ⎫
fortune, the,	das Glück.		⎬ Adject. nouns.
forward, Adv.,	vorwärts.	German, the (fem.)	die Deutsche ⎪
found, P. Part.,	gefunden.		
found, Impf.,	fand.	German, the (thing).	das Deutsche ⎭
fox, the,	der Fuchs.		
fraction, the,	der Bruch.	German (ancient),	der Germane.
fragrant, Adj.,	duftig.	Germany,	Deutschland, n.
France,	Frankreich, n.	get, to,	bekommen (st.v.).
Frederick,	Friedrich, m.	get, to (out of a carriage),	aussteigen (st.v.).
freeze, to,	frieren (st. v.)		
fresh, Adj.,	frisch.	get, to (up),	aufstehen (st. v.).
French, Adj.,	französisch;	girl, the,	das Mädchen.
—man; —woman, the,	der Franzose, die Französinn.	give, to,	geben (st. v.).
		give!	geben Sie!
Friday,	der Freitag.	give in, to,	nachgeben (st. v.).
Friderica,	Friederike, f.	given, P. Part.,	gegeben.
friend, the (male.)	der Freund.	gives, he,	er giebt.
		gladly, Adv.,	gern.
friend, the (fem.)	die Freundin.	glass, the,	das Glas.
		glazier, the,	der Glaser.
friendly, Adj.,	freundlich.	glorious, Adj.,	herrlich.
friends, to make,	sich befreunden.	glory, the,	der Ruhm.
friendship, the,	die Freundschaft.	go, to,	gehen, ziehen (st. vs.).
frog, the,	der Frosch.		
from, of,	von (Dat.).	go away, to,	weggehen, reisen.
fruit (orchard),	das Obst.	go out, to,	ausgehen.
fruit, the,	die Frucht.	go over to (cross),	übergehen.
fruittree, the,	der Obstbaum.	gone, P. Part.,	gegangen.
future, the,	die Zukunft.	gold, the; —en, Adj.,	das Gold; golden.
		goose, the,	die Gans.
		gooseberry, the,	die Stachelbeere.

g.

got, P. Part.,	erhalten.	have (ye or you)!	habet, or, habt!
grand, Adj.,	großartig.	hayfork, the,	die Heugabel.
granite, the,	der Granit.	hazelnut, the,	die Haselnuß.
grant, to,	verleihen (st. v.).	he, Pers. Pron.,	er, vid. Rule 54.
grape, the,	die Traube.	he (who), Dem. Pron.	derjenige etc., vid. Rule 66.
grass, the,	das Gras.		
gratitude, the,	die Dankbarkeit.	head, the,	der Kopf, das Haupt.
grave, the,	das Grab, die Gruft.		
		healthy, Adj.,	gesund.
great, Adj.,	groß.	hear, to,	{ hören (w. v.). vernehmen (st. v.).
great, a—deal of,	sehr viel.		
Great-Britain,	Großbritanien, n.		
green, Adj.,	grün.	heard, P. Part.,	gehört.
grey, Adj.,	grau.	hearing, the,	das Gehör.
groat, the,	der Groschen.	heart, the,	das Herz.
groats, the,	die Grütze.	heat, the,	die Hitze.
grocer, the,	der Krämer.	heaven, the,	der Himmel.
grow, to,	wachsen (st. v.).	heavy, Adj.,	schwer.
guardian, the,	der Vormund.	hemp, the,	der Hanf.
guest, the,	der Gast.	hemp-seed, the,	der Hanfsamen.
guild, the,	die Zunft.	hen, the, (fowl m. and fem.),	das Huhn.
h.			
		hen, the (fem.),	die Henne.
		henceforth, Adv.,	hinfort.
had, P. Part.,	gehabt.	Henry,	Heinrich, m.
hail, the,	der Hagel.	Henrietta,	Henriette, f.
hair, the,	das Haar.	herb, the,	das Kraut.
half, Adj.,	halb.	herd, the,	der Hirt(e).
half, the,	die Hälfte.	here, Adv.,	hier.
ham, the,	der Schinken.	herring, the,	der Hering.
hand, the,	die Hand.	hero, —ine, the,	der Held, die -inn.
hang, to, tr. v.,	hängen (w. v.).	Hesse, n.	Hessen, n.
hang, to, intr. v.,	hangen (st. v.).	hide, the,	die Haut.
happen, to,	geschehen, zu-stoßen, (st. v.).	high, Adj.,	hoch.
		hill, the,	der Hügel.
happened, Impf.,	geschah.	him (Dat.),	ihm.
happened, P. Part.,	geschehen.	his, Poss. Pron.,	sein, seiner, vid. R. 71, 75 & 76.
happiness, the,	das Glück.	history, the,	die Geschichte.
happy, Adj.,	glücklich.	hold, to,	halten (st. v.).
hard, Adj.,	hart.	hold under, to,	unterhalten (st. v.)
hare, the,	der Hase.		
hat, the,	der Hut.	holder, the,	der Halter.
hate, to,	hassen (w. v.).	Holland,	Holland, n.
hatred, the,	der Haß.	home, the,	die Heimath.
hatter, the,	der Hutmacher.	home, Adv.,	nach Hause, heim.
have (thou)!	habe!	home, at, Adv.,	zu Hause.

honest, Adj.,	ehrlich, redlich.
honour, the,	die Ehre.
honour, to,	verehren (Acc.), (w. v.).
hope, the,	die Hoffnung.
hope, I,	hoffentlich (Adv.).
horn, the,	das Horn.
horse, the,	das Pferd.
horseman, the,	der Reiter.
hospital, the,	das Hospital.
hospitable, Adj.,	gastlich.
hour, the,	die Stunde.
house, the,	das Haus.
how, Conj.,	wie.
however, Adv.,	indessen, indeß.
hungry, Adj.,	hungrig.
hunting, the,	die Jagd.
hurry, to,	sich beeilen (w. v.).
husband, the,	der Ehemann, der Mann, der Gemahl, der Gatte.
hyacinth, the,	die Hyacinthe.

I.

ice, the,	das Eis.
if, Conj.,	wenn.
if or whether, Conj.,	ob.
ignoble, Adj.,	unedel.
ill, Adj.,	krank.
immediately, Adv.,	gleich, sogleich.
in, Prep.,	in (Dat. and Acc.).
increase, to,	vermehren (w.v.).
Indian, the,	der Indianer.
influence, to,	beeinflussen (w. v.).
inhabitant, the,	der Einwohner.
ink, the,	die Tinte.
inkbottle, the,	die Tintenflasche. das Tintenfaß.
inkstand, the,	das Schreibzeug.
innocent, Adj.,	unschuldig.

interest, the,	der Zins.
iron, the,	das Eisen.
iron, of,	eisern, Adj.
insect, the,	das Insekt.
Ireland,	Irland, n.
island,	die Insel, das Eiland.
Italian, the,	der Italiener.
interesting, Adj.,	unterhaltend, anziehend.
its, Poss. Pron.,	sein, seiner etc., vid. Rules 70 and 75.

J.

Jane,	Johanna, f.
January,	der Januar.
jerkin, the,	das Wamms.
jesuit, the,	der Jesuit.
John,	Johann, m.
joiner, the,	der Tischler.
journey, the,	die Reise.
journeyman,	der Gesell.
joy, the,	die Freude.
July, the,	der Juli.
June, the,	der Juni.
just (of time), Adj.,	gerade.
just (please), Adv.,	mal, einmal.
just (right), Adj.,	gerecht.
just now, Adv.,	eben jetzt, soeben.

K.

key, the,	der Schlüssel.
killed, P. Part.,	getödtet.
kind, Adj.,	freundlich, gütig, liebenswürdig.
kindness, the,	die Güte.
king, the,	der König.
kingdom, the,	das Königthum. das Königreich.
knee, the,	das Knie.
knife, the,	das Messer.
knife, the gardener's,	das Gartenmesser.

A. v. Ravensberg, German Grammar. 3rd Ed.

knock, to,	klopfen (w. v.).	liberty, the,	die Freiheit.
know, to,	kennen, wissen, (st. vs.).	lie, to (stretched out),	liegen (st. v.).
known, P. Part.,	gekannt, gewußt.	lie down, to,	niederliegen, sich niederlegen.
known, Adj.,	bekannt.		
known, well, Adj.,	wohlbekannt.	lie, to (speak an untruth),	lügen (st. v.).
knows, Pres. Ind.,	kennt, weiß.		
		life, the,	das Leben.
l.		light, Adj.,	leicht.
		light, the,	das Licht.
labour, the,	die Arbeit.	lightning, the,	der Blitz.
lady, the young,	das Fräulein.	lily, the,	die Lilie.
lamb, the,	das Lamm.	lily of the valley, the,	das Maiblümchen.
land, the,	das Land.		
language, the,	die Sprache.	limb, the,	das Glied.
large, Adj.,	groß.	lion, the,	der Löwe.
lark, the,	die Lerche.	lip, the,	die Lippe.
last, Adj.,	letzt.	literal(ly), Adj. & Adv.,	wörtlich.
last (former), Adj.,	vorig.		
late, Adj.,	spät, (dead) verstorben.	lithographer, the,	der Lithograph.
		little, Adj.,	klein.
laugh, to,	lachen (w. v.).	little, Adv.,	wenig.
laundress, the,	die Wäscherinn.	live, to,	leben (w. v.).
lay, to,	legen (w. v.).	liver, the,	die Leber.
lay down,	niederlegen.	loaf, the,	das Brod.
lazy, Adj.,	faul.	lobster, the,	der Hummer.
lead, the,	das Blei.	lock, the,	das Schloß.
leader, the,	der Führer.	long (space), Adj.,	lang.
leaf, the,	das Blatt.	long (Adv. of time); — ago,	lange; schon längst.
leap, the,	der Sprung.		
learn, to,	lernen (w. v.).	look, to,	aussehen (st. v.).
learned, Adj.,	gelehrt.	lord, the,	der Herr.
leather, the,	das Leder.	lordly, Adj.,	herrlich.
leathermerchant, the,	der Lederhändler.	lost, P. Part.,	verloren.
		lot, the,	das Loos.
leave, to, (start),	reisen (w. v.).	loud, Adj.,	laut.
leave, to, (abandon),	verlassen (st. v.).	Louis,	Ludwig, m.,
		Louise,	Louise, f.,
leaves, he,	er läßt.	love, the,	die Liebe.
lemon, the,	die Citrone.	love, to,	lieben (w. v.).
lend, to,	leihen (st. v.).	loving, Pres. Part.,	liebend.
lense, lentil, the,	die Linse.	luck, the,	das Glück.
lesson, the,	die Aufgabe, die Schularbeit.	lucky, Adj.,	glücklich.
		luncheon, the,	das Frühstück.
letter, the,	der Brief.	lungs, the.	die Lunge, Sing.
letter, the (of the alphabet),	der Buchstabe.		

m.

machinery,	die Maschinerie.
made, P. Part.,	gemacht.
maiden, the,	die Jungfrau.
maid-servant, the,	die Magd.
make, to,	machen (w. v.).
makes, one,	man macht.
malady, the,	die Krankheit.
man (*male* and *female*),	der Mensch.
man, the old,	der Greis.
mankind, the,	die Menschheit.
manner, the,	die Sitte.
many, Adj.,	viel(e).
many a, Pron.,	mancher, -e, -es.
many, Noun,	die Menge.
marble, the,	der Marmor.
March,	der März.
march away, to,	abmarschiren (w. v.), ziehen, (st. v.).
marched away, P. Part.,	abmarschirt.
margin, the,	der Rand.
mark, the,	die Mark.
married, P. Part.,	geheirathet.
marry, to,	heirathen (w. v.).
masculine, Adj.,	männlich.
mast, the,	der Mast.
master, the,	der Herr.
matter, to be the,	fehlen (w. v.).
may, to be possible,	mögen (irr. v.).
May,	der Mai.
meal, the,	das Mahl, die Hafergrütze.
mean, to,	meinen (w. v.).
meaning, the,	die Bedeutung.
meat, the,	das Fleisch.
medicine, the,	die Medizin.
meerschaum, the,	der Meerschaum.
memory, the,	das Gedächtniß.
mention, to,	anführen (w. v.).
mention! Impf.,	führen Sie an!
merry, Adj.,	lustig.
metal, the,	das Metall.
midge, the,	die Mücke.
mid-day, the (noon),	der Mittag.
midnight, the,	die Mitternacht.
mignonette, the,	die Reseda.
might, the,	die Macht.
milk, the,	die Milch.
millet, the,	die Hirse.
milliner, the,	die Putzmacherin.
mind, the,	das Gemüth.
a mind,	Lust.
mine, Poss. Pron.	meiner etc.
vid. Rule 75.	
minute, the,	die Minute.
minute, Adj.,	ausführlich.
mirror, the,	der Spiegel.
misfortune, the,	das Unglück.
mist, the,	der Nebel.
mistake, to,	verkennen (st. v.).
mistaken, to be,	sich irren (w. v.).
mister, Mr.,	(der) Herr.
mistress, the,	die Herrinn.
Monday,	der Montag.
money, the,	das Geld.
month, the,	der Monat.
moon, the,	der Mond.
moor, the,	der Mohr.
more, Adj. & Adv.,	mehr.
morning, the,	der Morgen.
morrow, to-, Adv.,	morgen.
to-morrow's, Adj.,	morgend, morgig.
most, Adv.,	am meisten.
moth, the,	die Motte.
mother, the,	die Mutter.
mount, the,	der Berg, Hügel.
mountains, mountain-range, the,	das Gebirge.
mouse, the,	die Maus.
mouth, the,	der Mund.
mouth, the (of a beast),	das Maul.
much, Adj. & Adv.,	viel.
multitude, the,	die Menge.
murder, to,	ermorden (w. v.).
muscle, the,	der Muskel.
mustard, the,	der Senf.
muzzle, the,	das Maul.

21*

my, Poss. Pron.,	mein, vid. Rule 70.	number, the,	die Zahl.
		number, the,	die Anzahl.
		number, great,	die Menge.
	n.	numerous, Adj.,	zahlreich.
		nut, the,	die Nuſs.
name! Imp.,	nennen Sie!		
napkin, the,	das Tellertuch.		
narcissus, the,	die Narciſſe.		**o.**
naughty, Adj.,	unartig.		
necessity, the,	die Nothwendig=	oatmeal, the,	die Hafergrütze.
	keit.	oats, the,	der Hafer.
neck, the,	der Hals.	oblige, to,	verbinden.
necktie, the,	das Halstuch.	occupation, the,	die Beſchäftigung.
need, the		October,	der Oktober.
(distress),	die Noth.	of course, Adv.,	natürlich.
need, the (want),	das Bedürfniſs.	off, Adv.,	ab.
negro, the,	der Mohr, Neger.	offer, to,	darbringen, an-
neighbour, the,	der Nachbar.		bieten (st. vs.).
neither — nor,	weder — noch.	office, the,	das Amt.
nephew, the,	der Neffe.	official, the,	der Beamte.
nerve, the,	der Nerv.	often, Adv.,	oft.
nest, the,	das Neſt.	old, Adj.,	alt.
neuter, Adj.,	ſächlich.	old age,	das Alter.
never, Adv.,	nie, or, niemals.	on (at),	an (Dat. & Acc.).
new, Adj.,	neu.	once, Adv.,	einmal, einſt.
news, the,	die Kunde, Nach-	only, Adv.,	erſt, nur.
	richt.	open, Adj.,	offen.
next, Prep.,	nächſt, Dat.	open, to,	öffnen, aufmachen
nice, Adj.,	hübſch, ſchön, nett,		(w. v.).
	(of taste) ſchmack=	opera, the,	die Oper.
	haft.	opportunity, the,	die Gelegenheit.
niece, the,	die Nichte.	or, Conj.,	oder.
night, the,	die Nacht.	orange, the,	die Apfelſine.
nightingale, the,	die Nachtigall.	order, the,	der Orden.
no, none,	kein, keiner, vid.	origin, the,	der Urſprung.
Negative,	Rule 102.	orphan, the,	die Waiſe.
no! Interjection,	nein!	our, ours, Poss.	unſer, unſerer etc.,
noble, Adj.,	edel.	Pron.,	vid. Rules 70
nobody, Pron.,	niemand, keiner,		and 75.
	vid. Rule 95.	out of,	aus (Dat.).
north, the,	der Norden.	outside, Adv.,	draußen.
northwind, the,	der Nordwind.	over, Prep.,	über (Dat. &
nose, the,	die Naſe.		Acc.).
not, Neg. Adv.,	nicht.	over, Adv.,	herüber.
nothing, Pron.,	nichts.	own, Adj.,	eigen.
November,	der November.	ox, the,	der Ochs.
now, Adv.,	jetzt.	oyster, the,	die Auſter.

P.

paid, P. Part.,	bezahlt.
pansy, the,	das Stiefmütterchen.
parasol, the,	der Sonnenschirm.
pardon, to,	verzeihen (st. v.).
parents, the,	die Eltern.
parson, the,	der Pfaffe.
pass, to,	übergeben (st.v.).
pass over, pass by, to,	übergehen (st.v.).
past, the,	die Vergangenheit.
patience, the,	die Geduld.
pawn, the,	das Pfand; (chess) der Bauer.
pay, to,	zahlen, } (w. v.).
pay for, to,	bezahlen
pays, Pres. Ind.,	bezahlt.
pea, the,	die Erbse.
peace, the,	die Ruhe, der Friede.
pear, the,	die Birne.
peg, the,	der Stift.
pen, the,	die Feder.
pencil, the,	der Bleistift.
penetrate, to,	dringen (st. v.).
penholder, the,	der Federhalter.
penny, the,	der Pfennig.
people (nation), the,	das Volk.
people (men), the,	die Leute, plur.
people make, is or are made,	man macht.
pepper, the,	der Pfeffer.
perform, to,	vollbringen (st. v.).
perhaps, Adv.,	wohl, vielleicht.
permission, the,	die Erlaubniß.
peruse, to,	durchlesen (st.v.).
philosopher, the,	der Philosoph.
philosophy, the,	die Philosophie.
photographer, the,	der Photograph.
physician, the,	der Arzt.
picture, the,	das Bild.
piece, the,	das Stück.
pig, the,	das Schwein.
pigeon, the,	die Taube.
pike, the,	der Hecht.
pious, Adj.,	fromm.
pistol, the,	das Pistol, die Pistole.
pity, the,	das Mitleid.
place, the,	die Stelle, der Ort.
place, to,	stellen (w. v.).
place of interest, the,	die Sehenswürdigkeit.
plate, the,	der Teller.
play, the,	das Spiel.
play, the (theatre),	das Schauspiel.
play, to,	spielen (w. v.).
pleasant,	angenehm.
please!	bitte!
please, to,	gefallen (Dat.).
please, if you,	gefälligst, Adv.
pleased,	zufrieden.
pleasure, the,	das Vergnügen, die Lust.
pledge, the,	das Pfand.
plum, the,	die Pflaume.
plume, the,	die Feder.
plural, the,	die Mehrheit.
pocket, the,	die Tasche.
pocket-handkerchief, the,	das Taschentuch.
poetry, the,	das Gedicht.
Poland,	Polen, n.
poor, Adj.,	arm.
portmanteau, the,	der Mantelsack.
possessed, Impf.,	besaß.
possible, to be,	mögen (irr. v.).
possible, was,	mochte.
possible, been,	gemocht.
potatoe, the,	die Kartoffel.
pound, the,	das Pfund.
poverty, the,	die Armuth.
power, the,	die Macht.
pray, I,	ich bitte.
pray, to,	beten (w. v.).

praise, to,	loben (w. v.).	put (place), to,	stellen (w. v.).
precious, Adj.,	kostbar.	put (set), to,	setzen (w. v.).
presence, the,	die Gegenwart.	put (pull), to,	ziehen;
present, to,	verehren (Dat.),	— on, to,	anziehen;
	beschenken (Acc.).	— in, to,	einstecken (st. v.).
present, the,	das Geschenk.		
presented, Past Part.,	geschenkt.	queen, the,	die Königinn.
press, the,	der Schrank.	quick, Adj. & Adv.,	schnell.
press, the (in the wall).	der Wandschrank.		
pretty, Adj.,	hübsch, nett.	railway the,	die Eisenbahn.
price, the,	der Preis.	railwaytrain, the,	der Eisenbahn-
pride, the,	der Stolz.		zug.
priest, the,	der Pfaff(e).	rain, the,	der Regen.
prince, the,	der Fürst, der Prinz.	rain, to,	regnen (w. v.).
		raisin, the,	die Rosine.
princess, the.	die Fürstinn, die Prinzessinn.	rank, the,	das Glied.
		rat, the,	die Ratte.
principle, the,	der Grundsatz.	raven, the,	der Rabe.
prison, the,	das Gefängniß.	ray, the,	der Strahl.
prize, the,	der Preis, die Prämie.	reach, to,	erreichen (w. v.).
		read, to,	lesen (st. v.).
probable, Adj.,	wahrscheinlich.	read, P. Part.,	gelesen.
—, Adv.,	wohl.	read through, to,	durchlesen (st.v.).
proceed, to,	ziehen, fortfahren (st. v.).	ready, Adj.,	fertig.
		reason, the,	die Vernunft.
pronunciation, the,	die Aussprache.	reasonable, Adj.,	vernünftig.
		receive,to, -d, P.P.,	erhalten (st. v.).
property, the,	das Gut.	red, Adj.,	roth.
protestant, the,	der Protestant.	refute, to,	widerlegen
prudence, the,	die Klugheit.		(w. v.).
prudent, Adj.,	klug.	regent, the,	der Regent.
Prussia,	Preußen, n.	regiment, the,	das Regiment.
psalm, the,	der Psalm.	reigns,	herrscht.
public, Adj.,	öffentlich.	remember, to,	sich erinnern.
pull, to,	ziehen (st. v.);	require, to,	gebrauchen(w.v.),
— on (put on), to,	anziehen;		bedürfen
— off (take off), to,	ausziehen.		(irr. v.).
punish, to,	strafen (w. v.).	respect, the,	die Achtung.
purchased, Past Part.,	eingekauft.	rest, to,	ruhen, sich aus-ruhen.
pure, Adj.,	rein.	return, the,	die Rückkehr.
put, to,	thun (st. v.), stecken (w. v.).	return, to,	zurückkehren (w. v.),
put (hang), to,	hängen (w. v.).		heimkommen
put (lay), to,	legen (w. v.).		(st. v.).

reward, to,	belohnen (w. v.).	satisfied, Adj.,	zufrieden.
ribbon, the,	das Band.	satisfied, to be,	sich begnügen.
rice, the,	der Reis.	Saturday,	der Sonnabend,
rich, Adj.,	reich.		or der Samstag.
riches, the,	der Reichtum.	sausage, the,	die Wurst.
riddle, the,	das Räthsel.	saw, Impf.,	sah.
right (just),	gerecht.	say, to,	sagen (w. v.).
right, the,	das Recht.	say, to (to think,	meinen (w. v.).
right (very),	recht.	to mean),	
ring, the,	der Ring, Reif.	scholar, the,	der Schüler.
ripe, Adj.,	reif.	school, the,	die Schule.
river, the,	der Fluß.	Scotchman, m.,	der Schotte.
roast, the, -, to,	der Braten,	Scotch, Scottish,	schottisch.
	braten (st. v.).	Adj.,	
roastbeef, the,	der Rinderbraten.	Scotland,	Schottland, n.
robber, the,	der Räuber.	screen, the,	der Schirm.
roof, the,	das Dach.	sea, the,	die See, das
	das Zimmer,		Meer.
room, the,	die Stube,	seamstress, the,	die Nähterinn.
	das Gemach.	seated, to be,	sich niederjetzen
rose, the,	die Rose.		(w. v.).
round, Adj.,	rund.	second, the,	die Secunde.
royal,	königlich.	secure, Adj.,	sicher.
rude, Adj.,	roh, grob.	security,	die Sicherheit.
ruled, P. Part.,	geherrscht.	see, I,	ich sehe.
rules, Pres. Ind.,	herrscht.	see, to,	sehen (st. v.).
run away, to,	weglaufen(st.v.).	seem, to,	scheinen (st. v.).
Russia.	Rußland, n.	seems, it,	es scheint.
rye, the,	der Roggen.	seen, P. Part.,	gesehen.
		seize, to,	ergreifen (st. v.).
		seldom, Adv.,	selten.
S.		sell, to,	verkaufen
			(w. v.).
sad, Adj.,	traurig.	send, to,	schicken (w. v.),
safe, Adj.,	sicher.		senden (st. v.).
safety, the,	die Rettung;	sense, the,	der Sinn.
	Sicherheit.	sensible, Adj.,	vernünftig.
salmon, the,	der Lachs.	sent, P. Part.,	gesandt.
salt, the,	das Salz.	sentence, the,	der Satz.
salt, Adj.,	salzig.	September,	der September.
same,Pron. or Adj.,	selber.	serpent, the,	die Schlange.
same, the,	derselbe, dieselbe,	servant,the (man),	der Knecht, Die-
	dasselbe.		ner, Bediente
sanctuary, the,	das Heiligthum.		(adj. noun).
sand, the,	der Sand.	servant (maid),	die Magd, Die-
sang, Impf.,	sang.	the,	nerinn.
Saxony,	Sachsen, n.	served, P. Part.,	bedient.
sat, Impf.,	saß.		

set, to (put),	ſetzen (w. v.).
set over, to,	überſetzen (w. v.).
set out, to,	fortreiſen, abreiſen (w. v.).
several, Adj.,	mehrere.
sex, the,	das Geſchlecht.
shade, the	der Schatten.
shadowy, Adj.,	ſchattig.
sheep, the,	das Schaaf.
shepherd, the,	der Hirt.
shield, the,	der Schild.
shilling, the,	der Schilling.
shine, to,	ſcheinen (st. v.).
ship, the,	das Schiff.
shirt, the,	das Hemd.
shoemaker, the,	der Schuhmacher.
short, Adj.,	kurz.
shortsighted, Adj.,	kurzſichtig.
shoulder, the,	die Schulter, die Achſel.
show, to,	zeigen (w. v.).
shut, to,	zumachen (w. v.).
sickle, the,	die Sichel.
sight, the,	das Geſicht.
sign-board, the,	das Schild.
silver (of), Adj.,	ſilbern.
silver, the,	das Silber.
silver, the German,	das Neuſilber.
since, Prep.,	ſeit (Dat.).
since, Conj.,	da.
sinew, the,	die Sehne.
sing, to,	ſingen (st. v.).
singular, the,	die Einheit.
sister, the,	die Schweſter.
sister-in-law, the,	die Schwägerinn.
sixty, lot of,	das Schock.
skilful, Adj.,	geſchickt.
skin, the,	die Haut.
sky, the,	der Himmel.
sleep, the,	der Schlaf.
slow, Adj.,	langſam.
smell, the,	der Geruch.
smell, to,	riechen (st. v.).
smith, the; -y, the,	der Schmied, die -e.
snow, the,	der Schnee.
snow to,	ſchneien (w. v.).
so, Adv.,	ſo.
soft, Adj.,	weich.
solar system, the,	das Sonnenſyſtem.
sold, P. Part.,	verkauft.
soldier, the,	der Soldat.
sole, the,	die Sohle.
some, Pron.,	einige (Plur.).
somebody, someone, Pron.,	jemand, einer, vid. Rule 95.
son, the,	der Sohn.
song, the,	das Lied.
soon, Adv.,	bald.
sore, Adj.,	ſchlimm.
sorrow, the,	die Sorge.
soul, the,	die Seele.
sound, the,	der Klang.
soup, the,	die Suppe.
soup, the (broth),	die Fleiſchſuppe.
sour, Adj.,	ſauer.
source, the,	der Quell, die Quelle.
south, the,	der Süden.
southwind, the,	der Südwind.
southwestwind, the,	der Südweſtwind.
Spaniard, the,	der Spanier.
sparrow, the,	der Sperling.
speak, to,	ſprechen (st. v.).
speak!	ſprechen Sie!
spectre, the,	das Geſpenſt.
spider, the,	die Spinne.
splendid, Adj.,	glänzend, herrlich, prächtig.
spoken, P. Part.,	geſprochen.
spoon, the,	der Löffel.
spoon, the table-,	der Eßlöffel.
spoon, the tea-,	der Theelöffel.
spouse, the,	die Gattinn, Gemahlinn.
spring, the,	der Sprung.
spring, the (well),	die Quelle.
spring, the (season),	der Frühling.
st.v. = strong verb,	ſtarkes Verbum.
staid, Impf.,	blieb.
staid, P. Part.,	geblieben.

stand, to,	ſtehen (st. v.).	sultan, the,	der Sultan.
stands, Pr. Ind.,	ſteht.	sultaness, the,	die Sultaninn.
stand, to (endure),	ausſtehen (st. v.).	sun, the, summer, the,	die Sonne. der Sommer.
star, the,	der Stern.	Sunday,	der Sonntag.
state, the,	der Zuſtand.	sung, P. Part.,	geſungen.
stay, to,	bleiben (st. v.).	sure, Adj.,	gewiſs, ſicher.
steel, the,	der Stahl.	surround, to,	umgeben (st. v.).
steel pen, the,	die Stahlfeder.	surrounded, P. Part..	umgeben.
stepfather, the,	der Stiefvater.		
stick, the (cane),	der Stock.	swallow, the,	die Schwalbe.
stiff, Adj.,	ſteif.	swan, the,	der Schwan.
still, Adj.,	ſtill.		{der Degen,
still, Adv.,	noch.	sword, the,	{der Säbel,
stocking, the,	der Strumpf.		{das Schwert.
stone, the,	der Stein.	snowdrop, the,	das Schneeglöck-
stood, Impf.,	ſtand.		chen.
stool, the,	der Schemel.		
stop, to,	anhalten (st. v.).		t.
stork, the,	der Storch.		
storm, the,	der Sturm.	table, the,	der Tiſch.
story, the,	die Geſchichte.	table, the (long),	die Tafel.
straight through,	mitten durch.	tablecloth, the,	das Tiſchtuch.
strange,	fremd, ſonderbar, ſeltſam.	tablespoon, the, tailor, the,	der Eſslöffel. der Schneider.
stranger, the (male),	der Fremde.	take! take a walk, to,	nehmen Sie! ſpazieren gehen (st. v.).
stranger, the (female),	die Fremde.	take for, to,	für (Acc.) halten, (st. v.).
stranger, the (thing),	das Fremde.	taste, the,	der Geſchmack.
straw, the,	das Stroh.	taste, to,	ſchmecken, koſten
strawberry, the,	die Erdbeere.		(w. v.).
strength, the,	die Kraft, Stärke.	tea, the,	der Thee.
strict, Adj.,	ſtreng(e).	teaspoon, the,	der Theelöffel.
string, the,	die Schnur.	tell, to,	ſagen, erzählen
strong, Adv.,	ſtark.		(w. vs.).
student, the,	der Student.	than, Conj.,	als, denn.
study, to,	ſtudiren (w. v.).	that, Conj.,	daſs.
subject, the,	der Gegenſtand;	that, Dem. Pron.,	jener, -e, -es, der,
— (citizen),	der Unterthan.		die, das; vid.
such, Adv.,	ſolch.		Rule 62.
such, Pron.,	ſolcher, -e, -es.	that (which),	der-, -die, das-
suffered, P. Part.,	erlitten.		jenige (der, die,
suffering, the,	das Leid.		das); v. R. 65.
sugar, the.	der Zucker.	thaw, the,	der Thau.
suitable, Adj..	paſſend.	theatre, the,	das Theater.

(Adject. nouns.)

their, theirs, Poss. Pron.,	ihr, ihrer, etc., vid. Rules 70 and 76.	tooth, the,	der Zahn.
		torment, to,	quälen (w. v.).
		torn, P. Part.,	zerrissen.
then, Adv.,	dann.	towards, Prep.,	gegen (Acc.).
there, Adv.,	da, dort.	towel, the,	das Handtuch.
there is, there are,	es giebt (Acc.).	town, the,	die Stadt.
there was, there were,	es gab (Acc.).	train, the,	der Zug.
		transmigration of souls, the,	die Seelenwanderung.
therefore Adv.,	deshalb.		
thereupon. Adv.,	hierauf, darauf.	translate, to,	übersetzen (w. v.).
thief, the,	der Dieb.	travel, to,	reisen (w. v.).
thing, the,	die Sache, das Ding.	travel in, to,	bereisen (w. v.).
		traveller, the,	der Reisende.
think, to,	denken (st. v.).	travers, to (cross),	durchlaufen; überschreiten.
think, to (or believe),	glauben (w. v.).		
		treasure, the,	der Schatz.
think, to (to mean, to say),	meinen (w. v.).	tree, the,	der Baum.
		tried, P. Part.,	versucht.
thirsty, Adj.,	durstig.	trouble, the,	die Mühe.
this, Dem. Pron.,	dieser, -e, -es; vid. Rule 62.	trout, the,	die Forelle.
		true (faithful), Adj.,	treu.
thorn, the,	der Dorn.		
throat, the,	die Kehle.	true (real), Adj.,	wahr.
through, Prep.,	durch (Acc.).	trust, to	trauen (w. v.).
thunder, the,	der Donner.	truth, the,	die Wahrheit.
thunderstorm, the,	das Gewitter.	Tuesday,	der Dienstag.
Thursday,	(der) Donnerstag.	tulip, the,	die Tulpe.
		twig, the,	das Reis.
thus, Adj.,	also, so.		
tiger, the,	der Tiger.	**u.**	
tight, Adj.,	dicht, eng, fest.		
till, Adv.,	bis.	ugly, Adj.,	häßlich.
time, the, (number),	die Zeit, das Mal.	umbrella, the,	der Regenschirm.
		uncle, the,	der Oheim.
tin, the,	das Zinn.	under, Prep.,	unter (Dat. & Acc.).
to (till), Adv.,	bis.		
to (see persons), Prep.,	zu (Dat.).	understanding, the,	der Verstand.
to (see places), Prep.,	nach (Dat.).	unfortunate, Adj.,	unglücklich.
		unlucky, Adj.,	unheilbringend, unglücklich.
to-day, Adv.,	heute.		
toe, the,	die Zehe.	unkind, Adj.,	unfreundlich.
together, Adv.,	zusammen.	upon, Prep.,	auf (Dat. & Acc.).
to-morrow, Adv.,	morgen.	use, to,	gebrauchen, nützen, nutzen (w. vs.).
to-morrow, of, to-morrow's,	morgend, morgig, Adj.		
tongue, the,	die Zunge.	use, to be of (to avail),	nützen (w. v.).

useful, Adj.,	nützlich.	washer-woman, the,	die Waschfrau.
uses, one,	man nützt, man nutzt.	wasp, the,	die Wespe.
		watch, the,	die Taschenuhr, or, die Uhr.
V.		water, the,	das Wasser.
valet, the,	der Kammerdiener.	water, to,	bewässern (w. v.).
valley, the,	das Thal.	watering-place, the,	das Bad.
value, the,	der Werth.	weather, the,	das Wetter.
variegated, Adj.,	mannigfach, mannigfaltig, bunt.	Wednesday,	der Mittwoch.
various, Adj.,	verschieden.	week, the,	die Woche.
vegetables, the,	das Gemüse.	well, Adj.,	gesund, wohl.
vein, the,	die Ader.	well behaved, Adj.,	artig.
very, Adv.,	sehr.		
vessel, the,	das Gefäß.	wench, the,	das Mensch.
vessel, the (ship),	{das Schiff, das Fahrzeug.	went,	ging.
		went out,	ging aus.
vexation, the,	der Ärger.	west,	der Westen.
vice, the,	das Laster.	wether, the,	der Hammel.
Vienna,	Wien.	what ever,	was — auch.
villa, the,	das Landhaus.	wheat, the,	der Weizen.
village, the,	das Dorf.	wheel, the,	das Rad.
violet, the,	das Veilchen.	when? Adv.,	wann?
virtue, the,	die Tugend.	when (as),	wenn, als.
visit, to,	besuchen (w. v.).	whence,	woher.
voice, the,	die Stimme.	where,	wo.
		which, Pron.,	welcher, -e, -s; der, die, das; vid. Rules 87 and 91.
W.			
wages, the,	der or das Lohn.		
wait, to,	warten.	whither, Adv.,	wohin.
walk, to,	spazieren (w. v.).	who? Int. Pron.,	wer? vid. Rule 83.
wall, the (of the inner house),	die Wand.		
wallflower, the,	der Goldlack or, der Lack.	whole, Adj.,	ganz.
		wholesome,	gesund.
walnut, the,	die Wallnuß.	whom, whose, v. Rule 83.	wem, wessen, etc.
wander, to (err),	irren (w. v.).		
want, the (need),	das Bedürfniß.	why, Adv.,	warum, weshalb.
want, the (distress),	der Mangel.	wide, Adj.,	weit.
		widow, the,	die Wittwe.
want, to (wish),	verlangen (w. v.).	widower, the,	der Wittwer.
war, the,	der Krieg.	wild, Adj.,	wild.
warm, Adj.,	warm.	Wilhelmina,	Wilhelmine, f.
wash, to,	sich waschen (st. v.).	will (to wish, to want),	wollen (irr. v.).

willingly, Adv.,	gern.		worthy of notice,	sehenswürdig.
William,	Wilhelm, m.		wrath, the,	der Zorn.
wind, the,	der Wind.		wreath, the,	der Kranz.
window, the,	das Fenster.		write, to,	schreiben (w. v.).
wine, the,	der Wein.		written, P. Part.,	geschrieben.
winemerchant, the,	der Weinhändler.		wrong, the,	das Unrecht.
			w. v. (weak verb),	schwaches Verbum.
winter, the,	der Winter.			
wisdom, the,	die Klugheit.			
wise, Adj.,	weise.		**Y.**	
wish, the,	der Wunsch.			
wish, to,	wünschen (w. v.).		year, the,	das Jahr.
wish, to (want),	verlangen (w. v.).		yes, Int.,	ja!
with, Prep.,	mit (Dat.).		yesterday, Adv.,	gestern.
without, Prep.,	ohne (Acc.).		yesterday, of, Adj.,	gestrig (Adj.).
wolf, the,	der Wolf.		yet, Adv.,	noch.
woman, the,	{die Frau, das Weib, das Frauenzimmer.		yield, to,	nachgeben (st. v.).
			you, Pers. Pron.,	ihr, (thou) du, convent. form Sie; vid. Rule 55.
woman, the old,	die Greisin.			
wonderful,	wundervoll.		young, Adj.,	jung.
wood, the,	das Holz; der Wald.		young lady, the,	das Fräulein.
			your, Poss. Pron.,	euer, (thy) dein, convent. form Ihr; vid. Rules 70 & 73.
word, the,	das Wort.			
word for word, (literally),	wörtlich.			
work, the,	die Arbeit.		yours, Poss. Pron.,	eurer, (thine) deiner, convent. form Ihrer etc.; vid. Rules 75—77.
work, to,	arbeiten (w. v.).			
world, the,	die Welt.			
worm, the,	der Wurm.			
worship, to,	verehren (w. v.).			
worth, Adj.,	werth, Gen.		youth,	die Jugend.
worthy, Adj.,	würdig.		youth, the,	der Jüngling.

II.

GERMAN-ENGLISH.

A. a.

			aber,	but.
			abgereist,	departed.
Aal, der,	the eal.		abmarschirt,	marched away.
ab,	off.		abmarschiren,	to march away.
Abend, der,	the evening.		abreisen,	to set out.

Abtei, die, the abbey.
Abwesenheit, die, „ absence.
Ader, die, „ vein.
Adjutant, der, „ adjutant.
Affe, der, „ ape.
Ahn, der, „ ancestor.
all, all.
aller, -e, -es, all.
als, when, than, as.
also, thus, so.
alt, old.
Alter, das, old age.
Amt, das, the office.
Amerikaner, der, the American.
an, on, at.
anbieten, to offer.
Anfang, der, the commencement.
anführen, to mention.
angeklagt, accused.
angegriffen, attacked.
angekommen, arrived.
angenehm, pleasant.
angreifen, to attack.
Angst, die, the anxiety.
anhalten, (hold on), to stop.
anhalten, (keep on), continue.
anklagen, to accuse.
ankommen, to arrive.
anziehen, to pull *or* put on.
Apfel, der, the apple.
Apfelsine, die, „ orange.
Apotheker, der, „ apothecary.
April, der, April.
Arbeit, die, the labour, work.
arbeiten, to work.
Arbeiter, der, the workingman.
Ärger, der, the vexation.
Armuth, die, poverty.
arm, poor.
artig, well-behaved.
Arzt, der, the physician.

Asche, die, the ashes.
auch, also.
auf, upon.
Aufgabe, die, the lesson.
aufmachen, to open.
aufmerksam, attentive.
aufstehen, to get up.
Auge, das, the eye.
August, der, August.
aus, out of, from.
ausführlich, minute.
ausgehen, to go out.
ausgezeichnet, distinguished.
ausrufen, to cry out, to exclaim.
aussehen, to look.
Aussprache, die, the pronunciation.
aussteigen, to get out, to step·out.
ausstehen, to stand, to endure.
Auster, die, the oyster.
auszeichnen, to distinguish.
ausziehen, to pull *or* take out *or* off; remove.
Axt, die, the axe.

B. b.

Bad, das, the bath, watering-place.
baden, sich, to bathe.
Baier, der, Bavarian.
Baiern, n., Bavaria.
bald, soon.
Ball, der, the ball
Band, das, ribbon, tie.
Bank, die, the form, bank.
Bär, der, „ bear.
Barbier, der, „ barber.
Base, die, „ cousin, *fem.*
bat, begged.
bauen, to build, to cultivate.
der Baum, the tree, beam.

Beamte, der,	the official, officer.	bewundern,	to admire.
Beamter, ein,	an official.	bezahlen,	to pay for.
bedecken,	to cover.	bezahlt,	pays.
Bedeutung, die,	the meaning.	bezahlt,	paid.
bedient,	served.	bezwingt,	conquers.
Bedienter, ein,	a servant (*male*).	Biene, die,	the bee.
bedürfen,	to require.	Bier, das,	„ beer.
Bedürfniß, das,	the need, want.	Bild, das,	„ picture.
Beere, die,	the berry.	bilden,	to form.
beeilen,	to hurry.	binden,	to bind, to tie.
beeinflussen,	to influence.	Birne, die,	the pear.
befehlen,	to command.	bis,	till, to.
befreunden, sich,	to make friends.	bitte, ich,	I pray.
beginnt,	commences.	bitten,	to beg.
begleiten,	to accompany.	bitter,	bitter.
begleitet,	accompanied.	Blatt, das,	the leaf.
begnügen, sich,	to be satisfied.	blau,	blue.
bei,	at, with, at the house of.	Blei, das,	lead.
		bleiben,	to stay.
beide,	both.	Bleistift, der,	the pencil.
beinahe,	almost.	blieb,	staid.
bekannt,	known.	Blitz, der,	the lightning.
beklagen, sich,	to complain.	blühen,	to bloom.
bekommen,	to get.	Blume, die,	the flower.
belebend,	animating.	Blumenkohl, der,	„ cauliflower.
belohnen,	to reward.	Bohne, die,	„ bean.
bereisen,	to travel in.	Boot, das,	„ boat.
berühmt,	famous.	böse,	angry.
besaß,	possessed.	Braten, der,	the roast.
Beschäftigung, die,	the occupation.	Bratenmesser, das,	„ carving knife.
beschenken,	to present.		
beschießen,	to fire, to fire at.	braun,	brown.
		Braut, die,	the bride.
Beschreibung,	the description.	breit,	broad.
besiegen,	to conquer.	Brett, das,	the board.
besonder, Adv.; -s, Adv.	especial, -ly.	Brief, der,	the letter.
		bringen,	to bring.
besuchen,	to visit.	Brod, das,	the bread, the loaf of bread.
bestreiten,	to dispute, to assert the contrary.		
		Brodmesser, das,	the bread knife.
		Bruch, der,	„ fraction, breach.
beten,	to pray.		
betragen, sich,	to behave.	Bruder, der,	the brother.
Bett, das,	the bed.	Brücke, die,	„ bridge.
bewaffnet,	armed.	Brühe, die,	„ broth.
bewässern,	to water.	Brust, die,	„ breast.
		Buch, das,	„ book.

Buchbinder, der,	the bookbinder.	Diener, der,	the footman.
Buchhändler, der,	„ bookseller.	Dienstag, der,	Tuesday.
Buchstabe, der,	„ letter (of the alphabet.	Dienstmagd, die,	the servant-maid.
Bull(e), der,	the bull.	Ding, das,	the thing.
bunt,	motly, spotted, variegated.	Doktor, der,	the doctor.
		Dolch, der,	the dagger.
Butter, die,	the butter.	Donner, der,	„ thunder.
		Donnerstag, der,	Thursday.
C. c.		Dorf, das,	the village.
Celte, der,	the Celt.	Dorn, der,	„ thorn.
Christ, der,	„ Christian.	draußen,	outside.
Christentum, das,	Christendom, Christianity.	bringen,	to penetrate.
		duftig,	fragrant.
Citrone, die,	the lemon.	durch,	through.
Concert, das,	„ concert.	Durchlaufen,	to run through.
		durchlaufen,	to travers, cross.
D. d.		Durchlesen,	to read through.
		durchlesen,	to peruse.
da (Adv.),	there, then.	durstig,	thirsty.
da (Conj.),	as, since.		
Dach, das,	the roof.	**E. e.**	
Dankbarkeit, die,	gratitude.	eben,	just now.
dann,	then.	edel,	noble.
darauf,	thereupon, then.	ehe,	before.
darbringen,	to offer.	ehemals, früher,	formerly.
daß,	that.	Ehre, die,	honour.
dazu,	to it.	Ei, das,	the egg.
Degen, der,	the sword.	eigen,	own.
denken,	to think.	einernten,	to earn.
denn,	for.	eingekauft,	purchased.
derselbe, dieselbe, dasselbe,	the same.	Einheit, die,	the singular.
		einige,	some, a few.
deshalb,	therefore.	einmal,	once, just, please.
deutsch,	German.		
Deutsche, der,	the German (male).	einstecken,	to put in.
		Einwohner, der,	the inhabitant.
Deutsche, die,	the German (female).	Eis, das,	„ ice.
		Eisen, das,	„ iron.
Deutsche, das,	the German (thing).	Eisenbahn, die,	„ railway.
		Eisenbahnzug, der,	„ railway-train.
Deutschland, n.,	Germany.		
Dezember, der,	December.	eifern,	of iron.
Diamant, der,	the diamond.	Elephant, der,	the elephant.
dicht,	tight, close, dense.	Eltern, die,	„ parents.
		End(e), das,	„ end.
Dieb, der,	the thief.	endlich,	at last.

England, n.,	England.	Feld, das,	the field.
Engländer, der,	the Englishman.	Fenster, das,	„ window.
		fern,	far.
englisch,	English.	fertig,	done, ready.
Ente, die,	the duck.	fertig machen,	make ready, finish.
enterben,	to disinherit.		
entlassen,	to dismiss.	fest,	fast, fortified.
entweichen,	to escape.	Festland, das,	the continent.
Erbse, die,	the pea.	fett, -ig,	fat, greasy.
Erdbeere, die,	the strawberry.	Feuer, das,	the fire.
Erde, die,	„ earth.	finden,	to find.
ergreifen,	to seize.	findet,	finds.
erhalten,	to get, to receive.	Finger, der,	the finger.
		Fink, der,	„ finch.
erhalten,	received, got.	Fisch, der,	„ fish.
erinnern, sich,	to remember.	Flachs, der,	„ flax.
Erlaubniß, die,	permission.	Flamme, die,	„ flame.
erlauben,	to allow.	Flasche, die,	„ bottle.
erlitten,	suffered.	Fleisch, das,	„ flesh, meat.
ermorden,	to murder.	Fleischsuppe, die,	„ soup made of meat, broth.
erreichen,	to reach.		
erst,	only.	fleißig,	diligent.
Esel, der,	the ass.	Fliege, die,	the fly.
essen,	te eat, to dine.	fliegen,	to fly.
Essen, das,	the food, dinner.	Fluß, der,	the river.
Eßlöffel, der,	the table spoon.	folgend,	following.
		Forelle, die,	the trout.
F. f.		Forst, der,	„ forest.
		fortreisen,	to set out.
Fach, das,	the compartment.	fragen,	to ask.
		Frankreich, n.,	France.
Fahrzeug, das,	the vessel, ship.	Franzose, der,	Frenchman.
Fall, der,	the fall,	Französinn, die,	Frenchwoman.
Familie, die,	the family.	französisch, Adj.,	French.
fand,	found, *Impf.*,	Fräulein, das,	the young lady, Miss.
Faß, das,	the barrel,		
faul,	lazy.	Freiheit, die.	liberty.
Faust, die,	the fist.	Freitag, der,	Friday.
Februar, der,	February.	fremd,	strange.
Feder, die,	the plume, pen, feather.	Fremde, der,	the stranger (*male*).
Federmesser, das,	the pen knife.	Fremde, die,	the stranger (*female*).
fehlen,	to be the matter with, to fail.	Fremde, das,	the strange (*thing*).
Feige, die,	the fig.		
Feind, der,	„ enemy.	Friede, der,	peace.
Feindschaft, die,	„ enmity.	Friedrich,	Frederick.

Friedrike,	Friderica.	gebeten,	begged.
frieren,	to freeze.	Gebirge, das,	mountains, mountain-range.
frisch,	fresh.		
Freud-e, die, -ig.	joy, -ous.		
Freund, der,	the friend (male).	geblieben,	staid.
		gebraten,	roasted.
Freundinn, die,	the friend (fem.),	gebrauchen,	to require, to use.
freundlich,	friendly, kind.	gebunden,	bound.
Freundschaft, die,	friendship,	Geck, der,	the dotard, fopp.
fromm,	good, pious.	Gedächtniss, das,	„ memory.
Frosch, der,	the frog.	Gedicht, das,	„ poetry.
Frucht, die,	„ fruit.	Geduld, die,	patience.
früh,	soon, early.	Gefahr, die,	danger.
früher,	formerly.	Gefallen, der.	the favour.
Frühling, der,	spring.	gefälligst,	if you please.
Fuchs, der,	the fox.	Gefängniss, das,	the prison.
Frühstück, das,	„ breakfast.	Gefäss, das,	.. vessel.
Frühstück, das zweite,	,. luncheon.	Gefühl, das,	„ feeling.
		gefunden,	found.
führen Sie an!	mention!	gegangen,	gone.
Führer, der,	the leader.	gegeben,	given.
Fund, der,	„ find.	gegen,	towards, against.
für,	for.		
Furcht, die,	fear.	Gegenwart, die,	the presence.
fürchterlich,	dreadful.	gegessen,	eaten.
Fürst, der,	the prince.	gehabt,	had.
Fürstinn, die,	„ princess.	gehen,	to go.
Fuss, der,	„ foot.	gehen Sie!	go!
		geheirathet,	married.
G. g.		geherrscht,	ruled.
		Gehör, das,	the hearing.
gab,	gave.	gehört,	belong, -s, -ed; heard.
gab, es,	there was, there were.		
		gekauft,	bought.
Gabel, die,	the fork.	gekommen,	come.
Gans, die,	„ goose.	gekonnt,	been able.
ganz,	whole.	Geld, das,	the money.
Garten, der,	the garden.	Gelegenheit, die,	„ opportunity.
Gartenmesser, das,	„ gardener's-knife.		
		gelehrt,	taught, learned.
Gast, der,	the guest.	gelesen,	read.
gastlich,	hospitable.	Gemach, das,	the room.
Gastmahl, das,	the banquet.	gemacht,	made.
Gatte, der,	„ husband.	Gemahl, das,	the consort.
geben Sie!	give!	Gemahl, der,	„ consort.
geben,	to give.	Gemahlinn, die,	„ spouse.

A. v. Ravensberg, German Grammar. 3rd Ed.

Gemüſe, das,	the vegetables.	gewußt,	known.
Gemüth, das,	„ mind.	giebt, es,	there is, there are.
Genoſſe, der,	.. companion.		
genug,	enough.	giebt, er,	he gives.
gerade,	just.	ging,	went.
gerecht,	right. just.	Glas, das,	the glass.
Germane, der,	the German.	Glaſer, der,	„ glazier.
gern,	willingly. gladly.	Glaube, der, glauben,	„ faith. to believe, to think.
Geruch, der,	the smell.		
geſandt,	sent.	gleich, (sogleich),	alike, equal immediately.
Geſandte, der,	the ambassador.		
Geſandter, ein,	an ambassador.	Glied, das,	the limb, rank.
geſchah,	happened.	Glocke, die,	„ bell.
geſchenkt,	presented.	Glück, das,	(good) luck, happiness, fortune.
Geſchichte, die,	the story. history.		
geſchickt,	clever. skilful.	glücklich,	lucky, happy.
Geſchlecht, das,	the sex. gender.	Gold, das,	the gold.
Geſchmack, der,	„ taste.	golden,	gold(en).
geſchrieben,	written.	Goldlack, der,	the wallflower.
Geſchwiſter, das,	brother or sister.	Grab, das,	„ grave.
		Graf, der,	„ count.
geſehen,	seen.	Granit, der,	„ granite.
Geſelle, der,	the companion. fellow, journeyman.	Gras, das,	„ grass.
		grau,	grey.
		grauſam,	cruel.
Geſicht, das,	„ face, sight.	Greis, der,	the old man.
Geſpenſt, das,	„ spectre.	Greiſinn, die,	„ old woman (lady).
geſprochen,	spoken.		
geſtern,	yesterday.	Groſchen, der,	the groat.
geſtrig,	of yesterday, yesterday's.	groß,	large, great, big.
		großartig,	grand.
geſund,	sound, well, healthy. wholesome.	Großbritanien, n.,	Great-Britain.
		Gruft, die,	the grave.
geſungen,	sung.	grün,	green.
gethan,	done.	Grundſatz, der,	the principle.
getödtet,	killed.	Grütze, die,	„ groats.
getrunken,	drunk.	Gut, das,	„ estate, property.
Gewand, das,	the garment.		
geweſen,	been.	Güte, die,	kindness.
gewiß,	certain, surely.		
Gewitter, das,	the thunderstorm.	**H. h.**	
		Haar, das,	the hair.
gewöhnlich,	generally.	habe!	have (thou)!
geworden,	become.	haben,	to have.

habet, or habt,	have (ye *or* you)!	Henne, die,	the hen.
Hafer, der,	the oats.	Henriette,	Henrietta.
Hafergrütze, die,	„ oatmeal.	Herbst, der,	autumn.
Hagel, der,	„ hail.	Herr, der,	Mr., Lord, Master, Sir, Gentleman.
Hahn, der,	„ cock.		
halb,	half.	Hering, der,	the herring.
Hals, der,	the neck.	Herrinn, die,	the mistress.
Halstuch, das,	„ necktie.	herrlich,	lordly, splendid, glorious.
halten,	to hold.		
halten für,	to take for, to think.	herrscht,	reigns.
		herüber,	over.
Halter, der,	the holder.	Herz, das,	the heart.
Hammel, der,	„ wether.	Hessen, n.,	Hesse.
Hand, die,	„ hand.	Heugabel, die,	the hayfork.
handeln,	to deal, act.	heurig,	this year's.
Händler, der,	the dealer.	heute,	to-day.
Handlung, die,	„ action.	heutig,	to-day's, of to-day.
Handtuch, das,	„ towel.		
Handwerker, der,	„ artisan.	hiesig,	of this place.
Hanf, der,	„ hemp.	Himmel, der,	the sky, heaven.
hängen,	to hang, to put.	hinfort,	henceforth.
Hanfsamen, der,	the hemp-seed.	Hirse, die,	millet.
hart,	hard.	Hirte, der,	the herd.
Hase, der,	the hare.	Hitze, die,	„ heat.
Haselnuß, die,	„ hazelnut.	hoch,	high.
Haß, der,	hatred.	Hof, der,	the court.
hassen,	to hate.	hoffentlich,	I hope.
häßlich,	ugly.	Hoffnung, die,	hope.
Haupt, das,	the head.	Holz, das,	the wood.
Hauptstadt, die,	„ capital.	hören,	to hear.
Haus, das,	„ house.	Horn, das,	the horn, bugle.
Hause, nach,	home.	Hospital, das,	„ hospital.
Hause, zu,	at home, in.	hübsch,	pretty.
Haut, die,	the skin, hide.	Huhn, das,	the hen (*male and fem.*).
Hecht, der,	„ pike.		
Heiligtum, das,	„ sanctuary.	Hummer, der,	the lobster.
heim,	home.	Hund, der,	„ dog.
Heimat, die,	the home.	hungrig,	hungry.
heimkommen,	to come home, to return.	Hut, der,	the hat, bonnet.
		Hutmacher, der,	the hatter.
Heinrich,	Henry.	Hyacinthe, die,	„ hyacinth.
heirathen,	to marry.		
Held, der,	the hero.	**J. i.**	
helfen,	to assist.		
hell,	bright.	ihm,	(to) him.
Hemd(e), das,	the shirt.	ihn,	him.

22*

immer,	always.	Karpfen, der,	the carp.
in,	in.	Kartoffel, die,	„ potato.
indeß,	however.	Katholik, der,	„ catholic.
Indianer, der,	the Indian.	Katze, die,	„ cat.
Insel, die,	„ island.	Kehle, die,	„ throat.
Insekt, das,	„ insect.	kein, -e, -; -er, -e, no; none.	
irren,	to err, to wander.	-es,	
		Keller, der,	the cellar.
irren, sich,	to be mistaken.	kennen,	to know.
Irland, n.,	Ireland.	kennt,	knows.
Italiener, der,	the Italian.	Kind, das,	the child.
		Kirche, die,	„ church.
J. j.		Kirsche, die,	„ cherry.
		Klang, der,	„ sound.
ja,	yes.	Kleid, das,	„ dress.
Jagd, die,	the hunting.	klar,	clear.
Jahr, das,	„ year.	Klasse, die,	the class.
Januar, der,	January.	klein,	little.
je, or jemals,	ever.	klopfen,	to knock.
jeder,	each.	Kluft, die,	the cleft.
jedermann,	everyone.	klug,	prudent.
Jesuit, der,	the jesuit.	Klugheit, die,	the prudence, wisdom, cleverness.
jetzt,	now, at present.		
Johann,	John.		
Johanna,	Jane.	Knabe, der,	the boy.
Jugend, die,	youth.	Knecht, der,	„ servant.
Jüngling, der,	the youth.	Knie, das,	„ knee.
jung,	young.	Koch, der,	„ cook (*male*).
Jungfrau, die,	the maiden.	Köchinn, die,	„ cook (*fem.*).
Juli, der,	July.	König, der,	„ king.
Juni, der,	June.	Königinn, die,	„ queen.
		königlich,	royal.
K. k.		Koffer, der,	the box.
		Kohl, der,	„ cabbage.
Kaffe, der,	the coffee.	Kohle, die,	„ coal.
Käfig, der,	„ cage.	kommen Sie!	come!
Kalb, das,	the calf.	können,	to be able, can.
kalt,	cold.	konnte,	was able, could.
Käse, der,	the cheese.	Kopf, der,	the head.
Kaiser, der,	„ emperor.	Koncert, das,	„ concert.
Kaiserinn, die,	„ empress.	Korn, das,	„ corn.
Kameel, das,	„ camel.	kosten,	cost, taste.
Kammerdiener, der,	„ valet.	kostbar,	costly, precious.
Kampf, der,	„ battle.	Krabbe, die,	the crab.
Kanariensamen, der,	„ canary-seed.	Kraft, die,	„ strength.
Karl,	Charles.	Krähe, die,	„ crow.
Karoline,	Caroline.	krank,	ill.

Krankheit, die,	the malady, disease.	Leute, die,	the people.
Kranz, der,	the wreath.	Licht, das,	„ light.
Krämer, der,	„ grocer.	lieb,	dear (not *expensive*).
Kraut, das,	„ herb.	Liebe, die,	love.
Krebs, der,	„ crayfish.	lieben,	to love.
Krieg, der,	„ war.	liebend,	loving.
Küch(l)e(i)n, das,	chicken.	liebenswürdig,	amiable, kind.
Kukuk, der,	the cuckoo.	Lied, das,	the song.
Kugel, die,	„ ball, bullet.	liegen,	to lie.
Kuh, die,	„ cow.	liegt,	lies.
kühl,	cool.	Lilie, die,	the lily.
Kunst, die,	the art.	Linse, die,	lentil, lense.
Kupfer, das,	„ copper.	Lippe, die,	the lip,
kurz,	short.	Lithograph, der,	„ lithographer.
kurzsichtig,	shortsighted.		
		loben,	to praise.
L. l.		Loch, das,	the hole.
		Lohn, der or das,	„ wages.
lachen,	to laugh.	Löffel, der,	„ spoon.
Lachs, der,	the salmon.	Loos, das,	„ fate, lot.
lag,	lay.	Louise,	Louisa.
Lamm, das,	the lamb.	Löwe, der,	the lion.
Land, das,	„ land, country.	Luft, die,	„ air.
		Ludwig,	Louis.
Landhaus, das,	the villa.	Lüge, die,	the lie.
lang,	long (of space).	Lunge, die,	„ lungs.
lange, or, lang',	long (of time).	Lust (die),	lust, pleasure, desire, a mind.
längst (schon),	long ago.		
langsam,	show.	lustig,	merry.
Last, die,	the burden.		
Laster, das,	vice.	**M. m.**	
laut,	loud.		
leben,	to live.	machen,	to make.
Leben, das,	life.	man macht,	one makes. people make, there is, *or*, are made.
Leber, die,	the liver.		
Leder, das,	„ leather.		
Lederhändler, der,	„ leather-merchant.	Macht, die,	the might, power.
legen,	to put, to lay.	Mädchen, das,	the girl.
leicht,	light, easy.	Magd, die,	„ maid-servant.
Leid, das,	the suffering.		
leihen,	to lend.	Mal, das,	the time.
Lerche, die,	the lark.	Mahl, das,	„ meal.
lernen,	to learn.	Mai, der,	May.
lesen,	to read.	Maiblümchen, das,	the lily of the valley.
letzt,	last.		

Mais, der,	the Turkish corn.	mitten durch,	straight through.
Mandel, die,	lot of fifteen.	Mittag, der,	the mid-day, noon.
Mandel, die,	the almond.		
Mangel, der,	„ distress, want.	Mittagessen, das,	the dinner.
		Mitternacht, die,	„ midnight.
Mann, der,	the man, the husband.	mittheilen,	to communicate.
		Mittwoch, der,	Wednesday.
männlich,	manly, masculine.	mochte,	was possible (might).
Mantelsack, der,	the portmanteau.	mögen,	to be possible (may).
Mark, die,	mark (one shilling).	Mohr, der,	the more, negro.
Marmor, der,	the marble.	Monat, der,	the month.
März, der,	March.	Mond, der,	„ moon.
Maschinerie, die,	machinery.	Montag, der,	Monday.
Mast, der,	the mast.	morgen,	to-morrow.
Maul, das,	„ mouth. muzzle.	Morgen, der,	the morning.
		Motte, die,	„ moth.
Maus, die,	the mouse.	Mücke, die,	„ midge.
Medizin, die,	„ medicine.	Mühe, die,	„ trouble.
Meer, das,	„ sea.	Muhme, die,	„ aunt.
Meerschaum, der,	„ meerschaum.	Mund, der,	„ mouth.
		Muskel, der, or die,	„ muscle.
mehr,	more.	Muth, der,	„ courage.
mehrere,	several.	Mutter, die,	„ mother.
Mehrheit, -zahl, die,	the plural.		
meinen,	to mean, to think, to say.	**N. n.**	
meisten, am,	most.	nach,	to, after.
Melodie, die,	the air.	Nachbar, der,	the neighbour.
Menge, die,	the multitude, many.	nachdem,	after.
		nachgeben,	to give in, to yield.
Mensch, der,	man (*male* and *fem.*).	nachher,	afterwards.
Mensch, das,	the wench.	Nachmittag, der,	the afternoon.
Menschheit, die,	mankind.	Nachricht, die,	„ news.
messen, sich,	to compete.	Nacht, die,	„ night.
Messer, das,	the knife.	Nachtigall, die,	„ nightingale.
Metall, das,	„ metal.	nächst,	next.
Milch, die,	„ milk.	Naht, die,	the seam.
Minute, die,	„ minute.	Nähterin, die,	„ seamstress.
mit,	with.	Narcisse, die,	„ narcissus.
Mitgefühl, Mitleid, das,	pity, sympathy. compassion.	Narr, der,	„ fool.
		Nase, die,	„ nose.
		natürlich,	of course.

Nebel, der,	the fog, mist.	Oheim, der,	the uncle.
Neffe, der,	„ nephew.	ohne,	without.
nehmen Sie!	take!	Ohr, das,	the ear.
nein!	no!	Oktober, der,	October.
nennen Sie!	name!	Oper, die,	the opera.
Nerv, der,	the nerve.	Orden, der,	„ order.
Nest, das,	„ nest.	Osten, der,	„ east.
nett,	nice, pretty.		
neu,	new.	**P. p.**	
neulich,	the other day.		
Neusilber, das,	„ German silver.	passend,	suitable.
		Pfaffe, der,	priest, parson.
nicht,	not.	Pfand, das,	pawn, pledge.
nicht wahr?	is it not (true)?	Pfeffer, der,	the pepper.
nichts,	nothing.	Pfennig, der,	„ penny.
Nichte, die,	the niece.	Pferd, das,	„ horse.
niederlegen,	to lay down.	Pistol, das, or, die	„ pistol.
niederlegen, sich,	to lie down.	Pistole.	
niederliegen,	to lie down.	Pflaume, die,	„ plum.
nie, niemals,	never.	Pflicht, die,	„ duty.
niedersetzen, sich,	to be seated.	Pfund, das,	„ pound.
noch,	yet, still.	Philosoph, der,	„ philosopher.
Norden, der,	the north.	Philosophie, die,	„ philosophy.
Nordwind, der,	„ northwind.	Photograph, der,	„ photographer.
Noth, die,	„ need, distress.		
		platt,	flat.
Nothwendigkeit, die,	the necessity.	plump,	plump, clumsy.
November, der,	November.	Preis, der,	price, prize.
nur,	only.	Prinz, der,	the prince.
Nuss, die,	the nut.	Prinzessinn, die,	„ princess.
nutzen, nützen,	to avail, to be of use.	Preußen, n.,	Prussia.
		Putzmacherinn, die,	the milliner.
nützlich,	useful.	Protestant, der,	„ protestant.
		Polen, n.,	Poland.
O. o.		Psalm, der,	the psalm.
ob,	if, whether.	**Q. q.**	
Obst, das,	fruit (orchard).	Qual, die,	the torment.
Obstbaum, der,	fruit-or orchard-tree.	quälen,	to torment.
		Quell, der; -e, die,	the source, spring.
Ochs, der,	the ox.		
oder,	or.	**R. r.**	
Östreich, n.,	Austria.		
offen,	open.	Rabe, der,	the raven.
öffentlich,	public.	Rad, das,	„ wheel.
oft,	often.	Rand, der,	„ margin.

Räthsel, das,	the riddle.	rund,	round.
Ratte, die,	„ rat.	Rußland, n.,	Russia.
Räuber, der,	„ robber.		
rechnen,	to reckon, count.		
Rechnung, die,	the bill.	**S. s.**	
recht,	right, very.		
Recht, das,	the right.	Säbel, der,	the sword.
redlich,	honest.	Sache, die,	„ thing, affair, cause.
Regent, der,	the regent.		
Regen, der,	„ rain.	sächlich,	neuter.
Regenschirm, der,	„ umbrella.	Sachsen, n.,	Saxony.
Regiment, das,	„ regiment.	sagen,	to say, to tell.
regnen,	to rain.	sah,	saw.
reich,	rich.	Sahne, die,	the cream.
Reichtum, der,	the riches.	Salz, das,	„ salt.
reif,	ripe.	salzig,	salt (Adj.).
Reif, der,	the ring.	Sand, der,	the sand.
rein,	pure.	sang,	sang.
Reis, der,	the rice.	saß,	sat.
Reis, das,	„ twig.	Satz, der,	the sentence.
Reise, die,	„ journey.	sauer,	sour.
reisen,	to go away, travel.	Schaf, das,	the sheep.
		Schale, die,	„ cup, shell.
Reisende, der,	the traveller.	Schande, die,	the disgrace.
reiten,	to ride.	Schatten, der,	„ shade.
Reiter, der,	the rider, horseman.	schattig,	shady.
		Schauspiel, das,	the play.
reizend,	charming.	Schatz, der,	„ treasure.
Reseda, die,	the mignonette.	scheinen,	to shine, to seem.
Rettung, die,	„ safety.		
Rind, das,	„ cattle.	scheint, es,	it seems.
Rinderbraten, der,	„ roastbeef.	Schellfisch, der,	the cod.
Ring, der,	„ ring.	Schemel, der,	„ stool.
Rock, der,	„ coat.	schicken,	to send.
Roggen, der,	„ rye.	Schicksal, das,	the fate.
roh,	rude, rough.	Schiff, das,	„ ship.
Rose, die,	the rose.	Schild, der,	„ shield.
Rosine, die,	„ raisin.	Schild, das,	„ sign-board.
roth,	red.	Schilling, der,	„ shilling.
Ruhe, die,	the peace, rest.	Schinken, der,	„ ham.
ruhen,	to rest.	Schirm, der,	„ screen.
Ruhm, der,	the glory.	Schlaf, der,	„ sleep.
rücken,	to move (by degrees).	Schlange, die,	„ serpent.
		schlecht,	bad.
Rücken, der,	the back.	schlimm,	sore.
Rückkehr, die,	„ return.	Schloß, das,	the lock, castle.
rückwärts,	backward.	Schlüssel, der,	„ key.

schmackhaft,	tasty, nice.
schmecken,	to taste.
Schmerz, der,	the pain.
Schmetterling, der,	„ butterfly.
Schmied, der; -e, die,	„ smith; -y.
Schnee, der,	„ snow.
Schneeglöckchen, das,	„ snowdrop.
Schneider, der,	the tailor.
Schneiderinn, die,	„ dressmaker.
schneien,	to snow.
schnell,	quick.
Schnur, die,	string, cord.
Schock, das,	lot of sixty.
schon,	already.
schön,	beautiful.
Schönheit, die,	the beauty.
Schöpfung, die,	„ creation.
schottisch,	Scotch, Scottish.
Schottland, n.,	Scotland.
Schrank, der,	the press, cabinet.
schrecklich,	dreadful.
schreiben,	to write.
Schreibzeug, das,	the inkstand.
Schuh, der,	„ shoe.
Schuhmacher, der,	„ shoemaker.
Schularbeit, die,	„ lesson.
Schuld, die,	„ guilt, debt.
Schule, die,	„ school.
Schüler, der,	„ scholar, pupil.
Schulter, die,	the shoulder.
Schwager, der,	„ brother-in-law.
Schwägerinn, die,	the sister-in-law.
Schwalbe, die,	the swallow.
Schwan, der,	„ swan.
schwarz,	black.
Schwein, das,	the pig.
schwer,	heavy, difficult.
Schwert, das,	the sword.
Schwester, die,	„ sister.
Secunde, die,	„ second.
See, die,	„ sea.
Seele, die,	„ soul.
Seelenwanderung, die,	the transmigration of souls.
sehe, ich,	I see.
sehen,	to see.
sehenswürdig,	worthy of notice.
Sehenswürdigkeit, die,	the place of interest.
Sehne, die,	the sinew.
sehr,	very.
sehr viel,	a great deal of.
sei!	be (thou)!
seib!	be (ye or you)!
sein,	to be.
seit,	since.
selten,	rare, seldom.
seltsam,	strange.
senden,	to send.
Senf, der,	the mustard.
September, der,	September.
setzen,	to put, to set.
Sichel, die,	the sickle.
sicher,	secure, sure, safe.
Sicherheit, die,	security, safety.
Silber, das,	the silver.
silbern,	of silver.
singen,	to sing.
Sinn, der,	the sense.
Sitte, die,	„ custom, manner.
sobald,	as soon as.
Sofa, das,	the sofa.
Sohle, die,	„ sole.
Sohn, der,	„ son.
Soldat, der,	„ soldier.
Sommer, der,	„ summer.
sonderbar,	strange.
sondern,	but.
Sonne, die,	the sun.
Sonnenschirm, der,	„ parasol, sun-shade.
Sonnensystem, das,	the solar-system.
Sonnabend, der,	Saturday.
Sonntag, der,	Sunday.
sonst,	else.

Sorge, die,	the sorrow.
Spanier, der,	„ Spaniard.
spät,	late.
spazieren,	to walk.
spazieren gehen,	to take a walk.
Sperling, der,	the sparrow.
Spiegel, der,	„ mirror.
Spiel, das,	„ play, game.
spielen,	to play.
Spinne, die,	the spider.
Sprache, die,	„ language.
sprechen,	to speak.
sprechen Sie!	speak!
Sprung, der,	the spring, leap.
Staat, der,	the state.
Stachelbeere, die,	„ gooseberry.
Stadt, die,	„ town.
Stahl, der,	„ steel.
Stahlfeder, die,	„ steel-pen.
Stahlfederhalter, der,	„ penholder.
stand,	stood.
stark,	strong.
stecken,	to put.
steh-en; -t,	to stand; -s.
steif,	stiff.
Stein, der,	the stone.
Stelle, die,	„ place, situation.
stellen,	to place, to put.
Stern, der,	the star.
Stiefel, der,	„ boot.
Stiefmütterchen, das,	„ pansy.
Stiefvater, der,	the stepfather.
Stift, der; -, das,	„ peg; cloister.
still,	still.
Stimme, die,	the voice, vote.
Stirne, die,	„ forehead.
Stock, der,	„ stick, cane.
Stolz, der,	„ pride.
Storch, der,	„ stork.
strafen,	to punish.
Strahl, der,	the ray, jet.
streng,	strict.
Stroh, das	the straw.
Strumpf der,	the stocking.
Stube, die,	„ room.
Stück, das,	„ piece.
Student, der,	„ student.
studiren,	to study.
Stuhl, der,	the chair.
Stunde, die,	„ hour.
Sturm, der,	„ gale, storm.
Süden, der,	„ south.
Südwind, der,	„ southwind.
Südwestwind, der,	„ southwestwind.
Sultan, der,	the sultan.
Sultaninn, die,	„ sultaness.
Suppe, die,	„ soup.
süß,	sweet.

T. t.

tadeln,	to blame.
Tafel, die,	the (long) table, slate, (black) board.
Tag, der,	the day.
tapfer,	gallant, brave.
Tasche, die,	the pocket.
Taschentuch, das,	„ pockethandkerchief.
Taschenuhr, die,	the watch.
Tasse, die,	„ cup and saucer.
Taube, die,	the pigeon, dove.
that,	did.
Thal, das,	the dale, valley.
Thaler, der,	„ dollar.
Thau, der,	„ thaw, dew.
Theater, das,	„ theatre.
Thee, der,	„ tea.
Theelöffel, der,	„ teaspoon.
Theologie, die,	„ divinity.
theuer,	dear.
Thier, das,	the animal.
Thor, der,	„ fool.
Thor, das,	„ gate.
thun,	to do, put.
Thüre, die,	the door.

Teller, der,	the plate.	unedel,	ignoble.
Tellertuch, das,	„ napkin.	unfreundlich,	unkind.
Tiger, der,	„ tiger.	ungeschickt,	awkward.
Tinte, die,	„ ink.	Unglück, das,	bad luck, misfortune, accident.
Tintenfaß, das,	„ inkbottle.		
Tintenflasche, die,	„ inkbottle.		
Tisch, der,	„ table.	unglücklich,	unfortunate.
Tischler, der,	„ joiner.	unheilbringend,	unlucky.
Tischtuch, das,	„ tablecloth.	unschuldig,	innocent.
Tochter, die,	„ daughter.	unter,	under.
Tod, der,	„ death.	unterhalten,	to converse, to entertain.
todt,	dead.		
trank,	drank.	unterhalten,	to hold under.
Trank, der,	the drink.	unterhaltend,	interesting.
Traube, die,	„ grape.	Unterthan, der,	the subject.
trauen,	to trust.	Unrecht, das,	„ wrong.
Traum, der,	the dream.	unzufrieden,	dissatisfied.
traurig,	dreary, sad.	Ursprung, der,	the origin.
treu,	true, faithful.		
Treue, die,	faithfulness.	**V. v.**	
trinken,	to drink.	Vater, der,	the father.
trocken,	dry.	Veilchen, das,	„ violet.
trocknen,	to dry.	Verachtung, die,	„ contempt.
Tuch, das,	the cloth.	verbinden,	to oblige.
Tugend, die,	„ virtue.	verdenken,	to find fault with, to blame.
Tulpe, die,	„ tulip.		
		verehren,	to worship, to present, to honour.
U. u.			
über,	over.	Vergangenheit, die,	the past.
Überfluß, der,	the abundance.	vergessen,	to forget, forgotten.
überführen,	to convict, convince.		
		Vergißmeinnicht, das,	the forgetmenot.
überführen,	to lead over.		
übergeben,	to pass (over), pass by.	verkaufen,	to sell.
		verkauft,	sold.
übergehen,	to go over, cross.	verkennen,	to mistake.
		verlangen,	to want, to wish.
übersetzen,	to translate.	verlassen,	to leave, to abandon.
übersetzen,	to set over.		
Uhr, die,	the watch, clock.	verleihen,	to grant.
umgeben,	to surround, surrounded.	verloren,	lost.
		vermehren,	to increase.
umher,	about.	vernehmen,	to hear.
unartig,	naughty.	Vernunft, die,	the reason.
und,	and.	vernünftig,	reasonable, sensible.
und zwar,	and that.		

verschieden,	various.	Wasser, das,	the water.
Verstand, der,	the understanding.	warm,	warm.
		warten,	to wait.
verstorben,	deceased. late.	weder — noch,	neither — nor.
versucht,	tried.	weg,	away.
Vertrauen, das,	the confidence.	weggehen,	to go away.
verwandeln,	to change.	weglaufen,	to run away.
verzeihen,	to pardon.	wehen,	to blow.
Verzweiflung, die,	the despair.	Weib, das,	the wife, woman.
Vetter, der,	„ cousin. *m*.	weiblich,	womanly, feminine.
viel,	much.		
vielleicht,	perhaps.	weibisch,	effeminate.
Vogel, der,	the bird.	weich,	soft.
Volk, das,	„ people.	weil,	because.
voll,	full.	Wein, der,	the wine.
vollbringen,	to perform.	Weinhändler, der,	„ winemerchant.
vollenden,	to accomplish.		
von,	from, of.	weise,	wise.
vor,	ago, before.	Weizen, der,	the wheat.
Vorfahr, der,	the ancestor.	—, der türkische,	Turkish corn.
vorig,	last, former.	Welt, die,	the world.
vorkommen,	to appear.	wenn,	when, if.
Vormittag, der,	the forenoon.	wenn auch,	although.
Vormund, der,	„ guardian.	wenig,	little.
vorwärts,	forwards.	werde!	become (thou)!
		werdet!	become (ye or you).
W. w.			
		werden Sie!	become!
wachsen,	to grow.	werth,	worth, valuable.
Wagen, der,	waggon, carriage.	Werth, der,	the worth, value.
wahr,	true.	weshalb,	why.
Wahrheit, die,	the truth.	Wespe, die,	the wasp.
wahrscheinlich,	probable.	Westen, der,	„ west.
während,	during.	Wetter, das,	„ weather.
Waise, die,	the orphan.	widerlegen,	to refute.
Wald, der,	„ wood.	widersprechen,	to contradict.
Wallnuss, die,	„ walnut.	wie,	how.
Wamms, das,	„ jerkin.	wieder,	again.
Wand, die,	„ wall.	Wien,	Vienna.
Wandschrank, der,	„ press.	Wilhelm,	William.
wann,	when?	Wilhelmine,	Wilhelmina.
was auch,	what ever.	Wind, der,	the wind.
waschen,	to wash.	Winter, der,	„ winter.
Wäscherin, die,	the laundress.	wissen,	to know.
Waschfrau, die,	„ washerwoman.	Wittwer, der,	the widower.
		Wittwe, die,	„ widow.

wo,	where.	zeigen,			to show.
Woche, die,	the week.	zerbrechen,			to break (to pieces).
woher,	whence.				
wohl,	probably, perhaps, I think.	zerbrochen,			broken (to pieces).
wohlbekannt,	well known.	zerrissen,			torn.
Wohlthat, die,	the benefit.	ziehen,			to pull, draw, go, proceed, march.
wohlthätig,	benevolent.				
wohnen,	to dwell, to live.				
Wolf, der,	the wolf.	Zimmer, das,			the room.
Wolke, die,	„ cloud.	Zinn, das,			„ tin.
wollen,	(will) to wish, to want.	Zins, der,			„ interest.
		Zofe, die,			„ chambermaid.
Wort, das,	the word.				
wörtlich,	literally, word for word.	Zorn, der,			the wrath.
		zu,			to.
wundervoll,	wonderful.	Zucker, der,			the sugar.
Wunsch, der,	the wish.	zufällig,			by chance.
wünschen,	to wish.	zufrieden,			pleased, contented.
würdig,	worthy.				
Wurm, der,	the worm.	zufriedenstellend,			satisfying.
Wurst, die,	„ sausage.	Zukunft, die,			the future.
wußte,	knew.	Zug, der,			„ train.
		zumachen,			to shut.
3. z.		Zunft, die,			the guild.
		Zunge, die,			„ tongue.
Zahl, die,	the number.	zurück,			back.
zahlen,	to pay.	zurückkehren,			to return.
zahm,	tame.	zusammen,			together.
zahlreich,	numerous.	Zustand, der,			the state.
Zahn, der,	the tooth.	zustoßen,			to happen.
Zehe, die,	„ toe.	zwischen,			between.

FIFTH PART.

READING LESSONS.

a.

Specimens showing how the text should be prepared by the pupil and how to read the German properly.

Note. Pronounce the words connected by a hyphen like one, and put the stress on the most important part of each group.

I.

Die Sternthaler.
The star-dollars.

Es-war^1 einmal^2 ein-kleines^3-Mädchen, dem^4-war^5 Vater-und-Mutter gestorben^5, und es^6-war so-arm, daß-es kein-Kämmerchen^7-mehr^8 hatte, darin^9 zu-wohnen, und kein-Bettchen^{10}-mehr, darin^9 zu-schlafen und-endlich gar^{11}-nichts-mehr, als die^{12}-Kleider auf^{13}-dem^{14}-Leibe und ein-Stückchen-^{15}Brot in-der-Hand, das^{16} ihm^{17} ein-mitleidiges-Herz geschenkt-^{18}hatte. Es-war-aber gut-und-fromm. Und weil-es so von-^{19}aller-Welt verlassen^{20}-war, ging^{21}-es im^{22}-Vertrauen auf-^{13}den-lieben-Gott hinaus^{21}-ins^{22}-Feld. Da^{23} begegnete-^{24}ihm ein-armer-Mann, der sprach^{25}: ach, gieb^{26}-mir etwas zu-essen, ich-bin so-hungrig." Es-reichte^{27} ihm^{17} das-ganze-Stückchen^{15}-Brot und sagte^{28}: „Gott^{29} segne dir's" und ging^{21} weiter^{30}. Da-kam^{31} ein-Kind, das jammerte^{32} und sprach^{25}: „es-friert^{33}-mich-so an-meinen-Kopf, schenk^{34}-mir etwas, womit^{35} ich-ihn^{36} bedecken-kann^{37}. Da-that^{38}-es seine-Mütze ab^{38} und-gab sie^{39} ihm^{17}. Und als-es noch-eine-Weile ge=gangen^{40}-war, kam^{31} wieder ein-Kind und-hatte^{41} kein-Leibchen an^{41} und fror^{42}: da gab^{26}-es-ihm^{17} seins^{43}; und noch^{44}-weiter, da bat^{45} eins^{46} um^{45}-ein-Röcklein^{47}: das^{48} gab^{26}-es auch von^{49}-sich-hin^{49}. Endlich gelangte^{50}-es in-einen-Wald, und es^{51} war schon-dunkel-geworden; da kam^{31} noch^{52}-eins und-bat^{45} um-ein-Hemdlein^{53}, und das-fromme^{54}-Mädchen dachte^{55}: „es-ist dunkle^{56}-Nacht, da^{57} sieht^{58}-dich^{59} niemand, du-kannst^{60} wohl^{61} dein-Hemd^{62} weggeben und-zog^{63} sein-Hemd ab^{64} und-gab^{26}-es auch^{65} noch-hin^{66}. Und-wie^{67}-es so-stand^{68} und gar^{69}-nichts-mehr^{70} hatte, fielen^{71} auf-einmal^{72} die-Sterne^{73} vom^{74}-Himmel und waren^{75} lauter^{76} harte^{77}, blanke Thaler: und statt^{78} des^{79}-verschenkten-Hemdleins^{53} hatte^{41}-es ein^{80}-neues an^{41}, das war vom^{77}-allerfeinsten^{81} Linnen^{82}. Da^{23} sammelte^{83}-es die-Thaler hinein^{84} und war reich für^{85}-sein-Lebtag. Grimm.

1. Es, (*it*) there, war, Impf. Ind. of sein, war, gewesen, ich bin etc., to be. 2. einmal, Adv., once (upon a time). 3. kleines, Nom. neut. of klein, epithet to Mädchen, a Diminutive and neuter. 4. dem, Dat. neut. of Demonst. Pron. der, die, das, that, he, she, it etc., thus: to it, but here: *whose*; read also Note 6, cf. Rule 347. 5. war gestorben, Pluperfect Ind. of sterben, starb, gestorben, stirb! to die; cf. Rule 357. 6. es, Pers. Pron., third pers. neut., *it*, but here: *she*; Mädchen being neuter the pronouns representing it, or referring to it may also be neuter; but as the noun denotes a female being, the fem. forms of pronouns are more commonly used with such words. 7. kein Kämmerchen, Diminutive of Kammer, chamber, not even a small room; cf. Rule 152. 8. mehr, Adv., more, here: *left*. 9. darin, Relative Adv., therein, in it; cf. Note 2 Rule 55. 10. kein Bettchen, Dimin. of Bett, bed, not even a bed. 11. gar nichts mehr, Advs., left nothing, als, Conj., but. 12. die Kleider, pl. of das Kleid. 13. auf, Prep. with dat. and acc., on, upon. 14. dem Leibe, Dat. of der Leib, his body. 15. ein Stückchen (dim. of Stück) Brod, a small piece of bread. 16. das, Rel. Pron., Acc. neut., referring to Brod, n., which, that. 17. ihm, Dat. neut. of Pers. Pron. es, representing Mädchen; read note 4. 18. geschenkt hatte, Pluperfect Ind. of schenken, to present, give. 19. von, Prep. with Dat., of, from, but here: *by*; aller, Dat. fem. of all-er, -e, -es, all the. 20. verlassen, Perf. Part. of verlassen, verließ, verlassen, du, er verläßt, to abandon, forsake. 21. ging, Impf. Ind. of gehen, ging, gegangen, to go, walk: hinaus (out), Particle modifying the sense and belonging to the verb ging; thus: hinausgehen, Separable Compound, ging hinaus, hinausgegangen; cf. Rules 272 to 274. 22. im (in the), ins (into the), contractions of in dem and in das (cf. Rule 48): im Vertrauen auf (in the trust of) trusting in;

den lieben Gott, God; read Observation p. 311. 23. da, (then) Adv., it is important to notice that, as there are several words used both as adverbs and conjunctions, they are *Adv.* if the Verb is next to them, otherwise *Conj.*; such words are: da, dann, nun, so etc. 24. begegnete ihm, Impf. Ind. of begegnen with the dat., to meet; as, ich begegne einem Mann, less commonly, ein Mann begegnet mir, I meet a man; the past tenses are conjugated with sein; as, ich bin einem Mann begegnet, or ein Mann ist mir begegnet, I met a man. 25. sprach, Impf. Ind. of sprechen, sprach, gesprochen; sprich! to speak. 26. gieb, Imp. of geben, gab, gegeben; giebst, giebt; gieb! mir (me), Dat. of Pers. Pron. ich, I. 27. reichte, Impf. Ind. of reichen, reach, hand. 28. sagte, Impf. Ind. of sagen, to say, tell. 29. Gott, subject; segne Imp. 3rd pers. sing. of segnen, to bless; dir's, contraction of dir es (it to thee). — God bless you! 30. weiter, wider, further. Particle belonging to ging; thus, weitergehen, Sep. Comp., ging weiter, weitergegangen, to go on, proceed. 31. kam, Impf. Ind. of kommen, kam, gekommen, to come. 32. jammerte, Impf. Ind. of jammern, to lament, wail, Scotch *yammer*. 33. es friert mich (Pres. of Imp. Verb frieren, fror, gefroren, to feel cold) an meinen Kopf (at my head): my head is aching with cold. 34. schenk', Imp. of schenken, to give, present. 35. womit, Rel. Adv., wherewith, with which. 36. ihn, Acc. of er (he), referring to Kopf, *masc.*, here *it*. 37. kann, Pres. Ind. of können, konnte, gekonnt; ich kann, du kannst, er kann, to be able, can. 38. that, Impf. Ind. of thun, that, gethan, to do; ab (off), Particle qualifying and belonging to that, did off (old: doffed); here *took of*. 39. sie, Acc. of sie (she), referring to Mütze, *fem.*, here: *it*. 40. gegangen war, Plupf. Ind. of gehen (21), to go. 41. hatte, Impf. Ind. of haben, hatte, gehabt; du hast, er hat, to have; an (on), Particle qualifying and belonging to hatte; thus: an haben, Sep. Comp. hatte an, angehabt, to have on, wear, be dressed in; Leibchen (bodice), Dim. of der Leib, the body. 42. fror, Impf. Ind. of frieren, to feel cold, be shivering, freeze; vid. note 33. 43. seins for seines (its), referring to Leibchen, *neut.*; here: *her own*. 44. noch weiter, elliptical for: als sie noch weiter gegangen war, when she had proceeded a little further still. 45. bat, Impf. Ind. of bitten (um), to beg or ask (for). 46. eins, for eines, representing Kind, *neut.*, one. 47. Röcklein (little frock), Dim. Rock, frock. 48. das (that), Dem. Pron. representing the neut. noun Röcklein. 49. von sich (from or of herself), here connected with the verb gab and partc. hin, intensifying the idea of *give up, parting with*. NB. hin (hence, away, up), particle belonging to gab. 50. gelangte es, Impf. Ind. of gelangen, to arrive, reach or come. 51. es war geworden, Plupf. Ind. of werden, wurde or ward, geworden; du wirst, er wird; turn or grow. 52. noch eins (yet or still one), another: eins for Kind, n. 53. Hemblein (little shirt), Dim. of Hembe, shirt. 54. fromme, declined form of fromm, good, pious or gentle: 55. dachte, Impf. Ind. of denken, dachte, gedacht, to think. 56. bunfle, declined form of bunfel, dark. 57. ba, there, then. 58. ſieht, Pres. Ind. of ſehen, ſah, geſehen; ·ſich! to see. 59. dich, Acc. of du, thou. 60. kannſt (canst), Pres. Ind. of können, to be able, can. 61. wohl, particle, *well, surely, indeed*; here: du kannſt wohl weggeben, you may well (*i. e., without fear*) give away, part with. 62. dein Hemd, acc. neut., object to weggeben. 63. zog (related to *tug*), Impf. of ziehen, zog, gezogen, to pull; this is a very important verb, as it occurs both as simple verb and in connection with particles most frequently; its meanings may easily be understood if it be kept in mind that ziehen on the one hand signifies *to pull* or *to draw*, on the other *to go, march, proceed*. 64. ab (off) particle qualifying zog, read 63. 65. auch noch (also yet), likewise. 66. hin, an important Particle, implying a movement away from the speaker or person spoken of, opposed to her, which is used to express a movement towards the same; they are often not translatable, here say *up*. 67. wie, Conj. (familiar for als), as. 68. ſtand, Impf. Ind. of ſtehen, ſtand, geſtanden, to stand. 69. gar (at all), Adv. qualifying or here intensifying nichts, thus gar nichts, nothing at all. 70. mehr (more), left. 71. ſielen, Impf. Ind. plur. of fallen, fiel, gefallen; ich falle, du fällſt, er fällt, to fall. 72. auf einmal, Adv., all at once. 73. die Sterne, nom. pl. of der Stern, the star. 74. vom, contraction of von (from), Prep. w. dat., and dem (the), dat. of the def. Art. der, die, das. 75. waren, Impf. Ind. plur. of ſein, to be, second verb to the subject die Sterne. 76. lauter, Adv., nothing but, all. 77. harte, blanke, nom. plur. of hart, hard, blank, shining. 78. ſtatt (instead), Prep. w. gen. 79. des verſchenkten Hembleins, gen. to ſtatt, des (of the) gen. neut. of def. Art.; verſchenkten (given away), Perf. Part. of verſchenken, give away; and vid. 53. 80. ein neues (a new one), appositive to the neut. Hemblein. 81. allerfeinſten (very finest), intensified Superlative of fein; cf. Rule 169. 82. Linnen, n., linen. 83. ſammelte es, Impf. Ind. of ſammeln, to gather. 84. hinein, (into it), Partc. qualifying the verb ſammelte. 85. für ſein Lebtag (all her life), familiar for ſein Leben lang.

II.

Märchen[1] von[2] der Unke[3].

Ein-Waiſenkind[4] ſaß[5] an-der-Stadtmauer[6] und-ſpann[7]: da[8] ſah[9]-es eine-Unke[3] aus-einer-Öffnung[9] unten-an-der-Mauer[10] hervorkommen[11]. Geſchwind breitete-es[12] ſein-blau-ſeidenes-Halstuch[13] neben-ſich[14] aus[12], das[15] die-Unken gewaltig[16] lieben[17] und auf das[18] ſie allein[19] gehen[20].

Alsobald[21] die-Unke das[22] erblickte[23], kehrte-sie um[24], kam-wieder[25] und brachte[26] ein-kleines-goldenes-Krönchen[27] getragen[26], legte[23]-es darauf[28] und ging[29] dann wieder-fort[29]. Das Mädchen nahm[30] die-Krone auf[30]: sie glitzerte[23] und war von-zartem-Goldgespinnst[31]. Nicht-lange, so-kam[25] die-Unke zum-zweiten-Mal[32] wieder[25]: wie[33]-sie-aber die-Krone nicht-mehr-sah[9], kroch-sie[34] an-die-Wand[35] und-schlug[36] vor-Leib[37] ihr-Köpfchen so-[38]lange dawider[39], als[38]-sie-nur-noch[40] Kräfte[41]-hatte, bis-sie endlich todt dalag[42]. Hätte[43] das-Mädchen die-Krone liegen-lassen[43], so-hätte[44] die-Unke wohl[45] noch-mehr von-ihren-Schätzen[46] aus-der-Höhle herbeige-tragen[44].
Grimm.

1. Märchen, Fairy-tale, story. 2. von, of, about. 3. Unke, f., toad, *also* sprite. 4. Waisenkind, orphan (child). 5. saß, Impf. Ind. of sitzen, saß, gesessen, to sit. 6. an der Stadtmauer, at (or by) the wall of the city. *Note:* The buildings facing the city-walls were generally of the poorest description and chiefly inhabited by the humble classes. 7. spann, Impf. Ind. of spinnen, spann, gesponnen, to spin. 8. Vid. I (23). 9. sah es, Impf. Ind. of sehen, sah, gesehen; sieh! to see; aus, Prep. with Dat., out of; einer Oeffnung, Dat. fem., an opening, hole. 10. unten, Adv., below; an, Prep. with Dat. and Acc., at, in; der Mauer, Dat. fem., the wall. 11. hervor-kommen, Separable Compound Verb, Impf. kam hervor, P. Part. hervorgekommen, to come forth *or* out. 12. breitete es ... aus, Impf. Ind. of the Sep. Verb ausbreiten, breitete aus, ausgebreitet, to spread (out), (cf. breit, broad). 13. sein blauseidenes Halstuch, his *or* its neck-tie of blue silk (*lit.* blue-silken). 14. neben, Prep. with Dat. and Acc., near, beside; sich, Reflex. Pron. Dat. or Acc., himself or itself. 15. das (which), Relat. Pron. (referring to Halstuch), object to die Unken. 16. gewaltig, Adv. to lieben, mightily, very much; (cf. weald and walten). 17. lieben, Pres. Ind. of lieben, to love, like. 18. auf, Prep. with Dat. and Acc., on, upon; das, vid. 15. 19. allein (alone) attribute to auf das, upon which alone, *i. e.*, upon it and no other one. 20. sie gehen, Pres. Ind. of gehen, ging, gegangen, to go. 21. Alsobald, unusual for sobald (als), as soon as. 22. das, Object representing Halstuch (13). 23. The Infinitive of weak Imperfects and Participles is easily found by dropping their inflection -te, -test etc. and -(e)t, and substituting an -en; thus erblick-te, Impf. of erblick-en, to perceive, see. 24. kehrte sie um, Impf. Ind. of Sep. Verb umkehren, kehrte um, umgekehrt, to turn round. 25. kam wieder, Impf. Ind. of Sep. Verb, wiederkommen, kam wieder, wieder-gekommen, to come again, return. 26. brachte, Impf. Ind. of bringen, brachte, gebracht, to bring; connected with it is getragen, Perf. Partc.

of tragen, trug, getragen; du trägst, er trägt (cf. drag and tray); here it may be omitted in the translation. 27. Krönchen, n., diminutive of die Krone, the crown. 28. darauf (thereupon), Adv. for auf es (13), upon it. 29. ging ... fort, Impf. of Sep. Verb fortgehen, ging fort, fortgegangen, to go away, leave. 30. nahm ... auf, Impf. of Sep. Verb aufnehmen, nahm auf, aufgenommen; du nimmst auf, er nimmt auf; Imp. nimm auf! to take up, lift. 31. von (of), Prep. with Dat., zart-em, delicate, Goldgespinnst, gold-filigreen. 32. zum zweiten Mal, for the second time (cf. Rule 207). 33. wie, Conj. (more commonly als), when. 34. troch sie, Impf. Ind. of kriechen, kroch, gekrochen, to creep. 35. an die Wand, to the wall. 36. schlug, Impf. Ind. of schlagen, schlug, geschlagen; du schlägst, er schlägt, to strike, beat; (cf. slay, slew, slain). 37. vor Leid, with sorrow. 38. so ... als, as ... as. 39. dawider (more commonly dagegen), Adv. for wider sie, against it. 40. noch hatte, had left. 41. Kräfte, pl. of die Kraft, the strength. 42. da lag, Impf. Ind. of Sep. Verb daliegen, lag da, dagelegen. 43. Hätte ... liegen lassen, (Plup. Subj.) hypothetical for wenn ... liegen lassen hätte; lassen for gelassen (cf. Rule 384), allowed to. 44. hätte ... herbeigetragen, Plup. Subj. of Sep. Verb herbeitragen, to carry up, bring. 45. wohl, Particle, largely used, implying probability, and translatable by „I suppose, probably, I dare say. I think" and others. 46. von ihren Schätzen, von, Prep. with Dat.; Schätzen, Dat. Plur. of der Schatz, the treasure.

III.

Rechnungs-Exempel.
Arithmetical Puzzles.

Um-die-Osterzeit[1], wo[2] jede-Mutter ihren-Kindern gern[3] mit-ein-paar[4]-gefärbten[5]-Eiern[6] eine-Freude[7]-macht[3], verkauft[8] eine-Händlerinn[9] an-ihre-Nachbarsfrau[10] die-Hälfte von-allen-Eiern[6], die[11] sie hatte, und noch-ein-halbes-Ei dazu[12]. Aber wohlverstanden[13]! es-darf[14] keins[15] zerbrochen[16] oder getheilt[17]- werden. Es-kommt[18] die-zweite; diese[19] kauft vom-Reste wieder die-Hälfte und ein-halbes[20]-mehr. Am-Ende[21] hatte[22] die-Händlerinn noch ein-einziges-Ei übrig[22]. Jetzt ist die-Frage: wie-groß war ihr-Vorrath[23] von-Anfang-an[24]? —

Zwei-Schäfer begegnen-sich[25] mit-Schafen auf-der-Straße[26]. Hans sagt zu-Fritz: „Gieb[27]-mir eins-von-deinen-Schafen, alsdann[28] hab'-ich noch-einmal-soviel[29] als-du;" Fritz sagt zu-Hans: „Nein, gieb-du-mir eins-von-deinen[30], alsdann hab' ich so-viel als-du." Nun ist zu-errathen³¹ wie-viel ein-jeder hatte.

Ein-Mann hatte sieben-Kinder zu³²-einem-Vermögen, von-4900-Thalern. Da-gingen³³-ihn die-jüngern³⁴-Kinder öfters an³³, eine-Verordnung³⁵ darüber³⁶ zu-machen, damit³⁷-sie bei-der-Theilung³⁸ nach-seinem-Absterben³⁹ mehr-bekommen-sollten⁴⁰, als-die-ältern⁴¹. Das kam⁴² dem-guten-Vater hart an⁴², weil⁴³-er eins-von-seinen-Kindern liebte wie das-andere, und weil er-glaubte, Gott werde⁴⁴ den-jüngern, wenn-sie fleißig und gut gesinnt-wären⁴⁵ nach-seinem-Tode helfen⁴⁴, wie-er den-ältern bei-seinen-Lebzeiten geholfen-habe⁴⁶. Weil-sie-ihm-aber keine-Ruhe⁴⁷ ließen⁴⁸ und die-ältern es⁴⁹-auch zu-frieden-waren⁴⁹, so-machte⁵⁰-er folgende⁵⁰-Verordnung: — der-älteste-Sohn soll⁵¹ von-dem-ganzen-Vermögen 100 Thaler zum-Voraus⁵² haben und von-dem-übrigen⁵³ den-achten-Theil. Der zweite soll⁵¹ alsdann 200 Thaler wegnehmen⁵⁴ und von-dem-übrigen⁵³ wieder den-achten-Theil. Der-dritte soll⁵¹ 300 Thaler vor-dem-nachfolgenden⁵⁵ voraus-empfangen⁵⁶ und auch-wieder den-achten-Theil vom-Rest. Und-so soll⁵¹ jeder-folgende⁵⁷ 100 Thaler mehr, als der-erste, und dann von-dem übrigen⁵³ ein-Achtel erhalten, und der-Letzte bekommt, was übrig-bleibt⁵⁸-wie-überall! Damit⁵⁹ waren die-Kinder zufrieden. Nach-dem-Tode des-Vaters wurde⁶⁰ sein-letzter-Wille vollzogen⁶⁰ und es-ist⁶¹-nun auszurechnen⁶¹ wieviel ein-Jeder bekommen-habe.
Hebel.

1. Um, Prep. w. Acc.. at, about, around; die Osterzeit, Easter. 2. wo, Adv., where, when. 3. gern macht, likes to make; gern is very largely used with Verbs to express liking. 4. ein paar, with a small „p" is „a few"; with a capital (Paar) „a pair". 5. gefärbten, Part.-Adj. of färben, to dye. 6. Eiern, Dat. Plur. of Ei, governed by mit (with), prep. with dat. 7. Freude, f., joy, pleasure. 8. verkauft, Pres. Ind. of verkaufen, to sell. 9. Händlerinn, f., dealer, market-woman; related to handeln, to deal. 10. an, Prep. with dat. and acc., (on), to; Nachbarsfrau, neighbour. 11. die, Rel. Pron. to Eiern. 12. dazu (thereto), into the bargain. 13. wohl verstanden, (well understood), mark! 14. darf, Pres. Ind. of dürfen, durfte, gedurft; ich darf, du darfst, er darf, to be allowed (dare). 15. keins (none), Negat., nom. neut., representing Ei, n. 16. zerbrochen... werden, Pres. Inf. Pass. of zerbrechen, to break to pieces. 17. getheilt werden, Press. Inf. Pass. of theilen, to divide. 18. es kommt (there comes), imperson.

form Pres. Ind. of kommen, kam, gekommen, to come (cf. 261).
19. diese (she), Nom. Fem. of Dem. Pron. dies-er, -e, -es, this. 20. ein
halbes mehr (referring to Ei), another half. 21. Am Ende (in the
end), at last. 22. hatte ... übrig, Impf. Ind. of ü b r i g h a b e n, to
have over or left. 23. Vorrath, m.. stock. 24. von Anfang an,
from the beginning.
25. begegneten sich, Impf. Ind. of Refl. Verb sich begegnen, to
meet. 26. auf (upon, on, in), Prep. w. dat. and acc.; der Straße,
Dat. Fem. of die Straße, the street, road, strait. 27. vid. I 26.
28. alsdann, Adv., more commonly dann, then. 29. noch (yet) ein=
mal (once) so (so, as) viel, or viele (many), as many again. 30. deinen,
Dat. Plur. of poss. pron. dein-er, -e, -es, thine; Schafen being understood here; so viel (or viel[e]) als, as many as. 31. es ist zu
errathen, it is to be guessed, you must guess; notice the difference
in the voices of German Act. and English Pass.
32. zu (Prep. w. dat.) einem Vermögen, dat. neut., a fortune;
von 4900, read vier tausend, neunhundert; Thalern, Dat. Plur. masc.,
dollars. 33. gingen an, Impf. Ind. of Sep. Verb a n gehen, request,
desire. 34. jüngern, inflected comparative of jung. 35. Verordnung,
disposition. 36. darüber (thereover), Adv., anticipating the indirect
object namely the phrase: damit sie ... bekommen sollte (cf. Rule 289).
37. damit, Conj., in order that. 38. bei, Prep. w. dat., by, at, in; der
Theilung, dat. fem., (division). 39. Absterben, n., decease, death.
40. sollten, 3rd person Plur. Impf. Subj. of sollen, shall, are to;
thus, should or were to. 41. die ältern, Nom. Plur. of älter, comp.
of alt; Kinder understood. 42. kam ... an, Impf. of Sep. Verb
a n kommen, come on, come over, feel. 43. weil, Conj., because.
44. werde ... helfen (would help), Fut. Subj., dependent on „er
glaubte." 45. sie ... wären (they were), Impf. Subj. of sein, governed
by the Conj. wenn. 46. er ... geholfen habe (had helped), Perf.
Subj. (caused by the indirectness of the statement, vid. Rule 365)
of helfen, half, geholfen; hilf! 49. es (idiomatic for damit) zufrieden
waren, were agreed. 50. machte, Impf. of machen, to make, here:
execute; folgende, Partc. of folgen, to follow, here: subjoined.
51. soll (is to), Pres. Ind. of sollen, shall. 52. zum Voraus, before
the rest, in advance. 53. von dem übrigen (Vermögen, fortune,
understood), of the rest. 54. wegnehmen, Inf., Sep. Verb, nahm weg,
weggenommen, etc. 55. vor dem n a ch folgenden (Kinde, child, understood), before the following or next. 56. v o r a u s empfangen, Inf. to
„soll", receive before (the next). 57. jeder folgende, each next one.
58. ü b r i g bleibt, Pres. Ind. of Sep. Verb ü b r i g bleiben, to remain (over).
59. damit zufrieden, comp. 49. 60. wurde ... vollzogen, Impf. Pass.
of Insep. Verb voll-ziehen, -zog, -zogen, to execute. 61. es ist
a u s zurechnen, it is to be calculated; cf. 31.

b.

Specimens for Reading, showing, by hyphens, which words should be pronounced like one, and, by accents or spaced type which part of each group is important or most important and emphasized accordingly, with notes for translation etc.

I.

Die Erzäh'lung des thü'ringischen Candida'ten,
aus: Geschich'te Friedrichs des Gro'ßen, von F. Kugler.

Als-ich zum-erſten-Male im-Jahre-1766 nach-Berlin kam, wurden mir bei Viſiti'rung-meiner-Sachen auf-dem-Packhofe[1] 400-Reichsthaler Nürnberger-ganze-Batzen[2] weggenommen. Der-König, ſagte-man-mir, hätte-ſchon etliche-Jahre die Batzen ganz-und-gar verſchla'gen[3]-laſſen, ſie-ſollten in-ſeinem-Lande nichts-gelten, und ich-wäre ſo-kühn und-brächte die-Batzen hierher, in-die-königliche-Reſidenz', — auf-den — Packhof! — Con'trebande! — Con'trebande! — das-war ein-ſchöner-Willkommen! Ich-entſchuldigte-mich mit-der-Unwiſſenheit: käme aus-Thüringen, viele-Meilen[4]-Weges her, hätte-mithin ja-unmöglich wiſſen-können, was Seine-Majeſtät in-dero[5]-Ländern verbieten-laſſen[6].

Der Packhofsinſpector[7]: Das-iſt keine-Entſchuldigung. Wenn-man in-eine-ſolche-Reſidenz reiſen und daſelbſt ver-bleiben-will, ſo muſs-man-ſich nach-Allem genau-erkundigen und wiſſen, was-für-Geldſorten im-Schwange-gehen[8], damit-man-nicht durch-Einbringung verrufener-Münze Gefahr-laufe.

Ich[7]: Was ſoll-ich-denn anfangen? Sie-nehmen-mir[9] ja ſogar-unſchuldig die-Gelder weg! Wie und wovon ſoll-ich denn-leben?

Packhofsinſpector[7]: Da[10] muſs-Er zuſehen, und ich will-Ihm ſogleich-bedeuten[10]: wenn die-Sachen auf-dem-

Packhofe visitirt'-werden[11], so-müssen solche[12] von-der-Stelle geschafft-werden.

Es-wurde ein-Schiebkärrner[13] herbeigerufen, meine-Effec'ten[14] fortzufahren; dieser brachte-mich in-die-Judenstraße[15] in-den-weißen-Schwan[16], warf meine-Sachen ab und forderte vier-Groschen-Lohn. Die hatte-ich nicht. Der-Wirth kam-herbei, und-als er-sah, daß ich ein-gemachtes-Federbett[17], einen-Koffer-voll-Wäsche[18], einen-Sack-voll-Bücher und andere Kleinigkeiten-hatte, so bezahlte-er den-Träger und wies[19]-mir eine-kleine-Stube-im Hofe an[19]. Da könnte[20]-ich wohnen, Essen-und-Trinken wolle[20]-er mir-geben; — und-so lebte-ich-denn in-diesem-Gasthofe acht-Wochen-lang ohne einen[21]-blutigen-Heller, in-lauter-Furcht-und-Angst. In-dem-weißen-Schwan[16] spannen Fuhrleute[22] aus und logiren da, und so kam denn öfters ein-gewisser-Advokat-B. dahin und hatte sein-Werk[23] mit-den-Fuhrleuten; mit-diesem wurde-ich-bekannt und klagte-ihm meine-unglücklichen-Fata[24]. Er-verobligir'te[25]-sich, meine-Gelder wieder-herbeizuschaffen, und ich-versprach-ihm für-seine-Bemühungen einen Louisdor[26]. Den-Augenblick mußte-ich mit-ihm-fortgehen, und so kamen-wir in-ein-großes-Haus; da ließ B. durch-einen-Bedienten sich an'melden, und wir-kamen in continenti[27] vor den Minist'er. Der-Advokat' trug die-Sache vor und-sagte unter-Anderem: „Wahr-ist-es, daß der-König die-Batzen ganz-und-gar verschlagen[3]-lassen[6]; sie-sollen in-seinem-Lande nicht-gelten[28], aber das-weiß der-Fremde-nicht. Ohnehin extendirt-sich[29] das-Edict nicht-so-weit, daß-man den-Leuten ihre-Batzen weg'nehmen-soll".—Hierauf fing der-Minist'er an zu-reden: „Monsieur, seid-Ihr der-Mann, der meines-Königs-Mandate durchlöchern-will? Ich-höre, Ihr-habt-Lust auf die-Hausvogtei[30]! Redet weiter, Ihr-sollt zu-der-Ehre gelangen[31]". — Was-thut mein-Advokat? Er-submittir'te[32]-sich und ging zum-Tempel-hinaus[33]; ich hinter-ihm-her, und als-ich auf-die-Straße-kam, so-war-B. über[34]-alle-Berge; und-so hatte-er-denn meine-Sache ausgemacht[35] bis-auf-die-streit'igen-Punk'te. Endlich wurde-mir der-

Rath-gegeben, den-König supplicando³⁶-anzutreten; das
Memorial'-aber müsse²⁰ ganz-kurz, gleichwohl-aber die-
contenta³⁷ darinnen-sein. Ich-concipir'te³⁸-eins, mun=
dirte³⁹ es und-ging-damit mit-dem-Aufschlusse-des-
Thores⁴⁰, ohne-nur-einen-Pfennig-Geld' in-der-Tasche zu-
haben (der Verwegenheit⁴¹!), in-Gottes=Namen⁴² nach-Pots=
dam, und-da war-ich-auch so-glücklich, sogleich den-König
zum-ersten-Male zu-sehen. Er-war auf-dem Schlosplatze⁴³
beim-Exerciren⁴⁴-seiner-Soldaten. Als-dieses vorbei-war,
ging-er in-den-Garten und-die-Soldaten auseinander;
vier-Offiziere-aber blieben auf-dem-Platze und-spazier'ten
auf-und-nieder. Ich-wußte vor-Angst nicht, was-ich-
machen-sollte, und-holte die-Papiere aus-der-Tasche. Das-
war das-Memorial', zwei-Testimonia⁴⁵ und ein-gedruckter-
thüringischer-Paß. Das-sahen die-Offiziere, kamen gerade-
auf-mich-zu und fragten, was⁴⁶-ich-da für-Briefe-hätte.
Ich-communicir'te⁴⁷ solche¹² willig-und-gern. Da-sie-ge=
lesen-hatten, so-sagten-sie: „Wir-wollen-Ihm einen-guten-
Rath-geben. Der-König ist heute extragnädig⁴⁸ und
ganz-allein in-den-Garten-gegangen. Gehe-Er ihm auf-dem-
Fuße⁴⁹-nach, Er-wird-glücklich-sein". Das wollte⁵⁰-ich-
nicht; die-Ehrfurcht war-zu-groß; da griffen⁵¹-sie zu.
Einer nahm-mich beim-rechten, der-andere beim-linken-
Arm. Fort, fort' in-den-Garten! Als-wir-nun dahin-
kamen, so suchten-sie den-König-auf. Er-war bei einem
Gewächse mit-den-Gärtnern, bückte-sich und-hatte-uns
den-Rücken-zugewendet. Hier mußte-ich-stehen, und die-
Offiziere fingen-an in-der-Stille⁵² zu-commandiren:
„Den-Hut unter-den-linken-Arm. — Den-rechten-Fuß
vor⁵³! — Die-Brust heraus⁵⁴! — Den-Kopf in-die-
Höhe⁵⁵! — Die-Briefe aus-der-Tasche! — Mit-der-rechten-
Hand-hochgehalten⁵⁶! — So steht!" — Sie-gingen-fort und
sahen-sich immer-um, ob-ich-auch so-würde-stehen-bleiben.
Ich-merkte-wohl, daß-sie-beliebten, ihren-Spaß' mit-mir-
zu-treiben, stand-aber wie-eine-Mauer, voller-Furcht.

Die-Offiziere waren-kaum aus-dem-Garten-hinaus, so-
richtete-sich der-König auf und sah die-Maschi'ne⁵⁷ in-un=

gewöhnlicher Positur'⁵⁸ da ſteh en. Er-that⁵⁹ einen-Blick-auf-
mich; es-war⁶⁰, als-wenn-mich die-Sonne durchſtrahlte;
er-ſchickte einen-Gärtner, die-Briefe abzuholen, und als-er
ſolche¹² in-die-Hände bekam, ging-er in-einen-anderen-
Gang⁶¹, wo-ich-ihn nicht-ſehen-konnte. Kurz-darauf kam-
er wieder-zurück zu-dem-Gewächſe, hatte die-Papiere in-
der-linken-Hand aufgeſchlagen⁶² und winkte-damit⁶³, näher-
zu-kommen. Ich-hatte das-Herz und-ging gerade⁶⁴ auf-ihn-
zu. O, wie allerhuldreichſt⁶⁵ redete-mich der-große-Monarch
an: „Lieber-Thüringer! Er-hat zu-Berlin durch-fleißiges-
Informiren⁶⁶ der-Kinder das-Brod⁶⁷-geſucht, und ſie-haben
Ihm beim-Viſitiren der-Sachen auf-dem-Packhofe Sein-
mitgebrachtes-thüringer-Brod⁶⁸ weggenommen. Wahr iſt-
es, die-Batzen ſollen in-meinem-Lande nichts-gelten²⁸;
aber ſie-hätten auf-dem-Packhofe ſagen-ſollen: „„Ihr-ſeid
ein-Fremder und-wiſſet das-Verbot-nicht. Wohlan, wir-
wollen den-Beutel-mit-den-Batzen verſiegeln; gebt
ſolche¹² wieder-zurück nach-Thüringen und laſſet⁷⁰-Euch
andere Sorten ſchicken⁷⁰,"" aber nicht wegnehmen⁷¹.
Gebe-Er-ſich zufrieden; Er-ſoll ſein-Geld cum inter-
esse⁷² zurück-erhalten. Aber, lieber Mann, Berlin iſt-
ſchon⁷³ ein-heißes-Pflaſter; ſie-verſchenken-da nichts; Er-iſt
ein-fremder-Menſch; ehe-Er bekannt-wird und Information'⁷⁴ bekommt, ſo-iſt das⁷⁵-bischen-Geld verzehrt; was
dann?" — Ich-verſtand die-Sprache recht-gut; die-
Ehrfurcht war-aber zu-groß, daß-ich hätte⁷⁶ ſagen-können:
Ew.*) Majeſtät' haben⁷⁷ die-allerhöchſte⁷⁸-Gnade und ver-
ſorgen-mich. — Weil-ich-aber ſo-einfältig-war und um-
nichts-bat, ſo wollte-er-mir auch-nichts-anbieten. — Und-
ſo ging-er-denn von-mir-weg, war-aber kaum-ſechs-bis-acht-
Schritte gegangen, ſo-ſah-er-ſich nach-mir-um und-gab
ein-Zeichen, daß-ich mit'-ihm-gehen-ſolle. — Und-ſo ging-
denn das-Examen an:

 Der-König: Wo hat-Er-ſtudirt?
 Ich: Ew.-Majeſtät', in Jena.

---

*) Read: Euer and cf. Rule 73.

Der-König: Unter-welchem-Pro'rector ist-Er inscri=
birt'⁷⁹-worden?
Ich: Unter-dem-Professor-Theologiae Dr. Förtsch.
Der-König: Was-waren-denn sonst-noch für-Pro=
fesso'ren in-der-theolo'gischen-Facultät?
Ich: Buddä'us*), Danz*), Weissenborn*), Walch*).
Der-König: Hat-Er-denn auch-fleißig Biblica⁸⁰ gehört?
Ich: Beim-Buddä'o.
Der-König: Das-ist der, der mit-Wolffen**) so-viel-
Krieg-hatte?
Ich: Ja, Ew. Majestät'. Es-war —
Der-König: Was hat-Er-denn sonst-noch für-nützliche-
Colle'gia gehört?
Ich: E'thica⁸¹ et Exege'tica⁸² beim-Dr.-Förtsch,
Hermeneu'tica⁸³ et Polemica⁸⁴ beim-Dr.-Walch, He-
braica⁸⁵ beim-Dr.-Danz, Homiletica beim-Dr.-Weissen=
born, Pastorale⁸⁷ et Morale⁸⁸ beim-Dr.-Buddä'o.
Der-König: Ging⁸⁹-es-denn zu Seiner-Zeit noch-so-
toll in Jena her⁸⁹, wie-ehedem⁹⁰ die-Studen'ten-sich⁹¹
ohne-Unterlaß mit-einander katz'balgten⁹¹, daher der-be-
kannte-Vers kommt:

Wer von-Jena-kommt ungeschlagen,
Der⁹² hat von-großem-Glück zu-sagen.

Ich: Diese-Un'sinnigkeit ist ganz-aus-der-Mode
gekommen, und man-kann-dort anjetzt⁹³ sowohl', als auf
anderen Universitä'ten, ein stilles-und-ruhiges-Leben-führen,
wenn-man-nur das-dic-cur-hic? observiren-will. Bei-
meinem-Anzuge⁹⁵ schafften die Durchl.†) Nutrito'res⁹⁶
Academicae (Ernesti'nischer⁹⁷-Li'nie) die-sogenann'ten Re=
nommisten⁹⁸ aus-dem-Wege und ließen-sie zu-Eisenach⁹⁹ auf-
die-Wartburg¹⁰⁰ in-Verwahrung-setzen; da haben-sie
gelernt ru'hig-sein.

---

*) Names of distinguished professors.
**) Christian Wolff, the well-known philosopher, born 24. Jan.
1679, died 9. April 1754.
†) Read Durchlauchtigen, their Graces.

Und-da schlug-die-Glocke Eins'. „Nun muß-ich-fort", sagte-der-König, „sie-warten auf-die-Suppe." Und-da-wir aus-dem-Garten-kamen, waren die-vier-Offizie're noch gegenwär'tig und auf-dem-Schloßplatze, die-gingen mit-dem-Könige in's-Schloß-hinein und-kam-keiner wieder-zurück'. Ich-blieb auf-dem-Schloßplatze stehen, hatte in-27-Stunden nichts genossen, nicht-einen-Dreier[101] in-bonis[102] zu-Brode und-war in-einer-vehemen'ten[103]-Hitze vier-Meilen[4] im-Sande-gewa'tet. Da-war's-wohl eine-Kunst, das-Heulen zu-verbeißen.

In-dieser-Ban'gigkeit meines-Herzens kam ein-Kam'merhusar[104]-aus-dem-Schlosse und fragte: „Wo-ist der-Mann, der mit-meinem-Könige in-dem-Garten gewesen?" Ich-antwortete: „Hier!" Dieser führte-mich in's-Schloß in-ein-großes-Gemach, wo Pagen, Lakaien, und Husa'ren-waren. Der-Husar' brachte-mich an-einen-kleinen-Tisch, der-war-gedeckt, und-stand darauf: eine-Suppe, ein-Gericht-Rindfleisch, eine-Portion'-Karpfen mit-einem-Gartensalat', eine-Portion'-Wild'pret mit-einem-Gurkensalat'. Brod, Messer, Gabel, Löffel, Salz war-Alles-da. Der-Husar' präsentir'te-mir einen-Stuhl und-sagte: „Die-Essen, die hier auf-dem-Tische-stehen, hat-Ihm der-König auftragen-lassen und befohlen, Er-soll-sich satt-essen, sich an-Niemand-kehren und ich-soll serviren[105]. Nun[106]-also frisch-daran[106]!" Ich-war sehr-betreten und wußte-nicht, was zu-thun-sei, am-wenigsten wollte-mir's in-den-Sinn, daß des-Königs Kam'mer-husar' auch-mich bedienen-sollte. — Ich-nöthigte[107]-ihn, sich zu-mir zu-setzen; als-er sich-weigerte, that-ich, wie-er gesagt-hatte, und ging-frisch-daran, nahm den-Löffel und fuhr[108]-tapfer ein. Der-Husar' nahm das-Fleisch vom-Tische und setzte-es auf-die-Kohlenpfanne; e'benso con-tinuir'te[109]-er mit-Fisch und-Braten und schenkte Wein-und-Bier ein. Ich-aß-und-trank-mich recht-satt. Den Confect'[110], dito einen-Teller voll-großer-schwarzer Kirschen und einen-Teller voll-Birnen packte mein-Be-dienter in's-Papier' und senkte[111]-mir solche[12] in-die-

Tasche, auf-dem Rückwege eine Erfrisch'ung-zu-haben. Und-
so stand-ich-denn von-meiner-königlichen-Tafel auf, dankte-
Gott und dem-Könige von Herzen, daß-ich so-herrlich ge-
speiset-worden. Der Husar' räumte-auf! Den-Augenblick
trat ein-Secreta'rius herein und-brachte ein-verschlossenes-
Rescript an-den-Packhof nebst-meinen-Testimo'niis und
dem-Passe zurück, zählte auf-den-Tisch fünf Schwanz-
ducaten und einen-Fried'richsd'or: „Das schicke²⁰-mir
der-König, daß ich wieder-zurück nach-Berlin', kommen-
könnte."

Hatte¹¹²-mich-nun der-Husar' in's-Schloß-hineinge-
führt, so-brachte-mich der-Secreta'rius wieder bis-vor-das-
Schloß hinaus. Und-da-hielt ein-königlicher-Proviant-
wagen mit-sechs-Pferden-bespannt; zu-dem brachte-er-
mich-hin und-sagte: „Ihr-Leute¹¹³, der-König hat-be-
fohlen, Ihr-sollt diesen-Fremden mit-nach-Berlin'-fahren,
aber kein-Trink'geld von-ihm-nehmen." Ich-ließ¹¹⁴-mich
durch-den-Secreta'rium noch-einmal unterthänigst-be-
danken für-alle-königliche-Gnade, setzte-mich auf und-
fuhr davon.

Als-wir nach-Berlin'-kamen, ging-ich sogleich auf-den-
Packhof, gerade in-die-Expeditions'stube¹¹⁵, und-über-
reichte das-königliche-Rescript'. Der-O'berste¹¹⁶ erbrach-
es; bei-Lesung-desselben verfärbte-er sich, bald-bleich,
bald-roth, schwieg-still und gab-es dem-zweiten. Dieser
nahm eine-Prise-Schnupftabak, räusperte-und-schneuzte-
sich, setzte eine-Brille auf, las-es, schwieg-still und-gab-
es-weiter. Der-Letzte endlich regte-sich, ich-sollte-näher-
kommen und eine-Quittung-schreiben: Daß-ich für meine-
400 Reichsthaler ganze-Batzen so-viel an-brandenburger
Münzsorten, ohne-den-mindesten-Abzug, erhalten.
Meine-Summe wurde-mir sogleich'-richtig-zu'gezählt. Darauf wurde der-Schaffner¹¹⁷ gerufen, mit-der-Ordre: er-
sollte mit-mir auf-die-Jüdenstraße in-den-weißen-
Schwan gehen und-bezahlen, was-ich-schuldig-wäre und-
verzehrt-hätte, dazu gaben-sie-ihm 24-Thaler, und-wenn-
das nicht-zureichte, solle-er-kommen und-mehr-holen.

Das-war-es, daß der-König-sagte: „Er-soll seine-Gelder cum interesse wieder bekommen," daß der-Packhof meine-Schulden bezahlen-mußte. Es-waren-aber nur 10 Thaler[118] 4 Groschen[119] 6 Pfennige[120], die ich in-acht-Wochen verzehrt-hatte, und so-hatte-denn die-betrübende-Historie ihr erwünschtes-Ende.

1. Customhouse. 2. 400 dollars (about 3s. each), in Nürnberg batzen (about 2d. each). 3. recoin, decry. 4. One German mile is equivalent to $4^4{}_5$ English miles. 5. dero, obs. for derer: his, her, your. 6. laſſen, elliptic for Perf. Tense (habe gelaſſen); cf. Rule 384. 7. sagte, understood. 8. are current. 9. mir ja, from me, indeed. 10. That is your own look-out and I want you at once to understand (cf. Rule 55). 11. ſind, understood. 12. ſolche, for: ſie. 13. porter with his wheelbarrow. 14. luggage, traps. 15. Jüdenſtraße (Jews-street), street in the older part of Berlin much inhabited by Jewish small-tradesmen. 16. der weiße Schwan, hostelry called: the white swan. 17. a complete set of bedding. 18. linen. 19. wies mir ... an, showed me to. 20. Subj. mood, owing to indirect speech. sagte er, man, understood. 21. without as much as a farthing. 22. Sing. Fuhrmann, carter, waggoner. 23. work, dealings. 24. fata (Latin), fate; NB. the somewhat pedantic howbeit learned young curate and tutor is fond of Latin and other foreign terms as will be seen throughout the story. 25. (barbarous term) he obliged or bound himself, undertook. 26. Louidor, gold coin, about 16s. 6d. 27. together. 28. nicht gelten, have no currency. 29. extends, goes. 30. Luſt auf, a desire for, die Hausvogtei, a prison of that name in Berlin. 31. you shall (obtain) have that honour, namely to be taken to the Hausvogtei. 32. submitted, took the snubbing. 33. humorously: out of the lion's den. 34. über alle Berge, not to be seen, off. gone. 35. ausgemacht bis auf, won, carried, managed except. 36. supplicando anzutreten, to petition. 37. Latin, the contents, facts. 38. drew up. 39. made a clean copy of. 40. at the opening of the town-gate; formerly the gates of towns in Germany were locked during the night. 41. exclamation in the Genitive: fancy my boldness! 42. pious interjection: confidently, without fear. 43. Schloßplatz, the place or square in front of the Schloss (castle- or palace-square). 44. busy drilling. 45. Latin: testimonials, certificates. 46. was ... für, what kind of. 47. communicate, gave. 48. specially gracious. 49. auf dem Fuße, in his track, closely. 50. wollte ich, elliptic, thun, understood. 51. then they seized me. 52. in an undertone. 53. forward. 54. chest out! 55. up. 56. hold them up; about the use of the Part. instead of Imp. cf. Rule 383. 57. humorous: machine, engine, automaton; referring of course to his ludicrous position. 58. position. 59. (did) cast. 60. mir understood: I felt.

61. walk, alley. 62. opened-up. 63. (therewith) with them. 64. straight up to him. 65. how most graciously. 66. teaching. 67. to make a living. 68. savings. 69. hätten... sagen sollen, ought to have said. 70. lasset Euch... schicken, let them send you. 71. but ought not to have taken them away, sie hätten sollen understood. 72. with interest. 73. schon... Pflaster, a hot place, I fear. 74. teaching. 75. what little money you have. 76. hätte sagen können, for: sagen gekonnt hätte, could have said. 77. haben, Imp. may or will have. 78. allerhöchst, term applied to kings by their humble subjects, meaning: very great, royal, etc. 79. enrolled. 80. biblical theology. 81. ethics. 82. exegesis. 83. hermeneutics. 84. polemics. 85. Hebrew. 86. homiletics. 87. pastoral theology. 88. moral philosophy. 89. ging es... so toll... her, were things going on as madly or rowdily. 90. as formerly when. 91. were fighting. 92. der... sagen, he has to speak of great good luck, he may thank his stars. 93. anjetzt, obs., now. 94. die cur hic, say why are you here? i. e., remember what you are here for. 95. when I entered college. 96. (nursers) patrons of the university. 97. Ernestian line is the older, the ducal branch of the Saxon princely house (Coburg and Gotha, etc.) 98. bully, duellist, braggard; the term was specially applied to students of last century. 99. Eisenach, capital of Saxe-Weimar-Eisenach; Luther attented the Latin school there. 100. Wartburg, castle above Eisenach, situated at the northwest point of the Thuringian forest, famous through Luther's stay there and bible-translation. 101. farthing. 102. in bonis; in my fortune or possession. 103. scorching. 104. personal attendant of the king (dressed like a hussar). 105. wait on you. 106. Now, therefore, walk into it! 107. pressed. 108. made a gallant onslaught. 109. he continued, did. 110. sweetmeats. 111. (sunk) dropped. 112. just as the hussar had conducted me. 113. my lads! 114. Ich ließ... bedanken, I sent thanks to, I thanked the king. 115. forwarding-room, clearing-office. 116. head-official. 117. steward, porter. 118. 1 Thaler = 3 s. 119. 1 Groschen — 1¼ d. 120. 1 Pfennig -= ¹⁄₁₀ d.

II.

Böser Markt.*)
A Bad Bargain.

In-der-großen-Stadt-London und rings-um-sie-her gibt-es außerordentlich-viel gute-Narren, die an-anderer-

---
*) *Note.* Nouns which are mostly emphatic are easily recognisable by the capital with which all of them or their substitutes begin; they are therefore not always printed in special types.

Leute-Geld oder Sackuhren oder kostbaren-Fingerringen
eine-kindliche-Freude haben und nicht-ruhen, bis-sie die-
selben haben. Dies bringen-sie zuweg manch'mal durch-
List-und-Betrug, noch-öfter durch-kühnen-An'griff,
manchmal am-hellen-lichten-Tag und an-der-offenen Land=
straße. Einem geräth-es, dem-andern nicht. Der-
Kerkermeister zu-London und der-Scharfrichter wissen
davon-zu-erzählen. Eine-seltsame-Geschichte begegnete-
aber eines-Tags einem-vornehmen-und-reichen-Mann. Der
König und viele-andere-große-Herren-und-Frauen
waren an-einem-schönen-Sommertage in-einem-großen-königs
lichen Garten versammelt, dessen lange-gewundene-Gänge
sich in-der-Ferne in-einen-Wald verloren. Viele-andere-
Personen waren auch zugegen, denen-es-nicht auf-einen-
Gang und auf-ein-paar-Stunden an'kam, ihren-geliebten-
König und seine-Familie froh und glücklich zu-sehen.
Man-aß und-trank; man-spielte und-tanzte; man-ging-
spazieren in-den-schönen-Gängen und zwischen-dem-duften-
den-Rosengebüsch, paarweise und-allein, wie-es-sich-
traf. Da stellte-sich ein-Mensch, wohl-gekleidet, als
wenn-er auch-dazu gehörte, mit-einer-Pistole unter-dem
Rock, in-einer-ab'gelegenen-(Gegend an-einen-Baum, wo
der-Garten an-den-Wald grenzt, dachte, es-wird-schon Jemand
kommen. Wie-gesagt, so-geschehen, kommt ein-Herr
mit-funkelndem Fingerringe, mit klingenden-Uhrketten,
mit-diamantnen-Schnallen, mit-breitem-Ordensband und
goldnem-Stern, will-spazieren-gehn im-kühlen-Schatten,
und-denkt an-nichts. Indem-er an-nichts-denkt, kommt
der-Geselle hinter-dem Baum-hervor, macht dem-guten-
Herrn ein-bescheidenes Kompliment', zieht die-Pisto'le
zwischen-dem-Rock und Kamisol' heraus, richtet ihr-Maul
auf-des-Herrn-Brust, und bittet-ihn höflich, keinen-Lärm'
zu-machen, es-brauche Niemand zu-wissen, was-sie mit-
einander zu-reden-haben. Man-muß übel-dran-sein, wenn-
man vor-einer-Pisto'le-steht, weil-man nicht weiß, was-
d'rin-steckt. Der-Herr dachte vernünftig: „der-Leib ist
kostbarer als das-Geld; lieber den-Ring verloren, als den-

Finger;" und versprach zu-schweigen. „Gnädiger-Herr,"
fuhr jetzt der-Geselle fort. „wären-Euch Eure-zwei-goldenen
Uhren nicht-feil für gute Bezahlung? Unser-Schulmeister
richtet die-Uhr alle-Tage anders, man-weiß-nie wie-man-dran-
ist, und an-der-Sonnenuhr sind die-Zahlen verwischt."
Will der-reiche-Herr wohl-oder-übel, so-muß-er dem Ha-
lun'ken die-Uhren verkaufen für ein-Paar Stüber*) oder-
etwas, so-man kaum-ein-Schöpplein dafür trinken kann.
Und-so handelt-ihm der-Spitzbube Ring-und-Schnallen und
Ordenstern und-das-goldene-Herz, so**)-er vorne-auf-der-Brust
im-Hemd hatte, Stück-für-Stück ab, um-schlechtes-Geld,
und-immer mit-der-Pistole in-der-linken-Hand. Als-endlich
der Herr dachte: „Jetzt bin-ich absolvirt, Gottlob!"
fing der-Spitzbube von-Neuem an: „Gnädiger-Herr,
weil wir so-gut mit-einander zurecht-kommen, wolltet-Ihr
mir-nicht-auch von-meinen-Waaren etwas-abhandeln?" Der-
Herr denkt an-das Sprichwort, man-müsse zu-einem-bösen-
Markt ein-gutes-Gesicht' machen, und sagt: „Laßt-sehen!" Da-
zog der-Bursche allerlei-Kleinigkeiten aus der-Tasche-hervor,
so**)-er vom-Zweibatzen-Krämer†) gekauft oder auch-
schon auf-einer-ungewischten-Bank gefunden-hatte,††) und
der-gute-Herr mußte-ihm Alles-abkaufen. Als-endlich der-
Spitzbube nichts mehr als die-Pistole übrig-hatte, und-sah,
daß der-Herr noch-ein-paar-Dublo'nen in-dem-grünen-seidenen-
Geldbeutel-hatte, sprach-er-noch: „Gnädiger-Herr, wolltet-
Ihr-mir für-den-Rest, den Ihr da-in-den-Händen habt,
nicht die-Pistole abkaufen? Sie-ist-vom-besten-Büchsen-
schmied in-London, und zwei-Dublonen unter-Brüdern
werth." Der-Herr dachte in-der-Überraschung: „Du-
dummer-Dieb!" und kauft die-Pistole. Als-er-aber die-Pistole
gekauft-hatte, kehrte-er-den-Stiel um, und-sprach: „Nun
halt, sauberer-Geselle, und-geh'augenblicklich voraus, wohin
ich-dich-heißen-werde, oder ich schieße-dich auf-der-Stelle

---

*) A coin of small value, say: for a few coppers.
**) Obs. for welcher, -e, -es, which.
†) Penny-toyshop.
††) Humorous for: stolen.

tödt." Der-Spitzbube-aber nahm-einen-Sprung in-den-Wald, und sagte: „Schießt herzhaft los, gnädiger-Herr, sie-ist nicht-geladen." Der Herr drückte-ab, und es-ging-wirklich nicht-los. Er-ließ den-Lauf fallen, und-es war kein-Körnlein-Pulver darin. Der-Dieb-aber war unter=dessen schon tief-im Wald; und der-vor'nehme-Engländer ging scham'roth zurück, daß-er-sich-also habe in-Schreck-setzen-lassen, und dachte an-Vieles.   Hebel.

III.
Der-silberne-Löffel.
The Silver Spoon.

In-Wien dachte ein-Offizier: Ich will doch-auch-einmal im-rothen-Ochsen zu-Mittag-essen, und-geht in-den-rothen-Ochsen. Da-waren bekannte und unbekannte-Menschen, Vornehme und Mittelmäßige, ehrliche-Leute und Spitz=buben, wie überall'. Man-aß und-trank, der-Eine viel, der-Andere wenig. Man-sprach und disputir'te von-dem und-jenem, zum-Exempel von-dem-Stein'regen bei-Stannern-in-Mähren, von dem-Mach in-in-Frankreich, der mit-dem-großen-Wolf gekämpft-hat. — Als-nun das-Essen fast-vorbei-war, Einer und der-Andere trank noch-eine-halbe-Maas-Ungarwein zum-Zu'spitzen, ein-Anderer drehte Kügelein aus-weichem-Brod, als wenn er ein-Apothe'ker wär', und wollte Pillen-machen, ein-Dritter spielte mit-dem-Messer oder mit-der-Gabel, oder mit-einem-sil'bernen-Löffel; da-sah der-Offizier' von-ungefähr' zu, wie Einer, in-einem-grünen-Rock, mit dem-sil'bernen-Löffel-spielte, und wie-ihm der-Löffel auf-einmal in den Rock'ärmel hinein'schlüpfte und nicht-wieder-her aus-kam.

Ein-Anderer hätte-gedacht: Was geht's-mich-an? und wäre still-dazu-gewesen, oder hätte großen-Lärm an'gefangen. Der-Offizier dachte: Ich-weiß nicht, wer der-grüne-Löffelschütz ist, und was für-einen-Verdruß es geben kann, und war mausstill, bis. der-Wirth-kam und das-Geld'-einzog. Als der-Wirth kam und das-Geld-einzog, nahm der-Offizier'

auch einen-silbernen Löffel und steckte-ihn zwischen-zwei-
Knopflöcher-im-Rocke, zu-einem hinein' zum-andern hin=
aus', wie-es manchmal die-Soldaten im-Kriege machen,
wenn-sie den-Löffel mit'bringen, aber keine-Suppe.—Wäh'rend=
dem' der-Offizier' seine-Zeche-bezahlte, und der-Wirth schaute-
ihm auf-den-Rock, dachte-er: „Das ist ein-kurio'ser-Ver=
dienstorden, den der-Herr-da an'hängen-hat. Der muß-
sich im-Kampf mit-einer-Krebssuppe hervor'gethan-haben,
daß-er zum-Ehrenzeichen einen-silbernen-Löffel bekommen-
hat, oder ist's-gar einer von-meinen-ei'genen?" Als-aber der-
Offizier dem-Wirth die-Zeche bezahlt-hatte, sagte-er mit ernst=
hafter-Miene: „Und der-Löffel geht-ja-drein. Nicht wahr?
Die-Zeche ist theuer-genug dazu." Der-Wirth sagte: „so-
etwas ist mir noch-nicht-vor'gekommen. Wenn-Ihr keinen-
Löffel daheim habt, so will-ich-Euch einen-Patent'löffel
schenken, aber meinen-sil'bernen laßt-mir da." Da-stand
der-Offizier-auf, klopfte dem-Wirth auf-die-Achsel und
lächelte. „Wir-haben nur Spaß-gemacht," sagte-er, „ich und
der-Herr-dort in-dem-grünen-Rock. Gebt-Ihr Euern Löffel
wieder aus-dem-Ärmel heraus, grüner-Herr, so will-ich
meinen auch' wieder-her'geben." Als der-Löffelschütz merkte,
daß-er verra'then-sei, und daß ein-ehrliches-Auge auf seine-un=
ehrliche-Hand gesehen-hatte, dachte er: Lieber Spaß als
Ernst, und gab seinen Löffel ebenfalls' her. Also kam
der-Wirth wieder zu-seinem-Eigenthum, und der-Löffel=
dieb lachte-auch, — aber nicht-lange. Denn als die-
andern-Gäste das sahen, jagten-sie den-verrathenen-Dieb
mit-Schimpf und-Schande und ein paar-Tritten unter-
der-Thüre zum-Tempel-hinaus, und der-Wirth schickte-ihm
den Hausknecht mit-einer-Handvoll ungebrannter-Asche*) nach.
Den wackern-Offizier' aber bewirthete-er-noch mit-einer-
Flasche Ung'arwein auf-das-Wohlsein aller-ehrlichen-
Leute.

Hebel.

*) Humorous for: stick.

IV.

FOR RECITATION.

NB. The single accent (') is meant to indicate an important word or syllable, and the double accent (") the most important word in the sentence, to be stressed accordingly.

He'ro und Lean'der.

1. Seht-ihr dort die-al'tergrauen
Schlösser sich-entge'genschauen,
Leuch'tend in-der-Sonne-Gold',
Wo der-Hellespont' die-Wel'len
Brau'send durch-der-Dardanel'len
Hohe-Fel"senpforte rollt?
Hört-ihr jene-Bran'dung stürmen,
Die-sich an-den-Felsen bricht?
A'sien riß-sie von-Euro'pen;
Doch die-Lie"be schreckt'-sie-nicht.

2. Heros und Leanders Her'zen
Rührte mit-dem-Pfeil' der-Schmer'zen
A'mors heil'ge-Göt'termacht.
He'ro, schön wie-He'be blühend,
Er' durch-die-Gebirge ziehend
Rüstig im-Geräusch der-Jagd.
Doch der-Väter feindlich-Zür'nen
Trenn"te das-verbundne-Paar',
Und die-süße-Frucht-der-Lie"be
Hing am-Ab"grund der-Gefahr'.

3. Dort auf-Sestos'-Fel"senthurme,
Den mit-ew'gem-Wo"gensturme
Schäumend schlägt der-Hellespont',
Saß die-Jung'frau, einsam-grauend,
Nach-Aby'dos-Küste schauend,
Wo der-Heißgelieb'te wohnt.
Ach, zu-dem-entfern'ten-Strande
Baut-sich keiner-Brücke-Steg',
Und kein-Fahr'zeug stößt vom-Ufer,
Doch die-Lie"be fand' den-Weg.

4. Aus des-Labyrin'thes-Pfa"den
Leitet-sie mit-sicherm-Fa"den,
Auch den-Blö'den macht-sie klug,
Beugt ins-Joch die-wilden-Thie're,
Spannt die-feuersprüh'nden Stiere
An-den-diamant'nen Pflug,
Selbst der-Styx', der neun'fach fließet,
Schließt die-Wa'gende nicht-aus;
Mäch'tig raubt-sie das-Gelieb'te
Aus-des-Pluto finsterm-Haus.

5. Auch durch-des-Gewäs"sers-Fluthen
Mit-der-Sehn'sucht feur'gen Gluthen
Stachelt-sie Leanders-Muth.
Wenn des-Ta'ges heller-Schimmer
Bleichet, stürzt der-kühne-Schwim'mer
In-des-Pon'tus finstre-Fluth,
Theilt mit-starkem-Arm die-Wo'ge,
Stre'bend nach-dem-theuren-Strand,
Wo, auf-hohem-Söl'ler leuchtend,
Winkt der-Fa'ckel heller-Brand.

6. Und in-weichen-Lie'besarmen
Darf der-Glückliche erwar'men
Von-der-schwer bestandnen Fahrt',
Und den-Göt'terlohn empfangen,
Den in se'ligem Umfang"en,
Ihm die Lie'be auf'gespart,
Bis den-Säu'menden Aurora
Aus-der-Won'ne-Träu"men weckt
Und ins-kalte-Bett' des-Mee"res
Aus-dem-Schooß' der-Lie"be schreckt.

7. Und so-flohen dreißig-Son'nen
Schnell, im-Raub-verstohlner-Won'nen,
Dem-beglückten-Paar' dahin",
Wie-der-Braut"nacht süße-Freuden,
Die die-Göt"ter-selbst beneiden
E'wig-jung" und e'wig-grün".

Der' hat-nie das-Glück gekostet,
Der die-Frucht des-Him'mels nicht
Rau'bend an-des-Höl'lenflusses
Schau'ervollem-Ran"de bricht.

8. Hes'per-und-Auro'ra zogen
Wechselnd-auf am-Himmelsbogen,
Doch die-Glück'lichen, sie-sahn
Nicht den-Schmuck der-Blät'ter fallen,
Nicht aus-Nords' beeis'ten-Hal'len
Den ergrimm'ten Win"ter nahn.
Freu'dig sahen-sie des-Tages
Immer-kür'zern, kür'zern-Kreis;
Für-das-läng're-Glück der Näch'te
Dankten-sie bethört dem-Zeus.

9. Und es-gleichte-schon die-Wa'ge
An-dem-Himmel Nächt"-und-Ta'ge,
Und-die-holde-Jung'frau stand
Har'rend auf-dem-Fel'senschlosse,
Sah hinab die-Son'nenrosse
Fliehen an-des-Himmels-Rand'.
Und das-Meer' lag still-und-eben,
Einem-reinem-Spie'gel gleich,
Keines Win'des leises-Weben
Regte das-kryftall'ne Reich.

10. Lustige Delphi"nenschaaren
Scherz'ten in-dem-sil'berklaren,
Reinen-Element' umher,
Und in-schwärzlicht-grauen-Zü'gen
Aus dem-Meer"grund aufgestiegen,
Kam der-Te'thys buntes-Heer.
Sie, die-Ein'zigen, bezeugten
Den-verstohlnen-Lie'besbund;
Aber ihnen schloß auf-e'wig
He'kate den-stummen-Mund'.

11. Und sie-freu'te-sich des-schönen
Mee'res, und mit-Schmei'cheltönen

Sprach sie zu dem Element:
"Schöner Gott, du solltest trügen!
Nein, den Frevler straf' ich Lügen,
Der dich falsch und treulos nennt.
Falsch ist das Geschlecht der Menschen,
Grausam ist des Vaters Herz;
Aber du bist mild und gütig,
Und dich rührt der Liebe Schmerz."

12. "In den öden Felsenmauern
Müsst' ich freudlos einsam trauern
Und verblühn in ew'gem Harm;
Doch du trägst auf deinem Rücken,
Ohne Nachen, ohne Brücken,
Mir den Freund in meinen Arm.
Grauenvoll ist deine Tiefe,
Furchtbar deiner Wogen Fluth,
Aber dich erfleht die Liebe,
Dich bezwingt der Heldenmuth."

13. "Denn auch dich", den Gott der Wogen,
Rührte Eros' mächt'ger Bogen,
Als des gold'nen Widders Flug
Helle, mit dem Bruder fliehend,
Schön in Jugendfülle blühend,
Über deine Tiefe trug.
Schnell, von ihrem Reiz besieget,
Grifffst du aus dem finstern Schlund,
Zogst sie von des Widders Rücken
Nieder in den Meeresgrund."

14. "Eine Göttinn mit dem Gotte,
In der tiefen Wassergrotte,
Lebt sie jetzt unsterblich fort;
Hilfreich der verfolgten Liebe,
Zähmt sie deine wilden Triebe,
Führt den Schiffer in den Port.
Schöne Helle, holde Göttinn,
Sel'ige, dich fleh' ich an:

Bring' auch-heute den-Geliebten
Mir auf-der-gewohnten-Bahn!"

15. Und schon dunkelten die-Fluthen,
Und sie-ließ der-Fackel Gluthen
Von-dem-hohen-Söller wehn.
Leitend in-den-öden-Reichen
Sollte das-vertrau'te-Zeichen
Der-geliebte-Wand'rer sehn. — — —
Und es-saust' und-dröhnt' von-ferne,
Finster' kräu'selt-sich das-Meer,
Und es-löscht' das-Licht der-Sterne
Und es-naht gewit'ter-schwer.

16. Auf des-Pontus weite-Fläche
Legt-sich Nacht', und Wet'terbäche
Stürzen aus-der-Wolken-Schooß,
Blitze zucken in-den-Lüften,
Und aus-ihren-Fel'sengrüften
Werden alle-Stürme los,
Wühlen ungeheure-Schlünde
In-den-weiten Wasserschlund;
Gäh'nend, wie ein-Höl'lenrachen,
Öffnet-sich des-Meeres-Grund.

17. „Wehe, weh mir!" ruft die-Arme
Jam'mernd. „Großer-Zeus', erbar'me!
Ach, was wagt'-ich zu-erflehn!
Wenn die-Götter mich-erhören,
Wenn er-sich den-falschen Mee'ren
Preis'-gab in-des-Sturmes-Wehn!
Alle meer'gewohnten-Vögel
Ziehen-heim', in-eil'ger-Flucht;
Alle-sturm'erprobten-Schif'fe
Ber'gen-sich in-sichrer-Bucht".

18. „Ach, gewiß, der-Unverzag'te
Unter n a h m' das-oft-Gewag'te,
Denn ihn' trieb ein-mächt'ger-Gott'.
Er-gelob'te mir's beim-Scheiden

Mit der-Lie'be heil'gen-Eiden,
Ihn-entbin'det nur der-Tod.
Ach, in diesem-Augenblicke
Ringt-er mit-des-Sturmes-Wuth,
Und hinab in-ihre-Schlünde
Reißt-ihn die-empörte-Fluth!"

19. „Fal'scher-Pon"tus, deine-Stille
War-nur des-Verra'thes Hülle,
Einem-Spie'gel warst-du gleich;
Tück'isch ruhten deine-Wogen,
Bis du-ihn heraus'-betrogen
In-dein-falsches-Lü'genreich.
Jetzt, in-deines-Stromes-Mit'te,
Da die-Rückkehr sich-verschloß',
Lässest-du an-dem-Verrath'nen
Alle-deine-Schrecken los!"

20. Und es-wächst des-Sturmes-Toben,
Hoch, zu-Ber"gen auf'gehoben,
Schwillt das-Meer, die-Brandung bricht
Schäu'mend sich am-Fuß der-Klip'pen;
Selbst das-Schiff' mit-Ei'chenrippen
Nahte unzerschmet'tert nicht.
Und im-Wind erlischt die-Fack'el,
Die des-Pfades-Leuch'te war;
Schreck"en bietet das-Gewäs'ser,
Schreck"en auch die-Lan'dung dar.

21. Und sie-fleht zur-Aphrodi'te,
Daß sie dem-Orkan gebie'te,
Sänf'tige der-Wellen-Zorn,
Und gelobt', den strengen-Winden
Reiche-Op'fer anzuzünden,
Einen-Stier' mit-goldnem-Horn.
Alle-Göt'tinnen der-Tiefe,
Alle-Götter in-der-Höh'
Fleht-sie, lindernd-Öl' zu-gießen
In-die-sturm'bewegte-See'.

22. „Höre meinen-Ruf erschal'len,
Steig' aus-deinen-grünen Hal'len,
Se'lige-Leuko'thea!
Die der-Schiffer in-dem-öden
Wel'lenreich, in Stur'mesnöthen
Rettend oft erschei'nen-sah.
Reich' ihm deinen-heil'gen-Schleier,
Der, geheim'nissvoll gewebt,
Die ihn tragen, un'verletz'lich
Aus-dem-Grab der-Fluthen hebt!"

23. Und die-wilden-Winde schwei'gen,
Hell an-Himmels-Rande steigen
Eos'-Pfer'de in-die-Höh'.
Friedlich in-dem-alten-Bet'te
Fließt das-Meer' in-Spiegelglätte,
Heiter lächeln Luft-und-See.
Sanf'ter brechen-sich die-Wellen
An-des-Ufers Fel'senwand,
Und sie-schwem'men, ruhig-spie'lend,
Einen-Leich"nam an-den-Strand.

24. Ja, er-ist's, der auch-entsee'let
Seinem-heil'gen-Schwur' nicht feh'let!
Schnellen-Blicks erkennt'-sie ihn.
Keine-Kla'ge läßt-sie schallen,
Keine-Thrä'ne sieht-man fallen,
Kalt, verzweifelnd starrt-sie hin.
Trost'los in-die-öde-Tie'fe
Blickt-sie, in-des A'thers-Licht,
Und ein-ed'les-Feu'er röthet
Das-erbleichte-An'gesicht.

25. „Ich-erkenn' euch, ernste-Mächte!
Streng'e treibt-ihr eure-Rechte,
Furcht'bar, un'erbitt'lich ein.
Früh-schon ist mein-Lauf beschlossen;
Doch das-Glück' hab'-ich genossen,
Und das schön'ste Loos war mein'.

Lebend hab'-ich deinem-Tempel
Mich-geweiht als Prie"sterinn;
Dir ein-freu'dig-Op'fer sterb'-ich,
Ve'nus, große-Königinn!"

26. Und mit-flie'gendem-Gewan'de
Schwingt-sie von-des-Thurmes Rande
In-die-Meer'fluth sich hinab.
Hoch in-seinen-Flu'thenreichen
Wälzt-der-Gott die-heil'gen-Leichen,
Und er-sel'ber ist ihr-Grab'.
Und mit-seinem-Raub zufrie'den,
Zieht-er freu'dig fort' und gießt
Aus-der-un'erschöpften-Ur'ne
Seinen-Strom', der e'wig-fließt.

Schiller.

V.
A'mor als Land"schaftsmaler.

Saß'-ich früh auf-einer-Fel"senspitze,
Sah mit-starren-Au'gen in den Ne"bel;
Wie ein-grau-grundir'tes-Tuch" gespan'net
Deckt'-er Alles in-die-Breit' und Höhe.

Stellt ein-Kna"be-sich mir-an-die-Sei'te,
Sagt: Lieber-Freund, wie magst-du starrend
Auf-das-leere-Tuch" gelassen-schau'en?
Hast-du-denn zum-Malen und-zum-Bilden
Alle-Lust auf-e'wig wohl-verloren?

Sah-ich-an' das-Kind und dachte heimlich:
Will das-Bübchen doch den-Mei"ster machen!
Willst-du immer trüb'-und-müßig bleiben,
Sprach der-Kna'be, kann nichts-Klu'ges-werden:
Sieh, ich-will-dir gleich ein-Bild'chen malen,
Dich ein-hübsches-Bildchen malen-leh'ren:
Und er-richtete den-Zei'gefinger,
Der so-röth"lich-war wie-eine-Rose,

Nach-dem-weiten aus'gespannten Tep"pich,
Fing mit-seinem-Finger an' zu-zeich"nen:
O'ben malt'-er eine-schöne-Son"ne,
Die mir in-die-Augen mächtig-glänz'te,
  Und den-Saum'-der-Wolken macht'-er gol"den,
Ließ die-Strah'len durch-die-Wolken dringen,
Malte-dann die-zarten-lichten-Wipfel
Frisch-erquickter-Bäu"me, zog die-Hü"gel,
Ei'nen nach-dem-an'dern, frei-dahin'ter;
Un'ten ließ-er's-nicht an-Was'ser-fehlen,
Zeichnete den-Fluß so-ganz-natür'lich,
Daß er-schien im-Son'nenstrahl zu gli"tzern,
Daß er-schien am-hohen-Rand' zu rau"schen.
  Ach", da-standen-Blu'men an-dem-Flusse,
Und da-waren Far'ben auf-der-Wiese,
Gold und Schmelz' und Pur'pur und ein-Grünes,
Alles wie Smaragd" und wie Karfun"kel!
Hell'-und-rein lasirt"'-er d'rauf den-Him"mel
Und die-blauen-Ber"ge fern-und-ferner,
Daß ich ganz-entzückt und neugeboren
Bald den-Maler, bald das-Bild" beschaute.
  Hab'-ich-doch, so-sagt'-er, dir-bewie'sen,
Daß-ich dieses-Handwerk gut-verste'he;
Doch es-ist das-Schwer'ste noch-zurü"cke.
  Zeichnete danach mit-spitzem-Finger,
Und mit-großer-Sorgfalt an-dem-Wäldchen,
Grad' an's En'de, wo die-Sonne kräftig
Von dem-hellen-Boden wi"derglänzte,
Zeichnete das-allerlieb'ste-Mäd"chen,
Wohlgebil'det, zierlich-an'gekleidet,
Frische-Wangen unter-braunen-Haaren,
Und die-Wang'en waren von-der-Farbe,
Wie das-Fing"erchen, das sie gebildet.
  O du Knabe! rief-ich, welch'-ein-Meister
Hat in-seine-Schule dich-genommen,
Daß-du so-geschwind' und so-natür'lich
Alles klug-beginnst' und gut-vollen'dest?

Da-ich noch-so-re'de, sieh", da-rühret
Sich-ein-Wind'chen und-bewegt die-Gip'fel,
Kräu'selt alle-Wellen auf dem-Fluſ'ſe,
Füllt den-Schleier' des-vollkomm'nen-Mädchens,
Und-was mich-Erſtaunten mehr-erſtaunte,
Fängt das-Mädchen an' den Fuß zu-rühren,
Geht zu-kom'men, nä'hert-ſich dem-Or'te,
Wo-ich mit-dem-loſen-Lehrer ſitz'e.
  Da-nun Al'les, Al'les ſich-bewegte,
Bäume, Fluß und Blumen und der-Schleier,
Und der-zarte-Fuß' der-Allerſchön"ſten:
Glaubt'-ihr-wohl, ich-ſei auf-meinem-Felſen
Wie ein-Felſen ſtill'-und-feſt" geblieben?

Goethe.

14, Henrietta Street, Covent Garden, London; and
20, South Frederick Street, Edinburgh.

WILLIAMS AND NORGATE'S
LIST OF

French, German, Italian, Latin and Greek,

AND OTHER

SCHOOL BOOKS AND MAPS.

French.

FOR PUBLIC SCHOOLS WHERE LATIN IS TAUGHT.

Eugène (G.) **The Student's Comparative Grammar of the French Language**, with an Historical Sketch of the Formation of French. For the use of Public Schools. With Exercises. By G. Eugène-Fasnacht, French Master, Westminster School. 11th Edition, thoroughly revised. Square crown 8vo, cloth. 5s.

Or Grammar, 3s.; Exercises, 2s. 6d.

"The appearance of a Grammar like this is in itself a sign that great advance is being made in the teaching of modern languages..... The rules and observations are all scientifically classified and explained."—*Educational Times.*

"In itself this is in many ways the most satisfactory Grammar for beginners that we have as yet seen."—*Athenæum.*

Eugène's **French Method**. Elementary French Lessons. Easy Rules and Exercises preparatory to the "Student's Comparative French Grammar." By the same Author. 9th Edition. Crown 8vo, cloth. 1s. 6d.

"Certainly deserves to rank among the best of our Elementary French Exercise-books."—*Educational Times.*

Delbos. **Student's Graduated French Reader**, for the use of Public Schools. I. First Year. Anecdotes, Tales, Historical Pieces. Edited, with Notes and a complete Vocabulary, by Leon Delbos, M.A., of King's College, London. 3rd Edition. Crown 8vo, cloth. 2s.

—— The same. II. Historical Pieces and Tales. 3rd Edition. Crown 8vo, cloth. 2s.

Little Eugène's **French Reader**. For Beginners. Anecdotes and Tales. Edited, with Notes and a complete Vocabulary, by Leon Delbos, M.A., of King's College. 2nd Edition. Crown 8vo, cloth. 1s. 6d.

2000/9/89

Krueger (H.) Short French Grammar. 6th Edition. 180 pp. 12mo, cloth. 2s.

Victor Hugo. Les Misérables, les principaux Episodes. With Life and Notes by J. Boïelle, Senior French Master, Dulwich College. 2 vols. Crown 8vo, cloth. Each 3s. 6d.

—————— **Notre-Dame de Paris.** Adapted for the use of Schools and Colleges, by J. Boïelle, B.A., Senior French Master, Dulwich College. 2 vols. Crown 8vo, cloth. Each 3s.

Boïelle. French Composition through Lord Macaulay's English. I. Frederic the Great. Edited, with Notes, Hints, and Introduction, by James Boïelle, B.A. (Univ. Gall.), Senior French Master, Dulwich College, &c. &c. Crown 8vo, cloth. 3s.

Foa (Mad. Eugen.) Contes Historiques. With Idiomatic Notes by G. A. Neveu. 3rd Edition. Crown 8vo, cloth. 2s.

Larochejacquelein (Madame de) Scenes from the War in the Vendée. Edited from her Mémoirs in French, with Introduction and Notes, by C. Scudamore, M.A. Oxon, Assistant Master, Forest School, Walthamstow. Crown 8vo, cloth. 2s.

French Classics for English Schools. Edited, with Introduction and Notes, by Leon Delbos, M.A., of King's College. Crown 8vo, cloth.

No. 1. Racine's Les Plaideurs. 1s. 6d.
No. 2. Corneille's Horace. 1s. 6d.
No. 3. Corneille's Cinna. 1s. 6d.
No. 4. Molière's Bourgeois Gentilhomme. 1s. 6d.
No. 5. Corneille's Le Cid. 1s. 6d.
No. 6. Molière's Précieuses Ridicules. 1s. 6d.
No. 7. Chateaubriand's Voyage en Amérique. 1s. 6d.
No. 8. De Maistre's Prisonniers du Caucase and Lepreux d'Aoste. 1s. 6d.
No. 9. Lafontaine's Fables Choisies. 1s. 6d.

Lemaistre (J.) French for Beginners. Lessons Systematic, Practical and Etymological. By J. Lemaistre. Crown 8vo, cloth. 2s. 6d.

Roget (F. F.) Introduction to Old French. History, Grammar, Chrestomathy, Glossary. 400 pp. Crown 8vo, cl. 6s.

Foreign School Books and Maps. 3

Kitchin. Introduction to the Study of Provençal. By Darcy B. Kitchin, B.A. [Literature—Grammar—Texts—Glossary.] Crown 8vo, cloth. 4s. 6d.

Tarver. Colloquial French, for School and Private Use. By H. Tarver, B.-ès-L., late of Eton College. 328 pp., crown 8vo, cloth. 5s.

Ahn's French Vocabulary and Dialogues. 2nd Edition. Crown 8vo, cloth. 1s. 6d.

Delbos (L.) French Accidence and Minor Syntax. 2nd Edition. Crown 8vo, cloth. 1s. 6d.

———— Student's French Composition, for the use of Public Schools, on an entirely new Plan. 250 pp. Crown 8vo, cloth. 3s. 6d.

Vinet (A.) Chrestomathie Française ou Choix de Morceaux tirés des meilleurs Ecrivains Français. 11th Edition. 358 pp., cloth. 3s. 6d.

Roussy. Cours de Versions. Pieces for Translation into French. With Notes. Crown 8vo. 2s. 6d.

Williams (T. S.) and J. Lafont. French Commercial Correspondence. A Collection of Modern Mercantile Letters in French and English, with their translation on opposite pages. 2nd Edition. 12mo, cloth. 4s. 6d.
For a German Version of the same Letters, vide p. 4.

Fleury's Histoire de France, racontée à la Jeunesse, with Grammatical Notes, by Auguste Beljame, Bachelier-ès-lettres. 3rd Edition. 12mo, cloth boards. 3s. 6d.

Mandrou (A.) French Poetry for English Schools. Album Poétique de la Jeunesse. By A. Mandrou, M.A. de l'Académie de Paris. 2nd Edition. 12mo, cloth. 2s.

German.

Schlutter's German Class Book. A Course of Instruction based on Becker's System, and so arranged as to exhibit the Self-development of the Language, and its Affinities with the English. By Fr. Schlutter, Royal Military Academy, Woolwich. 5th Edition. 12mo, cloth. (Key, 5s.) 5s.

Möller (A.) A German Reading Book. A Companion to Schlutter's German Class Book. With a complete Vocabulary. 150 pp. 12mo, cloth. 2s.

Ravensberg (A. v.) Practical Grammar of the German Language. Conversational Exercises, Dialogues and Idiomatic Expressions. 3rd Edition. Cloth. (Key, 2s.) 5s.

—— **English into German.** A Selection of Anecdotes, Stories, &c., with Notes for Translation. Cloth. (Key, 5s.) 4s. 6d.

—— **German Reader,** Prose and Poetry, with copious Notes for Beginners. 2nd Edition. Crown 8vo, cloth. 3s.

Weisse's Complete Practical Grammar of the German Language, with Exercises in Conversations, Letters, Poems and Treatises, &c. 4th Edition, very much enlarged and improved. 12mo, cloth. 6s.

—— **New Conversational Exercises in German Composition,** with complete Rules and Directions, with full References to his German Grammar. 2nd Edition. 12mo, cloth. (Key, 5s.) 3s. 6d.

Wittich's German Tales for Beginners, arranged in Progressive Order. 26th Edition. Crown 8vo, cloth. 4s.

—— **German for Beginners,** or Progressive German Exercises. 8th Edition. 12mo, cloth. (Key, 5s.) 4s.

—— **German Grammar.** 10th Edition. 12mo, cloth. 4s. 6d.

Hein. German Examination Papers. Comprising a complete Set of German Papers set at the Local Examinations in the four Universities of Scotland. By G. Hein, Aberdeen Grammar School. Crown 8vo, cloth. 2s. 6d.

Schinzel (E.) Child's First German Course; also, A Complete Treatise on German Pronunciation and Reading. Crown 8vo, cloth. 2s. 6d.

—— **German Preparatory Course.** 12mo, cloth. 2s. 6d.

—— **Method of Learning German.** (A Sequel to the Preparatory Course.) 12mo, cloth. 3s. 6d.

Apel's Short and Practical German Grammar for Beginners, with copious Examples and Exercises. 3rd Edition. 12mo, cloth. 2s. 6d.

Sonnenschein and Stallybrass. German for the English. Part I. First Reading Book. Easy Poems with interlinear Translations, and illustrated by Notes and Tables, chiefly Etymological. 4th Edition. 12mo, cloth. 4s. 6d.

Foreign School Books and Maps.

Williams (T. S.) Modern German and English Conversations and Elementary Phrases, the German revised and corrected by A. Kokemueller. 21st enlarged and improved Edition. 12mo, cloth. 3s. 6d.

—— and O. Cruse. German and English Commercial Correspondence. A Collection of Modern Mercantile Letters in German and English, with their Translation on opposite pages. 2nd Edition. 12mo, cloth. 4s. 6d.

For a French Version of the same Letters, vide p. 2.

Apel (H.) German Prose Stories for Beginners (including Lessing's Prose Fables), with an interlinear Translation in the natural order of Construction. 12mo, cloth. 2s. 6d.

—— German Prose. A Collection of the best Specimens of German Prose, chiefly from Modern Authors. 500 pp. Crown 8vo, cloth. 3s.

German Classics for English Students. With Notes and Vocabulary. Crown 8vo, cloth.

Schiller's Lied von der Glocke (the Song of the Bell), and other Poems and Ballads. By M. Förster. 2s.
—— Maria Stuart. By M. Förster. 2s. 6d.
—— Minor Poems and Ballads. By Arthur P. Vernon. 2s.
Goethe's Iphigenie auf Tauris. By H. Attwell. 2s.
—— Hermann und Dorothea. By M. Förster. 2s. 6d.
—— Egmont. By H. Apel. 2s. 6d.
Lessing's Emilia Galotti. By G. Hein. 2s.
—— Minna von Barnhelm. By J. A. F. Schmidt. 2s. 6d.
Chamisso's Peter Schlemihl. By M. Förster. 2s.
Andersen's Bilderbuch ohne Bilder. By Alphons Beck. 2s.
Nieritz. Die Waise, a German Tale. By E. C. Otte. 2s. 6d.
Hauff's Mærchen. A Selection. By A. Hoare. 3s. 6d.

Carové (J. W.) Mærchen ohne Ende (The Story without an End). 12mo, cloth. 2s.

Fouque's Undine, Sintram, Aslauga's Ritter, die beiden Hauptleute. 4 vols. in 1. 8vo, cloth. 7s. 6d.

Undine. 1s. 6d.; cloth, 2s. Aslauga. 1s. 6d.; cloth, 2s.
Sintram. 2s. 6d.; cloth, 3s. Hauptleute. 1s. 6d.; cloth, 2s.

Latin and Greek.

Cæsar de Bello Gallico. Lib. I. Edited, with Introduction, Notes and Maps, by Alexander M. Bell, M.A., Ball. Coll. Oxon. Crown 8vo, cloth. 2s. 6d.

Euripides' Medea. The Greek Text, with Introduction and Explanatory Notes for Schools, by J. H. Hogan. 8vo, cloth. 3s. 6d.

—— **Ion.** Greek Text, with Notes for Beginners, Introduction and Questions for Examination, by Dr. Charles Badham, D.D. 2nd Edition. 8vo. 3s. 6d.

Æschylus. Agamemnon. Revised Greek Text, with literal line-for-line Translation on opposite pages, by John F. Davies, B.A. 8vo, cloth. 3s.

Platonis Philebus. With Introduction and Notes by Dr. C. Badham. 2nd Edition, considerably augmented. 8vo, cloth. 4s.

—— **Euthydemus et Laches.** With Critical Notes and an Epistola critica to the Senate of the Leyden University, by Dr. Ch. Badham, D.D. 8vo, cloth. 4s.

—— **Symposium,** and Letter to the Master of Trinity, "De Platonis Legibus,"—Platonis Convivium, cum Epistola ad Thompsonum edidit Carolus Badham. 8vo, cloth. 4s.

Sophocles. Electra. The Greek Text critically revised, with the aid of MSS. newly collated and explained. By Rev. H. F. M. Blaydes, M.A., formerly Student of Christ Church, Oxford. 8vo, cloth. 6s.

—— **Philoctetes.** Edited by the same. 8vo, cloth. 6s.

—— **Trachiniæ.** Edited by the same. 8vo, cloth. 6s.

—— **Ajax.** Edited by the same. 8vo, cloth. 6s.

Dr. D. Zompolides. A Course of Modern Greek, or the Greek Language of the Present Day. I. The Elementary Method. Crown 8vo. 5s.

Kiepert's New Atlas Antiquus. Maps of the Ancient World, for Schools and Colleges. 6th Edition. With a complete Geographical Index. Folio, boards. 7s. 6d.

Kampen. 15 Maps to illustrate Cæsar's De Bello Gallico. 15 coloured Maps. 4to, cloth. 3s. 6d.

Italian.

Volpe (Cav. G.) Eton Italian Grammar, for the use of Eton College. Including Exercises and Examples. New Edition. Crown 8vo, cloth.   4s. 6d.

——— Key to the Exercises.   1s.

Rossetti. Exercises for securing Idiomatic Italian by means of Literal Translations from the English, by Maria F. Rossetti. 12mo, cloth.   3s. 6d.

——— Aneddoti Italiani. One Hundred Italian Anecdotes, selected from "Il Compagno del Passeggio." Being also a Key to Rossetti's Exercises. 12mo, cloth.   2s. 6d.

Venosta (F.) Raccolta di Poesie tratti dai piu celebri autori antichi e moderni. Crown 8vo, cloth.   5s.

Christison (G.) Racconti Istorici e Novelle Morali. Edited for the use of Italian Students. 12th Edition. 18mo, cloth.   1s. 6d.

Danish—Dutch.

Bojesen (Mad. Marie) The Danish Speaker. Pronunciation of the Danish Language, Vocabulary, Dialogues and Idioms for the use of Students and Travellers in Denmark and Norway. 12mo, cloth.   4s.

Williams and Ludolph. Dutch and English Dialogues, and Elementary Phrases. 12mo.   2s. 6d.

Wall Maps.

Sydow's Wall Maps of Physical Geography for School-rooms, representing the purely physical proportions of the Globe, drawn in a bold manner. An English Edition, the Originals with English Names and Explanations. Mounted on canvas, with rollers:

1. The World. 2. Europe. 3. Asia. 4. Africa. 5. America (North and South). 6. Australia and Australasia.   Each 10s.

——— Handbook to the Series of Large Physical Maps for School Instruction, edited by J. Tilleard. 8vo.   1s.

Miscellaneous.

De Rheims (H.) Practical Lines in Geometrical Drawing, containing the Use of Mathematical Instruments and the Construction of Scales, the Elements of Practical and Descriptive Geometry, Orthographic and Horizontal Projections, Isometrical Drawing and Perspective. Illustrated with 300 Diagrams, and giving (by analogy) the solution of every Question proposed at the Competitive Examinations for the Army. 8vo, cloth. 9s.

Fyfe (W. T.) First Lessons in Rhetoric. With Exercises. By W. T. Fyfe, M.A., Senior English Master, High School for Girls, Aberdeen. 12mo, sewed. 1s.

Fuerst's Hebrew Lexicon, by Davidson. A Hebrew and Chaldee Lexicon to the Old Testament, by Dr. Julius Fuerst. 5th Edition, improved and enlarged, containing a Grammatical and Analytical Appendix. Translated by Rev. Dr. Samuel Davidson. 1600 pp., royal 8vo, cloth. 21s.

Strack (W.) Hebrew Grammar. With Exercises, Paradigms, Chrestomathy and Glossary. By Professor H. Strack, D.D., of Berlin. Crown 8vo, cloth. 4s. 6d.

Hebrew Texts. Large type. 16mo, cloth.
Genesis. 1s. 6d. Psalms. 1s. Job. 1s. Isaiah. 1s.

Turpie (Rev. Dr.) Manual of the Chaldee Language: containing Grammar of the Biblical Chaldee and of the Targums, and a Chrestomathy, consisting of Selections from the Targums, with a Vocabulary adapted to the Chrestomathy. 1879. Square 8vo, cloth. 7s.

Socin (A.) Arabic Grammar. Paradigms, Literature, Chrestomathy and Glossary. By Dr. A. Socin, Professor, Tübingen. Crown 8vo, cloth. 7s. 6d.

Bopp's Comparative Grammar of the Sanscrit, Zend, Greek, Latin, Lithuanian, Gothic, German and Slavonic Languages. Translated by E. B. Eastwick. 4th Edition. 3 vols. 8vo, cloth. 31s. 6d.

Nestle (E.) Syriac Grammar. Literature, Chrestomathy and Glossary. By Professor E. Nestle, Professor, Tübingen. Translated into English. Crown 8vo, cloth. 9s.

Delitzsch (F.) Assyrian Grammar, with Paradigms, Exercises, Glossary and Bibliography. By Dr. F. Delitzsch. Translated into English by Prof. A. R. S. Kennedy, B.D. Crown 8vo, cloth. 15s.

Williams and Norgate's School Books and Maps.

Williams (T. S.) Modern German and English Conversations and Elementary Phrases, the German revised and corrected by A. Kokemueller. 21st enlarged and improved Edition. 12mo. cloth 3s

Williams (T. S.) and C. Cruse. German and English Commercial Correspondence. A Collection of Modern Mercantile Letters in German and English, with their Translation on opposite pages. 2nd Edition. 12mo. cloth 4s 6d

Apel (H.) German Prose Stories for Beginners (including Lessing's Prose Fables), with an interlinear Translation in the natural order of Construction. 2nd Edition. 12mo. cloth 2s 6d

—— **German Prose.** A Collection of the best Specimens of German Prose, chiefly from Modern Authors. A Handbook for Schools and Families. 500 pp. Crown 8vo. cloth 3s

German Classics for English Schools, with Notes and Vocabulary. Crown 8vo. cloth.

Schiller's **Lied von der Glocke** (The Song of the Bell), and other Poems and Ballads, by M. Förster 2s
—— **Minor Poems.** By Arthur P. Vernon 2s
—— **Maria Stuart**, by Moritz Förster 2s 6d
Goethe's **Hermann und Dorothea**, by M. Förster 2s 6d
—— **Iphigenie auf Tauris.** With Notes by H. Attwell. 2s
—— **Egmont.** By H. Apel 2s 6d
Lessing's **Minna von Barnhelm**, by Schmidt 2s 6d
—— **Emilia Galotti.** By G. Hein 2s
Chamisso's **Peter Schlemihl**, by M. Förster 2s
Andersen (H. C.) **Bilderbuch ohne Bilder**, by Beck 2s
Nieritz. **Die Waise**, a Tale, by Otte 2s
Hauff's **Mærchen.** A Selection, by A. Hoare 3s 6d

Carové (J. W.) Mæhrchen ohne Ende (The Story without an End). 12mo. cloth 2s
Fouque's Undine, Sintram, Aslauga's Ritter, die beiden Hauptleute. 4 vols. in 1. 8vo. cloth 7s 6d
Undine. 1s 6d; cloth, 2s. Aslauga. 1s 6d; cloth, 2s
Sintram. 2s 6d; cloth, 3s. Hauptleute. 1s 6d; cloth, 2s

Latin, Greek, etc.

Cæsar de Bello Gallico. Lib. I. Edited with Introduction, Notes and Maps, by ALEXANDER M. BELL, M.A. Ball. Coll., Oxon. Crown 8vo. cloth *2s 6d*

Euripides' Medea. The Greek Text, with Introduction and Explanatory Notes for Schools, by J. H. Hogan. 8vo. cloth *3s 6d*

—— **Ion.** Greek Text, with Notes for Beginners, Introduction and Questions for Examination, by the Rev. Charles Badham, D.D. 2nd Edition. 8vo. *3s 6d*

Æschylus. Agamemnon. Revised Greek Text, with literal line-for-line Translation on opposite pages, by John F. Davies, B.A. 8vo. cloth *3s*

Platonis Philebus. With Introduction and Notes by Dr. C. Badham. 2nd Edition, considerably augmented. 8vo. cloth *4s*

—— **Euthydemus et Laches.** With Critical Notes, by the Rev. Ch. Badham, D.D. 8vo. cloth *4s*

—— **Convivium, cum Epistola ad Thompsonum,** "De Platonis Legibus," edidit C. Badham. 8vo. cloth *4s*

Dr. D. Zompolides. A Course of Modern Greek, or the Greek Language of the Present Day. I. The Elementary Method. Crown 8vo. *5s*

Kiepert New Atlas Antiquus. Maps of the Ancient World, for Schools and Colleges. 6th Edition. With a complete Geographical Index. Folio, boards *7s 6d*

Kampen. 15 Maps to illustrate Cæsar's De Bello Gallico. 15 coloured Maps. 4to. cloth *3s 6d*

Italian.

Volpe (Cav. G.) Eton Italian Grammar, for the use of Eton College. Including Exercises and Examples. New Edition. Crown 8vo. cloth (Key, 1s) *4s 6d*

Racconti Istorici e Novelle Morali. Edited, for the use of Italian Students, by G. Christison. 12th Edition. 18mo. cloth *1s 6d*

Rossetti. Exercises for securing Idiomatic Italian, by means of Literal Translations from the English by Maria F. Rossetti. 12mo. cloth *3s 6d*

—— **Aneddoti Italiani.** One Hundred Italian Anecdotes, selected from "Il Compagno del Passeggio."

www.ingramcontent.com/pod-product-compliance
Lightning Source LLC
Chambersburg PA
CBHW051244300426
44114CB00011B/877